A Nation Beyond Borders

A Nation Beyond Borders

Lionel Groulx on French-Canadian Minorities

Michel Bock

Translated by Ferdinanda Van Gennip

University of Ottawa Press 2014

The University of Ottawa Press acknowledges with gratitude the support extended to its publishing list by Heritage Canada through the Canada Book Fund, by the Canada Council for the Arts, by the Federation for the Humanities and Social Sciences through the Awards to Scholarly Publications Program and by the University of Ottawa.

The UOP would also like to acknowledge La Fondation Lionel-Groulx as well as the Centre de recherche en civilisation canadienne-française (CRCCF) for providing the photographs used in this book. Contributions from La Fondation Lionel-Groulx include the cover image as well as photographs used in chapters 1 to 5. Contributions from the CRCCF include the frontispiece as well as the photograph used in chapter 6.

Copy editing: Lisa Hannaford-Wong
Proofreading: Joanne Muzak
Typesetting: Édiscript Enr.
Cover design: Édiscript Enr.

Library and Archives Canada Cataloguing in Publication
Bock, Michel, 1971-
[Quand la nation débordait les frontières. English]
A nation beyond borders: Lionel Groulx on French-Canadian minorities/Michel Bock; translated by Ferdinanda Van Gennip.

Translation of: Quand la nation débordait les frontières.
Includes bibliographical references and index.
Issued in print and electronic formats.
ISBN 978-0-7766-0821-1 (pbk.).
ISBN 978-0-7766-2157-9 (pdf).
ISBN 978-0-7766-2156-2 (epub).

1. Groulx, Lionel, 1878-1967--Political and social views. 2. Canadians, French-speaking—Ethnic identity. 3. Linguistic minorities—Canada. 4. Nationalism—Canada. 5. Canadians, French-speaking—Ontario. 6. Canada—Ethnic relations. 7. Nationalism—Canada—Historiography. 8. Canada—Ethnic relations—Historiography. 9. Historians—Canada—Biography. 10. Historians—Québec (Province)—Biography. I. Gennip, Ferdinanda van, 1948-, translator II. Title. III. Title: Lionel Groulx on French-Canadian minorities.

FC151.G76B6213 2014 971:4007202 C2014-901914-9
C2014-901915-7

Printed in Canada

Table of Contents

Translator's Note

A FEW POINTS OF CLARIFICATION regarding the style and terminology used in this book may be useful. While the lack of inclusive language may offend some, it was felt that in a work of historiography such as this, it would be too jarring to translate, for example, *les hommes* as "men and women" rather than "men," or to translate *il* as "they," rather than "he" and that the tone should reflect the mindset of Groulx and the thinking of his day. It is also hoped that the extensive use of quotation marks throughout the book will not be a distraction. Terminology is of central importance in this book. Was the Confederation compact a "pact" or not? Were the French minorities "persecuted"? Was the French-Canadian nation an "organism"? Did it really have an "apostolic mission"? The author has used quotation marks to remind the reader that these terms are being used specifically in the way that either Groulx or another historian used them and with the meaning that they attached to them. Especially the word *race* has by and large been kept in quotation marks, as in Groulx's ideology its meaning is equivalent to that of nation, nationality, ethnic group or people. In this work, "America" (*Amérique* in the original) refers not to the United States of America, but to the New World, the North American continent, for that is what Groulx meant by it. For the word *survivance*, a decision was made to retain the French, as its meaning is not limited to "survival," for which the French word would be *survie*. The *survivance* of a people is not only about continuing to exist and entails more even than cultural and spiritual survival. It refers to a truly viable nation with its own strong sense of identity.

I found the original French work to be one of exceptional clarity and cohesion, and I hope I have done justice to it in this English version. It was a great privilege to translate this book, which manages to be at the same time intellectually stimulating and rich in the kind of vivid detail that brings history to life.

I wish to thank the publishers for their gracious assistance and patience throughout this project and, especially, the author, Michel Bock, for his timely and helpful replies to all my queries.

Ferdinanda Van Gennip
Windsor, Ontario
September 2013

Preface

IN 2004, when this book was originally published, the historiographical debates surrounding the ideology of Abbé Lionel Groulx (1878–1967) were once again heating up. As French Canada's most influential nationalist intellectual from the 1920s to the 1950s, the interest Groulx has elicited over the past sixty years among historians, as well as various other commentators, has been cyclical, with each generation choosing to see something new or different in his œuvre. Groulx's power to fascinate has always been remarkable and suggests that, as an historical figure, there is very little, if anything, about him, that can be considered banal or trivial. From a strictly quantitative point of view, his production as an intellectual is, quite simply, staggering: dozens of books and brochures covering many genres, hundreds of articles of all kinds, a collection of personal correspondence comprised of thousands of letters, numerous unedited manuscripts and more. From a qualitative point of view, Groulx's life's work has, of course, been the subject of many controversies, both during his lifetime and afterward. Here was a man, born and raised in the nineteenth century in a very modest habitant home, whose initiation to the world of culture and ideas would come from his classical education and his exposure to the ideals of philosophical traditionalism. Here was a man who would be thrust quickly into the position of leader of the French-Canadian nationalist movement at a time when Québec's social structure had begun to undergo tremendous upheaval as a result of rapid industrialization and urbanization, and of the increasingly important role American capital had come to play in the Canadian and Québec economies. These things worried him. The reasons for this apprehension were numerous, but what it all boiled down to was a fear that French Canada, as a culturally autonomous national entity, would be unable to negotiate these very far-reaching social and economic changes on an equal footing with those who seemed, in his eyes, to be determining the rules of the game on their own.

As historians, there are many ways for us to approach the analysis of Abbé Groulx's ideology. One is to see him simply as a reactionary who rejected change, idealized the past and was out of touch with the realities of his time. Another is to attempt to penetrate the man's intellectual and cultural universe, one which is vastly different, in many ways, from our own, in order to decipher its logic and decode its own particular "language." This is perhaps more difficult to accomplish, as it requires that the historian strike a more delicate balance between comprehension and judgment (and/or condemnation). It also calls for a very refined understanding of the cultural context that provides the backdrop against which these issues played out. This can be achieved only through a great deal of patience and humility. With respect to Groulx, this means understanding that every aspect of his thought and his actions, including his nationalism, was subordinated to (though inseparable from) his Catholicism, which remained the backbone of his life's work, and not the other way around. The French-Canadian nation, in his view, remained instituted not within the state—not even within the Québec state—but within the Church, as it had been since the 1840s (or, in Groulx's understanding of things, since the birth of New France). The state could certainly be a tool put at the disposal of the nation but could never assume the task of structuring it, a task which belonged to the Church alone. The transcendent role Groulx attributed to Catholicism in French Canada's historical development and national existence kept him at distance from extreme right-wing ideologies and thinkers in Europe, especially those of the French *Action française* movement of Charles Maurras, contrary to what a certain historiographical tradition has maintained.[1] It also kept him from considering the idea of state corporatism or fascism during the 1930s, as he aligned himself, instead, with the school of thought that looked toward social corporatism as the solution to the woes of the Great Depression.[2]

In fact, Groulx devoted precious little time to thinking about the question of which political regime would best suit French Canadians, whose national problems were more spiritual, in his view, than political or institutional.[3] Only by renewing their commitment to the apostolic mission he believed Providence had laid out for them and by being peaceful beacons of Catholicism in the New World would they succeed in rising above the obstacles they faced as a national collective. The nature of the regime was thus of very little concern to him on the whole. One also needs to keep this in mind when considering his so-called "separatism." Unable, for essentially theological reasons, to invoke the principle of nationalities in order to justify the independence of an eventual "French state,"

1. For a survey of the studies devoted to the question of Groulx's so-called Maurrassisme, see Michel Bock, "L'influence du maurrassisme au Canada français: Retour sur le cas de Lionel Groulx," in Olivier Dard, ed., *Charles Maurras et l'étranger. L'étranger et Charles Maurras* (Berne: Peter Lang, 2009), p. 135–152. See also: Michel Bock, "Lionel Groulx devant la France catholique: Contacts, échanges et collaboration," *Études d'histoire religieuse*, vol. 79, No, 1 (2013), p. 31–44; Michel Bock and Hugues Théorêt, "Les revues traditionalistes canadiennes-française devant les droites radicales européennes. L'exemple de *L'Action nationale* et de *Tradition et progrès* (1945 à 1970)," in Olivier Dard, ed., *Supports et vecteurs des droites radicales au XXe siècle (Europe/Amériques)* (Berne: Peter Lang, 2013), p. 169–185.
2. See E.-Martin Meunier and Michel Bock, "Essor et déclin du corporatisme au Canada français (1930–1960): Une introduction," in Olivier Dard, ed., *Le corporatisme dans l'aire francophone au XXe siècle* (Berne: Peter Lang, 2011), p. 179–200.
3. See the pioneering work of Jean-Claude Dupuis on this topic, "La pensée politique de *L'Action française* de Montréal (1917–1928)," *Les Cahiers d'histoire du Québec au XXe siècle*, No. 2 (Summer 1994), p. 27–43.

Groulx's separatism was "timid,"[4] to say the least. Yet, a certain historiographical current has made him out to be a radical "isolationist," a "provincialist" and indeed a "separatist." Such a thesis, in my view, needed to be re-examined.

This book began as a doctoral thesis I undertook at the University of Ottawa in the late 1990s, first under the supervision of professor Pierre Savard until his untimely passing in 1998, and then under professors Jean-Pierre Wallot and Gaétan Gervais. Growing up as a Franco-Ontarian in Sudbury, Ontario, during the 1970s and 1980s, I had always been fascinated (and at times disconcerted) by the ambiguous relationship between Québec and French-Canadian minorities, a relationship that had come under considerable strain during the Quiet Revolution of the 1960s. My study of Groulx first originated from a desire to gain a better understanding of the processes that had led to the construction and the transformation of the French-Canadian cultural and national project over the course of the twentieth century, given that much of the historiography, once again, presented him as an isolationist and a separatist with little or no regard for those French-Canadian communities living outside Québec. It became abundantly clear to me that this thesis would not hold up to closer scrutiny. Indeed, the very intense feeling of national solidarity that Groulx maintained vis-à-vis those he called his *frères de la dispersion* never wavered, not even after the Second World War and the Quiet Revolution, when French Canada would undergo a significant institutional and ideological transformation. Moreover, I discovered that the study of the place held by French-Canadian minorities in Groulx's ideology was a very effective way of addressing many of the issues discussed above, whether it be the role he attributed to the Church, as opposed to the state, in maintaining French Canada's institutional cohesiveness beyond provincial borders, the importance he attributed to Catholicism as the very "lifeblood" of the nation, his consequent (though relative) anti-statism, his presumed isolationism and separatism, or, through the study of his relationships with his contemporaries and disciples, the reformulation of French-Canadian nationalist discourse as the Quiet Revolution drew ever closer.

Since the book's initial publication in French, the historiography has progressed, as has my own view on the original source material. It was tempting to revisit and further elaborate on the issues it raises as my understanding of them has broadened, hopefully, over the years. But this is a translation, not a revised edition, and I quelled the urge to begin anew. I do believe the book has retained its relevance and I am very grateful for the opportunity to have it reach a wider audience. Many people are to be thanked for this, including, first of all, the Canada Council for the Arts, which is largely responsible for the funding of the project. My thanks also go to the publisher of the original French-language version of the

4. *Ibid.*

book, les Éditions Hurtubise, as well as to the University of Ottawa Press for the time and care they have invested in the production of this book. Finally, I must thank the book's translator, Ferdinanda Van Gennip. Entrusting another person with a work that one has laboured over for so many years can be a bit daunting. On some level, a translation is, of course, an interpretation. Luckily, I felt from the beginning that the book was in very capable and professional hands. I am grateful to Ms. Van Gennip for the quality of her work, and for the great respect she has shown the original source material.

MICHEL BOCK
Gatineau, December 16th, 2013

Introduction

"The dominant fact about French life in America, during the past century, is without a doubt that it became dispersed. French Canada can no longer be defined as a geographical expression limited by the borders of Québec."[1] Those were the parameters used by Lionel Groulx in 1935 to describe the French-Canadian nation. This small excerpt from his vast study on the French minority schools, written while he was at the peak of his influence, alone reveals a major aspect of Abbé Groulx's nationalist doctrine. The priest, who later became Canon Groulx, was the nationalist school's intellectual leader from the 1920s to the 1950s. Throughout his long career as a professor, historian, lecturer, publisher, intellectual and polemicist, he became one of the chief advocates of the *survivance* of the French minorities in Canada.

However, this element of his thought remains largely unknown. Since the sixties, historiography has tended to give the French minorities little coverage and to present Groulx as a "Québécois" nationalist, sometimes a "separatist" nationalist, who cared only about obtaining greater political autonomy for Québec—inside or outside of Confederation. Similarly, the great political and ideological debates that Québec has experienced since the Quiet Revolution are reflected in the writings of its historians and intellectuals, with primacy commonly given to the "Québécois" nation and the French minorities receiving a certain indifference. In fact, during the 1960s, relations between the French Canadians of Québec and those of the other provinces underwent a dramatic shift. In Québec, the upheavals of the Quiet Revolution transformed traditional French-Canadian nationalism and recast the discourse about identity in terms of the territory of Québec alone. This metamorphosis provoked a serious political, ideological and institutional break with the French minorities. From René Lévesque's "dead ducks" to Yves Beauchemin's "still warm corpses," this break stood in singular contrast to the intense feeling of national solidarity which, for a century, had generally characterized relations between nationalist groups in Québec and the French minorities in the other provinces.[2]

1. Lionel Groulx, *L'Enseignement français au Canada: Tome II: Les Écoles des minorités* (Montréal: Librairie Granger Frères, 1935), p. 71.
2. On the "break" with French Canada, see Marcel Martel, *Le Deuil d'un pays imaginé: Rêve, luttes et déroutes du Canada français* (Ottawa: Presses de l'Université d'Ottawa, 1997), 203 p.; Gaétan Gervais, *Des gens de résolution: Le passage du Canada français à l'Ontario français* (Sudbury: Prise de parole, 2003), 230 p.

With a great number of historians subscribing to the paradigm of the *Québécois* nation, however, a large portion of the history of the *French-Canadian* nation, as conceived by Abbé Groulx, was overlooked. A study of the place Canada's French minorities held in his ideology constitutes an excellent means to better grasp the foundations of French-Canadian nationalism in its most common form prior to the 1950s and 1960s. It would have been logically impossible for the dispersal of the French "race" in America to escape the preoccupations of a historian such as Groulx. In his view, the linguistic, cultural and religious "persecution" suffered by the French minorities represented not only a threat to them but a threat to the French-Canadian nation as a whole. Groulx presented the anti-French and anti-Catholic measures adopted by several provincial governments as a series of violent acts betraying the confidence that French Canadians had placed in the good faith and the spirit of fair play of their English-Canadian partners at the—solemn—moment of the signing of the Confederation "pact" of 1867. If he used this constitutional argument frequently to come to the defence of the French minorities, his reasoning was nevertheless not limited to it. Minority rights were not, in his mind, just the result of the deliberations and negotiations that had led to the adoption of the British North America Act, but rather of the historical experience of the French-Canadian nation since the arrival of the first French in the sixteenth and seventeenth centuries. Rather than considering Confederation as the source in which the rights of the French minorities were grounded, Groulx saw in it the political and constitutional recognition of their historical experience on the North American continent. Certainly, to deprive the minorities of their linguistic and religious rights represented for him an attack on Canadian constitutional law. But worse still, he saw in this a violation of the natural right—understood here in its traditionalist sense—of a people to develop in accordance with their own "national genius." It was, in a word, an affront to the providential plan that had birthed the French-Canadian nation, and he deemed its authority infinitely superior to that of mortals.

While the minorities certainly constituted for Lionel Groulx the outposts or the ramparts of the French-Canadian nation, they represented far more than that to him: they were also—and especially—the remnant, the still living witnesses of the great "French Empire of America." Groulx recognized in them the descendants (if not always genealogically, at least spiritually) of the heroes of New France who had opened up the country, even the continent, to a European and Christian, French and Catholic civilization. He felt that, for this reason, they deserved more respect than they received in several of the provinces with English majorities. The historian would never deviate from this principle. Similarly, the Compact theory of Confederation or the national duality of Canada, as Groulx conceived it, cannot be understood in all its complexity without relating it to the role he attributed to the minorities within the French-Canadian nation.

Why this unflagging resolve to demonstrate and invoke the historical origins of the French minorities in order to defend their right to *survivance*? Granted, Groulx had made history his trade and his calling, but that in itself does not explain such deep ideological convictions. His nationalism, as we shall see, generally conformed to traditionalist currents of thought, whose origins dated back to the nineteenth century. A community bound together by language, culture, tradition and faith—Groulx's concept of nation—was the fruit of both "providential" design and a long historical evolution. The nation that had been formed in New France during its finest hours, he always said, was an entity characterized by its essence, not its territory, and could therefore flout political borders. This logic allowed the French minorities in Canada (and the United States) to make the same claims as their compatriots in Québec. To Groulx, whose ideology resembled political romanticism on this point, the "nation" was something analogous to an "organism" endowed with a distinct "personality." From this idea flowed another: that Québec, as a national "ancestral home," had specific duties toward the French minorities who lived beyond its borders. In fact, excluding the minorities from the "fold" would have been tantamount, in his eyes, to inviting self-destruction: Québec could not turn in on itself and ignore its "scattered brethren" without sapping its own strength in the process.

As a very young man, Lionel Groulx was exposed to the situation of the French minorities, as his parents were before him. At the age of thirteen, his mother, Philomène Pilon, worked as a domestic servant for a Franco-American family in Detroit. It was there that she met the man who would become her second husband, Guillaume Émond. He, moreover, worked many winters in the lumber camps, at times along the Ottawa River, at times in the United States.[3] As a child, Lionel learned his first lessons in patriotism from his mother. In the evening, she would read to him lengthy excerpts from the newspapers of the day, particularly around the time of the Riel affair, which had a profound influence on the young boy's mind. Much later he would write in his *Mémoires*:

> It was through these readings that in 1886, I was made aware of the Riel affair, an "affair" that made us, little school boys that we were, ardent chauvinists. Days of tension during which would be revealed to our young minds the duel between the races in Canada. A strange quiver of pity and anger passed through the land of Québec. They had to hear us, in the school yard, in the streets of the village, singing at the top of our lungs, to the melody of the *Marseillaise* of France, the "Marseillaise of Riel," the first quatrain of which has remained fixed in my memory:
>
> *Enfants de la Nouvelle-France*
> *Douter de nous n'est plus permis,*

3. See Lionel Groulx, *Mes Mémoires: Tome 1: 1878–1920* (Montréal: Fides, 1970), p. 17–19, 29.

Au gibet Riel se balance
Victime de nos ennemis![4]

The sons and daughters of New France are we,
You shall not doubt us anymore,
The great Riel was hanged for all to see,
The victim of our mortal foe!

In a journal he kept during his student years at the Séminaire de Sainte-Thérèse in Valleyfield, Groulx frequently referred to the friendships he formed with Franco-Ontarian and Franco-American classmates. He also wrote in it about some of the visits the missionaries from the Northwest would occasionally make to the students at the *collège*.[5] In 1896, the year of the Laurier-Greenway agreement regarding the separate schools of Manitoba, the *séminaire* received a prestigious visit from the Archbishop of Saint-Boniface, Adélard Langevin. The young Groulx, deeply impressed, noted how discouraged the prelate appeared but how, despite everything, he refused to give in and give up the struggle: "the Bishop spoke to us. He looked tired . . . . The enemies of the faith have put sorrow in his soul but he has hope, and nothing can shake his hope. 'The faith will triumph,' he told us, 'because the matter in dispute is a matter for God.'"[6] This parallel that Langevin had drawn between the "matter" of the French minorities and the project he believed God had mapped out for the French Canadians in America would later constitute the cornerstone of Lionel Groulx's ideology and the intellectual justification for his nationalist commitment.

Some fifteen years later, in 1912, Langevin sent Groulx a message to congratulate him on the release of his first book, *Une Croisade d'adolescents*, which recounts the beginnings of the Association catholique de la jeunesse canadienne (ACJC) in Valleyfield[7] at the start of the century: "This work contains," the Franco-Manitoban prelate wrote, "very admirable fervour and a high degree of religious and intellectual culture which pleases me."[8] Groulx's contact with the French minorities grew rapidly once he became better known within the French-Canadian nationalist movement. However, very early on already, he had shown interest in the problems they faced as they struggled against linguistic and cultural assimilation and fought to retain their religious faith. These contacts contributed powerfully, as we shall see, to the development of his own nationalist ideology.

4. *Ibid.*, p. 36.
5. Lionel Groulx, *Journal, 1895–1911: Tome I* (Montréal: Presses de l'Université de Montréal, 1984), p. 205–206.
6. *Ibid.*, p. 202–203.
7. Lionel Groulx, *Une Croisade d'adolescents* (Québec: L'Action sociale limitée, 1912), 264 p.
8. Letter from Adélard Langevin to Lionel Groulx, Bibliothèque et Archives nationales du Québec (hereinafter BAnQ), Fonds Lionel-Groulx (hereinafter FLG), P1/A,2063, October 29, 1912.

* * *

In terms of method, this study will consist in applying qualitative research analysis to the nationalist ideology of Lionel Groulx as it relates to the French minorities of Canada.[9] By 1950, Abbé Groulx had entered the ranks of the principal ideologues or "definers" of French-Canadian nationalism. The product of a rural background and the classical Catholic education system, he made himself the spokesman for a profoundly conservative nationalism situated at the intersection of several intellectual influences, including the counter-revolutionary tradition, ultramontanism, the Church's social doctrine and parliamentarism, ideologies that he wove together into a delicate and original synthesis. Not that his work encompassed French-Canadian nationalism in its entirety. There were others besides him who went ahead with their own interpretation of the French-Canadian nation and French-Canadian nationalism, including, to his left, Olivar Asselin and, to his right, Robert Rumilly. Nevertheless, Abbé Groulx's thought represents an enormous and vital segment of French Canada's intellectual history, by virtue of both the impact the priest-historian had on several generations of intellectuals and the longevity of his career, which extended from the beginning of the twentieth century to the Quiet Revolution of the 1960s. Even after his death, the name Groulx continued to ignite controversies and arguments, attested a few years ago by the appearance of Esther Delisle's book, *Le Traître et le juif*, and, more recently, Gérard Bouchard's *Les Deux Chanoines*.[10] Today, we are seeing an increase in the number of analyses of his work, concurrently with a growth in the field of intellectual history. It is an area of Canadian historiography that was neglected by researchers between the 1960s and the 1980s out of a preference for social and quantitative history.

Throughout his career, Lionel Groulx witnessed the radical transformations that Canada underwent socially and economically: still largely rural and agricultural at the turn of the century, it had become, by the time of Groulx's death in 1967, one of the richest countries in the world. It is therefore necessary when studying his thought to take great care to situate it in its historical context. The importance Groulx attached to the concept of tradition in building French-Canadian national identity betrayed the anxiety he felt in the face of the process of

9. Although the scope of this study is limited, generally speaking, to the French minorities of Canada, it is nevertheless useful and necessary at times to consider the case of the Franco-American émigrés in New England. However, for a fuller analysis of the place of the Franco-Americans in the work of Canon Groulx, one may consult Damien-Claude Bélanger, *Lionel Groulx et la Franco-Américanie*, master's thesis (history), Université de Montréal, 2000, 184 p.

10. See Esther Delisle, *Le Traître et le juif: Lionel Groulx, Le Devoir et le délire du nationalisme d'extrême droite dans la province de Québec, 1929–1939* (Outremont: L'Étincelle, 1992), 284 p. For an interesting analysis of this book and the controversy it provoked, consult Gary Caldwell, "La controverse Delisle-Richler," *L'Agora*, June 1994, p. 17–26; Gérard Bouchard, *Les Deux Chanoines: Contradiction et ambivalence dans la pensée de Lionel Groulx* (Montréal: Boréal, 2003), 313 p.

modernization (i.e., of industrialization and urbanization) that the country was undergoing. He believed this process threatened to impose on his *petit peuple* a single cultural model, that of the Anglo-Saxon group that held the reins of economic power. If, because of this, he sang the praises of tradition, it was not in order to deprive French Canadians of the material progress that modernization could bring and whose importance he had never denied, but rather to protect them from the curse of acculturation.

A study of the ideology of Lionel Groulx provides us, then, with an excellent pretext for analyzing the tensions that characterized the development of the French-Canadian nationalist movement of the twentieth century, as well as the significance of the place the French minorities occupied within it. The context for our approach is the more general issue of the social function of the intellectual's role. An intellectual is defined by Jacques Julliard and Michel Winock as an individual "who applies to the political order a high profile acquired elsewhere" and "who . . . seeks to propose to society as a whole an analysis, a direction and a moral compass that their previous work qualifies them to formulate."[11] In other words, to consider someone an intellectual means quite simply to choose to insert them into a *social category* and does not necessarily mean that the historian passes judgment on their work.[12] It is rather the notion of *social engagement* that needs to be retained in identifying intellectuals. However, this engagement is located outside the partisan politics framework: if *politics* is what interests the politician, it is rather the *political* that is the domain of the intellectual. Although intellectualism has long been associated with the left, the definition used by Julliard and Winock seems to apply perfectly to the work of Lionel Groulx, a man of the right. As a historian, he relied largely on his own work to formulate the direction—the political, economic, social and cultural reform project—that he proposed to French Canadians. His preferred reform targets included the French-Canadian (and English-Canadian) political class in particular, but also—and this may seem more astonishing coming from a priest in whom the ultramontane spirit had not yet been entirely extinguished—the Catholic clergy.

Groulx's intellectual evolution involved a whole network of relationships and acquaintances. In addition to analyzing several aspects of his ideology, this study will try to reconstruct the social network that Lionel Groulx was able to build for himself among the French minorities. This endeavour will tell us much about the influence his peers had on him and the struggles he got involved in. In dealing with a writer and polemicist as prolific as Lionel Groulx, source material poses a problem only by virtue of its abundance. The numerous books, articles, speeches and brochures that Groulx published during his long career are among

11. "Introduction," in Jacques Julliard and Michel Winock, ed., *Dictionnaire des intellectuels français* (Paris: Seuil, 1996), p. 12.
12. "Il y a des intellectuels idiots," in the words of Jean d'Ormesson (*Le Figaro littéraire*, Thursday, September 26, 1996, p. 4).

the principal documents that we consulted. Furthermore, it has been possible to study at length and in great detail the correspondence received and sent by the Canon from the beginning of the century to his death in 1967. This enormous documentary collection—of which historians have as yet made little use—contains several hundred, if not thousands, of items, not to mention the handwritten drafts and copies of a great many unpublished speeches and talks.[13] Although we have sometimes cited texts written by Groulx at the start of the twentieth century, we have dedicated our chief research effort to roughly the period following 1910. It was from that point forward that Groulx, then in his early thirties, found himself thrust into a leading role in the French-Canadian nationalist movement. His numerous interventions in the Franco-Ontarian schools crisis (1912–1927), his appointment in 1915 as the first Chair of Canadian history at Université Laval de Montréal and his taking on the directorship of *L'Action française* in the 1920s propelled his ascension in French Canada's intellectual world.

The study of Lionel Groulx's thought sheds a great deal of light on the French-Canadian intellectual context of the first two thirds of the twentieth century. The present study fits into that current of intellectual history which postulates that ideologies are much more than just "superstructures," to borrow a term from Marxism, and that they participate in social change and act upon history. As Fernand Dumont already explained more than forty years ago, ideologies, by interpreting human activity, take a direct part in it:

> Ideology is an explicit definition of the situation by the groups, especially the classes, that are involved in it; the history of ideas cannot be reconstituted therefore in isolation. Not that ideologies are some kind of *reflection* of the social structure. Rather, they fill in the indeterminate areas, they give coherence, they fix the objectives of action. They take part in the social mechanisms.[14]

In effect, the ideological convictions of Lionel Groulx drove him to become actively involved alongside the minorities who, in return, could complete his education on the subject of French-English relations and contribute to the fine-tuning of his own ideology. In so doing, the historian-turned-polemicist managed to build for himself in minority circles a very complex network of contacts, colleagues and often comrades-in-arms, a network that in practical terms facilitated the rapprochement of nationalist groups from all over French Canada.

This study will seek therefore to analyze an important dimension of French-Canadian nationalism as defined by Groulx, that is, the relationship between

13. These handwritten and unpublished documents are conserved in Montréal, Québec at the Bibliothèque et Archives nationales du Québec.
14. Fernand Dumont, "Quelques réflexions d'ensemble," in Fernand Dumont *et al.*, ed., *Idéologies au Canada français, 1850–1900* (Québec: Presses de l'Université Laval, 1971), p. 1.

Québec and the French minorities. We will try to show that the deep sentiment of "national" solidarity that nationalist groups in Québec manifested toward their "dispersed brethren" during the Groulx era was due to an organic concept of the French-Canadian nation that placed the notion of tradition above all else, above any territorial consideration and above political structures. According to this concept, all those who had "inherited" the French-Canadian tradition were part of the national "organism" and, as members of a single body, had the responsibility and even the duty to interact harmoniously with one another. The French-Canadian identity, as Groulx construed it, dictated to Québec an urgent duty of national solidarity with the French minorities. After the Second World War, this definition of French Canada became marginalized and was gradually replaced by a more territorial and Québécois concept of the nation which, in due course, would tend to give priority to political and economic structures. Studying the place of the French minorities in Abbé Groulx's work will therefore give us a better understanding of the tensions accompanying the evolution of the nationalist movement after 1945.

The outline that we have adopted for this book is both thematic and chronological. The first chapter is an appraisal of the historical studies to date of French-Canadian nationalism, Canon Groulx's writings and the French minorities. As we have pointed out, historians of French-Canadian nationalism have for the last fifty or sixty years tended to overlook the issue of the French minorities. What must be seen in this phenomenon is that a considerable number of researchers subscribe to the paradigm of the "Québécois" nation, which, of necessity, leaves in the shadows the study not only of the minorities but also of a good part of what was historically called the "French-Canadian" nation. In fact, an in-depth study of Groulx's nationalism cannot be carried out without an analysis of the place occupied by the French minorities in his work.

In the second chapter, we shall try to identify the "parameters," or "boundaries," to borrow from the sociologists' jargon, that, according to Lionel Groulx, made it possible to identify or recognize the French-Canadian nation. Groulx's thought emerged, to a very large extent, out of traditionalist currents of thought. Among the many dimensions of these ideas, there were at least two that Groulx explored abundantly. First of all, traditionalist thinkers often granted Providence an organizing and directing role in the birth and historical experience of nations. Then there is the fact that they defined natural law as the right of human beings to develop themselves in accordance with their "national genius," that is to say, their culture of origin. Groulx, for his part, subscribed fully to the theory of the providential creation of nations, a conviction that led him to conclude that French Canadians had an apostolic mission. Being the historian that he was, he believed he was observing the constant and faithful accomplishment of this mission from the foundation of New France through to the moment of the "birth" of his *petit peuple*. From the first explorers to the missionaries and martyrs, and to the settlers of the nineteenth and twentieth centuries, the French-Canadian nation appears in Groulx's historical works as the greatest civilizing force that the North American continent had known: the French Canadians in his view had been the first to introduce Christianity and European civilization to the New World. He was known to repeat frequently that there was no place in America that had not been watered by the blood and shaped by the labour of the French "race."

Thus by citing both the providential mission of the French Canadians and the fact that the ancestry of almost the entire continent was rooted in New France, he was able to defend the right to *survivance* of the French minorities throughout the country. As the descendants of those who opened up the vast French colonial empire, they possessed a birthright in America that he believed no one could legitimately violate. It was likewise this reasoning that led him to regard French Canadians as one of the country's two founding peoples—a stance also taken by one of his first intellectual mentors, Henri Bourassa. This great principle, which he saw as the basis of the constitution of 1867, overshadowed all other considerations for him, including the principle of provincial autonomy, which he did however brandish with great conviction when he believed that Québec's interests were threatened.

The "organic" vision of French Canada held by Groulx dictated to its various members a duty of national solidarity and mutual assistance, for the members of a single body could not, logically speaking, act in a manner that would be harmful to another member. Everywhere and at all times, the nation should behave as a harmonious whole. Accordingly, Groulx believed that an attack directed against any part whatsoever of this body was an attack on the organism as a whole. His nationalism therefore assigned to Québec, which he depicted as the nation's "ancestral home," certain duties and responsibilities toward the French minorities who were grappling with the assimilating ambitions of the Anglo-Protestant majority. The third chapter will tackle this question by studying the relationship that Groulx hoped Québec would cultivate with the French minorities in the other provinces. To his dismay, he observed instead that the national "ancestral home" often displayed extreme indifference toward its "dispersed brethren." Groulx singled out Québec's political class as being among the guiltiest. He accused them of systematically placing the interests of the party, whether red or blue, ahead of the interests of the nation. These observations were partly responsible for his conclusion that "fratricidal" partisan battles not only increased national divisions and deprived the minorities of the indispensable framework Québec could offer but had also dealt a severe blow to the unity of the nation. Groulx, for his part, devoted himself with all the zeal of a man of faith to uniting the "ancestral home" and the "vanguard" of the nation. He saw this as a necessary goal and made it his top priority, especially once he became director of the monthly review, *L'Action française* during the 1920s.

The last three chapters will deal with issues whose parameters are more defined by chronology. The fourth will study the substantial intervention of Abbé Groulx during the Regulation 17 crisis between 1912 and 1927. This regulation forbade the teaching *of* French and teaching *in* French in Ontario schools. Starting around 1910, Groulx built numerous and deep friendships among the French-Canadian nationalist elite in Ontario, particularly in the federal capital and in Kent and Essex counties in the southern part of the province. Very quickly, Groulx became a fully committed member of the resistance to Regulation 17 and wholeheartedly took on a key role in the schools crisis. At the same time, the Franco-Ontarian crisis helped push him into the foreground of the nationalist movement: he would become one of its principal intellectual leaders by the early 1920s. During this turbulent period, which coincided with the First World War and the conscription crisis of 1917, Groulx took every opportunity to denounce the Ontario provincial government and to make Québec aware of the disgrace of Regulation 17. He churned out more and more articles and speeches and even dedicated a novel, *L'Appel de la race*, to the tragic situation of Franco-Ontarians. As well, the director of *L'Action française* made the schools crisis one of the main stories that the review would follow during the 1920s.

The fifth chapter will follow the controversy surrounding the vague notions of "separatism" that Abbé Groulx was presumed to have during the interwar period and their consequences for his relationship with the minorities. In 1922, *L'Action française* undertook an extensive study on the political future of French Canada, in which it envisaged a more or less immediate break with the Confederation pact and the creation of an independent "French state." Very quickly, numerous public figures, including Henri Bourassa, brought accusations of "separatism" against Groulx and his acolytes. The French minorities themselves were panic-stricken by this controversy, some of them fearing that Québec would abandon them for good. The director of *L'Action française* spared no effort to reassure them, both in the pages of the review and through personal correspondence. An examination of Groulx's conduct throughout the period of the "French state" controversy—which went on until the end of the 1930s—lets us, in turn, better grasp the foundation of the French-Canadian identity as he understood it.

The final chapter will be dedicated to the study of Canon Groulx's thought from 1944 to 1967, the year of his death, a period that coincides with the aftermath of the war and the Quiet Revolution. The degree of defiance and ideological turmoil these years produced was unprecedented and gave rise to several intellectual movements representing a more or less open split with the legacy of the traditional nationalist school and with Groulx's legacy in particular. There were several factors that would lead to the French minorities being abandoned by the new nationalist discourse: a redefinition of the nationalist discourse in terms that sought to be more "modern" (that is to say, less imbued with "consoling myths"), massive intervention by the Québec government, as of 1960, in social, cultural and economic areas, and the *québécisation* of the French-Canadian national identity. The development is all the more interesting because some of the main architects of this discursive mutation had been recruited among Groulx's disciples. Where did the old master stand in relation to all this upheaval? What was his assessment of the neo-nationalism of the Quiet Revolution and the fate awaiting the French minorities in the new "Québécois" national cosmogony? Did he approve of the project undertaken by his own disciples, some of whom were claiming to adhere at the same time to his school of thought? Did he maintain, over and against the neo-nationalist intellectuals, his "faith" in the *survivance* of the minorities? The study of Groulx's thought—and of the place the minorities held in it—during these turbulent years will allow us to get the measure of both the continuity and the discontinuity between the "French-Canadian" and "Québécois" identities. The intellectuals of the postwar period may not have completely rejected the organic definition that Groulx had proposed to the French-Canadian nation. However, the neo-nationalist movement as a whole would now strive to put forward, more than ever before, a "territorial" and "Québécois" understanding of the "national" identity.

⋆ ⋆ ⋆

An analysis of the ideology that has historically characterized relations between the French minorities and nationalist groups seemed imperative. For some fifty years now, the abandonment of the traditional French-Canadian identity has given rise, in Québec, to the "provincialization" or *québécisation* of nationalist discourse. The intellectual and political upheavals it produced have left French-language communities in other parts of the country anxiously wondering just what nation, culture or collective identity they belong to, the concept of "French Canada" having been virtually banished from all speech. The fact that conceptual problems such as these still exist shows that researchers are far from having exhausted the issue of the intellectual relationship between the two branches of the French-Canadian tree, between Québec and the French minorities. The present book seeks to do some of the spadework that we hope will contribute to furthering this field of study.

Chapter One

The French Minorities in the Work and Thought of Lionel Groulx: The Blind Spot of Historians of French-Canadian Nationalism

THE FRENCH-CANADIAN NATIONAL IDENTITY issue is one that historians rarely seem to tire of. There is in our historiography—from François-Xavier Garneau to Gérard Bouchard, including Fernand Dumont and, of course, Lionel Groulx—a tradition which, despite different interpretive and methodological frameworks, makes the nation one of our preferred subjects of study. Is this just the normal reflex of a minority afloat in a vast Anglo-Saxon sea, anxious about its own precarious state? A partial explanation, no doubt, but a passion for national history has evidently not been the preserve of French Canada alone.

Immediately after the Second World War, two competing historical interpretations of the national question placed the matter of the economic inferiority of French Canadians at the centre of their concerns.[1] The first, the *École de Montréal*, attributed their current situation to the Conquest of 1760, which, by robbing *Canadien* elites of control of the political and economic levers, had created a veritable national catastrophe. The *École de Québec* approached the issue instead with a severe critique of the *Ancien Régime* mentality of French Canadians, an attitude embodied even in the twentieth century by "clerico-nationalism." This, they felt, is what had delayed the economic development of French Canadians by steering them clear of modernity and devaluing material progress.

In the decades that followed, history as a discipline underwent the breakup and fragmentation imposed on it by the ascendancy of social history, and retreated somewhat from the national issue. The new generations of historians, deeming national, political or traditional history too narrow and elitist, shifted their focus, instead, to the history of workers, women, ethnocultural minorities, regions, social practices and so forth. Traditional national history therefore lost its preponderance among researchers. In spite of this shift in priorites, however, nationalism, as a field of historical analysis in search of its own autonomy, experienced an appreciable upswing. In fact, since the 1950s, the field has always had one researcher or another studying either the apparatus and institutions of French-Canadian nationalism or its principal ideologues, including of course

1. See Jean Lamarre, *Le Devenir de la nation québécoise selon Maurice Séguin, Guy Frégault et Michel Brunet* (Sillery: Septentrion, 1993), 561 p.; Ronald Rudin, *Making History in Twentieth-Century Quebec* (Toronto: University of Toronto Press, 1997), 294 p.

Lionel Groulx who, being the "national" historian that he was, himself became transformed into a subject of historical study.

While interest in the issue of the nation and nationalism is continually renewed, this does not always benefit historical knowledge. Redefining the concept of nation in terms of the territory of Quebec alone, which we have seen happening for some decades now, entails the risk at times of transposing contemporary issues into a past that to a great extent had not yet encountered them. There is no more convincing example of this development than the treatment given to the French minorities, starting in the 1950s, by most historians of French-Canadian nationalism. The historiography of the last sixty years neglects the place of the minorities in traditional nationalist ideology, most studies reducing them, more often than not, to near invisibility. This relative indifference toward the minorities and toward the issue they represent no doubt stems from the emergence of a new paradigm among historians, intellectuals and politicians during the postwar period and *a fortiori* during the 1960s, the paradigm of the "Québécois" nation. The great political and intellectual debates that have gripped Québec since the Quiet Revolution are also evident in the academic writing of a good many of its researchers. This type of methodological, or even ideological, approach, in which the "nation" is defined in terms of the territory of the Québec state, goes hand in hand, however, with an immense conceptual problem, for it overlooks a large area in the history of the "French-Canadian" nation. The relationship it depicts between nationalist circles in Québec and those in the other provinces is at best incomplete.

This first chapter seeks to identify the principal trends in the historiography of French-Canadian nationalism and, more precisely, to determine the importance given to the French minorities of Canada in this area of study. Since the 1950s, a good many historians of French-Canadian nationalism, despite their disagreement on a number of other issues, have adhered to the theory of "provincialism" concerning Lionel Groulx and the movement he led. They were no doubt influenced in this regard by the way nationalist discourse had been transformed following the Second World War. More recently the theory of the "Americanity" of Québec, which has stirred up some stormy debates among historians and intellectuals, has contributed to obscuring even further the issue of relations between Québec and the French minorities. It is only in the last twenty years that a handful of historians have broadened their perspective by seeking to better define the ties, both ideological and institutional, uniting the French minorities and the nationalist groups in Québec.

French-Canadian Nationalism and the Emergence of the Theory of Provincialism

The 1940s and 1950s, ideologically speaking, represent a turbulent period in French Canada. In the aftermath of the political, social and economic upheavals of the economic crisis of the 1930s and especially of the Second World War, Canada, like so many Western countries, entered a period of unprecedented economic growth. Demographically, this prosperity brought a spectacular increase in the birthrate—the baby boom. It was an era that saw the democratization of the automobile, the rise of suburbs, the growth of urban centres and the development of new means of communication, the television being its iconic symbol. In such a context of modernization, urbanization and economic development, and in accordance with the Keynesian principles that were becoming more widely accepted, governments took on an increasingly prominent role in social and economic planning as part of an effort to avoid a return to the extreme poverty of the 1930s. Furthermore, in Canada, the federal government, feeling empowered by its war experience and the recommendations of the Rowell-Sirois Commission on federal-provincial relations (1937–1940), henceforth sought to concentrate in its own hands powers and responsibilities that, from a strictly constitutional point of view, normally fell under the jurisdiction of the provinces. Thus began a lengthy dispute between the federal government and certain provincial governments surrounding the question of the centralization of powers. In Québec, the Union Nationale premier, Maurice Duplessis, sang the praises of provincial autonomy by systematically refusing to participate in several shared-cost programs designed and implemented by the central government. In 1954, he also imposed a provincial income tax despite Ottawa's opposition.

It was in this context that certain intellectuals began to criticize traditional nationalist ideology, which in their view had not adapted to the socioeconomic climate or to the challenges of modernity. According to historian Michael Behiels, the critique was organized into two camps. On the one hand, there were the "neo-liberals" gathered around the *Cité libre* review and supported by the union movement and the social sciences faculty of Université Laval. On the other, there were the "neo-nationalists" who gravitated around the daily, *Le Devoir*, the monthly, *L'Action nationale*, and the history department of Université de Montréal.[2] In both groups, it was deemed that traditional nationalist ideology, by idealizing *agriculturisme* and disparaging economic, industrial and urban progress, had been maintaining the economic inferiority of French Canadians compared to Anglo-Saxon society. Both movements condemned what they considered to be the clericalism and anti-statist sentiment of the traditional ideology. They preferred to see in the state a mainstay that French-Canadian society could no longer do without.

2. Michael D. Behiels, *Prelude to Quebec's Quiet Revolution: Liberalism Versus Neo-Nationalism, 1945–1960* (Kingston and Montréal: McGill-Queen's University Press, 1985), 366 p.

On the national question, however, liberals and neo-nationalists stood diametrically opposed. While both groups wanted to secularize society and reinforce the role the state would play in it, one looked to Ottawa and the other to Québec. The liberal and *citélibriste* intellectuals condemned nationalism in all its forms—including Duplessis's *autonomisme*—which they held responsible for the economic inferiority of French Canadians. By contrast, for the neo-nationalists, nationalism was not harmful in itself. It just had to be adapted to the needs of a society that had become largely industrial and urban. The importance they accorded to strengthening the provincial state, however, made them espouse a nationalism that was limited to the territory of Québec and thus excluded the French minorities in the other provinces.[3]

This was the intellectual atmosphere in which the first studies of French-Canadian nationalism were carried out. There may have been nothing novel about the issue of the nation in the 1950s, but the study of nationalism as an ideology still remained unexplored. The earliest historians to examine French-Canadian nationalism came from the anglophone world, the first being Mason Wade, who, in 1955, published his voluminous synthesis of the history of French Canada from the time of the Conquest of 1760.[4] Although his work does not deal exclusively with the development of the nationalist movement, the author nevertheless devotes numerous pages to the ideology that was put forward by those principally responsible for defining nationalist doctrine during the interwar period, and offers the theory of a split in the nationalist movement during the aftermath of the First World War. On the one side were the "pan-Canadian" nationalists, led by Henri Bourassa and on the other, the "provincialist" nationalists, led by Abbé Lionel Groulx.

The very next year, in 1956, historian Michael Oliver produced an important doctoral thesis dealing exclusively with nationalist discourse during the interwar period. Like his predecessor Wade, Oliver frequently applies the theory of provincialism to Groulx and *L'Action française*. Originally entitled *The Social and Political Ideas of French Canadian Nationalists*, it would finally be published, some thirty-five years later, as *The Passionate Debate: The Social and Political Ideas of Quebec Nationalism*.[5] This semantic shift from *French Canadian* to *Quebec* reveals the central paradigm of the study, namely, the provincialism of the French-Canadian nationalists of the interwar period. The shift is all the more telling as no substantial modification

3. See Jean Lamarre, *Le Devenir*, p. 416; Marcel Martel, "'Hors du Québec, point de salut!' Francophone Minorities and Quebec Nationalism, 1945–1969," in Michael D. Behiels and Marcel Martel, ed., *Nation, Ideas and Identities: Essays in Honour of Ramsay Cook* (Toronto: Oxford University Press, 2000), p. 130–140. We shall return to these questions in the last chapter of this study.
4. Mason Wade, *The French Canadians, 1760–1945* (Toronto: Macmillan, 1955), 1136 p.
5. Michael Oliver, *The Social and Political Ideas of French Canadian Nationalists, 1920–1945*, doctoral dissertation, McGill University, 1956, 370 p.; Michael Oliver, *The Passionate Debate: The Social and Political Ideas of Quebec Nationalism, 1920–1945* (Montreal: Véhicule Press, 1991), 284 p. We refer, in the following pages, only to the published version of this study.

was made to the original thesis in the preparation of the published version. For Oliver, as for Wade, the two notions are definitely synonymous.

Both of these books allege a clear dichotomy between the Bourassa and Groulx schools of thought, their disagreement taking the form of a conflict between an attitude of openness and one of intolerance, between a progressive and a reactionary spirit. According to Wade, the Groulx nationalists were dangerous "extremists," filled with "bitter feeling":

> The term 'ultranationalist' will henceforward be used to describe the extremists of the Groulx school; though it must be remembered that the term 'nationalism' is a misnomer for the movement after the First World War, which was an intense provincialism complicated by ethnic and religious factors, rather than the true nationalism professed by Henri Bourassa, in his early days, and now largely adopted by forward-looking English Canadians.[6]

Groulx's nationalism, heavily influenced, according to Wade, by the racist theorist Gobineau, "was a much narrower and headier doctrine than the broad traditional nationalism of Bourassa." The author does not explain in what way Bourassa's nationalism was more "true" than the brand promoted by Groulx and his colleagues, which he terms "a narrow nationalism" and denigrates as "the dream of a separate French-Canadian state, 'Laurentia,' [that] haunted some hotheaded minds." The historian cites here the famous "French state" controversy and the extensive study organized by *L'Action française* in 1922 on the political future of French Canada. The author expresses the opinion that, during the 1920s, Groulx was at heart a separatist, although outwardly he would have rejected this option.[7]

Like Mason Wade, Michael Oliver makes no effort to hide his admiration for Bourassa, presenting him as the promoter of a form of "cultural and ethnic social pluralism." In the same breath, he attacks Lionel Groulx as one extolling a "narrow," "extremist," "intransigent" and "exclusivist" nationalism.

> It must be concluded that Bourassa's nationalism [contrary to that of Groulx] was not directed towards exclusively French Canadian ends. He consistently supported the concept of a state in which two cultures existed as partners, and in which other national groups had a place too. This Canadian state was desirable in itself, and was the one which was politically available. The difficult dualistic pattern of growth which Canada had to follow was inherently a strength rather than a weakness.[8]

6. Mason Wade, *The French Canadians, 1760–1945*, p. 865.
7. *Ibid.*, p. 865, 867, 880, 882, 887–888.
8. Michael Oliver, *The Social and Political Ideas of French Canadian Nationalists, 1920–1945*, p. 31.

Oliver goes on to state that Bourassa, in contrast to Groulx, was more interested in promoting the political and juridical independence of Canada from Great Britain than in making English Canada accept "a rigid compact theory of Confederation." In summary, Wade and Oliver paint an unflattering portrait of Groulx. But what must especially not be forgotten is that they were the first historians to put forward the theory of the "provincialism" of Groulx's ideology. They maintain that the collaborators of *L'Action française* rarely turned their gaze beyond the borders of Québec, thus explaining their "obsession" with independence. Deeply "isolationist," at least during the 1920s, a period when they were apparently "turned in on themselves," Groulx's followers are alleged to have been unable to show the same broadmindedness as Bourassa. It is very tempting to see in this analysis a transposition of the debate, which at the time of publication of their works, had placed the *citélibriste* liberals and the neo-nationalists in opposite camps.

The theory of provincialism they develop diverts their attention from the place the minorities occupied in Groulx's thought. However, their analysis of Bourassa's "pan-Canadian" nationalism did not develop this issue strongly either: there is barely a mention of the old leader's attacks, made repeatedly throughout his career, against English Canada's desecration of French minority rights. Bourassa's pan-Canadianism seems to be limited simply to an absolute and radical rejection of the separatism of the Groulx school. Wade and Oliver pay amazingly little attention to the crusade undertaken by the founder of *Le Devoir* to demand respect for biculturalism from one end of the country to the other. Their interpretation is only valid to the extent that a relationship of equivalence is established between French Canada and Québec. Promoting an exclusively French-Canadian nationalism—as Groulx and his acolytes did—would then mean limiting it to the territory of Québec.

The ideological gap that separated Groulx and Bourassa was also apparent, according to Oliver, in the discourse of the institutions that were founded in the wake of their respective militant involvements. The Ligue nationaliste, founded at the start of the twentieth century by Olivar Asselin and others, in fact considered Bourassa as its spiritual leader. In Asselin's view, the ideology spread by the Ligue encompassed the whole of Canada. Conversely, the Association catholique de la jeunesse canadienne (ACJC), which came into existence at the same time thanks in part to the efforts of the young Abbé Groulx, was considered to be primarily focused on seeking respect for "French-Canadian particularism" in Québec. However, the author fails to mention the numerous funding campaigns organized by the ACJC to assist the French minorities in their school battles (although he acknowledges that it supported the efforts of the Ligue nationaliste in this regard). Similarly, Oliver perceives the Ordre de Jacques-Cartier, a secret society founded in 1926, also known as *La Patente*, as an example of applied Groulxism. He concludes that the Ordre was a "separatist" organization based on the study of a single speech and a few articles in *L'Émerillon*, the voice of *La Patente*. Oliver does not make it clear that the organization had been founded in Ottawa to promote access by French Canadians to the senior levels of the federal public service and to provide support to the French minorities. It was even strongly criticized for this by Québec nationalists decades later.

In Mason Wade's defence, it must be said that the French minorities are not entirely excluded from his interpretation of Groulx's "new nationalism," whose origin he attributes partially to the schools crises of 1905 (in the new provinces of Alberta and Saskatchewan) and 1912 (in Ontario). He also emphasizes the numerous journeys made by the director of *L'Action française* among the French minorities in Canada and the United States "seeking to promote a reunion of the 'race.'" The review, he points out, also protested the ever-increasing number of obstacles placed by the federal government in the path of French Canadians who wanted to settle in the Western provinces.[9] However, the limited recognition of these events does not amount to a systematic analysis of the place occupied by the minorities in the ideology of Abbé Groulx, who is still always presented as fundamentally "provincialist." Wade's comments on the nationalist historian's first novel, *L'Appel de la race*, are highly revealing of this casual treatment. Despite the novel being set in Ottawa, in the midst of the Regulation 17 crisis, Wade is more interested in the "intransigent nationalism and racism," which, in his view, "permeate" the novel. He believes that the hero, Lantagnac, is living in Ottawa as a *déraciné*, a view that seems to subtly reiterate the notion of Groulx's provincialism. Oliver concurs with Wade in this and claims that the novel defended "separatist values."[10]

Oliver adds that Groulxist nationalism "limited" the individual, barring him from the path to the universal and confining him to a cultural "particularism."[11] As we shall see in the next chapter, Groulx had, however, developed a traditional nationalism according to which the embodiment of the person in a culture or a nation in itself represented a witness to the universality of the human condition. Did he oppose this "internationalism?" What he questioned, rather, was that a human being should have to go against their nature, to deny their origins and the cultural context that had given them life in order to know the universality of their human condition. Cultural and national identity, according to Groulx, did not constitute an obstacle to "internationalism" and could even be an ideal means of accessing it.

In any event, Oliver's study, like Wade's, gives short shrift to the issue of the French minorities, which is hardly raised, even in his analysis of Bourassa's "pan-Canadianism." The manifestations of solidarity by nationalists toward

9. Mason Wade, *The French Canadians, 1760–1945*, p. 877, 891.
10. Michael Oliver, *The Social and Political Ideas of French Canadian Nationalists, 1920–1945*, p. 100–103, 220.
11. *Ibid.*, p. 120–121.

the minorities during the interwar period constitute for him nothing more than anomalies that went against the "provincialist" nationalist current of the majority:

> French Canadian nationalism during both the 1920s and 1930s focussed narrowly on Quebec. There were exceptions to this: Bourassa, *La Relève* after the publication of its "Préliminaire à un manifeste pour la patrie," and such institutions as the Congrès de la langue française [of 1912], which treated French Canadians as a unity regardless of geographic location. But the main concern in *L'Action française*, *L'Action nationale*, and *La Nation*, and among the members of Jeune[-]Canada, [l]es Jeunesses patriotes and [l]'Action libérale nationale was the *État national*, whether in loose affiliation with, or separated from, the rest of Canada.[12]

Could this chasm between Bourassa and Groulx not be at least partially bridged by a more systematic analysis of the place of the French minorities in their respective ideologies? Might this not give us a more nuanced understanding of the dichotomy between the "pan-Canadianism" of the one and the "provincialism" of the other? Subsequently, their positions might appear less incompatible. Mason Wade and Michael Oliver presume that because Groulx advocated a "French-Canadian" rather than a "Canadian" nationalism, it obliged him to limit the field of his activity to Quebec. This view exempted them from having to make the minorities a subject of study in itself. Their conclusion seems to stem from a certain conceptual confusion resulting in a failure to grasp the essence of Lionel Groulx's idea of the French-Canadian nation. We repeat that it is very tempting to see in this interpretation of the thought of Groulx and Bourassa the influence of the debate between the *citélibristes* and the neo-nationalists that was stirring up French-Canadian and Quebec society around the same time.

The Historians and *L'Action française*

Reaction to the theories of Mason Wade and Michael Oliver were not unanimous. By the end of the 1960s, following on the heels of the institutional, political and ideological upheavals of the Quiet Revolution and the rise of the sovereignty movement in Québec, historians had begun to periodically revisit the nationalist movement of the interwar period, either to study new aspects of it or to refute the theories of Wade and Oliver outright. The considerable number of studies, in itself, clearly attests to the fact that there was no consensus among these historians—and prevents us from reviewing all of them. On certain fundamental questions, however, opinions diverged significantly. While some sought to confirm the portrait that Wade and Oliver had painted of an archaic and xenophobic Groulxism, there were also those who roundly criticized it. Nevertheless, on

12. Ibid., p. 148.

other questions that were just as fundamental, the conclusions of these studies from the 1950s were accepted almost indiscriminately, there being no call for further analysis. This was the case regarding the place of the French minorities in French-Canadian nationalist discourse in general and in the thought of Lionel Groulx in particular. The theory of provincialism would live a long and happy life indeed.

The first major study to appear during the 1960s was that of Mireille Badour who, in 1967, wrote a master's thesis on *Le Nationalisme de* L'Action nationale.[13] This study does not propose an exhaustive analysis of the discourse of *L'Action française* and *L'Action nationale* (which Badour treats as one and the same) and seeks only to determine what theoretical model fits the review's conception of the French-Canadian nation. Badour identifies two possible models: the "political conception" and the "cultural and ethnographic conception" of the nation. The first model "is defined . . . principally in political terms and presents the identification of *State and Nation* as its ideal." The cultural model, on the other hand, sees the nation as a "natural community" that is independent of the state. In contrast to the political model, "nationality becomes . . . an *inherent trait* in the individual and not the result of a choice." The two models represent, then, although the author does not explicitly say so, a confrontation between individualism, liberalism and modernity on the one hand and tradition and communitarianism on the other. The ideology of *L'Action nationale*, Badour explains, belonged to the "cultural" concept of nationhood.

If the nation, for the review, was basically "cultural," without formal ties to the state, one might have expected the author to acknowledge and study the place of the French minorities in it. Somewhat in the manner of Michael Oliver, who was—and this deserves to be mentioned—her research director, Badour maintains that the cultural nationalists sought, out of necessity, to have a state. Is there a contradiction here? Are not the nation and the state, according to Badour's cultural model, in principle independent of each other? The cultural nation, the author continues, would go so far as to bring about the "deification" of the state, realizing in this way a certain form of totalitarianism. We should clarify that these statements are made in the context of the discussion on the theoretical models of nationhood and that the author does not seek, subsequently, to show that *L'Action française* and *L'Action nationale* adhere to such totalitarian principles. Conversely, Badour believes there was no hesitation on the part of the nationalists to demand Québec independence, which in their view constituted "the political expression of French Canada." By taking better account of the place held by the minorities in the review's discourse, this study might have better reflected the connections between the concepts of "nation" and "state." The minorities, in any case, receive

13. Mireille Badour, *Le Nationalisme de* L'Action nationale, master's thesis (political science), McGill University, 1967, 152 p.

only a single mention, apart from a brief discussion on the Franco-Americans and the famous Sentinelle crisis.[14]

A few years later, in 1974, Donald Smith published a short study on what he called the "first" *Action française*, which ran from 1917 to 1921, a period when Lionel Groulx's predecessor, journalist Omer Héroux, was its director.[15] Smith offers a succinct but highly readable overview of the five principal themes developed by the review: family, education, religion, political life and the nation, the latter taking precedence over all the others. The French minorities, for their part, are not the subject of any particular analysis. The topic resurfaces occasionally when the aforementioned themes are being discussed. For example, under education, Smith points out that the review wanted to preserve the humanist training offered by the classical colleges "in the province and elsewhere." The review is also said to have promoted bilingualism outside Québec, in keeping with its defence of minority rights. Finally, Smith acknowledges that, for *L'Action française*, "the French-Canadian nation is not limited to Québec, but [that] its members are dispersed throughout the Canadian territory."

Smith's study is of interest to us for two reasons. In contrast to Wade and Oliver, he avoids demonizing Lionel Groulx and *L'Action française*, which allows him to present a more balanced analysis of their ideology. We cannot help but note, further, that although his essay is essentially a summary, it gives more attention to the minorities than either Wade or Oliver. Nonetheless, this attention is still limited to a few brief—and minor—comments.

These remarks apply equally to the next two studies of *L'Action française*. Susan Mann Trofimenkoff's work, which appeared in 1974, and Jean-Claude Dupuis's master's thesis, submitted some twenty years later in 1992, are, however, more substantial.[16] Trofimenkoff analyzes the review's discourse, the birth of the movement it was associated with and the numerous deliberations held behind the scenes unbeknownst to its readers. The author recounts the review's numerous "hesitations" as it found itself torn between, on the one hand, the forces of change (industrialization and urbanization) and, on the other, its attachment to a traditional way of life that had become obsolete. The review's fundamental inability to choose its camp, and its sentimental attachment to a bygone era, seriously hampered the efficacy of its interventions. Dupuis's study was intended, at least in part, as a riposte to Trofimenkoff's study. Dupuis felt Trofimenkoff had not sufficiently appreciated the ideology professed by Groulx and *L'Action française*, especially regarding their critique of industrialization and urbanization:

---

14. *Ibid.*, p. ii, 16–18, 32–34, 64.
15. Donald Smith, "*L'Action française*, 1917–1921," in Fernand Dumont *et al.*, *Idéologies au Canada français: 1900–1929* (Québec: Presses de l'Université Laval, 1974), p. 345–367.
16. Susan Mann Trofimenkoff, *Action Française: French Canadian Nationalism in the Twenties* (Toronto: University of Toronto Press, 1975), 157 p.; Jean-Claude Dupuis, *Nationalisme et catholicisme: L'Action française de Montréal (1917–1928)*, master's thesis (history), Université de Montréal, 1992, 329 p.

> We set out from the hypothesis that the ideological conflict separating liberal and Catholic thought in the Québec of the 1920s was not between partisans of the future and defenders of the past. In reality, the two ideological families that clashed were looking toward the future and sought progress for French Canada. But they did not understand this progress in the same way. The liberals favoured a modern society founded on the values of individualism and materialism while *L'Action française*, the leading voice for Catholics, preferred a modernization that rested on the traditional collective values of family, country and Church.[17]

Thus, to highly value tradition, to criticize materialism, to condemn the most pernicious effects of industrialization and urbanization, these, the author points out, are not at odds with progress. In fact, Dupuis's analysis brings major and very welcome nuances to the position that the ideology of *L'Action française* was archaic, which a good many researchers, including Mason Wade and Michael Oliver and, to a lesser extent, Susan Mann Trofimenkoff, had maintained. Dupuis points out that the review was more avant-garde than was generally thought, in that it "represented, rather, a force of protest against the status quo in a society dominated by liberal ideology and unfettered capitalism."[18]

In addition, Dupuis provides certain conceptual explanations that are lacking in the previous works, such as the definition of "nation" embraced by *L'Action française*. He recalls that, for the collaborators of the review, the nation was considered an organic entity that flowed from the sharing of a common historical and cultural heritage and national traditions:

> In the thinking of *L'Action française*, the nation is a living organism, an independent entity, comparable to a person or, rather, to a family. The tradition is in some sense the soul of this organism.
>
> . . . The nation is made up therefore of a sociological element—the common characteristics of language, religion, customs, territory, etc., and a historical element—the bond that unites the generations and which may be called tradition.[19]

With this definition in mind, one which values tradition much more highly than belonging to a well-defined territory, what place does Dupuis accord to the French minorities in his analysis of the review's discourse? "The question of the education rights of French Canadians outside Québec was a frequent topic in *L'Action française*," he tells us. Dupuis recognizes that the founding, in 1913, of the Ligue des droits du français (renamed Ligue d'Action française four years later) came about as a reaction against, among other things, the government of

17. Jean-Claude Dupuis, *Nationalisme et catholicisme: L'Action française de Montréal* (1917–1928), p. 7–8.
18. *Ibid.*, p. 16.
19. *Ibid.*, p. 102, 104.

Ontario's adoption of Regulation 17 the previous year. The review regularly reiterated its support for the minorities of Ontario and the West, where their educational rights were being systematically violated by intolerant provincial governments.

As in the Dupuis study, the French minorities come up several times in the Trofimenkoff account. The hanging of Louis Riel and the schools crises in the West and Ontario all served as motivating factors in the founding of not only *L'Action française*, but also a good many nationalist institutions in the early twentieth century, including the Association canadienne-française d'éducation d'Ontario (ACFEO), *Le Droit*, a nationalist newspaper published in Ottawa (which had "inspired" *L'Action française*) and the Congrès de la langue française of 1912, to name only a few. In French-Canadian intellectual circles in Montréal, during the second and third decades of the twentieth century, the educational and religious problems experienced by the minorities had often dominated discussions, especially at the Mile End rectory, where Abbé Philippe Perrier, who had Henri Bourassa in his parish, regularly welcomed several of nationalism's heavyweights from Québec and the other provinces.

While Trofimenkoff and Dupuis mention that the schools crises were frequently discussed in the pages of *L'Action française*, most of the attention their studies give to the minorities is focused on two specific questions: the famous Sentinelle crisis in New England, which earned a group of Franco-American militant nationalists a sentence of excommunication, and especially the "French state" dispute. The controversy surrounding the review's leanings toward *indépendantisme* and the creation of a "French state," let us repeat, had started in 1922 at the time *L'Action française* published its extensive study on "our political future." At that time, the review's collaborators anticipated the breakup of Confederation as the country faced the combined pressures of galloping Americanization and increasing economic disparity between Western and Central Canada. The French minorities, Trofimenkoff tells us, expressed deep reservations about the validity of this analysis, fearing they would be left in the lurch by their Quebec compatriots. The review relied on several arguments to calm their anxiety: *L'Action française* in no way promoted separatism, but believed that other factors beyond its control would likely provoke the breakup of Confederation; Québec's participation in the Canadian federation had not prevented provincial governments from "persecuting" the French minorities; finally, the spread of the French culture in America would come about only through the political reinforcement of Québec, ancestral home of the French-Canadian nation.

In conclusion, Trofimenkoff states that "[n]ever would [*L'Action française*] break with French Canadian minorities beyond Quebec," and that this position represented one of the many "hesitations" of the review.[20] However, with respect

20. Susan Mann Trofimenkoff, *Action Française: French Canadian Nationalism in the Twenties*, p. 119.

to the review's "separatism" and its treatment of the Sentinelle crisis, the analysis of the place the minorities held in the discourse of Groulx and his colleagues receives only marginal attention: the minorities seem important only to the extent that they could provide a better understanding of the French state dispute. As such, the minorities do not constitute the subject of any analysis, despite the fact that the author recognizes the importance of the schools crises in the birth of the Groulxist movement. No analysis of how the French minorities were represented in the review, or of what role they were seen to have in the nationalist cosmogony, is provided.

Dupuis in turn deals with the question of the review's separatism and the anxiety this argument caused among the French minorities. The sad fate that they would have been left to were an independent "French state" to be created constituted one of the many arguments advanced by Henri Bourassa in his condemnation of the separatist inclinations of Groulx and *L'Action française*. Independence, according to the founder of *Le Devoir*, would quite simply have meant Québec's abandonment of the French minorities. Nevertheless, in Dupuis's view, the conflict between Groulx and Bourassa, on this question and others, was not as serious as was believed. In reality, the thinking of the two nationalist leaders contained far more points of convergence than difference. At most, they clashed, quite simply, over how to achieve "their common national ideal, a French, Catholic ideal." *L'Action française*, generally speaking, subscribed to the idea of a bicultural Canada, an idea Bourassa had vigorously defended, and its version of separatism remained, by that very fact, a "hesitant" one. With regard more specifically to the minorities, Bourassa was wrong to accuse *L'Action française* of endorsing their abandonment. Dupuis holds that the review did not renounce the "idea of French *survivance* outside Québec; on the contrary, it [had made] it an essential aspect of its doctrine."[21]

The study by Jean-Claude Dupuis is no doubt the one that grants the greatest importance to the place of the French minorities in the discourse of *L'Action française*. The progress made since the works by Mason Wade and Michael Oliver in this respect is not to be ignored. It is also interesting to note that it is in the context of a study more sympathetic toward Lionel Groulx and *L'Action française* than previous ones that one finds this openness to the minorities issue. That said, the studies by Dupuis and Trofimenkoff do not analyze the representation of the minorities in the review's discourse any more systematically than the previous studies did. Yet, the interest that *L'Action française* and Lionel Groulx showed in the minorities extended far beyond the education question and the French state debate. Perhaps the studies that were entirely dedicated to the thought of the *L'Action française* director, Lionel Groulx, were more productive in this regard.

21. Jean-Claude Dupuis, *Nationalisme et catholicisme: L'Action française de Montréal* (1917–1928), p. 205.

The Historians and the Thought of Lionel Groulx

The early 1970s witnessed the appearance of the first books and articles dedicated entirely to the work of Lionel Groulx, who had died a few years earlier in 1967. It is easy to recognize, upon reading several of them, the political and ideological context of that turbulent period, marked as it was by the spread of Quebec nationalism and the resulting dramatic break between Québec and the French minorities, the rise of sovereignty fervour and the modernization of Québec society. The questions therefore of Québec independence and of the obstacles to modernity resurfaced frequently among the concerns addressed by historians of nationalism. Was Groulx a separatist? Was he a French-Canadian nationalist or a Québec nationalist? Was his ideology outmoded to the point of being completely obsolete in the context of the Quiet Revolution or was there still something relevant to be salvaged from it?

The first major historical study of Groulx's thought, Jean-Pierre Gaboury's *Le Nationalisme de Lionel Groulx*, appeared in 1970, barely three years after the Canon's death.[22] Gaboury uses the yardstick of modernity, which he clearly champions, to assess Groulx's thought, at times with sharp criticism, targeting in particular its economics. Inspired by the theories of German sociologist Max Weber, Gaboury interprets Groulx's economic thought as manifesting a "traditional" and "feudal mentality." The Canon's classical, humanist model of the education system was thought to be unsuited to a society in the midst of industrial expansion, and his Catholicism was seen as radically opposed to the material progress that the Protestant religion easily endorsed. It was this retrograde ideology, Gaboury maintains, that prevented the French Canadian nation from occupying its rightful place in the economic sphere:

> This basic premise of Weber's [according to which Protestants place a higher value on material progress than Catholics] seems to bear out perfectly in French Canada, where the directors and shareholders of the large financial and business corporations were for the most part adherents of the Protestant religion, and the less lucrative jobs were shared among the Catholics. Lionel Groulx truly embodies this "traditional" morality, as attested moreover by his "humanist" notion of education and his clear rejection of the industrial revolution.[23]

The theme of economic catch-up, a leitmotif of the architects of the Quiet Revolution, emerges here with resounding clarity, as does the anticlerical bias of the sixties and the seventies. Although Gaboury is severely critical of the nation/religion synthesis that is so central to Groulx's thought, he nevertheless proposes an interesting theoretical discussion of nation. The French-Canadian nation, in the

22. Jean-Pierre Gaboury, *Le Nationalisme de Lionel Groulx: Aspects idéologiques* (Ottawa: Presses de l'Université d'Ottawa, 1970), 226 p.
23. *Ibid.*, p. 163.

mind of the Canon, was similar to the idea of community developed by German sociologist Ferdinand Tönnies. Over and against modern, industrial society, which relied on the notion of contract as its unifying force, the Groulxist nation relied on its organic and natural bonds.

Does this organicist interpretation of Groulx's thought lead the author to give some attention to the issue of the French minorities? Or are we being presented with yet another reiteration of the theory of provincialism? It would seem indeed to be the latter that serves as the background for Gaboury's work, although this historian, in contrast to Mason Wade and Michael Oliver, sees nothing deplorable in it. Generally speaking, the terms "Québec" and "French Canada" appear interchangeable, although as early as the first chapter the author offers the following clarification: "We shall use the term French-Canadian rather than Québécois, because this is the term Lionel Groulx constantly used and his reference was always to the French-Canadian reality and not just the reality of Québec."[24] That Gaboury felt the need to include this cautionary note speaks volumes about the disfavour the concept and term "French Canadian" had already fallen into by 1970 in certain segments of the population of Québec. If it is true that, despite substantial overlap in meaning, the terms "Québec" and "French Canada" are not synonymous, one is obliged to conclude that the author's clarification only partially saves him from lapsing into presentism. Take the following excerpts, for example:

> We know there are in French Canada, in the field of nationalism as in the field of history, two distinct trends: one grants primacy to French Canada (now, rather, Québec), the other to Canada.
>
> The fundamental question in this debate was to know whether the history of French Canada should promote Québec nationalism or harmonious relations between Canadians. For Abbé Groulx, the answer was easy.[25]

Gaboury thus finds himself in the rather incongruous position of making Abbé Groulx an advocate of "Québecois" nationalism although the author himself admits that the priest-historian never made use of the term. The minorities, for their part, receive only scant coverage in his analysis. After a brief initial comment on the schools crises, which, he writes, had an influence on Groulx's thought, the author embarks on a lengthy discussion of his fictional work. In addition to *L'Appel de la race* which appeared in the early 1920s, Groulx published a second novel, *Au Cap Blomidon*, some ten years later. Once again, the action takes place in a minority setting, this time in Acadia. However, this point does not hold Gaboury's attention. He seeks only to demonstrate that Groulx's literary work was part of a campaign and constituted a "popular extension of his commitment

24. *Ibid.*, p. 2, n. 2.
25. *Ibid.*, p. 42, 103.

as a historian and propagator."[26] While the author explains that the context and raw material for the first novel had been provided by the Franco-Ontarian schools crisis, he does not exploit this opportunity to explore further the specific place the French minorities held for Groulx in his ideology. The discussion, on the contrary, is confined to an enumeration of the themes developed in Groulx's novels (the spinelessness of the French-Canadian bourgeoisie, the weaknesses of the education system, the dangers of exogamy, fidelity to tradition and to the ancestors, and so forth) and an account of how they were received in literary circles.

The minorities make another appearance in Gaboury's work—in a section on Groulx's critique of the federal government's centralizing policies. Groulx, he writes, vigorously defended Québec's autonomy vis-à-vis the federal government. Yet, he demanded that it repudiate the provincial governments' anti-French and anti-Catholic school laws. He wanted it to intervene in order to compel the provinces to uphold the principle of the two founding peoples. Gaboury found Groulx's logic here to be fundamentally contradictory:

> If the federal government must protect the "rights of the French," even though education falls under the jurisdiction of the states, would it not also have the right to intervene in the affairs of Québec on behalf of the English minority? The *autonomiste* thought of Abbé Groulx involves a dangerous inconsistency here.[27]

The Compact theory of Confederation and the principle of provincial autonomy are said here to be incompatible, something Groulx was considered not to have understood. Gaboury's manner of reasoning assumes that in order to protect Québec effectively against infringements by the federal government, it would have been preferable for Groulx to, quite simply, abandon the French minorities of the other provinces. Gaboury comes across as extremely critical towards Groulx's hesitation to openly approve of Québec independence, on the one hand, and his feeling of nostalgia for the bygone era of New France, on the other:

> [Groulx], who studied the French Empire of America at length and with great admiration, had some difficulty conceiving of a French Canada reduced to the limits of Québec's borders. By a kind of irredentism, found in the writings of Tardivel, it seems that his "French state" relates to all the French of America, or at least of Canada. . . . The independent "French state" had the drawback of abandoning the French minorities, in whose favour he had often fought and whom he did not wish to abandon. . . . A true separatist does not believe in the *survivance* of the French minorities[28].

26. Ibid., p. 75.
27. Ibid., p. 154–155.
28. Ibid., p. 159.

Too reticent toward separation, too preoccupied over the fate of the French minorities and too unaware of the inherent contradiction. This, in a few words, summarizes Gaboury's analysis of the place of the minorities in Lionel Groulx's work. The priest-historian's attitude toward the separatist movement of the 1930s also drew the attention of another researcher, Robert Comeau. In an article on *La Nation* (1936–1938), Comeau sets out to clarify the ideological relationship between Groulx and the editors of the *indépendantiste* newspaper, who openly claimed to be followers of Groulx's teachings.[29] The author disagrees with Gaboury, who concludes, he says, that the Canon was a separatist. If, as Comeau believes, Groulx never explicitly professed to favour independence, it was, in the author's view, because the French state he dreamed of represented more of a "mystical" reality than a program of political action in the strict sense of the term. Consequently, radical separatists, just as easily as more moderate nationalists who respected the federal regime, could draw on Groulx's vision and find there something supporting their own. By all accounts, Comeau subscribed to the theory of the apolitical nature of Groulx's thought, a theory we shall return to shortly.

With respect to the French minorities, the author points out that Paul Bouchard, "the leader" of *La Nation*, was delighted that Abbé Groulx had "admirably demolished the sentimental argument of the sparse French minorities in the Dominion" put forward by the detractors of the separatist project.[30] Comeau, however, does not show the discrepancy between this theory of Bouchard's and Groulx's actual position regarding the minorities. On this question, he is content to quote the nationalist leader's words as he addressed *La Nation*'s adversaries, stating that "independence did not mean isolating, any more than abandoning, the minorities."[31]

In 1974, André-J. Bélanger published an important work, *L'Apolitisme des idéologies québécoises*, which dedicated a full chapter to Groulx's thought during the economic crisis of the 1930s.[32] This study, as the title indicates, picks up the theory of the apolitical nature of the nationalist movement, put forward two years earlier by Robert Comeau. Groulx's ideology was considered apolitical because he sought to develop a "Québecois mystique" rather than a political action program, in the full and complete sense of the word "political." Groulx had always had a deep mistrust of the state and partisan politics, Bélanger tells us. He had only ever seen it as a condemnable source of division. His concept of the nation as an organic entity rested, instead, on the notions of consensus, harmony and corporatism. The

29. Robert Comeau, "Lionel Groulx, les indépendantistes de *La Nation* et le séparatisme (1936–1938)," *Revue d'histoire de l'Amérique française* (hereinafter RHAF), Vol. 26, No. 1 (June 1972), p. 83–102.
30. Paul Bouchard, cited in *ibid.*, p. 90.
31. *Ibid.*, p. 98.
32. André-J. Bélanger, "Lionel Groulx, une mystique québécoise," in *L'Apolitisme des idéologies québécoises: Le grand tournant de 1934–1936* (Québec: Presses de l'Université Laval, 1974), p. 191–255.

national interest, which he defined as separate from the concepts of statehood and political conflict, was at all times to take precedence over party interests.

This interpretation needs to be nuanced somewhat today. Groulx's nationalism valued the notion of tradition above all else. In this sense, it is true that he considered French Canada an organic entity, to which partisan politics brought division. But that analysis does not take into account Groulx's proposed "political" interpretation of the history of the French-Canadian nation as the story of a slow political liberation that went from the Conquest of 1760 to the Québec Act of 1774, to the establishment of the parliamentary system in 1791, and to the Confederation of 1867. Certainly, the political ascension of the French-Canadian nation was due, in his mind, to the actions of great men who had known how to glue together the partisan factions of the time. But these were, nevertheless, actions that had a political context. Groulx's thought was only apolitical to the extent that one limits politics to partisan conflicts.

This chapter by Bélanger is dedicated to the period in Groulx's career that immediately followed the publication of two of his most important books focused on the minorities, the novel *Au Cap Blomidon* (1932) and the second volume of his *Enseignement français au Canada* (1935). The author, however, makes no mention of the place the minorities occupied in his work. According to Bélanger, "all [Groulx's] thought revolves around the autonomy granted to Québec since the Union [of 1841] was dissolved." What is more, the author expressly omits Ottawa's *Le Droit* from the institutions, media agencies and intellectuals he studies. He justifies that decision by saying that while the newspaper "appeared to have been well established," it is "automatically excluded by virtue of "being outside Québec."[33] It is hard not to see in this bias another case of the theory of provincialism at work and another example of the very contemporary semantic confusion between the concepts of "French Canada" and "Québec."

However, certain themes developed by Bélanger in this study could have allowed for some breakthroughs. The author makes much, for example, of Groulx's notion of the "apostolic vocation" of French Canada but fails to draw the conclusions he might have made with respect to the role and representation of the French minorities in his nationalism. As we shall try to show below, the burden of French-Canadian messianism, according to Groulx, was mainly carried by the French minorities, whom he considered the remnant, or the extension, of the great "French Empire of America." In Bélanger's mind, Groulx made the apostolic vocation of French Canada the exclusive affair of the French explorers who had travelled across America during the short century between the discovery of Canada by Jacques Cartier and the erection of the first permanent settlements in the Saint-Lawrence Valley. In the ensuing struggle between the imperative to

33. *Ibid.*, p. 22, 250.

explore and the imperative to colonize, it was the latter that won out in Groulx's historical work, according to Bélanger. From a strictly historical perspective, the era of great explorations was considered to have ended with the start of colonization: The first colonists put down roots in their new land and, once settled, went about accomplishing their agricultural vocation without further ado. However, Bélanger explains that Groulx, the propagandist, by exalting the myth of the explorer, frequently contradicted Groulx, the historian. "The spirit of conquest was an ideal [Groulx] advised his contemporaries to develop, for he felt that was something they were sorely lacking in."[34]

This essential opposition between the ideals of exploration and colonization proceeds, in Bélanger's analysis, from the premise—by now familiar to us— that "provincialism" was an inherent part of Lionel Groulx's nationalism. Since, according to this idea, French Canada is confused with Québec, how could one not see in exploration and the desire for territorial expansion a negation of the imperative of colonization? Would integrating the French minorities into this debate not help to nuance it and make the dichotomy between exploration (or migration, at the very least) and colonization less irreducible? In Groulx's mind, as we shall see, the two processes were not always in opposition. He believed that the work of the explorers and missionaries had made it possible to establish French-Canadian communities everywhere in the country and, far from being limited to the era of discovery, continued, in some places, up to the nineteenth century. Thus, the Tachés and the Langevins, who, in his view, had opened the West to French Catholic civilization, were just as much a part of the national pantheon as the Champlains of New France. The desire to explore and evangelize served not only to spread the vital strength of the nation; it could also push the boundaries of the nation's influence ever further.

The theory of provincialism will resurface again, in the late 1970s, in the writings of two other historians of Groulx's thought, Georges-Émile Giguère and Guy Frégault. Giguère and Frégault alike, when discussing the French minorities, seem to do so mainly to show that the problems the minorities encountered in resisting assimilation had driven Lionel Groulx to espouse a strictly Québecois concept of the French-Canadian nation and abandon the pan-Canadian one he had held. In 1978, Giguère published a short biography of Lionel Groulx.[35] In the feverish atmosphere of the Parti Québécois's initial mandate and the discussions surrounding the referendum to be held on the sovereignty of Québec, the author seeks to better define the nature of Groulx's nationalism and to determine, like Gaboury and Comeau before him, whether his thought was that of a true separatist. The conceptual confusion regarding the use of the terms "French Canada"

34. *Ibid.*, p. 206.

35. Georges-Émile Giguère, *Lionel Groulx: Biographie: "Notre État français, nous l'aurons!"* (Montréal: Bellarmin, 1978), 159 p.

and "Québec" becomes apparent once again in this work, the author going so far as to call Groulx a "son of the Québec nation." In this respect, Giguère is manifestly sympathetic to the independence movement and picks up the old interpretation of Mason Wade and Michael Oliver in his analysis of the conflict between Henri Bourassa and Lionel Groulx. It is tempting to compare this conflict with the one that was raging at the time between Pierre Elliott Trudeau and René Lévesque.

Giguère does not disregard the existence of the French minorities, who recur often enough in his work. However, the author brings them into play principally in order to show how the injustices they suffered had prompted Lionel Groulx to construct a strictly Québécois nationalism (the term "Québécois" being substituted more often than not, in this work, for the term "French-Canadian"). He believes Groulx understood very early on in his career that, from the hanging of Louis Riel to the crisis of Regulation 17, Canada had shown it was basically incapable of respecting either the spirit or the letter of the Constitution or of respecting the rights of the minorities. "How could we be surprised," Giguère asks, "that a Lionel Groulx should reach the point of wondering whether the country might not rather be Québec, and the nation, the Québécois?"[36]

Was Groulx's nationalism separatist after all? Not necessarily, says Giguère, who provides an honest answer to this question. The ideal for Groulx, he explains, had been respect for Québec autonomy, in keeping with the agreement of 1867. Was that brand of nationalism Québécois? The answer this time seems to be yes and there's the rub. Giguère, like others before him, frequently confuses the concepts of "French Canada" and "Québec," which inevitably leads him to see as equivalent the provincial autonomy principle and the founding-peoples principle, an equivalence that all but completely eliminates the issue of the French minorities from Groulxist thought. This approach does not seem to pose the same problems for Giguère as for Jean-Pierre Gaboury. Gaboury, as we have seen, observes a "dangerous inconsistency" in Groulx's defence of provincial autonomy and his appeal to the founding-peoples theory to defend the minorities. Evidently, a closer analysis of these two concepts and of their reciprocal relationship in Groulx's thought is needed.

According to Giguère, the minorities, or rather the difficulties they had experienced, had served only to push Abbé Groulx to re-evaluate the foundations of the nation, which in his mind had become the Québécois nation. His study seems to tell us more about the political and ideological context of the Québec of the late 1970s than about Groulx's real thought concerning the French minorities. These comments may also be applied, almost in their entirety, to Guy Frégault's *Lionel Groulx tel qu'en lui-même*, also published in 1978.[37] This essay cannot be considered

36. *Ibid.*, p. 42.
37. Guy Frégault, *Lionel Groulx tel qu'en lui-même* (Montréal: Leméac, 1978), 237 p.

a historical analysis, in the strict sense of the term, of Groulx's thought. It is, rather, a personal reflection offered by the author on the writing of his former mentor. Like Giguère before him, Frégault notes the significant role played by the Métis rebellions and the education battles of the minorities in the intellectual formation of Groulx and the nationalists of his generation. He also highlights the place the minorities held in his historical works and in the numerous talks he gave in various parts of French Canada. When reading Frégault's essay, however, one gets the impression that these experiences served only to reinforce a pessimism that had already taken hold in Groulx's mind with regard to the minorities. His major study on the minority schools, done at the beginning of the 1930s, is reported as having led him to conclude that it was impossible for a French-Canadian nation to be spread throughout the entire country:

> Instead of the "duality" he tried so hard to find in "the spirit of 1867," he discovered in the facts the inequality of the two peoples; instead of seeing *la francophonie* "expand right across Canada," he saw it pushed back to inside Québec—that Québec whose provincial "shortcomings" limited "the accomplishment of that dream." He concludes with bitterness that there will henceforth be, "before the constitution, two Canadas: a French Canada respectful of the freedom of all, but limited to its Québec "reserve," and an Anglo-Protestant Canada, unable to tolerate, except in minute doses, the teaching of the Catholic faith and the French language."[38]

Frégault, who pulls this quote from Groulx's study of the minority schools, attributes this conclusion to Groulx himself. However, after a more careful reading of the cited text, one notices that Groulx's intention, rather, was to summarize the logic behind the anti-French and anti-Catholic policies of the English-Canadian political class. Frégault could have cited, from the same work, another passage which no doubt better expresses what Groulx really thought on this topic and which we cited in the introduction: "The dominant fact about French life in America, during the past century, is without a doubt that it became dispersed. French Canada can no longer be defined as a geographical expression limited by the borders of Québec."[39] In any case, Frégault speaks freely of Groulx's "Québécois" nationalism and patriotism, which he terms a "spontaneous feeling,"[40] while stressing at the same time and at length the "excellent" writings of Richard Arès which had already reported the irrevocable decline of French presence outside Québec since the Second World War. The acculturation of the minorities became particularly blatant, he explains, during the 1970s.[41]

38. *Ibid.*, p. 74–75.
39. Lionel Groulx, *L'Enseignement français au Canada: Tome II: Les Écoles des minorités* (Montréal: Librairie Granger Frères, 1935), p. 71.
40. Guy Frégault, *Lionel Groulx tel qu'en lui-même*, p. 86–87, 128, 192–193.
41. *Ibid.*, p. 78–81.

Frégault does not fail to mention the French state debate of the 1920s and 1930s. While he recalls the anxiety it produced among the French minorities and the reassuring words Groulx and his collaborators at *L'Action française* offered them, the author nevertheless concludes that "the Groulx of the twenties is the better Groulx," no doubt because it was during that period that he was most candid about his vision for the creation of an independent "French state."

If Giguère and Frégault, despite a few reservations, offer a sympathetic portrait, on balance, of the figure and the thought of Lionel Groulx, the same cannot be said of Phyllis Senese. In a very critical article, Senese maintains that Groulx tried to create an illogical and incoherent, if not impossible, synthesis between two notions which in her view were by definition mutually exclusive: nationalism and Catholicism.[42] Although Senese acknowledges that the former is, in Groulx's thought, subordinate to the latter, she still concludes that

> [h]e frequently confounded patriotism and nationalism and failed to recognize or appreciate the extent to which nationalism by its very nature became an agent of secularisation. And this habit of thought, of uncritically linking Catholicism and nationalism, bedevilled Groulx's work more and more after the wartime traumas of 1917.[43]

However, Groulx was often called upon to explain and justify the links that he believed were essential between Catholicism and the life of the French-Canadian nation. To reduce the question to what Senese considers a lack of critical thinking on Groulx's part seems a poorly nuanced analysis of an otherwise complex issue. Nationhood, according to Groulx, rested on the notion of tradition, rather than on some kind of political bond. As an "organic" entity, it was, as we shall see shortly, a providential creation. In essence, then, there is no opposition between Catholicism and nationalism, as long as we know what kind of nationalism we are talking about.

This conceptual confusion prompts Senese to venture dubious interpretations of other questions, particularly when she states that the fusion between faith and nation is so complete in Groulx's mind that he considered only French Canadians could be true Catholics. The author advances only one point to illustrate this—namely, Groulx's first novel, *L'Appel de la race*. She maintains that Groulx doubted the sincerity of Maud's religious convictions, Maud being the Catholic but English-Canadian spouse of his hero, Lantagnac. This is how she explains the breakup of their marriage:

42. P. M. Senese, "Catholique d'abord!: Catholicism and Nationalism in the Thought of Lionel Groulx," *Canadian Historical Review*, Vol. 60, No. 2 (June 1979), p. 154–177. Jean-Claude Dupuis offers an interesting reply to Senese in "La pensée religieuse de l'Action française [sic] (1917–1928)," *Études d'histoire religieuse*, 1993, p. 73–88.
43. P. M. Senese, "Catholique d'abord ! . . . ," p. 163.

> Catholicism was French; Maud could never be a Catholic no matter how sincere and deep her conversion. It was precisely this religious separatism that was the most dangerous implication of the novel. Rather than counsel Catholic solidarity against secular values, *L'Appel de la race* seemed to sanction the animosities of nationalities specifically condemned by Benedict XV and Pius XI.[44]

Yet, upon reading the novel, it is abundantly clear that the marital breakup is not due to weak religious conviction on Maud's part but rather to her inability to tolerate Lantagnac's crusade against the provincial regulation outlawing the French language in Ontario schools, a measure supported, however, by a good number of English-language Catholic bishops. To hold that for Groulx Catholicism was the exclusive domain of French Canadians is rather problematic. In his mind, it was French Canadians who were necessarily Catholic, not the other way round.

It is important to take into account Senese's interpretation of the links between faith and nation in Groulx's thought when considering her view of his treatment of the French minorities. Obviously, she writes, other Catholics did not welcome the claims to Catholic exclusivity that Groulx ascribed to French Canadians. "In the end, he seemed to exclude even French Catholics outside Québec."[45] Is this a new instance of the provincialism theory? Let us consider the following, very telling, excerpt:

> More than anything else, the acrimonious debates of the war years [the First World War] and his loss of confidence for the prospects of Catholicism in North America persuaded Groulx to consider French Canada's destiny as lying exclusively within the province of Quebec. Whatever fleeting possibilities he had previously seen in regarding Quebec as vital to the maintenance of Canada or even in the existence of Canada [were] swept away in the flood of hostility directed at Quebec by the rest of the country as a consequence of the war. What Quebec and the Québécois needed in order to survive became his preoccupation in the years after 1917. By 1928 he would describe himself less as a French Canadian and ever more as a Québécois.[46]

The confusion surrounding French-Canadian and Québec identities is total here. The theory of Groulx's exclusion of the French minorities and his conversion to "Québecois" nationalism is all the harder to accept given that Senese provides no evidence of it, other than two unreferenced examples taken out of context, where Groulx spoke of "Québécois" rather than of "French Canadians."[47]

---

44. *Ibid.*, p. 170–172.
45. *Ibid.*, p. 167.
46. *Ibid.*, p. 165.
47. *Ibid.*, p. 165, n. 47.

We must mention, as we conclude this section, the recent and very interesting work of Frédéric Boily on Groulx's nationalist thought.[48] This study mainly seeks to cast doubt on the idea that Groulx's thought is an ideology of "biological racism." While admitting that his discourse, in certain highly specific contexts, was not always entirely free of xenophobic, and even anti-Semitic, elements, Boily maintains that the deeper logic of his nationalism was first and foremost cultural, and borrowed from the romantic and organicist philosophy of Johann Gottfried Herder. This is a perspective that would let us gain a better grasp of his concept of history, education, the relationship between nationalism and Catholicism and so forth. In the final chapter of the book, the author seeks to demonstrate that certain aspects of Lionel Groulx's work have survived him, notably in the thought of some of the intellectuals who succeeded him, like Michel Brunet and Fernand Dumont, but also—and this will surely surprise many—Charles Taylor and Gérard Bouchard. Nevertheless, although Boily rightly highlights the organic character of the Groulxist nation and draws attention to its disregard for territorial and political borders, his study, just like those that preceded it, still remains largely silent, save for a few references, on the question of the French minorities and their place in Groulx's thought.

Modernity, "Americanity" and the French Minorities

This historiographic overview would be incomplete if it discounted the emergence of the "Americanity of Québec" theory, considering the role it played in the debate over the nature of the Québécois nation. Recently, this question took on the character of a genuine controversy with the publication of Ronald Rudin's book, *Making History in Twentieth-Century Quebec*.[49] In this work, the author states that, since the end of the 1970s, a "revisionist" school, seeking to show how Québec constitutes and has always constituted a "normal" society, rallied several historians if not the majority of them. The central paradigm of this school would be the rejection of the idea that Québec was late in entering modernity. Thus, according to the "revisionists," the Quiet Revolution of the 1960s does not really

48. Frédéric Boily, *La Pensée nationaliste de Lionel Groulx* (Sillery: Septentrion, 2003), 232 p. Among the most recent studies of Groulx's thought, we must also count Stéphane Pigeon, *Lionel Groulx, critique de la Révolution tranquille (1956–1967)*, master's thesis (history), Université de Montréal, 1999, 119 p.; Sylvie Beaudreau, "Déconstruire le rêve de nation: Lionel Groulx et la Révolution tranquille," *RHAF*, Vol. 56, No. 1 (Summer 2002), p. 29–61; Marie-Pier Luneau, *Lionel Groulx: Le mythe du berger* (Montréal: Leméac, 2003), 226 p. Note that later in this chapter we shall visit Gérard Bouchard's work, *Les Deux Chanoines: Contradiction et ambivalence dans la pensée de Lionel Groulx* (Montréal: Boréal, 2003), 313 p.

49. Ronald Rudin, *Making History in Twentieth-Century Quebec*, p. 171–218. Regarding this controversy, one may read the sometimes virulent remarks exchanged between Rudin, Fernand Harvey and Paul-André Linteau in *Revue d'histoire de l'Amérique française*: Fernand Harvey and Paul-André Linteau, "Les étranges lunettes de Ronald Rudin," *RHAF*, Vol. 51, No. 3 (Winter 1998), p. 419–424, 429; Ronald Rudin, "Les lunettes différentes," *RHAF*, Vol. 51, No. 3 (Winter 1998), p. 425–428, 429. Serge Gagnon also takes Rudin to task in *Le Passé composé: De Ouellet à Rudin* (Montréal: VLB Éditeur, 1999), 192 p. See also Sébastien Parent, "Ronald Rudin et l'historiographie dite 'révisionniste': Un bilan," *Bulletin d'histoire politique*, Vol. 9, No. 1 (Fall 2000), p. 169–183.

represent a turning point in the history of Québec, but simply the acceleration of a process of cultural, economic and political modernization entered during the nineteenth century. Consequently, Québec's historical evolution is presented as being similar to that of most other North American societies. That is how, according to Rudin, these historians choose to define the notion of "normal."

Rudin is of the opinion, however, that this search for a "normal" society tends to minimize the ethnic, cultural and religious particularities of the "Québec nation"—distinctive characteristics that represent as many demons, which the "revisionists" wanted to exorcize from Québec's history. Furthermore, he says it is this choice to retain the territory of Québec, rather than French Canada, as their single field of analysis that allows these historians to sustain their theory. It could be argued that the importance they accorded to the territory of Québec was explainable, at least in part, by the ascendancy of quantitative methods of analysis among historians since the 1960s. Practitioners of social history in particular might require a more defined territorial framework, given the nature of their studies. Be that as it may, the Québec of the "revisionists," according to Rudin, would be made up essentially of individuals whose ethnocultural identity was no longer of any significance in the process of defining identity. The economic progress made by some would belong to all, without discrimination, and the theory of the economic inferiority of French Canadians, long held by academics, would be quietly discarded.

Among the principal representatives of this school, Rudin cites Paul-André Linteau, René Durocher and Jean-Claude Robert who, in 1979 and 1986, published their famous and authoritative *Histoire du Québec contemporain*.[50] In this vast synthesis, which deals with several dimensions of Québec's history, the authors maintain that "any study that uses the Quiet Revolution or even the Second World War as its point of departure for understanding present-day Québec would be a short-sighted analysis."[51] Industrialization, urbanization, modernity in literature and in the arts, all these developments, the authors explain, find their origin in the nineteenth century and attest to the fact that Québec was never substantially behind the other Western and North American societies, prior to 1960, except in the matter of modernizing its state apparatus. What about the French-Canadian nationalist movement in this narrative of Québec's ever-growing modernization? In the 300 pages or so covering the period from 1896 to 1929, the authors devote about eight, it must be noted, to the study of the ideas of the nationalists of the

50. Paul-André Linteau, René Durocher and Jean-Claude Robert, *Histoire du Québec contemporain: De la Confédération à la crise* (Montréal: Boréal, 1979), 658 p. In 1986, François Ricard joined the team for the publication of the second volume of this work, *Histoire du Québec contemporain: Le Québec depuis 1930* (Montréal: Boréal, 1986). Subsequent references to this study will be to the revised edition of 1989: Linteau, Durocher and Robert, *Histoire du Québec contemporain: Tome I: De la Confédération à la crise (1867–1929)* (Montréal: Boréal, 1989), 760 p.; Linteau, Durocher, Robert and Ricard, *Histoire du Québec contemporain: Tome II: Le Québec depuis 1930* (Montréal: Boréal, 1989), 840 p.

51. Linteau *et al.*, *Histoire du Québec contemporain: Tome II*, p. 805.

early part of the century. The following passage summarizes their principal observation well:

> The clerico-nationalist project is systematically turned towards the past. It is characterized by the rejection of new values and the falling back on French-Canadian and Catholic tradition. Its spokespersons are convinced that in order to survive as a people, the French Canadians must hang on to these traditional values and preserve them as a precious heritage.[52]

If Québec has been a modern society for a long time already, these clerico-nationalist elites necessarily look like a group of reactionary intellectuals with more or less retrograde ideas. According to the authors, "clerico-nationalism" seems to represent no more than a minority ideological current, not very representative of Québec society as a whole and situated in opposition to its overall development. Needless to say, a vision of a "nation" or, at the very least, a "society" that limits itself to the territory of Québec will not feature the French minorities very prominently. On this question, Linteau and his colleagues reconstitute the difference of opinion, found in much of the previous historiography, that seemingly distinguished Bourassa's "Canadian" and "bi-ethnic" nationalism from the ideology of Groulx and *L'Action française*: they portray Bourassa as willingly coming to the aid of the French minorities all across the country, while Groulx and the review, for their part, experienced "a brief independence phase in 1922" and developed "a nationalism centred particularly on Québec."[53]

Gérard Bouchard is among those who, more recently yet, have examined in the greatest detail and with the greatest clarity the issue of the "Americanity" of the "Québécois" nation. This theme, in fact, constitutes the main thread of a good portion of Bouchard's academic and, we might add, polemical work.[54] In his view, there existed a chasm as deep as it was unfortunate between the traditional French-Canadian elites, who projected "false identities," and the general Québécois population who had already become reconciled to their "Americanity" a long time ago. Bouchard judges that by defining the French-Canadian nation as an "organic" and homogenous entity, by glorifying the founders and heroes of New France, by making Catholicism and *agriculturisme* the foundations of the national identity, by favouring French and European culture to the detriment of its North American counterpart, by harbouring a suspicious attitude toward the

52. Linteau *et al.*, *Histoire du Québec contemporain: Tome I*, p. 700.
53. *Ibid.*, p. 704–706.
54. Bouchard tackled this question many times, in fact. The reader may consult the following titles for a good general survey of his principal ideas: *Genèse des nations et cultures du Nouveau Monde: Essai d'histoire comparée* (Montréal: Boréal, 2001), 504 p.; *Entre l'Ancien et le Nouveau Monde: Le Québec comme population neuve et culture fondatrice* (Ottawa: Presses de l'Université d'Ottawa, 1996), 56 p.; "Ouvrir le cercle de la nation: Activer la cohésion sociale," *L'Action nationale*, Vol. 87, No. 4 (April 1997), p. 107–137; *La Nation québécoise au futur et au passé* (Montréal, VLB Éditeur, 1999), 159 p.

state, economic progress and urbanization, these elites knowingly placed themselves at the periphery of the development experienced by the other peoples of the continent and, by that very fact, assured their own obsolescence. This falling behind occurred in the aftermath of the Rebellions of 1837–1838. The defeat of the insurgents brought the collapse of the modern, political dimension of the national project, which consequently fell back on an archaic discourse that emphasized ethnicity and turned toward the past. It was only during the 1960s that the gap between the discourse of the elites and the "American" reality lived out by the great majority of the population of Québec began to close. The Quiet Revolution, as Bouchard understands it, therefore represents a much greater turning point than it does in the Linteau, Durocher and Robert narrative. Basically, however, and discounting this divergence of opinions on the actual influence of the traditional elites, Bouchard and the "revisionists" agree: Québec is and always has been an "American" society whose general course is (or, according to Bouchard, should have been) like that of the other "new" populations on the American continent.

In Gérard Bouchard's recent book, devoted to analyzing the thought of Lionel Groulx, he has taken the same approach. Featuring an intriguing title, *Les deux chanoines*, this study holds that Groulx's thought was basically "contradictory" and "ambivalent" and that his work, in the end, had proved to be a "failure": "In other words, Groulx seems to me like the spokesperson for a society or, to be more precise, for a fragment of society, that could not manage to understand itself clearly or take an effective place in history on the basis of its own principles."[55] The judgment delivered by Bouchard on the nationalist historian's work could hardly be more severe. He considers his thought to show "equivocation" in the sense that it "proposes a world view that does not correspond to the facts and urgencies of the time."[56] Whether it concerns his understanding of history or his always ambiguous positions on tradition, modernity and the importance of the state in the development of the French-Canadian nation, his prevarications are seen to systematically undermine the coherence of his interventions. With regard to the French minorities outside Québec, Bouchard suggests there was again contradiction between his organic idea of the nation and his desire to see it become an autonomous or independent state.

After denouncing this "organic" concept of nationhood and minimizing the importance of tradition in defining national identity, the author is hardly disposed to be concerned about the place of the French minorities in the "national" history. In the Bouchardian model, the Québécois nation is a "North American francophonie," in other words, a nation that would retain nothing but the French language as its shared cultural element:

55. Gérard Bouchard, *Les deux chanoines*, p. 21.
56. *Ibid.*, p. 23.

> We think Québec has a collective space in which to found a cultural nation—and just as easily, a national culture or a national identity—that is viable and legitimate, taking into account a very flexible interpretation of these notions. This space is fragile, to be sure: it is to a large extent in the process of being formed, but it exists. It is defined by the French language, as matrix or common denominator, whether as mother tongue, working language or second or third language. On a cultural level, this framework designates the primary space in the francophonie of Québec, which everyone can participate in and belong to by virtue of their mastery of the language.[57]

Language, on which Bouchard hopes to found this "cultural" nation, is thus reduced to only its instrumental dimension, without regard for the historical context that determined its evolution over the centuries. One can imagine the scope of the debate that this ideological stance has, for some time, been causing. If language now has only a pragmatic value, and if in reality it serves only to facilitate communication (understood here in the strictest sense) between the individuals who make up the "nation," then what point would there be in giving the French language priority over another in Québec, over English, for example, spoken by the majority of North Americans? Serge Cantin, supported by Fernand Dumont, proposes this reply to the question:

> [I]magine for an instant that the French language in Québec no longer had anything "organic" about it for francophones of French extraction themselves, that it was no longer for them anything but an instrument of communication; in that situation, what would justify their continuing to speak that language? "Why defend the French language, why promote its use or its restoration," asks [Fernand] Dumont, "if not because it comes from the past and is rooted in an inherited identity? Otherwise, one might as well speak the English language, which has spread throughout all of America."[58]

It is therefore the territorial paradigm that wins out over almost every other consideration in Bouchard's model. The nation must no longer be "French-Canadian": it can only be "Québécois," that is, composed of individuals all communicating in French and confined within the borders of Québec. The historian states that he wants to establish what he calls the "Québécois space of the nation's history." This statement raises a number of important epistemological questions.

57. Gérard Bouchard, *La Nation québécoise au futur et au passé*, p. 63.

58. Serge Cantin, "Nation et mémoire chez Fernand Dumont: Pour répondre à Gérard Bouchard," *Bulletin d'histoire politique*, Vol. 9, No. 1 (Fall 2000), p. 48. We might also add here that Cantin rejects Bouchard's "ethnicizing" interpretation of Fernand Dumont's theories; he believes Dumont subscribed rather to a "cultural" definition of the nation. This understanding would make it possible, he explains, to be open to other communities, without ignoring or dismissing altogether the historical and cultural dimension of the French language (*ibid.*, p. 41).

While it is no doubt true that historians cannot completely dispel the shadow of the present in their appreciation of the past and that, as Bouchard claims, citing Michel Foucault, "discontinuity [is] engraved in the heart of historic duration," "presentism" may also turn the historian's gaze away from certain portions of a group's history. By transposing the individualistic and territorial Québec paradigm into a past where it would not have had the same resonance, one risks eventually losing sight of historical issues whose importance we may not suspect.[59]

The way historians deal with the French minorities outside Québec is typical here. The leap from "establishing the Québécois space of the nation's history" to ignoring the existence, even the historic existence, of a "French-Canadian nation" based on a different paradigm is easy to make. Serge Cantin evokes a similar idea when he uses the image of "flight" to describe the behaviour of those sovereigntists today who rally in large numbers to Bouchardian theories: "It is a troubling paradox of sovereigntist thought, engaged in a constant impetuous flight to escape its shameful 'ethnic' nationalist past, a past which the adversaries of sovereignty, furthermore, do not fail to cruelly remind our *post-nationalist* sovereigntists is theirs, whatever they may think of it."[60]

While the foundations of the theory of "Americanity" may be part of an otherwise laudable effort aiming to "open up the circle of the nation" to those outside, they nevertheless force this nation to withdraw into itself in a different respect, namely, with regard to the French minorities. The Bouchard model seems to exclude the study of the French-Canadian nation as it was built historically, opting instead to study a "nation" whose advent, ironically, is still to come.

Québec and the French Minorities in Recent Historiography

Most major studies of Lionel Groulx's thought, French-Canadian nationalism and the Québec "national" issue tackle the question of the French minorities only superficially, if they tackle it at all. However, we must point out that a new historiographical trend has emerged recently: in the last twenty years or so (with some earlier exceptions) certain historians have sought to make the French minorities, and especially their relationship with Québec, a subject of analysis in itself. Although they are not numerous, they have started to fill the glaring gap we have observed.

As early as 1979, A.-N. Lalonde published a study on the position of Québec's "intelligentsia" with regard to the emigration of French Canadians to the West between 1870 and 1930.[61] It shows that the development evoked various reactions, ranging from enthusiasm to suspicion. In general, the West was considered a

59. Gérard Bouchard, *La Nation québécoise au futur et au passé*, p. 95, 96.
60. Serge Cantin, "Nation et mémoire chez Fernand Dumont: Pour répondre à Gérard Bouchard," p. 51.
61. A.-N. Lalonde, "L'intelligentsia du Québec et la migration des Canadiens français vers l'Ouest canadien, 18701930," *RHAF*, Vol. 33, No. 2 (September 1979), p. 163–185.

destination that was preferable to New England, at least until the Manitoba schools crisis broke out in the 1890s. Subsequently, the French-Canadian elites would have thought Nouvel-Ontario a better bet. While the article is interesting, it is limited to the analysis of a single question, emigration. It is also worth noting that, although his study ends in 1930, Lalonde includes neither Bourassa nor Groulx among his "intelligentsia."

A few years later in 1982, Arthur Silver published *The French-Canadian Idea of Confederation*.[62] This is a study of the various interpretations of federal union proposed by the French-Canadian press of Québec between 1864 and 1900. The author aims to demonstrate that the Compact theory appeared late in the media conversation and was absent at the time of the negotiations that culminated in the British North America Act, only appearing some thirty years later. The Métis rebellions in the West and the Manitoba schools crisis prompted Québec to become aware of the precariousness of the religious and educational rights of the French Canadians in the other provinces, while the rights and privileges of their own Anglo-Protestant minority were constantly being enhanced. Silver states that, in 1867, Québec was still unaware of the existence of the French minorities. The BNA Act, rather than constituting a "pact" between English Canadians and French Canadians, had simply represented an agreement between three provinces, the United Canadas, New Brunswick and Nova Scotia. Even Québec, according to Silver, had held to this interpretation, at least in 1867. By the start of the twentieth century, however, the French-Canadian elites had become convinced that Confederation was a "pact" between two "founding peoples" which protected the rights of the French minorities, and that the future of the country would necessarily be worked out on the basis of respect for this guiding principle.

It would not be until the 1990s that the start of a certain predilection among historians for the study of the French minorities and, in particular, of their relationship with Québec, can really be observed. The collection published in 1993 under the direction of Cornelius Jaenen on Franco-Ontarians, *Les Franco-Ontariens*, includes a brief but very interesting article by Pierre Savard dealing with the question of their relations with Québec in the twentieth century.[63] From Regulation 17 (1912–1927), "which will trigger the most spectacular movement of solidarity between the Québécois and Franco-Ontarians," to the Estates General of French Canada (1966, 1967, 1969), during which "the split [between the two groups] became clear," Savard analyzes the development of relations between French Canadians on either side of the Ottawa River.[64] During the first half of the twentieth century, their relations were characterized by solidarity, as evidenced by the

62. A. I. Silver, *The French-Canadian Idea of Confederation, 1864–1900* (Toronto: University of Toronto Press, 1982), 257 p.

63. Pierre Savard, "Relations avec le Québec," in Cornelius J. Jaenen, ed., *Les Franco-Ontariens* (Ottawa: Presses de l'Université d'Ottawa, 1993), p. 231–263.

64. Ibid., p. 234, 247.

support that several journalists, intellectuals and politicians had given to the Franco-Ontarians during the schools crisis—Lionel Groulx and *L'Action française* among them.

Until the 1950s, Pierre Savard tells us, there were also several organizations formed for the purpose of promoting cooperation between the two groups, such as the Sociétés Saint-Jean-Baptiste (SSJB), the Association catholique de la jeunesse canadienne-française (ACJC), the Ordre de Jacques-Cartier (OJC), the clubs Richelieu, the Association canadienne des éducateurs de langue française (ACELF), the Conseil de la vie française en Amérique (CVFA) and so forth. This institutional network was supported by French-Canadian nuns and clergy, who came from Québec to run the schools, hospitals and charitable institutions, at the same time solidifying relations between Québec and Franco-Ontarians. The 1960s, however, brought profound changes in the relations between French Canadians from Québec and Ontario. The earlier solidarity, which few differences had truly managed to dent, was henceforth shattered, with the nationalist movement presenting Québec as French America's one and only hope of salvation.

In 1993 as well, the Acadian review *Égalité* published two articles on relations between the minorities and Québec in the context of the Quiet Revolution, articles in which the theme of breakup also has a prominent place. The first, by Angéline Martel, on the "*étatisation* of relations between Québec and the French-speaking Acadian communities," shows how the spectacular growth of the Québec state during the 1960s was a "cause of distancing" between the two groups.[65] Given these developments, it was the Québec government that took over the French-Canadian institutional network, which at the time was falling apart, and promised that it would maintain relations with the French minorities. The creation of the Service du Canada français d'outre-frontières [department of extra-territorial French Canada] and of Maisons du Québec in several provinces was one persuasive example that demonstrated, in the author's view, the Québec government's willingness to cultivate relations with the minorities. However, the outcome was the opposite:

> Nevertheless, irony of ironies, this so impressive plan, intended to ensure that Québec would not desert those francophones residing outside its territory, contributed, by the very process of *étatisation*, to the realization of the problem it sought to avoid: a distancing between the two groups.[66]

The second article, written by Lawrence Olivier and Guy Bédard, picks up a similar idea, but takes a greater interest in the symbols through which Québec

65. Angéline Martel, "L'étatisation des relations entre le Québec et les communautés acadiennes et francophones: Chroniques d'une époque," *Égalité: Revue acadienne d'analyse politique*, No. 33 (Spring 1993), p. 13–79.
66. *Ibid.*, p. 48.

nationalism has been expressed since the 1960s.[67] The authors, foreshadowing in this way the works of Ronald Rudin, make it clear that the promoters of this ideology considered themselves "modern" and sought to separate themselves from what they perceived as the "ethnicism" of French-Canadian nationalism. The break then was not only structural but also—and perhaps especially—ideological: the existence of the minorities takes the "Québécois" back to an image of themselves that they seek to replace, if not erase, from their own history. According to Olivier and Bédard, in the eyes of Québec nationalists, the minorities represent the traditional values that clash with the rational approach of modernity (defined in terms of progress, individualism, civil society, a valuing of political life, etc.) achieved by the Quiet Revolution. Thus, to show interest in the "ethnicity" of the French-Canadian minorities, just when the new nationalist elites were trying to wipe away all trace of their "ethnic" past and to understand the "nation" strictly in civic terms, would, besides resurrecting old demons, seem to them a contradictory enterprise. As a consequence, the sometimes pessimistic discourse of Québec nationalists on the future of the French minorities is not the result of a detached analysis of the balance of power to which the latter are subject, but rather,

> of a desire to repress this image of themselves represented by the Acadians and the francophones of Canada. It is not so much the traditional society with which they are identified that creates the problem, but rather the image of themselves that resurfaces into the void left by modern society and by the Québécois identity.[68]

In a brief but interesting overview of relations between Québec and the minorities since the nineteenth century, Fernand Harvey too takes up the theme of the breakup, or the "split," of the 1960s.[69] The author explains that immediately following Confederation, the nationalists interpreted the migration of French Canadians to Ontario and the Western provinces by drawing up a "so-called traditional concept" of French Canada, founded on the French language and the Catholic faith.[70] According to Harvey, a great many thinkers applied themselves to developing this nationalist ideology. One of them was Lionel Groulx:

> In his *Histoire du Canada français* [published in four volumes between 1950 and 1952], Lionel Groulx considered that after 1867 French Canada was no longer confused with Québec. He believed that French Canada had at that point ceased to be a

67. Lawrence Olivier and Guy Bédard, "Le nationalisme québécois, les Acadiens et les francophones du Canada," *Égalité: Revue acadienne d'analyse politique*, No. 33 (Spring 1993), p. 81–100.
68. Ibid., p. 98.
69. Fernand Harvey, "Le Québec et le Canada français: Histoire d'une déchirure," in Simon Langlois, ed., *Identité et cultures nationale: L'Amérique française en mutation* (Sainte-Foy: Presses de l'Université Laval, 1995), p. 49–64.
70. Ibid., p. 51.

> geographic entity "in order to become a national and cultural entity, spread across all of Canada."
>
> . . . Lionel Groulx makes himself the ardent defender of a French Canada that includes the minorities. Thus, he deplores the injustices that have victimized these minorities in the field of education, and condemns the partisan mindset that has always divided French Canadian politicians both inside Québec and in the federal parliament and even within the various francophone communities.[71]

From the time of the Quiet Revolution, which marked "the start of the great identity split within the French-Canadian nation," the Québec state supplanted the religious and cultural foundations of this national identity. In Québec, the discourse on the "Québécois" nation rallied the vast majority of intellectuals, journalists and politicians, with, however, some notable exceptions, such as André Laurendeau. If Québec, generally speaking, viewed this transformation in a positive light, the minorities, for their part, felt they had been left in the lurch.[72]

The most thorough studies of the relationship between the minorities and Québec, done by Marcel Martel and Gaétan Gervais, likewise deal with this issue of the structural and ideological breakup of French Canada. Martel, in a work carrying the evocative title of *Le Deuil d'un pays imaginé*, analyzes the development of the French-Canadian institutional network. He highlights the Comité permanent de la survivance française, which was created in 1937 and became the Conseil de la vie française en Amérique in 1952.[73] Until the 1960s, it was in fact the Conseil that coordinated the French-Canadian nationalist movement's action. The Conseil and the Ordre de Jacques-Cartier together constituted the primary means enabling Québec to assist the French minorities in their various projects. With the Quiet Revolution, however, it was the Québec state that took over from this organization and created the Service du Canada français d'outre-frontières. Nevertheless, support from the Québec government fizzled out quickly: by the end of the decade, the minorities had to turn to the federal government, whose language policies offered them unprecedented possibilities of socio-cultural growth. These developments resulted in a seemingly impenetrable wall being built between Québec and the minorities. Québec exchanged the theory of the two founding peoples for the principle of associated states, and the minorities saw in this discursive metamorphosis the end of an argument

71. *Ibid.*, p. 51, 52.
72. When studying specifically the case of the Acadians, Harvey takes up some of the same ideas he expresses in "Les relations culturelles Québec – Acadie: Analyse d'une mutation," *Les Cahiers des Dix*, No. 53 (1999), p. 235–250. See also Fernand Harvey and Gérard Beaulieu, ed., *Les Relations entre le Québec et l'Acadie de la tradition à la modernité* (n.p.: IQRC and Éditions de l'Acadie, 2000), 300 p. (See especially Harvey's essay, "Les historiens canadiens-français et l'Acadie, 1859–1960" (p. 19–48), which naturally deals with Groulx's contribution to Acadian historiography.)
73. Marcel Martel, *Le Deuil d'un pays imaginé: Rêves, luttes et déroute du Canada français* (Ottawa: Presses de l'Université d'Ottawa, 1997), 204 p.

that had been widely used since the nineteenth century to justify their right to exist.

Gaétan Gervais's method, on the other hand, consists of analyzing in depth the Franco-Ontarian participation in the great French-Canadian patriotic conferences that took place between the end of the nineteenth century and the 1960s.[74] In his view, these gatherings, which he sees as "symbols" of the nation, created a "conference culture" in French Canada.[75] For almost a century, such meetings allowed French-Canadian elites to reiterate those fundamental values on which the French-Canadian national identity rested (language, culture, faith and common history). Whether local, provincial or national (as was the case for the French language conferences of 1912, 1937 and 1952), they also provided the French-Canadian elites of Québec with the opportunity to express the solidarity that connected them to the French minorities in the other provinces.

However, the last of these great meetings, the Estates General of French Canada (1966, 1967, 1969), represents, in Gaétan Gervais's opinion, "an episode in the history of French-Canadian nationalism, indeed, its final act."[76] The traditional, nationalist ideology collapsed under the weight of the immense Québec majority at the Estates General, a majority already largely acquired through the paradigm of the "Québécois" nation and the independence project. Confronted by this exclusion, the Association canadienne-française d'éducation d'Ontario (ACFEO), which sponsored the Franco-Ontarian delegates, decided to withdraw in dramatic fashion from the 1969 conference:

> At the Estates General, there was an attempt to muzzle the minorities, they were prevented from expressing their views on constitutional issues, they were given second-class status and treated with condescension and a patronizing attitude. When the minorities went to sit at the main table, they were assigned the little benches along the wall. Thus, the only honourable thing for them to do was withdraw. That was the decision ACFEO finally adopted after two years of hesitation. The French minorities finally came to realize that they were just being used as puppets to back the political schemes aimed at Québec separation.[77]

The Estates General gave rise, Gervais explains, to a clash between two ideologies, the one basically conservative and Catholic, and the other more focused on

74. Gaétan Gervais, "L'Ontario français et les grands congrès patriotiques canadiens-français (1883–1952)," *Cahiers Charlevoix 2: Études franco-ontariennes* (Sudbury: Société Charlevoix and Prise de parole, 1997), p. 9–155; and "L'Ontario français et les 'États généraux du Canada français,'" *Cahiers Charlevoix 3: Études franco-ontariennes*, Société Charlevoix and Prise de parole, 1998, p. 231–364. These articles were published as a collection in Gaétan Gervais, *Des gens de resolution: Le passage du Canada français à l'Ontario français* (Sudbury: Prise de parole, 2003), 230 p.

75. Gaétan Gervais, "L'Ontario français et les grands congrès . . . " p. 13–26.

76. Gaétan Gervais, "L'Ontario français et les 'États généraux . . . '" p. 233.

77. Ibid., p. 364.

identifying with the territory and political institutions of Québec. The minorities, at the end of the day, had to throw in the towel and concede defeat. Their French-Canadian identity had been replaced by gloomy discussions on the unwelcome burden they now represented for Québec nationalists.[78]

⋆ ⋆ ⋆

This overview of the principal studies of French-Canadian nationalism, while incomplete, has allowed us to identify certain trends. Starting in the 1950s, historians developed the theory of the "provincialism" of the nationalists of the inter-war period, a theory that would be picked up more or less in its entirety by the majority of researchers who were interested, after them, in either *L'Action française* or the thought of Lionel Groulx.[79] Furthermore, the theory of the "Americanity" of Québec, by imposing on historians a territorial and individualist paradigm, complicates the study of the ideological and institutional relationship that existed historically between Québec and the French minorities, not to mention the inter-cultural and interethnic dynamic within Québec. If Gérard Bouchard, shows a greater sensitivity to it, it is only to better emphasize the weaknesses of the traditional elites and to prevent any resurgence of a certain "ethnic" understanding of the nation.

It was not until the 1990s that more significant studies, still few and far between for that matter, were produced on relations between Québec and the minorities and on the place of the latter in French-Canadian nationalist discourse. In the majority of cases, historians agree on the theory of the breakup, which occurred during the 1960s, between French Canadians from Québec and those from elsewhere. Before the Quiet Revolution, relations between the two groups were characterized mainly by a strong sentiment of national solidarity.[80] The reformulation of the national project by the neo-nationalists of Québec provoked a schism that manifested itself in the weakening of the traditional institutional network. It was evidenced by the increase in the role of governments in the life of the various French communities, in Québec as elsewhere, and by the rejection of the Compact theory, at least in its traditional form, in favour of the associated-states principle.

The theory of the breakup of the 1960s is not, however, unanimously accepted. Yves Frenette, in his *Brève histoire des Canadiens français*, holds that the process

78. Ibid., p. 235–236.

79. We must however point out the recent and very interesting master's thesis of Damien-Claude Bélanger on the place of the Franco-Americans in Groulx's work, a study that challenges the long held theory of the "provincialism" of Groulx's ideology. See Damien-Claude Bélanger, *Lionel Groulx et la Franco-Américanie*, master's thesis (history), Université de Montréal, 2000, 184 p.

80. Also consulted will be the thesis of Jeffrey Marcil, who studies the coverage the minorities received from the Montréal press in 1905 and 1906 (Jeffrey Marcil, *"Les Nôtres": Franco-Américains, Canadiens français hors Québec et Acadiens dans la grande presse montréalaise de langue française, 1905–1906*, master's thesis (history), Université d'Ottawa, 1998, 158 p.).

leading up to the breakup had been under way since the 1920s, when the French-Canadian nationalist movement, Groulx included, began withdrawing into Québec.[81] Gaétan Gervais, on the other hand, relativizes the actual consequences of the breakup which, in his view, are situated only on the level of representations. Although discourse on French-Canadian national identity has been marginalized, the factors of cultural reproduction still remain, in his opinion, more numerous than the elements of division. Thus, the "Franco-Ontarian identity," like the "Québécois identity," despite deep divisions, will never be anything other than the extension of the "French-Canadian identity," itself the extension of the "French identity."[82]

Despite all this, the historical analysis of the place of the French minorities in traditional French-Canadian nationalism still remains a neglected field. In the pages that follow, we shall try partially to fill this gap by analyzing the place of the minorities in the work of Lionel Groulx, prolific intellectual and mentor to the French-Canadian nationalist movement for many decades. This is an ideal way to more clearly identify the ties that united the French minorities and Québec nationalist groups. It is a method that will challenge the idea that Groulx's ideology was essentially "provincialist" and allow for a better grasp of the nature and logic of French-Canadian nationalism as it existed before the Quiet Revolution.

81. Yves Frenette, *Brève histoire des Canadiens français* (Montréal: Boréal, 1998), 216 p.

82. Gaétan Gervais, "Aux origines de l'identité franco-ontarienne," *Cahiers Charlevoix: Études franco-ontariennes* (Société Charlevoix and Prise de parole, 1995), p. 125–168.

Chapter Two

The French Minorities, Remnant of an Empire: French Canada, Its Apostolic Vocation and Founding Mission

WE HAVE OBSERVED, in the preceding chapter, that the vast majority of historians of French-Canadian nationalism and of Lionel Groulx's thought tend to ignore the issue of the French minorities. The theory of "provincialism," first proposed in the 1950s, has only in the last twenty years been seriously contested. Many historians misunderstood the ideology developed by Lionel Groulx because they exaggerated the importance he gave to the territorial factor in his definition of the French-Canadian nation. They very often transposed the paradigm of the "Québécois" nation into French Canada's past. This was a common paradigm in French-Canadian political and intellectual circles immediately following the Second World War and *a fortiori* during the Quiet Revolution of the 1960s. It is difficult not to recognize the presentist character of this approach and to see how it sowed confusion in the minds of researchers trying to understand the issue of the French minorities in Groulxist nationalism.

In the following pages, we shall try to shed more light on the place Lionel Groulx accorded the minorities in his conceptual framework. In fact, to clearly understand many of the most important themes in his nationalism, including French-Canadian messianism and the founding-peoples theory, they need to be seen in direct relation to the minorities issue. On several levels, Groulx's ideology was "reactionary" in the strict sense of the term. It was critical, at times virulently so, of the growing paradigm of modernity which, since the end of the eighteenth century, had progressively marginalized Providence and the sacred as the guiding and organizing principle of human societies. This is not the place to entertain a theoretical debate on the idea of modernity. Let us simply define it as that set of economic, political, cultural and intellectual developments that accompany the passage of a "traditional" society (that is, one that is essentially rural and agricultural) into the era of urbanization and industrialization. As a consequence of this progressive transition, the breakdown of the old communal solidarities of traditional society is accelerated, and certain of its social relationships become redefined within a system of intermediary and homogenizing institutions, the most important of which are, no doubt, the bureaucratic state and the mass media. The rise of individualism, which goes hand in hand with this transition, in its loosening of the former traditional and organic bonds, precipitates what some philosophers have called the "destruction of the metaphysical" and the "low-water mark of the sense of the sacred," all in the interest of scientific reason and a more materialistic and naturalistic understanding of reality:

> The rhetoric of modernity finds its hegemonic expression in the amplifying redundancy of the economic and social imperatives that are constituted by the power of mass media over opinions, attitudes and social (but also cultural and psychological) *habitus*, which become as many generators of needs, desires and aspirations, in the form of currents of opinion, modes of thought and styles of life . . . . Truth itself is essentially interpreted, in this game, as exactness of representation in the natural sciences, the human sciences and the technologies of techno-science, for purposes of technical domination of natural, economic and social processes and conformity to attitudes, behaviours, mentalities and social *habitus*, these being consensually validated by public opinion and by modern society, whose functional imperatives and needs, it seems, must ultimately become *law*. [translation][1]

We shall see, in the final chapter of this book, that Lionel Groulx's vigorous criticism of the materialist dimension of modernity came to a head in the aftermath of the Second World War and during the Quiet Revolution. It relied heavily, however, on the ideological system he had begun to construct early in the twentieth century. The mistrust that he sometimes harboured toward modernity and the democratic principle was not due to some sort of disdain for the "people," as some have nevertheless maintained.[2] Coming from a modest rural background himself, Groulx only ever felt toward his *petites gens* a respect that verged on worship, even though he was quite capable of strongly criticizing them. What perturbed him about modernity was that it invalidated the sacredness of society for the benefit of the increasingly widespread paradigm of universalism, individualism and materialism. He also noted that modernity was accompanied by another development, far more troubling, on an ethical level, namely, the supplanting of memory or tradition as the foundation of French-Canadian identity. In his mind, individualistic universalism reduced man to an uprooted being, with no regard given to the national or cultural context into which he had been born. Now, Groulx was a firm believer in the providential creation of nations and attributed cultural diversity, in the final analysis, to a divine plan. Western modernity had become obsessed, in his view, by the idea of a universalism that was abstract, materialist and contrary to humanity's deeper nature. Within a minority cultural context, like that of French Canada, he believed that universalism and individualism could lead only to acculturation and apostasy. Resistance to this "pestilence" was for

1. "Modernité," *Encyclopédie philosophique universelle, Vol. II: Les Notions philosophiques, Tome II* (Paris: Presses universitaires de France, 1990), p. 1655–1658.
2. See Esther Delisle, *Le Traître et le juif: Lionel Groulx, Le Devoir et le délire du nationalisme d'extrême droite dans la province de Québec, 1929–1939* (Outremont: L'Étincelle, 1992), 284 p.

him a duty dictated by Providence, as was the national solidarity that he hoped would take root among all members of the French-Canadian nation, wherever they were. He believed that the *survivance* of the French minorities was an integral part of a divine plan: Providence had entrusted to the French-Canadian people a founding mission, that of propagating the Catholic faith and French civilization in America. This was the deeper logic of Groulx's nationalist thought and of his attitude toward the French minorities outside Québec.

Lionel Groulx's ideology presented nations as organic entities, analogous to living beings, each with their own national "genius." The diversity of nations was the work of Providence, and Providence did not tolerate the possibility of legitimating the absorption of the weakest by the strongest. This dimension of Groulx's thought took the form of the conviction that French Canada had been endowed by Providence with a mission to be an instrument of civilization. This conviction was shared likewise by the colonial powers of the late nineteenth and early twentieth centuries. He believed that the French, and after them, the French Canadians, had faithfully accomplished their mission, which had started with the founding of New France. He believed it was the missionary ideal that accounted, more than anything else, for the expansion of the French-Canadian people to the four corners of America. In line with this thinking, he saw the minorities as the remnant of the great "French Empire of America" and as the surviving witnesses of the providential mission of the "French race" on the North American continent. According to Groulx, the founding-peoples principle was the logical and incontrovertible corollary to the civilizing mission of the French Canadians. Being the historian that he was, he came to the conclusion that the British North America Act represented the political and constitutional recognition of that historical reality and that Confederation was to be the guarantor, in principle, of the cultural survival of the French minorities throughout the country. However, between the spirit of the "pact" of 1867 and its concrete application, Groulx noted an abyss that he always criticized sharply. He saw two reasons behind the efforts of certain English-Canadian circles to assimilate the minorities: on the one hand, French Canada had difficulty getting English Canada to accept its status as a founding people of the entire country and, on the other, the French-Canadian political class showed a lack of backbone by always being ready to sacrifice the higher interests of the nation on the altar of electioneering.

The French-Canadian Nation According to Lionel Groulx: Conceptual Clarifications

Nation and State in Groulxist Nationalism

Lionel Groulx was born in 1878. His philosophical and intellectual education was classical and Catholic. To be more precise, Groulx was completely immersed in the organicist and traditionalist schools of thought of the nineteenth century. In his recent work, Frédéric Boily labels Groulx's nationalism as the French-Canadian manifestation of the Romantic thought of Johann Gottfried Herder.[3] Although it appears Groulx never read the works of the German philosopher—something Boily, moreover, acknowledges—it is possible to establish a parallel, in certain regards at least, between his thought and some of the broad lines of political Romanticism. This school of thought was first of all a radical critique of the "contractualist" interpretation of society that had been proposed in the eighteenth century by the philosophers of the Enlightenment and had become widely accepted by virtue of the military successes of the French Revolution and the Napoleonic Empire. In lieu of the individualistic concept of society professed by the French Revolutionaries, the Romantics proposed a more "organic" definition—one based on the tradition manifested in the history, language and literature of a people. If for the Enlightenment philosophers, the nation—which they equated with the state—was the result of individuals freely entering into a social contract, the Romantics argued that the nation was a natural entity that predated the state. Thus, against the voluntarism, mechanism and universalism of the contractual nation, the Romanticist nation set its determinism, organicism and particularism.[4]

According to the Romanticist definition, what made humans "human" was their incarnation in a particular national or cultural context, while the "universal man" of the Enlightenment philosophers represented merely a dehumanizing abstraction devoid of meaning. Although the Romantic philosophers were undoubtedly not among Groulx's intellectual influences, there is a measure of resemblance between his thought and theirs in that he adopted an organicist understanding of national identity. While he defined the nation as a "natural" entity, that is, one that existed prior to the establishment of governmental structures, he saw it as flowing from a "supernatural" or providential power. This aspect of his thought was borrowed from the French counter-revolutionary tradition, which was disseminated in French Canada during the nineteenth century by, among others, Félicité de Lamennais and Joseph de Maistre, and according to which the authority of Providence carried more weight than that of the people.

Nevertheless, French-Canadian traditionalism was not just a borrowed ideology, as historian Pierre Trépanier points out. In a text of rare density, he explains that traditionalist thought had been transformed in French Canada after the Conquest of 1760, upon contact with British parliamentarism and certain values specific to English political liberalism.[5] Accordingly, traditionalist thinkers of the

3. Frédéric Boily, *La Pensée nationaliste de Lionel Groulx* (Sillery: Septentrion, 2003), 232 p.
4. Alain Renaut, "Postérité de la querelle entre Lumières et romantisme," in Alain Renaut, ed., *Lumières et romantisme* (Paris: Calmann-Lévy, 1999), p. 370.
5. Pierre Trépanier, *Qu'est-ce que le traditionalisme? Causerie-débat tenue à Montréal, le samedi 8 juin 2002* (n.p.: Club du 3 juillet, [2002]), 53 p.

nineteenth century had created an original and typically French-Canadian doctrinal synthesis: while maintaining their faith in the divine origin of authority, they had been able to adapt to political representative institutions, whose legitimacy they ultimately attributed to Providence. The monarchism of their French confreres was removed from the doctrine of traditionalists here who could henceforth see in the exercise of power, albeit by the people, the will of God. As Trépanier tells us, it was Louis-François Richer Laflèche, Bishop of Trois-Rivières, who, during the nineteenth century, developed this doctrine most explicitly. But many thinkers ensured its spread in subsequent decades, Lionel Groulx among them. Trépanier calls him "the traditionalist intellectual leader par excellence from the 1920s through to the 1940s." Moreover, this French-Canadian interpretation of the democratic principle should be kept in mind when evaluating the sometimes harsh criticism that Groulx directed at parliamentary institutions. What he lamented was not the idea that the people could express themselves under a democratic political regime, but rather that this sovereignty of the people could be exercised without any regard for the authority of Providence, to which, he believed, it owed its existence.

In Groulxist nationalism, every people and every nation possesses its own "sensibility," its own spirit or "collective soul." Groulx readily professed to be a follower of the thought of Joseph de Maistre, whom he admired for what he saw as his lucidity and balanced views. In an article appearing in *L'Action française* in 1917 to commemorate the fiftieth anniversary of Confederation, he approvingly repeated the ideas of the French thinker according to whom "an arbitrary gathering of men does not a nation make."[6] Following this reasoning, the existence of the Canadian federation did not guarantee the existence of a Canadian nation. This failure to understand the concept of nation, he insisted, betrayed the "congenital weakness of our federation" which ought to be considered binational. Groulx did not hesitate to combat the liberal and individualist thinking that flouted a people's traditions and submitted them, in his opinion, to a dogmatic utilitarian logic. Among the principal proponents of this doctrine, Groulx listed not only John Stuart Mill and Jeremy Bentham, but Paul Henri d'Holbach, Condorcet and Jean-Baptiste Say as well. He considered these thinkers the authors of a mechanical and alienating concept of society that ran totally counter to what he believed to be humanity's deeper nature:

> These jurists and philosophers carry in their head a mechanical concept of society and a political ethic based on the interest of the greatest number. All they want to see in society is an artificial conglomeration of individualities; this makes them

6. Lionel Groulx, "Ce cinquantenaire," *L'Action française* (hereinafter AF), July 1917, p. 193–203. See also Lionel Groulx, "Nos devoirs envers la race," *Dix ans d'Action française* (Montréal: Bibliothèque de l'Action française, 1926), p. 231.

> cheapen national traditions and the collective soul. From the principle of utility, of total happiness conceived as the sum total of individual happinesses, they deduce the moral superiority of a democratic evolution. Where might these principles and these deductions not lead them? When there is a conflict between the interest or the happiness of two groups, they do not hesitate: the interests of the majority win out.[7]

This social mechanism risked bordering on tyranny; it pandered to the whims of the majority at the expense of the rights of the minority. Groulx considered that in nineteenth-century England, it was utilitarian liberalism that had produced a generation of imperialists like Lord Durham, who had judged the common good through the distorting lens of quantitative reason:

> Reread the Durham Report now bearing in mind the philosophy of "Radical Jack" and his theory of utilitarianism which is founded on the interest of the greatest number . . . and you will understand by what sleight of hand the noble lord was able—radical as he was and devout as he may have been in his religion of popular freedoms—to sacrifice a little people to the voracious appetite of imperialism.[8]

Groulx's ideological convictions prevented him from brushing aside concerns of a cultural and moral order which, although intangible and difficult to quantify, were not therefore any less real in his view. Herein undoubtedly lies one of the greatest points of contention between the nationalism he defended and the philosophy of utilitarian liberalism. It was this reasoning also, as we shall see later, that prompted him to come to the defence of the French minorities in the other provinces, even after the Second World War, when some of the historians who had been his disciples thought differently. They argued Québec should abandon its "dispersed brothers" on the basis of a "scientific" analysis of human societies that was founded largely on a certain form of historical materialism. For now, however, let us simply remember that in Groulx's nationalism, it was impossible to confuse the concepts of state and nation, as each retained full autonomy from the other. He saw the former as carrying out the "political drudgery" of maintaining "order rather than developing any particular kind of life." Nations, he felt, existed separately from the state, against which they would at times even have to fight in order to defend their right to exist. This logic subjected the rights of the nation and the rights of the state to a strict hierarchical order, subordinating the latter to the former:

7. Lionel Groulx, "Durham et son époque," *Notre Maître le passé, Tome III* (Ottawa: Éditions internationales Alain Stanké, 1978 (1944)), p. 171. (This article was originally published in *Le Devoir* in January 1938.)
8. *Ibid.*, p. 172–173.

> If the state has as its sole purpose the bringing together, for a common purpose, of undetermined wills, if all it is for them is an external force in the service of order, then would not the national organism, on the other hand, carrying within itself customs and morals of supreme educational virtue, that are apt to stabilize in the wills almost irresistible hereditary habits, would it not by its moral action, merit priority over the state?[9]

Although Groulx considered the state a legitimate institution, even an important means of development, it remained in his eyes an artificial construct. The nation, conversely, was a natural "organism," a living "being," and represented a much deeper and immutable reality. Groulx did not hesitate to concede to the state the "incontestable right to claim political assimilation," but this did not guarantee it any right to "ethnic assimilation."[10] That was the message he delivered in 1935 to the Société Saint-Jean-Baptiste of Manchester, New Hampshire. A few years earlier, the famous Sentinelle crisis had revealed to Franco-Americans the inherent difficulty of maintaining this distinction between being a member of a nation and a member of a state, between nationality and citizenship. The question had erupted in 1927 when a group of nationalist militants, united behind the *La Sentinelle* newspaper, had dragged the Bishop of Providence, Rhode Island, William Hickey, before the civil courts. He had been trying, since 1922, to win the right to build an English diocesan college using the financial reserves of the Franco-American parishes. The impertinence of his Franco-American detractors earned them nothing less than a sentence of excommunication. Before the *Sentinellistes* developed more radical methods of protest, Groulx and *L'Action française* (the review he directed from 1920 to 1928) had not only unequivocally supported their claims but had gone so far as to propose the naturalization of Franco-Americans as a way of solving the crisis. They reasoned that if the Franco-Americans were to obtain American citizenship, this would not have meant they were being assimilated. On the contrary, it could even contribute to preventing it: a block of several hundred thousand Franco-Americans would undoubtedly have given pause to those politicians bold enough to consider taking or supporting measures contravening their "national" interests. Groulx had made suggestions of this kind to Franco-Americans as early as 1922. During a conference of the Congrès de la Fédération catholique des sociétés franco-américaines, he said,

> I have already taken the liberty of telling you in *L'Action française*: "A people does not choose its roots any more than does a tree." If nationality is determined by the

9. Lionel Groulx, "L'histoire et la vie nationale," *Dix ans d'Action française*, p. 236, 265. See also Lionel Groulx, "Nos devoirs envers la race," *Dix ans d'Action française*, p. 227–228; Lionel Groulx, "Nos responsabilités intellectuelles," *Orientations* (Montréal: Éditions du Zodiaque, 1935), p. 23.
10. Lionel Groulx, "Notre avenir en Amérique," *Orientations*, p. 282.

> blood, the soul, and the language one shares with one's extended family, or—to use the terminology of ethnologists and philosophers—by physiological, psychological and moral identity, you cannot, in spite of your American nationality, act as if you do not also have the French-Canadian nationality.[11]

Actually, out of respect for the complexity of his own thought, Groulx should have spoken of American "citizenship," rather than "nationality." But no matter. The ease with which Groulx and his colleagues endorsed the naturalization of Franco-Americans clearly revealed the distinction they were establishing between citizenship and nationality: the former, in their mind, was merely a political structure, while the latter retained an inalienable "organic" character.

Therefore, no basic incompatibility existed, according to Abbé Groulx, between American citizenship and Franco-American or French-Canadian nationality. Likewise, in Canada, one could be a member of the Canadian state without ever losing anything of one's French-Canadian nationality. Morally, he insisted, the state was prohibited from acting as a usurper and demanding that French Canadians assimilate to the culture of the majority. This conviction stemmed from a certain traditionalist understanding of natural law in which a person's right to develop in accord with their national or cultural "genius," unimpeded in any way by a structure as artificial as a state, is a priority of the highest order. Again in Manchester, in 1935, Groulx, citing Jesuit theologian Lucien Brun, developed this idea most explicitly:

> Listen to the opinion of a Catholic philosopher who is a theologian as well . . . : "To make use of all the vital resources offered to us by the milieu into which we are born is thus for each of us a natural right. The right to culture, the right to maintain cultural particularities, is thus the right to a full and natural life, the right to satisfy tendencies more or less deeply rooted in our nature and, furthermore, good in themselves. Is this not a natural right?" "The currently prevailing interpretation in official circles," the philosopher notes, fully safeguards the essential rights of cultural groups, "the right to remain attached to their mother tongue, their ancestral customs and their cultural origins."[12]

The ancestral tradition was, in Groulx's nationalism, the glue that held the French-Canadian nation together and preserved its integrity. This insistence on the past and on tradition grew out of his criticism of the modern arguments that

11. Lionel Groulx, "L'Amitié française d'Amérique," *Dix ans d'Action française*, p. 181. See Michel Bock, "'Suicide de race' ou 'vocation apostolique'? La représentation des Franco-Américains dans *L'Action française* de Montréal (1917–1928)," in Jean-Pierre Wallot, ed., with the collaboration of Pierre Lanthier and Hubert Watelet, *Constructions identitaires et pratiques sociales* (Ottawa: Presses de l'Université d'Ottawa and Centre de recherche en civilisation canadienne-française, 2002), p. 175–200.
12. Lionel Groulx, "Notre avenir en Amérique," *Orientations*, p. 282. See also Lionel Groulx, "Notre destin français," *L'Action nationale* (hereinafter AN), March 1937, p. 130–142.

claimed to support the idea of progress. It was not that Groulx opposed progress. Quite the contrary. He did wonder, though, if complete and utter disdain for tradition was really a necessary prerequisite for progress.[13] To a minority people like the French Canadians, continually at risk of drowning in an Anglo-Protestant world, the rejection of tradition and an inordinate zeal for liberalism and individualism represented a major threat. To them, its "constants," its "lines of force," which allowed it to preserve its uniqueness in the world and remain something infinitely precious, were endangered. As we shall see in the following chapters, Groulx never deviated from this conviction, not even when the postwar nationalists and the Quiet Revolution nationalists questioned this fundamental dimension of his intellectual heritage. Groulx never stopped hounding his contemporaries to rid their minds of the false dichotomy between tradition and progress. Progress, he would repeat to them, ought to be an ideal based on construction, not demolition. It should be built on the historical experience of the preceding generations. To turn one's back on one's ancestors, to ignore the wisdom tradition contained, this, in his eyes, could only be destructive. Let us consider this passage from a famous speech he gave in 1937 at the Deuxième Congrès de la langue française de Québec (which earned him many accusations of separatism), evocatively entitled "L'histoire, gardienne des traditions vivantes":

> Tradition means delivery, transmission. And since we are speaking here about the transmission of a moral legacy and about transmission by a constantly evolving living organism, inevitably it is the transmission of a moral legacy which one may presume remains identical to itself in its foundation, but, from generation to generation, does not fail to be modified and enriched by new elements. To summarize, to speak of tradition is to speak of continuity, constant advancement, perpetual enrichment; and by this very process, it would be impossible to understand by tradition anything other than living tradition. In the most general sense of the word, what is it if not the characteristics, the main orientation of a history? It has been rightly said: they are the "constants" of a people, its lines of force. And the word evokes the inner thought, the architectural plan according to which a people builds its history, while, faithful to the specific impulses of its soul, it lives, creates, evolves, but without ever separating from its roots, remaining consubstantial with its past, with its ancestors, with the genius of its race.[14]

13. See the excellent study by Jean-Claude Dupuis, *Nationalisme et catholicisme: L'Action française de Montréal* (1917–1928), master's thesis (History), Université de Montréal, 1992, 329 p.
14. Lionel Groulx, "L'histoire, gardienne des traditions vivantes," *Directives* (Montréal: Éditions du Zodiaque, 1937), p. 208–209. Commentaries of this type are too numerous to list. However, we refer the reader to the following texts: Lionel Groulx, "L'éducation nationale," *Directives*, p. 142; "Le patriotisme des jeunes," *Notre Maître le passé, Tome I* (Ottawa: Éditions internationales Alain Stanké, 1977 (1924)), p. 19-20; "Jacques Cartier à Hochelaga," *Notre Maître le passé, Tome II* (Ottawa: Éditions internationales Alain Stanké, 1977 (1936)), p. 20; "Le malaise canadien-français," *Paroles à des étudiants* (Montréal: Éditions de l'Action nationale, 1941), p. 34–35; "Vers l'avenir," *Paroles à des étudiants*, p. 43, 46.

Clearly then, tradition was the foundation on which the nation was built; it guaranteed stability to a perpetually evolving national organism. Abbé Groulx was known to have said, in his more lyrical flights of oratory, that it was the "blood that courses through our veins" and the "heredity with which our being has been endowed" that determined the nation, that "predestined" French Canadians to "certain ways of thinking and feeling."[15] But the deeper logic of his nationalism placed the real emphasis, in his definition of French-Canadian national identity, on the notion of tradition—passed on from generation to generation rather than transmitted biologically. Consequently, that identity applied to all those who, wherever they might be, had received a share of the French-Canadian tradition. "A teacher worthy of his or her role could not fail to constantly keep in mind, it seems to me, this primary guiding idea: *The child I am to raise is not an abstract child but a little French Canadian.*" These words spoken by Groulx in 1934 could have been his leitmotif. Faithful to the principles of his traditionalism, he opposed a universal abstraction that plucked the person out of their context and saw in them only an individual stripped of cultural and historical foundations. The culture and the nation, rather than representing an obstacle to universalism constituted ideal paths to achieve it. These realities provided the human being with "a means of improvement," the means to achieve their "human purpose." For, in the final analysis, what humans had in common without exception was their embodiment in a particular culture.[16]

It was on the basis of this ideological conviction that Groulx justified his occasionally harsh criticism of the "universalist" claims of certain French-Canadian groups. Artists' circles, or at least some of them, were made to take the brunt of it. In 1918, in a speech given at the newly founded *L'Action française*—whose directorship he would assume two years later—Groulx lambasted them for tending all too frequently to ignore their "deeper nature" under the pretext of preferring "universalism" over "regionalism." He gave this speech shortly after the appearance of his first literary work, *Les Rapaillages*, a collection of stories written to celebrate the abundant virtues and deep wisdom he had witnessed in French-Canadian rural communities. In 1920, he explained to Georges Courchesne, future archbishop of Rimouski, that he worried about the fact that "exoticism here seems to stem less from passion for universal ideas and general themes than from an almost total ignorance of things concerning our own country." He did not go so far, however, as to try to recruit artists to march "under the banner of patriotism or regionalism." As he pointed out in 1935, "we do not seek to impose, . . . through orders to be followed blindly, the aim of the French-Canadian mission. But would it be too

15. Lionel Groulx, "L'éducation nationale," *Directives*, p. 143. This text originally appeared in the March 1934 issue of *L'Action nationale*.
16. Lionel Groulx, "L'éducation nationale à l'école primaire," *Orientations*, p. 119; Lionel Groulx, "Le national et le religieux," *AN*, February 1934, p. 93.

much to wish that the anonymous personality or the cosmopolitan soul not be, under the pretext of artistic freedom, the final word of the artistic personality?"[17]

Groulx also brought this crusade against universalist abstraction into ecclesiastical territory. He took to task those who believed Catholicism should, by definition, exist at the margins of or, rather, above, the relatively secular ideas of nation and culture. As a priest, he conceded a certain logic in this reasoning, but even if the Church was a divinely created universal institution, he believed it was human and incarnate in the culture of its faithful. Respect for national cultures, he insisted, was the best tool the Church had at its disposal for increasing its influence: "A Catholic is not an abstract being," he said in 1935; "and it would be illusory to expect to graft the faith onto a human ghost."[18] The purely artificial conflict between the national and the religious, such as the one between rootedness and universalism, originated, in his opinion, in a false debate. These reflections were triggered by a controversy that followed the speech given in 1910 by Msgr. Francis Bourne, Archbishop of Westminster, at the Eucharistic Congress in Montréal. Bourne had maintained that, in America, the Church had to adopt English as its principal operating language in order to foster expansion. At the time, French-Canadian nationalist circles, which included Henri Bourassa, had condemned the prelate's argument outright. This episode, to which we shall return later, had deeply influenced Groulx's thought. He would always remain sceptical of this separation that certain parties wanted to maintain between the national and the religious. In 1938, he voiced this concern to Father Charles Charlebois. Charlebois was a key participant in the resistance to Regulation 17 (1912–1927), which, under pressure from a segment of the Irish clergy, had been imposed by the Ontario government in order to prohibit the French language in the province's schools: "They don't want to hear us mention 'national' under the pretext of Catholicism . . . . Let us stop this absurdity and let us also assure ourselves that if Canada is a country in America, there is also such a thing as French Canada and French Canadians in Canada."[19]

Essential Conditions: Tradition and Will

In Lionel Groulx's logic, to try to drive a wedge between a people and their "national genius" or traditional culture, even if only for the purpose of fostering the spread of the Catholic church, was equivalent to committing a transgression against natural law as he understood it. Tradition was one of the principal

17. Lionel Groulx, "Pour l'Action française," *Dix ans d'Action française*, p. 68–69; Lionel Groulx, *Les Rapaillages. Vieilles Choses, vieilles gens* (Montréal: Éditions du Devoir, 1916), 159 p.; letter from Lionel Groulx to Georges Courchesne, Bibliothèque et Archives nationales du Québec (hereinafter BAnQ), Fonds Lionel-Groulx (hereinafter FLG), Pi/A,889, January 27, 1920; Lionel Groulx, "Nos positions," *Orientations*, p. 271–272.
18. Lionel Groulx, "L'éducation nationale à l'école primaire," *Orientations*, p. 154. See also Lionel Groulx, "Pour qu'on vive...," AN, September 1935, p. 52–63.
19. Letter from Lionel Groulx to Charles Charlebois, BAnQ, FLG, Pi/A,746, March 22, 1938.

foundations of the French-Canadian nation according to Groulx, but not the only one. To this "material element" he also added a "formal element" or, in plainer language, a "will to live." The one was made up of all the cultural traits shared by all the members of the nation collectively, while the other expressed the will to live in accordance with the "genius" of the nation to which one belonged. In 1934, he defined these two conditions for the existence of nations in the following way:

> Two elements constitute nationality. The first, which the philosophers call material, is defined as the possession in common of a heritage of memories, glory, traditions, cultural and ethnic similarities. The other element, the formal and principal one, may be defined as the will to live together on the basis of the physical and moral solidarities indicated above, the will to preserve the national heritage, on the sole basis of its value for assuring the human personality's development.[20]

The nation was both a subjective and an objective reality. The "material" element (which Groulx sometimes called "substantial") comprised cultural traditions and institutions which, over the years, had served as the scaffolding for the French-Canadian identity. He was referring to traditions that dated back to the seventeenth century, to the founding of New France. French Canada represented to him an outgrowth of European French civilization, with all that went with it in the way of nobility, grandeur and the missionary ideal. Clearly Groulx saw a remarkable cultural continuity between the mother country and the colony that had taken shape in the valley of the St. Lawrence. It is possible to draw certain parallels between this analysis and the *fragment societies* theory of Louis Hartz.[21] New France did indeed represent for Groulx what the political scientist would have called an ideological "fragment," born of *Ancien Régime*, Catholic France. The parallel is limited, however. Contrary to what Hertz would undoubtedly have concluded, Groulx considered the France of the Grand Siècle the only one that could be deemed the authentic repository of the French "soul." The "other" France, the one born of the French Revolution and the Third Republic, could not claim this title since it had, in his opinion, strayed from its deeper nature under the impulse of the individualist, universalist and, of course, anticlerical ideal. In the following passage, which appeared in a 1921 issue of *L'Action française*, Groulx establishes a direct filial relationship between French Canada and the France of the *Ancien Régime*:

20. Lionel Groulx, "Pour qu'on vive," *Orientations*, p. 224. See also Lionel Groulx, "Notre avenir en Amérique," Orientations, p. 276–277; "Labeurs de demain," *Directives*, p. 122–123; "L'éducation nationale," *Directives*, p. 139, 155–156; "L'Amitié française d'Amérique," *Dix ans d'Action française*, p. 187; "La bourgeoisie et le national," AN, April 1939, p. 291–301.
21. Louis Hartz, *The Founding of New Societies. Studies in the History of the United States, Latin America, South Africa, Canada and Australia* (New-York: Harcourt, Brace & World, 1964), 336 p.; André-J. Bélanger uses the Hartz model in "Lionel Groulx, une mystique québécoise," *L'Apolitisme des idéologies québécoises: Le grand tournant de 1934–1936* (Québec: Presses de l'Université Laval, 1974), p. 191–255.

> Our entire doctrine may be summed up in this brief formula: we wish to reconstitute the fullness of our French life. We wish to find once more, seize again, in its integrity, the ethnic type that France brought to our shores and that one hundred and fifty years of history then formed. . . . And it is this French type, clearly distinguished, dependent on a history and a geography, having its ethnic and psychological heredities, it is this type we wish to continue, on which we rest the hope of our future, because a people, like any person growing up, can only develop what they have in them, can only develop those strengths whose living seed they already contain.[22]

"Ethnic and psychological heredities," "living seed": all these concepts seem to work toward predetermining the very essence of French Canada. The Groulxist nation expanded not just in space but also in time. Accordingly, it formed an organic body, a "being," at the start of the French regime which always continued, in his view, to be directed toward the realization of its temporal destiny. But the "personality" of the nation, he insisted, remained essentially the same in spite of its evolution. This "ethnic type" that he sought to recover was to draw from two cultural and spiritual sources in order to reach the fullness of its destiny: France, certainly, but also Rome. A Latin character, comprising French and Catholic points of reference, was thus ranked first among the national traits of French Canadians:

> For our intellectual elite, we claim the Roman and the French cultures. The first will give us teachers of truth, who can provide us with spiritual rules, to set aglow those lofty principles without which there is no firm direction, no intangible social foundation, no permanent order, no people assured of its purpose. In the natural order, the culture of France, immortal educator of our thoughts, will achieve the rigorous training of their minds.[23]

This was the vision Abbé Groulx held out to all French Canadians, in particular, "all our brothers in the other Canadian provinces and in the United States who feel, as we do, that our pressing duty is to build up the energy of our national life." If the French Catholic culture had been able to survive its journey across the Atlantic, how could it not adapt to a migration beyond the borders of Québec? In a talk entitled "La France d'outre-mer" that he gave in Paris the following year, Groulx picked up this theme of French Canada belonging to the universal French culture: "These men bring into New France an integral element of the French nation," he explained to his hosts. He also contended that his people should be able to develop "their Latin orientation" and lamented "the present indifference

22. Lionel Groulx, "Notre doctrine," *AF*, January 1921, p. 25–26.
23. *Ibid.*, p. 28.

of many of the French . . . toward this group of the French family, the largest, after all, outside of France."[24] One of the most striking testaments to this cultural continuity with seventeenth-century France was, according to Groulx, the high priority that had been given to the teaching of the classical humanities in the French-Canadian school system for three centuries. The "treasures" of the Greek, Roman and French cultures, these were considered by Groulx to be in perfect "harmony with our inherited psychological predispositions, with the deep innate requirements of the French intelligence." France, in his mind, sat at the apex of humanism and European civilization. And French Canadians would have been wrong to reject such a heritage, since they were every bit as dependent on it for their cultural development in the present as they were during the French regime.[25] Groulx assigned to metropolitan France an important role of cultural diffusion and encouraged the intellectual and academic elites of French Canada to reconnect with the former mother country. Rather than studying at "foreign" universities like McGill, Harvard or Oxford, they should attend institutions "in harmony with our intellectual traditions," like those in Paris, but also Louvain and Fribourg.

> May the French intellect continue to rely, in our nation, on the inherited virtues and may the integrity of that intellect be attained and sustained by borrowing from the original family, this . . . is what we ask. No one, to our knowledge, has been foolishly persuaded that our insufficiency could be sufficient for us, or that the accumulation of intellectual capital from France over three centuries should leave us indifferent.[26]

The French Canadians were, nevertheless, more than just a group of French people transplanted into the New World: "We believe that the French Canadians constituted, not a French people living in Canada, nor a people of 'simply Canadians,' but an entity of French origin, who through three hundred years of battles, adaptation and conquests, have acquired a distinct national personality."[27] These lines appeared in 1927 in *L'Action française*. Ten years later, in an article appearing in *L'Action nationale*, his opinion had not changed. "What is a French Canadian?" he asked:

24. Lionel Groulx, "La France d'outre-mer," *Notre Maître le passé, Tome II*, p. 257, 298–303.
25. See Lionel Groulx, *L'Enseignement français au Canada, Tome I: Dans Le Québec* (Montréal: Éditions Albert Lévesque, 1931), p. 35–36, 194–197. See also Lionel Groulx, "Notre avenir en Amérique," *Orientations*, p. 286; Lionel Groulx, "Préparation des jeunes à leurs tâches prochaines," *Directives*, p. 247; Lionel Groulx, "Labeurs de demain," Directives, p. 95–96; Lionel Groulx, "Notre avenir en Amérique," *Orientations*, p. 287–288.
26. Lionel Groulx, "Méditations patriotiques," *Dix ans d'Action française*, p. 88. This article originally appeared in *Le Devoir* on June 24, 1920.
27. L'Action française, "Les modes d'action nationale," *AF*, December 1927, p. 321. Although this text is signed by the review's directorship, it comes, by all appearances, from the desk of Lionel Groulx.

> The definition comes from the name: A Canadianized Frenchman. A Frenchman in origin and culture, but changed and diversified by three hundred years of existence in an original historical and geographical milieu. In defining our ethnic or national character, the accent must be placed squarely on the qualifier "French." Stronger than its adherence to the country Canada, its adherence to the French culture situates it in a particular spiritual family, gives it its orientation and depth of soul, sets a seal on its human type. . . . We must even add that our people can only gain access to the culture of France, which is the source of our own and an essential supplement to it, through its institutions . . . . In summary, our national cultural milieu cannot be an artificial one, like that of a plant in a greenhouse, that has to survive in a simulated atmosphere with synthetic sunlight. France cannot be that for us, some kind of loan that we rely on from them; no, our corner of the world is French Canada, with its own potential for civilization.[28]

So, the nation was "French-Canadian" even though Groulx accorded greater importance to the qualifier "French" than to the noun "Canadian." In a way, one could say that he was fighting against the "pan-Canadian" national identity, too abstract and disembodied for his liking, with as much conviction as the Romantics had fought against the universalist abstraction of the Enlightenment philosophers. Groulx presented French Canada as the offspring, or the extension of, France in America, as a child who, having reached adulthood, could now fly on its own wings. The relationship between the French and the French Canadians was a filial one to be sure, but not one of dependence or submission. Groulx attributed the autonomy obtained by the French-Canadian nation to the unique character of its history, its religious and cultural traditions, as well as the political, social, legal and intellectual institutions it had developed over more than three centuries. As a historian, he applied himself diligently to retracing the origin of the traditions and institutions on which the French-Canadian identity was founded. His first major effort in this regard was made during the 1918–1919 academic year in the context of the history courses he gave at Université Laval de Montréal. The theme he chose that year was "Birth of a race." By his own admission, he designed this series of studies less as a political or colonial history of the French Regime than as an analysis of the conditions and factors that had produced, right from the seventeenth century, a distinct and autonomous French people in America.[29] "Every true story must culminate in a collective psychology," he told his audience, by way of introduction. "The facts and exploits of times gone by would not be worth the trouble of such arduous research if they did not reveal at the end a state of the soul, a form of humanity." His account comprised three major sections. To begin with, he studied the provincial origin of the first settlers who came from France

28. Lionel Groulx, "Notre destin français," AN, March 1937, p. 130–142.
29. Lionel Groulx, *La Naissance d'une race* (Montréal: Bibliothèque de l'Action française, 1919), 284 p.

in order to explain how they had mingled in America to give rise to a homogenous culture. Next, he analyzed the earliest religious, social and cultural institutions that they had established. Finally, he offered a lengthy commentary demonstrating the originality of the "new race" thus founded.

In his *Mémoires*, written after the Second World War, he showed he was aware that the concept of "race" had fallen into disfavour: "I admit the too frequent use of the vocabulary of my day," he wrote, explaining that the almost interchangeable terms "race," "nation" and "people," had a less specific meaning in the era when he used them. He added that it had never "occurred to him to speak of *race* based purely on *blood*, in the animal or biological sense." Rather, he had wanted to found the French-Canadian "race" "on a substance of culture or civilization, that is, on the essential elements that constitute the nation."[30] Although he admitted he had "included a hereditary aspect" in his definition of the French-Canadian nation, he explained, in his own defence, that other well-respected thinkers had also made use of the term, "race," Louis-Adolphe Pâquet and André Siegfried among them.

Furthermore, in the first few pages of *La Naissance d'une race*, he took care to qualify his use of the word "race," which he used simply in the sense of "ethnic group." Later, in 1936, addressing the Jeunesses patriotes, he positively condemned cultural aloofness and isolation, stressing the need for French Canadians to be open to "otherness"—to borrow a very popular contemporary term: "The genius of a people," he told them,

> is not something fixed or static; it is an essentially dynamic reality, with the potential for indefinite development and enrichment. In order for it to be possible and legitimate to limit oneself to one's nation, that nation would have to contain all human good.[31]

However, he went on, art, literature, philosophy—none of that was the exclusive domain of a single nation. "Not only must no one people exclude other peoples; but none has the right to condemn itself to such isolation." Even the Anglo-Saxon people, whose formidable power of absorption, moreover, Groulx dreaded, could, in his view, offer French Canadians possibilities of cultural enrichment, as long as the latter were able to maintain the integrity of their own cultural identity. Groulx shared concerns of a similar nature with Father Charles Charlebois in 1941. He told him he was anxious about the immigrant situation as it seemed to him the French-Canadian political class had given up and left to others the responsibility of managing and controlling immigration to the country. Immigration represented to him an excellent way of increasing the numbers of the French-Canadian population:

30. Lionel Groulx, *Mes Mémoires, Tome III: 1926–1939* (Montréal: Fides, 1972), p. 52.
31. Lionel Groulx, "Labeurs de demain," *Directives*, p. 97.

> A people that is the least bit concerned about its national interests would a long time ago have applied itself to conquering these newcomers [immigrants] who, together with the thirty percent of the population that we represent, would give us a majority in Canada. A long experience should have taught us to turn in that direction and to seek our support there . . . . But this enormous task of rapprochement and conquest cannot be accomplished, as you can well understand, artificially. It would need to be the natural consequence of our power of attraction. In other words, immigrants can only orient themselves toward the French group if to them we appear, in our province, to be the strongest, most civilized and most promising group.[32]

In 1928, Groulx had made remarks stressing the same point: he stated that it was "the intellectual and moral elements, culture, faith, traditions and customs, rather than biological heredity, that gave a human type its original physiognomy or character."[33] Frédéric Boily reflects this view in his comments that despite certain statements, which seem at first glance to point to the "racial" character of Groulx's thought, the deeper logic of his nationalism was much more cultural.[34]

This long digression deserves a far more nuanced and in-depth treatment than the scope of this study allows. But let us retain quite simply that French Canada, in the mind of Abbé Groulx, was first and foremost a cultural entity generated by a long historical tradition. He often had occasion to pursue his analysis of the factors that had fashioned the French-Canadian "type." For example, in 1923, he gave a talk on "The French-Canadian family," enumerating its countless virtues. He credited François de Laval, the first bishop of Québec, with having seen to the moral purity of the pioneers of New France by establishing a parish framework. The parish and the family were the two most important social cells of the young colony. Despite their cultural isolation, these colonists had not, in his estimation, yielded to any slackening of moral standards, scrupulously upholding marriage when it would have been relatively easy for them to slide into dissolute living. The first generations enjoyed remarkable birthrates (especially among "our Acadian brothers," who doubled their ranks every sixteen years); illegitimate births were rare and had constituted culpable anomalies: the father possessed an authority whose origin was recognized by all members of the family to be divine. "On this kind of authority, supported by the supernatural," he concluded, "the education of the French-Canadian family will produce beautiful fruit, as do all things that are in harmony with truth." Groulx also lent great importance to the geographic environment in the formation of the French-Canadian "type": fresh air,

32. Letter from Lionel Groulx to Charles Charlebois, BAnQ, FLG, Pi/A,746, July 12, 1941.
33. Lionel Groulx, "Nos responsabilités intellectuelles," *Orientations*, p. 17. See also Lionel Groulx, *Mes Mémoires*, Tome III, p. 98.
34. Frédéric Boily, *La Pensée nationaliste de Lionel Groulx*, p. 31–46.

the work of clearing the land, and agriculture were the elements that he believed had fashioned a robust and vigorous people. He also made much of the religious homogeneity of the first generations of French Canadians, the political and ecclesiastical authorities of France having forbidden the Huguenots to emigrate to New France. From this he concluded that "our ancestors felt they were the sons of one same Church before they felt they were the subjects of one state, and it was the bond of faith that was the first bond of nationality."[35]

Physical health, moral health, work ethic, modesty, spirituality and respect for the established order; these were the dominant characteristics that Abbé Groulx observed when he scanned the historic origins of his *petit peuple*: "These men and these women of long ago know very well that they are founding a country and a race. They fully accept the consequences of this lofty duty: the race they found, they want it to be noble, loyal and pure, up to the standard of its origins."[36] It is obvious that the portrait Groulx painted of the pioneers of New France had been idealized to the point of seeming bland and rather naïve to our contemporary eyes. However, what we should draw primarily from this approach is the historian's desire for the cultural uniqueness of the French-Canadian people to be understood, so that their right to exist might be better defended.

Thus far, we have taken into account what Groulx meant by the "material" element that served as the foundation of his definition of the concept of nation. Let us remember that he had also identified a second, "formal," element, indispensable to the existence of any nation. It was not sufficient, therefore, that a collective group aspiring to the status of nation should share a set of cultural traditions and a common historical experience: it needed also to have awareness of that commonality and to express the "will" to exist as a national community. We should not read into this form of voluntarism an allusion to the contractualist understanding of nation that the Enlightenment had developed in the eighteenth century. Nor did Groulx's "will to live" resemble in any way the "daily plebiscite" of Ernest Renan or the "social contract" of Jean-Jacques Rousseau, who saw in the nation only some sort of amalgamation of individuals making an arbitrary choice to live in society. Groulx's voluntarism consisted rather of the individual's "choice" to remain faithful to the deeper nature of his or her people or, to put it differently, to recognize that they belong to a genealogical line plotted around the "formal" elements of the nation. While the nation here is understood as a "natural" and "organic" entity, the individuals who comprised it still had the prerogative of turning their back on it and rejecting the historical and cultural legacy

35. Lionel Groulx, "La famille canadienne-française: Ses traditions, son rôle," *Notre Maître le passé, Tome I*, p. 115–151, 124–125; Lionel Groulx, "L'éducation nationale," *Directives*, p. 142–143; Lionel Groulx, "Conclusion: Ce que nous devons au catholicisme," *Notre Maître le passé, Tome I*, p. 272; Lionel Groulx, "La France d'outre-mer," *Notre Maître le passé, Tome II*, p. 258–259; Lionel Groulx, "François de Laval," *Notre Maître le passé, Tome I*, p. 10; Lionel Groulx, "Conclusion. Ce que nous devons au catholicisme," *Notre Maître le passé, Tome I*, p. 275–276.

36. Lionel Groulx, "Marguerite Bourgeoys," *Notre Maître le passé, Tome I*, p. 38 (Groulx wrote this text in May 1918).

that natural law guaranteed them. This explanation may help resolve the contradiction observed by Gérard Bouchard between the two "motors"—human freedom and Providence—of the history of the French-Canadian nation according to Groulx.[37] This "will to live," what was it if not nationalism? Abbé Groulx therefore treated this "formal" element as the *sine qua non* condition of the *survivance* of peoples and, even more so, of minority peoples struggling against the pressures of assimilation coming at them from all sides:

> And that is how we know . . . , he said to the Franco-Americans in 1935, that it exists, this supreme element of nationality, the collective will-to-live, the will to persist in our cultural and historical soul. . . . And if I were to call to mind the last hundred years of the history of nationalities, each nationality would testify that their awakening and their *survivance* were not the fruit of chance but the result of a conscious act of will.[38]

Groulx contended that even the smallest peoples could expect to survive and flourish, if only they desired it. This faith in the will to live kept him from backing down in the face of the structural determinism that, after 1945, started rallying young intellectual nationalists, increasingly inclined to advocate that Québec should abandon the French minorities in the other provinces. The intellectual leader would have none of it. The "will to live" was "the distinctive feature of the personality seeking to liberate itself from all outside pressures, all illegitimate determinism."[39] Groulx placed the burden of responsibility for developing this "collective will to live" on the shoulders of the elites. His nation was an organism: every group that was an element of it carried specific and inalienable responsibilities. Accordingly, he considered the elites somewhat as the "thinking head" of the nation, charged with coordinating and directing the activity of the other members of the national organism. In French Canada, in his view, the religious and intellectual elites were doing a good job of meeting their responsibilities in this regard. However, he felt the political elites too often acted like mere clowns, as we shall see in the next chapter, and this worried him greatly for he saw the consequences as disastrous. The masses, thus left adrift, were at risk of drowning: "Experience, alas, has shown this all too well: both intellectually and morally, peoples left to their own devices tend to give up."[40] Groulx believed the solution to this "plague" lay to a large extent with the French-Canadian educational

37. Gérard Bouchard, *Les deux chanoines: Contradiction et ambivalence dans la pensée de Lionel Groulx* (Montréal: Boréal, 2003), p. 57–66.
38. Lionel Groulx, "Notre avenir en Amérique," *Orientations*, p. 280, 295. See also Lionel Groulx, "Labeurs de demain," *Directives*, p. 96–102; Lionel Groulx, "Nos positions," *Orientations*, p. 241.
39. Lionel Groulx, "L'histoire et la vie nationale," *Dix ans d'Action française*, p. 238.
40. Lionel Groulx, *L'Enseignement français au Canada, Tome I*, p. 51. See also Lionel Groulx, "Notre avenir en Amérique," *Orientations*, p. 297–298; "Pour l'Action française," *Dix ans d'Action française*, p. 62–63.

system: the political elites could not agree to assume their natural role unless they first received an adequate national education. In 1934, he asked,

> In clear terms, what is it we want? To renew our sense of nation or our national consciousness and to strengthen our collective will-to-live. In other words, we want to restore among ourselves the formal element of nationality. Now, to undertake a project like this, what group of workers is the largest in number, the most active and the most powerful, if not teachers, if by teachers, I mean all teachers from the country school house teacher to the university professor?[41]

It will surprise no one that Groulx, being a professor and a historian, wanted to augment the role played by history in the educational institutions of French Canada. If the nation was essentially a historical entity, if its existence depended directly on the will manifested by its members to belong to it, it was natural that Groulx should wish to develop the "historical consciousness" of his people: in order to want to belong to a nation, one first had to get to know it. That was the argument he developed in 1925 during a stirring lecture he gave, entitled "History and the life of the nation":

> History is the genealogy of a people. How could this marvellous little phrase fail to impress on us that one is not isolated in life or in time, but attached to a moral person, ancient and august? . . . There does not exist, in fact, any moral or spiritual inheritance as such; at best, there are simply dispositions, the result of physical heredity. But then there is history, the past and traditions, gathered and condensed. History can carry to all minds all the glorious booty it has gleaned along the routes of the fatherland. It can welcome the least sons of the race who possess their spiritual heritage, keep them in close relationship with the best of the ancestors, recreate for them indefinitely the moral atmosphere in which the heroes lived. Come now, is there anything more effective to ensure that the sons will resemble their fathers, that their inherited traits can be read on their faces and in their souls?[42]

The Minorities and French-Canadian Messianism

French Canada and the Theory of the Providential Creation of Nations

Some might think that of all the cultural traditions of the French-Canadian people, Groulx placed its religious tradition at the top of the list. In reality, this is

41. Lionel Groulx, "Pour qu'on vive...," AN, September 1935, p. 52–63.
42. Lionel Groulx, "L'histoire et la vie nationale," *Dix ans d'Action française*, 261–262. See also Lionel Groulx, "Nos devoirs envers la race," *Dix ans d'Action française*, p. 225–227; "Nos positions," *Orientations*, p. 260; "L'éducation nationale à l'école primaire," *Orientations*, p. 140; "Le patriotisme des jeunes," *Notre Maître le passé, Tome I*, p. 21.

only half true. Catholicism, for this man of faith, was considerably more than just a cultural tradition. It represented for him something more all-encompassing and more "transcendent." In 1937, he voiced this conviction at the Congrès de la langue française de Québec:

> Catholicism has created everything here, animated everything in us; often it has rectified everything, healed everything. Let us see in it much more than our great tradition. It transcends our entire life, it gives life to our whole being. And because of the supreme role it plays, I hesitate to list as one of our traditions that which permeates them all as their very soul.[43]

This is why we accord special treatment to the question of religion and the Church in this analysis of the Groulxist understanding of the French-Canadian nation.

In Lionel Groulx's ideology, nations "are not built by chance, according to geographical determinism or randomness, through political and economic adventures."[44] They were, on the contrary, the work of Providence. This was a belief from which he never departed. Let us recognize, however, that Groulx was not the first to subscribe to it. It was a much more ancient idea, which the European Romantics, in particular, had already developed in the nineteenth century. Without going so far as to establish a direct relationship between Groulx's thought and theirs, one is nevertheless tempted to draw a parallel between them. To cite philosopher Robert Legros, the Romantic movement conceived society as a "natural, normative and supernatural community": it was natural because it did not depend on a "social contract," normative because it presumed conformity to a cultural tradition that had evolved over the course of history, and supernatural because it had, at the same time, been engendered by a "supra-human" power or, to put it more simply, a divine power.[45] Groulx said nothing to contradict this. Seen from this perspective, national (or cultural) diversity would also appear to be the result of providential design. Groulx was able to transform this idea into a powerful instrument of combat against those who, in North America, wanted to assimilate the French Canadians. As early as 1900, when he was still a student at the *collège*, Groulx wrote this reflection in his journal:

> For anyone who believes in Providence, is it so difficult to understand that, given the certainty of divine action, action governing the peoples, God did not give to the different actors in the drama of history the same character or the same national genius? Would this same Creator God who cast so much variety into the rest of

43. Lionel Groulx, "L'histoire, gardienne des traditions vivantes," *Directives*, p. 210–211. See also Lionel Groulx, "La famille canadienne-française: Ses traditions, son rôle," *Notre Maître le passé, Tome I*, p. 286.
44. Lionel Groulx, "Le national et le religieux," *AN*, February 1934, p. 93–98. See also Lionel Groulx, "L'annexionnisme au Canada français," *Notre Maître le passé, Tome III*, p. 233–234.
45. Robert Legros, "Le romantisme politique," in Alain Renaut, ed., *Lumières et romantisme*, p. 285.

> creation for the sake of universal harmony, have abstained from imbuing the higher level of his great work likewise with nuances of tone and colouring?[46]

Groulx developed this idea frequently throughout his career. In a course he gave in 1916 on the constitutional history of the English regime, he appealed to it as justification for the French-Canadian struggle, at the time, against the assimilating designs of the British and the English Canadians. The "too vast hegemonies," he said, were "as contrary to the divine plan as they were to the interests of humanity": "The originality and the variety of the races desired by Providence, whatever our little primary-culture assimilators may think of it, remain necessary to perpetuate the beauty of the world . . . ." In 1935, to encourage the Franco-Americans in Manchester to remain steadfast and resist assimilation, he would say, for example: "I observe, despite everything, that humanity was not made from a uniform pattern . . . . God, who made the countries and the races, wanted them diverse for the diversity of talents and the exchange of services."[47] Although he appreciated cultural diversity, Groulx did not hesitate to claim there were "sun-peoples" who existed in order to "enlighten the less privileged nations."[48] Thus, he did not break with certain prejudices of his day, his "cultural relativism," so to speak, being no doubt largely confined to the Western societies of the Judeo-Christian tradition. Not only did he not reject proselytizing, but he presented the evangelization of the North American continent as the greatest achievement of the French-Canadian nation, as we shall see shortly.

Groulx's reasoning on the intervention of Providence in the destiny of nations had other ramifications too. He believed divine authority had willed cultural diversity. He believed it had likewise entrusted a particular mission to each of the nations it had created. By working in concert with one another, the nations of the world were working towards the realization of a great supernatural plan to which Providence alone held the secret. Groulx's thought was therefore deeply ontological in that it attributed to the cultural experience of the human person a purpose belonging to the metaphysical order: it postulated that the past had a direction and that history allowed us to observe the movement toward this purpose, if not this purpose itself. On this question of the providential mission of the French Canadians, Groulx was only following the reasoning of certain of his predecessors, including Jules-Paul Tardivel, Msgr. Louis-Adolphe Pâquet and Henri Bourassa.[49] In 1900, once again in the diary he kept as a *collège* student, he wrote,

46. Lionel Groulx, *Journal, 1895–1911: Tome II* (Montréal: Presses de l'Université de Montréal, 1984), p. 559–560.
47. Lionel Groulx, *Nos luttes constitutionnelles V: Les Droits du français* (Montréal: Le Devoir, [1916]), p. 21; Lionel Groulx, "Notre avenir en Amérique," *Orientations*, p. 293–294. See also Lionel Groulx, "L'histoire et la vie nationale," *Dix ans d'Action française*, p. 239; "Intention apostolique ou hypocrisie politique?," *Notre Maître le passé, Tome III*, p. 51.
48. Lionel Groulx, *Journal, 1895–1911: Tome II*, p. 559–560.
49. See Réal Bélanger, "Le nationalisme ultramontain: le cas de Jules-Paul Tardivel," in Nive Voisine and Jean Hamelin, ed., *Les Ultramontains canadiens-français: Études d'histoire religieuse présentées en hommage au professeur Philippe Sylvain* (Montréal: Boréal, 1985), p. 267–303, 342–347; Louis-Adolphe Pâquet, "La vocation de la race française

> Not all peoples can teach, not all peoples are talented in business. Not everyone can be a soldier. Nor is it possible to be or to do only those things, to the exclusion of any other mission, but all can work in accordance with their particular genius towards the fulfillment of the providential plan, a plan shaped and defined before the beginning of time, the final secret of which will be revealed only when God himself has precipitated the dénouement of the drama and has said: The End!"[50]

Some thirty years later, this conviction remained intact: "All nations have a mission to fulfill here below, which is to put themselves at the service of truth."[51] And the French-Canadian nation as he understood it was not exempt. He believed that from the time of the founding of New France, it had received a mission that could not have been clearer: to ensure the spread of Catholicism and French civilization in America. This conviction made French Canada the natural heir, in the New World, of the mission that in Europe fell to France, "the eldest daughter of the Church." "It is said," he stated in 1922, before an audience of Parisians, "that this French force is being established in America in order to serve Catholicism there."[52] During a talk given in Montréal in 1925, he spoke of the French-Canadian nation as a "chosen race":

> Whatever we believe about the motive of the kings of France for founding the colony, there is one major fact that cannot be contested: that the idea of mission caused the idea of colonization to triumph. French penetration into the heart of the continent was as much an advance of the Catholic apostolate as it was commercial penetration. And if we could read the providential plan above, which inclined our ancestors from France to come to the Northern part of America rather than to the sunny beaches of the South, perhaps we would learn that the winds of heaven pushed the French caravels towards the vast hunting grounds and the great river routes, where the most populous indigenous nations lived and where there was the greatest potential for apostolic work.[53]

The French-Canadian nation was thus destined by Providence to work toward the "conquest of souls" in America. The dignity of this mission, Groulx added,

en Amérique," edition annotated by Dominique Foisy-Geoffroy, *Mens: Revue d'histoire intellectuelle de l'Amérique française*, Vol. 3, No. 1 (Fall 2003), p. 61–95; Henri Bourassa, *Religion, langue, nationalité: discours prononcé à la séance de clôture du XXI*e *Congrès eucharistique à Montréal, le 10 septembre 1910* (Montréal: Le Devoir, 1910), 30 p.; Fernand Dumont, Genèse de la société québécoise (Montréal: Boréal, 1996 (1993)), p. 271–275.

50. Lionel Groulx, *Journal, 1895–1911, Tome II*, p. 559–560.
51. Lionel Groulx, "Nos responsabilités intellectuelles," *Orientations*, p. 29; Lionel Groulx, *L'Enseignement français au Canada: Tome I*, p. 314–315.
52. Lionel Groulx, "La France d'outre-mer," *Notre Maître le passé, Tome II*, p. 262, 296. See also Lionel Groulx, "Le patriotisme des jeunes," *Notre Maître le passé, Tome I*, p. 12, 23; "Intention apostolique ou hypocrisie politique?," *Notre Maître le passé, Tome III*, p. 52–53.
53. Lionel Groulx, "L'histoire et la vie nationale," *Dix ans d'Action française*, p. 267–268. See also Lionel Groulx, "Jacques Cartier à Hochelaga," *Notre Maître le passé, Tome II*, p. 7–21.

citing Pascal, could not be measured in material or quantitative terms. "True civilization" is not manifested in "commerce or glory" but rather in the "dignity of the customs."[54] As we shall see shortly, the historian believed he was able, in his studies of the French and English regimes, to ascertain that this apostolic mission was being constantly and faithfully accomplished. It was impossible for him to separate the existence of the French Canadians from their mission as Catholics and apostles, for it was this mission that provided their reason for being in America. Groulx, however, hesitated to posit a direct relationship between language and faith: "That a people or an individual who loses their language would automatically lose their faith, I don't think any of us has ever stated anything so completely absurd."[55] But in the same breath he added that "it [was] also an exaggeration to declare that one's linguistic milieu was irrelevant to the faith question." In other words, when a person abandoned their national culture to be integrated into a different one, Providence might not preserve for them the supernatural gift of faith: assimilation always involved the risk of apostasy. Nevertheless, Groulx believed it was still granted to the *petits peuples*, to the least numerous, to the least endowed with material riches, to live in accordance with their "national genius," on condition that they accept the mission Providence had entrusted to them: "God cannot will our national undoing," he said in 1934, because it would never be part of the providential plan that a Catholic people, no matter how small, should die, or even lose the least of its spiritual values."[56] In his eyes, the missionary zeal of the French Canadians throughout America, since the founding of New France, was one of the most eloquent manifestations of the French-Canadian nation's accomplishment of its providential mission. The French minorities of the other provinces represented the remnant, the surviving witnesses of the former grandeur of the French Empire. In 1922, to a group of Franco-Americans gathered in Lowell, he expressed that conviction in these terms:

> Those peoples who, by serving God, accomplish the supreme purposes, can, more than other peoples, rest in the certainty of their future. Heirs of the highest civilization that the modern era has known, sons of the most apostolic nation to which the Church has given birth, remaining worthy of this noble ancestry by virtue of our religious expansion, it would indeed seem to be by a design of God that we have been sent to all corners of the continent to found Catholic apostolic centres, to defend, against the new barbarism, humanity's most beautiful heritage.[57]

54. Lionel Groulx, "Conclusion. Ce que nous devons au catholicisme," *Notre Maître le passé, Tome I*, p. 274–275. See also Lionel Groulx, "La vie religieuse au temps de Talon," *Notre Maître le passé, Tome III*, p. 68–73.
55. Lionel Groulx, "Notre avenir en Amérique," *Orientations*, p. 290. See also Lionel Groulx, "L'économique et le national," *Directives*, p. 66, 74–76.
56. Lionel Groulx, "Pour qu'on vive," *Orientations*, p. 223.
57. Lionel Groulx, "L'Amitié française d'Amérique," *Dix ans d'Action française*, p. 201. See also L'Action française, "Le problème religieux," *AF*, January 1927, p. 4–14.

Providence, History and French America

In Lionel Groulx's nationalism, the French-Canadian nation's claim to its right to exist was founded on the pivotal idea that almost the whole of the North American continent had belonged to the French colonial empire of its ancestors. The French Canadians, therefore, had to be considered as the legitimate heirs of New France, as a "founding" people, in the sense that it was they, in his understanding, who had been chosen by Providence to introduce Christianity and European civilization to America. He could not imagine that the desecration of their fundamental rights would not constitute defiance of natural law and of the divine plan.

Groulx believed that French Canadians, right up to his own day, were endowed with an apostolic mission in the New World, a mission they could fulfill only by remaining faithful to their deeper "nature," which consisted of their Frenchness (Canadianized Frenchness, of course) and Catholicity. His historical work consisted to a very large extent of trying to rekindle in the mind of his compatriots the former grandeur of the "French Empire of America." This historical project, in turn, fuelled his work as a nationalist militant, particularly his efforts to win a guarantee that the ancestral rights of French Canadians, in Québec and the other parts of America to which they had spread, would be respected. It proved extremely difficult at times to distinguish between the historian and the polemicist on this question.

It was in 1915 that Université Laval de Montréal appointed Abbé Groulx as its first Chair of Canadian History. While his first public courses dealt mainly with the period of the English Regime, the young professor soon turned his attention to New France. He made one of his first forays into this area in 1917, when he gave a talk in Montréal entitled simply "L'Histoire acadienne." The evening had been organized by the Société Saint-Jean-Baptiste (SSJB) around this talk, allowing funds to be raised for the rebuilding of the church in Grand-Pré, where numerous Acadians had been gathered, in 1755, before being exiled.[58] Groulx made a point of retracing, although succinctly, the historical origins of Acadian colonization, emphasizing the religious and missionary zeal that had fired the hearts of its architects. The ancestral rootedness of the Acadians in the North American continent, he reflected, had only added to the humiliation of the *Grand Dérangement*: "Well before us, the Acadians understood that the fatherland is the country of one's birth and of life, the land where the ancestors sleep, and that only to it did they owe the love in their hearts, the strength in their arms and the blood in their veins."

It is interesting to note that Groulx, in this extract, makes a distinction between "them" and "us," between the Acadians and the French Canadians. Did he consider these "brothers" as a people making up part of the French-Canadian

58. Lionel Groulx, *L'Histoire acadienne* (Montréal: Éditions de la Saint-Jean-Baptiste, 1917), 32 p.

nation? In the same breath, he stated that it was in Acadia that "the duel of our [italics are ours] history" had begun, thus implying a rapprochement between the two groups. This willingness to be identified with the Acadians, followed by a view of them as a distinct people, this passing from the objective to the subjective, makes Groulx's thought in this regard extremely tortuous and difficult to grasp. At the time of the French regime, the Acadiens and the *Canadiens* were separated, explained Groulx, by forests and huge distances. They were cut off from the metropolis by policies that were "stingy" and "arbitrary": consequently, French immigration was halted, for all intents and purposes, in 1686, and any demographic growth among the Acadians after that was attributable entirely to their own fecundity—which, incidentally, was remarkable. "Already," he concluded, "all the characteristics of a distinct people were evident." Distinct from whom? From the French, certainly, but also, we are no doubt meant to understand, from the French Canadians. Groulx goes even further when he explains that already, when the Treaty of Utrecht was signed in 1713, definitively ceding Acadia to the English, "a new race was born." However, the conclusion to his presentation on Acadian history, leaves his line of reasoning hazy once again:

> This history is a chapter in our own; it is therefore a part of our moral heritage. If this past has known so many trials, so many tragic catastrophes, it must be because a French race is not forged like any other. Because we carry in a fragile vessel a superior ideology, we need greater strength of resistance. And the strength to resist, the virtue of pride, is found in the beauty of the history that lends the race its nobility.[59]

On this question of the "national" relationship between the two branches of the "French family" of America, Groulx always demonstrated great ambiguity, hesitating to incorporate the Acadians unequivocally within the French-Canadian nation. In 1915, with Oblate Rodrigue Villeneuve of Ottawa, he made a long journey to Acadia which showed him the immensity of the gulf that seemed to separate the two "fraternal" peoples. The log book he kept during his tour revealed he was astounded by the cold reception he noted some Acadians gave their French-Canadian visitors. Although he was pleased that the elites had become closer since the "Acadian renaissance" of the 1880s, it remained a fact, he felt, that among the "ordinary people," Acadians had a hard time concealing their genuine distrust of "big brother Québec." Let us examine this extract from the journal:

> Why not admit it? We French Canadians have not always understood that a political situation different from our own, a particular historical manifestation, has made

59. *Ibid.*, p. 30.

> the French person in Acadia a quite distinct nationality type. The first priests we sent to them did not always take into account these differences and these legitimate sensitivities. . . . [They] refused to accept that the Acadiens did not want to become obedient little *Canadiens*; we mocked their flag, their national feast day, their language . . . . All these tactical errors must have hurt and created a negative disposition in a *petit peuple* who possessed a very lively national sentiment and who, through their long and drawn out misfortunes, had become easily vulnerable and distrustful. For a long time, we spoke of big brother Québec as of the great taskmaster or, at least, an over-zealous tutor, treating with condescension a protégé who did not ask for any protection.[60]

Keen to avoid offending the sensitivities of his Acadian hosts and to establish warmer relations with them, Groulx tried to dispel their scepticism. When he passed through Moncton, he used the opportunity to speak to the members of Paroisse de l'Assomption who were studying the possibility of founding a circle of the Association catholique de la jeunesse canadienne (ACJC). In his journal, he reported the stormy debate that the project had sparked in the local press, some people fearing that it was just another ploy to absorb the Acadians into the great French-Canadian whole. Groulx tried to reassure the most sceptical among them with two arguments. First of all, extending the Association to Moncton would in no way impinge on Acadian specificity: "Acadian you are, . . . Acadian you shall remain when you enter the A.C.J.C." On the other hand, he stressed the things that, despite the particularities of any given group, would allow them to forge a powerful bond of solidarity:

> We have things that distinguish us, we have none that divide us. We have the same faith we wish to confess; we have the same language to defend—the French language, which is threatened all around us . . . . [W]e have therefore enough reasons to shake hands and forget the past.[61]

Also in Moncton, in a speech given on August 15, on the occasion of the feast of Our Lady of the Assumption, patron saint of the Acadians, he once more did his utmost to regain their confidence and break down the wall that had formed between the Acadians and the French Canadians. Besides praising their courage and calling them "the chosen people of God," he wanted to reassure them of the honest intentions of the French-Canadian nationalists concerning them. In his view, the Acadians had written an "epic page in the Christian martyrology

60. Lionel Groulx, *Visions acadiennes*, BAnQ, FLG 12 12, fonds Pi, p. 28–31.
61. *Ibid.*, p. 32, 33–34. See also Lionel Groulx, *Mes Mémoires: Tome I: 1870–1920* (Montréal: Éditions Fides, 1970), p. 232–233. Fernand Harvey also evokes this passage of Groulx [speaking] in Acadia (see Fernand Harvey, "Les historiens canadiens-français et l'Acadie, 1859–1960," in Fernand Harvey and Gérard Beaulieu, ed., *Les Relations entre le Québec et l'Acadie de la tradition à la modernité* (n.p.: IQRC and Éditions de l'Acadie, 2000), p. 30–34).

of peoples": even for this reason alone, the *Canadiens* owed it to them to show respect rather than condescension:

> Acadians of today, like your Évangéline, continue to embrace your country, your dear old Acadia, with an immense gaze of love. But when your gaze reaches the western borders of your country, look with confidence even farther, to the old province of Québec. You will see that over there, you have brothers and friends, brothers who may have appeared to forget you in the bad days, but who, now, more aware of the realities of their history, come back to you and understand you. Guard in your hearts and in your homes the traditions that are your most cherished asset after your faith.[62]

Even though he recognized the Acadians' unique sense of identity, Groulx did not hesitate in the same breath to include their historical experience, like that of all the French minorities, in the great history of French Canada, in the *je me souviens* litany: "I remember 1755; I remember 1760, 1776, 1812, 1837, 1840; I remember 1872 in New-Brunswick, I remember 1890 in Manitoba, I remember 1905 in the West, I remember 191[2] in Ontario."

In Lowell, Massachusetts, in 1922, Groulx gave a famous talk entitled "L'Amitié française d'Amérique." The purpose of the event was to define the foundations of the French-Canadian nation as he conceived it, while at the same time firmly establishing the duties and responsibilities that were incumbent upon Québec, as the nation's "ancestral home," toward the French minorities. While this talk was intended primarily for the Franco-Americans who came to listen, it also concerned all the other minorities of the continent, including the Acadians. If Québec, in its interventions, had to respect the autonomy of all its "dispersed brothers," and never impose on them its point of view, there were two groups who deserved special status within the "French friendship of America," namely, the Franco-Americans and the Acadians:

> We have had time to learn also that two of these groups, the Acadian group and yours, are entitled to a fuller autonomy than the others.
>
> The Acadians have their unique history; their race has been deeply marked by its misfortunes and its humiliation; it has legends, customs and traditions that are particular to it. The set of virtues thus historically developed constitute for it a heritage and sacred strength that deserve more than respect. And if the Acadians have their place, like the others, in the French friendship of America, it can only be in order to thereby preserve before all else the integrity of their national soul.[63]

62. Lionel Groulx, "Aux Acadiens. Discours prononcé à Moncton, le dimanche 15 août, par M. l'abbé L.-A. Groulx," *Le Devoir*, September 11, 1915, p. 9.
63. Lionel Groulx, "L'Amitié française d'Amérique," *Dix ans d'Action française*, p. 171–172.

His use of that second-last word was almost like saying there was a distinct Acadian nation! However, almost at the same time, Groulx stated the opposite: French Canadians were "the oldest race" in America and the "heirs and continuation of New France." All "French groups" gathered within French Canada—including the Acadians—had special entitlement in America by virtue of their long history there, and no one had the power to contest it.

This long digression has allowed us to establish that Groulx's preference would no doubt have been to clearly include the Acadians in the French-Canadian nation: their history, although distinct, was in many respects, similar to that of the other members of the great "French family of America." The historian saw the Acadians as the first occupants of their corner of the country and, despite the events of 1755, the Maritime provinces had always constituted their legitimate heritage. Between the breakup of 1713 and the so-called "reunification" of 1867, Acadians and French Canadians had evolved separately, to be sure. However, they had evolved in parallel fashion. Groulx believed that the fight for Acadian *survivance* was identical to the fight French Canadians were engaged in elsewhere in the country, against acculturation and apostasy. (Moreover, the theme of the Acadian reconquest served as a background for Groulx's second novel, *Au Cap Blomidon*, published in 1932.[64] The principal character, Jean Bérubé, tries to take back possession of a plot of land that belonged to his grandfather before the *Grand Dérangement*.) Groulx hesitated, though, to offend the sensibilities of the Acadians, preferring to grant them a special place, albeit it a very ill-defined one, within the French-Canadian nation.[65] He never managed to shed this ambiguity entirely, which leads one to believe he may even have cultivated it. However, this sensitivity did not prevent him from seeing in Acadian history a manifestation of the apostolic mission that, in his view, Providence had entrusted to the entire "French race of America."

The studies he produced between 1917 and 1922 continued to make abundant use of this argument. He praised the "efflorescence of beautiful supernatural souls," as well as the chivalrous virtues of the founders of Ville-Marie. In a piece devoted to the work of Marguerite Bourgeoys, he described with pride the spread of Christian education which, even in the midst of the country's colonization, had constituted a priority for the pioneers of New France.[66] In a speech he gave in Paris in 1922, Groulx made a point of developing this theme meticulously. He began by

64. Alonié de Lestres [pseudonym of L. Groulx], *Au Cap Blomidon* (Montréal: Le Devoir, 1932), 239 p.

65. Generally, in Groulx's lexicon, the terms "race," "nation," "nationality," and even "ethnocultural group," are all synonymous. However, in certain cases, notably when he addressed the Acadians, he referred only to the French "race" and the French "family," while at the same time being willing to speak of an Acadian "nationality."

66. Lionel Groulx, "Ville-Marie," *Notre Maître le passé, Tome I*, p. 32; Lionel Groulx, "Marguerite Bourgeoys," *Notre Maître le passé, Tome I*, p. 37–47. See also "Au Long-Sault," *Notre Maître le passé, Tome I*, p. 53–60; "Montréal, son histoire singulière," *Notre Maître le passé, Tome III*, p. 22–24; "La traite des fourrures à Montréal," *Notre Maître le passé, Tome III*, p. 107–119; "Le départ de Maisonneuve," *Notre Maître le passé, Tome III*, p. 47; Lionel Groulx, "Les femmes dans notre histoire," *Notre Maître le passé, Tome I*, p. 268.

recounting the exploits of the French explorers, who had made the first overtures of European civilization in America. Close on their heels, there had followed a legion of missionaries committed to evangelizing the Amerindian populations:

> This story, which is all about boldness [the boldness of the explorers], is exceeded in beauty and grandeur only by the story of those who came to evangelize. The missionaries accompanied the explorers almost everywhere they went; often they preceded them; always they followed. The man of God wishes to be the first to greet the nations without faith, and he knows that all land that becomes French is promised to Catholicism. . . . As French strength was rebuilt, it placed itself of its own accord at the service of Catholicism. We believe that we inherited from the old France its apostolic gifts. . . . It is our people who organized the religious life of all the provinces in the Dominion, from the Atlantic to the Pacific. Our missionaries cleared the path; our nuns soon followed them; and then apostolic vicars of the French race organized these primitive churches. It was like this everywhere and it is still like this.[67]

Given that the structural anthropology of Claude Lévi-Strauss and the deconstructionist theories of Michel Foucault, among others, have become part of general consciousness since the Second World War, we cannot accept Groulx's attitude without batting an eyelid. It is, to say the least, condescending toward the Amerindian cultures, which he considered to be "without faith." Let us acknowledge, however, that on this question, Groulx was merely reflecting an intellectual position that was very widespread in Western societies in his day. In fact, if he had shown greater broad-mindedness, it would have been astonishing prior to the publication of Lévi-Strauss's earliest works at the end of the 1940s, which pushed Western academic and intellectual circles to question many of their biases toward indigenous peoples throughout the world. Before the Second World War, the old dichotomy between "civilization" and "primitiveness," while it is unfortunate and easy to criticize today, still had currency in most places in the Western world: if we are to be completely honest, it cannot be attributed to Lionel Groulx.

In *L'Action française*, during the 1920s, Abbé Groulx frequently used the argument of the apostolic mission of the French-Canadian people to encourage the Franco-Americans of New England to remain steadfast and resist Americanization. These people, he wrote, "h[ad] only to glance at a map of their country to learn that a large part of its early history is actually French."[68] The United States, he went on, was indebted to the French for being the first to explore the vast stretches

67. Lionel Groulx, "La France d'outre-mer," *Notre Maître le passé, Tome II*, p. 271, 296–297; See also "François de Laval," *Notre Maître le passé, Tome I*, p. 108–111; "La famille canadienne-française: Ses traditions, son rôle," *Notre Maître le passé, Tome I*, p. 150; "La situation religieuse au Canada français vers 1840," *Notre Maître le passé, Tome III*, p. 180–225; "Les leçons d'histoire au bord du S[ain]t-Maurice," *AF*, August 1927, p. 102–112.

68. Lionel Groulx, "Les Franco-Américains et nous," *AF*, June 1922, p. 366.

of its territory, as evidenced by the French toponymy still found there: "How can Franco-Americans, who are looking for reasons to be proud, wait any longer," he asked, "before taking ownership of these memories?"

Similarly, in an article Groulx devoted to the expedition of explorers Louis Jolliet and Jacques Marquette, who had set out to conquer the Mississippi two and a half centuries earlier, he wrote, "What a future that expedition was about to prepare! An immense territory was opened up for the Gospel and a great empire for France. In the footsteps of the first discoverers, a legion of others would set out to create, in the heart of the continent, a marvellous epic."[69] In his speech on "French friendship in America," Groulx dedicated many more lengthy passages to the theory of French-Canadian messianism. He explained to the Franco-Americans who came to hear him that, in America, "where we are the oldest race and where that must necessarily count for something," those who embodied the "continuation of New France" could legitimately demand that their right to *survivance* be respected. He then reviewed how long each French minority had lived in its part of the continent since putting down roots there. The Acadians were, he proclaimed, "the earliest owners, and the only legitimate ones," of the land of their birth. The Franco-Ontarians, for their part, could claim a similar title: "There, in the upper part of the country, old Huronia will remind [them] that the soil of Ontario, more than any other, was the soil of the martyrs, the land of the glorious missionaries who went so far as to die for the civilization of Christ." The immense plains of the West too were marked by French Catholic civilization before the other peoples from Europe ever set foot there:

> Well before the wave of immigrants, which included their persecutors, men of their race [the race of "our brothers of the prairies"] had unlocked the mystery of the great plain, and missionaries had, by their blood, prepared it to receive civilisation. That is the history of the West. That country belongs first to Canadians of the French race. The ruins of the old French forts, the bases of thousands of old crosses still buried in the ground, attest to a right.[70]

Groulx was extremely irked that the initial possession of the West by French-Canadian clergy and explorers remained a fact completely ignored by the federal authorities, who, immediately after Confederation, penetrated the country as usurpers. The way the Métis were treated, he felt, made this abundantly clear. This faith in the providential mission of the French-Canadian nation, and in

69. Lionel Groulx, "La découverte du Mississipi," *AF*, April 1923, p. 212. See also Lionel Groulx, "Jacques Marquette," AN, December 1939, p. 232–237.
70. Lionel Groulx, "L'Amitié française d'Amérique," *Dix ans d'Action française*, p. 193–194. Groulx took these pages from "L'Amitié française d'Amérique" and used them as an epilogue to the first volume of *Notre Maître le passé*, a work that appeared in 1924 (see Lionel Groulx, "Pour qu'on écrive l'histoire," *Notre Maître le passé, Tome I*, p. 289–296).

the primarily "mystical" character of the French colonial enterprise in America, served as a major source of ammunition for Groulx and *L'Action française* in their struggle to defend the French minorities. The French Canadians, he stated repeatedly in the review, could not be considered as recent arrivals to the country; they did not constitute an ethnic group like so many others who had come to Canada during and after the great wave of immigration at the beginning of the century. As the first explorers and the first evangelizers of a good part of the New World, they deserved greater respect than they received in several of the provinces with an English majority. The French-Canadian nation, Groulx declared, had paid with its labour and its blood for its right to exist everywhere in America.[71] He reasoned from this that it was a grave injustice toward all of French Canada to deprive the French minorities of their educational and religious rights. In the midst of the Regulation 17 crisis in Ontario, one of the most faithful collaborators of *L'Action française*, Hermas Bastien, also evoked the apostolic mission of the French Canadians to claim respect for the educational rights of Franco-Ontarians: "People who are not open to constitutional arguments would listen to a historical argument and would accept the fact that the descendants of the explorers of the land have the right to some regard."[72] Upon his return from a trip made in 1924 to Kent and Essex counties in Southern Ontario, Abbé Groulx's alter ego, Jacques Brassier, nostalgically recalled the toponymy of that corner of the country which clearly still bore the stamp of New France:

> And on the map, one reads these names of French resonance: Belle-Rivière, Pointe-aux-Roches, Pointe-aux-Bouleaux, Grande-Pointe, Paincourt, Rivière-aux-Canards . . . The traveller who has consulted history is reminded that he is in fact entering old French territory. As early as the year 1752, while on the opposite shore, Lamothe Cadillac's settlement had been growing for half a century, some twenty families had already established their homes on the south shore of the Detroit River. In 1816 the Bishop of Québec found three parishes there and a population of 2600 souls. English emigration was not much inclined to move to that area until around 1830, which means that one could say Essex belonged to the French Canadians.[73]

Around the same time, Groulx wrote a piece about the solemn ceremony of June 14, 1671 that brought together representatives of both the colonial authorities and some of the Amerindian tribes at Sault Ste. Marie, enabling the French to take possession of the major part of the Western territories:

71. Lionel Groulx, "Nos martyrs," AF, June 1925, p. 369–376.
72. Hermas Bastien, "L'Ontario français," AF, April 1924, p. 238.
73. Jacques Brassier [pseudonym of L. Groulx], "Dans Kent et Essex," AF, May 1924, p. 297.

> Did we not do the right thing to sign it? The event that took place that day makes June 14, 1671 one of the great days of our history. It was the definitive impetus toward the expansion of New France. It was the hour when several thousand men would set out on this epic enterprise of embracing the immensity of an entire continent.[74]

French Canadians possessed in Ontario a birthright that was in no way reconcilable with the persecution visited on them by the provincial government and its Regulation 17. Groulx and *L'Action française* did not limit their application of this historical argument to Ontario. The French Canadians in the West were likewise entitled, as we have already established, to such rights—rights that were again being all too casually scoffed at. The heroes of the West occupied a special place in Groulx's national pantheon, no doubt because colonization in this region did not go nearly as far back. No need to travel back to the seventeenth century to find the apostles of Christianity and French civilization west of the Great Lakes. The names of these men, though they were born much later, were not for that reason any less inspiring, he insisted, than those of Champlain or Brûlé. Provencher, Taché and the numerous missionaries who travelled the length and breadth of the West had won his admiration, even his veneration. The director of *L'Action française* considered Msgr. Taché in particular as "one of the most glorious sons of the French-Canadian fatherland." Deeply moved by the work of Taché, he did not hesitate to raise the prelate to the rank of the great heroes of the French-Canadian people:

> The scene is filled with majesty and takes us back to our heroic times. The only work in our history that might be comparable to the work of the Oblates in the Northwest would be that of the Jesuits in old New France. Like the great French founding fathers before him, [Taché] adapted his work to the scale of the continent. In a country where politicians were astute, it would have been obvious early on that the greatest work accomplished in the West was the claim staked in the country by this man of the Church. Before the immigrants invaded, he had everywhere ignited the flame of the highest civilization.[75]

Groulx wanted of course to see the teaching of history developed in such a way as to reveal to French Canadians the grandeur and nobility of their own history. He wanted at the same time that it should show them the premises on which their

74. Lionel Groulx, "Une grande date (June 14, 1671)," *Notre Maître le passé, Tome I*, p. 82–83. See also Lionel Groulx, "Les grandeurs historiques de l'Outaouais," *Notre Maître le passé, Tome II*, p. 55–60; "Le dossier de Dollard," *Notre Maître le passé, Tome II*, p. 41.

75. Lionel Groulx, "Monseigneur Taché," *AF*, October 1923, p. 211, 214, 223. In 1924, the Archbishop of Saint-Boniface, Arthur Béliveau, provided *L'Action française* with a text in which he used a similar idea (See Arthur Béliveau, "Les Canadiens français et le rôle de l'Église catholique dans l'Ouest," *AF*, May–June 1924, p. 362).

rights were based. He suggested many times that every school in French Canada should be equipped with a "triumphal map" illustrating the "apostolic journeys" of the French explorers and missionaries, as well as the continental immensity of ancient New France.[76] It was the continuity of the French presence in America that the historian believed his people needed to grasp. In 1935, he echoed this thought to the Franco-Americans in Manchester: "No one is more rooted in this America than we are," he told them, [no one] has identified more with this continent."[77]

The Minorities and the Compact Theory of Confederation

The Minorities and the Pact of 1867

A missionary people who had received from Providence the duty to evangelize the North American continent: that is what Abbé Groulx believed he saw in the history of the French-Canadian nation. Their long presence in the northern part of the New World, the fact that they had been the first to introduce Christianity and European civilization there had conferred on them a right to "national *survivance*" that Groulx considered inalienable. He believed, moreover, that the parliamentary debates of the nineteenth century that had culminated in the adoption of the British North America Act had allowed French Canadians to finally obtain political recognition of their long history as a "founding people."

The Confederation of 1867, in this sense, was the translation, into Canadian constitutional law, of a fundamental principle of natural law. But, in Groulx's mind, there was no doubt that the latter should at all times take precedence over the BNA Act: constitutional law was a human construction and could consequently be manipulated, or even rejected, but it was Providence itself that had written the law that conferred the right to live in accordance with one's national "genius." The Anglo-Protestant majority might well try to remove the 1867 provisions or, at the very least, interpret them in a minimalist fashion, but Groulx considered that they did not have the ability to flout "natural" law in order to justify cultural assimilation. The first courses Groulx gave at Université Laval de Montréal in 1915, furthermore, were dedicated to the history of Canadian constitutional law. The new professor found it quite difficult to hide his nationalist convictions, which came through loud and clear:

> Should we be defeated before all the courts and all the parliaments, it would still be our duty to take refuge on the mountain tops of this inalienable right, determined to maintain to the end every last one of our claims. Let the persecutor tear up then,

76. Lionel Groulx, "L'éducation nationale," *Directives*, p. 170–171; "Notre destin français," AN, March 1937, p. 130–142; "L'histoire, gardienne des traditions vivantes," *Directives*, p. 223.
77. Lionel Groulx, "Notre avenir en Amérique," *Orientations*, p. 278. See also L'Action française, "Le problème de notre vie morale," AF, July 1927, p. 5–16.

> if it pleases him, the *scraps of paper*, let him deny or cross out the most solemn signatures; never, let us be bold enough to tell him, will he erase, from the bottom of the ever valid charter of our natural right, the signature of God.[78]

Even if, as we shall see later, Groulx believed the spirit of the BNA Act was eventually perverted, he nevertheless hailed its coming into force in 1867 as an important national victory: it was the culmination of a long series of struggles the French Canadians had engaged in ever since the British Conquest a century earlier to assert their right to exist as a distinct collective entity. Groulx studied the measures taken by the conquerors immediately following the Treaty of Paris to try to stifle the *petit peuple* of the St. Lawrence Valley. The first, he explained, was to "carve up" the territory of ancient New France: before the Conquest, the French and the *Canadiens* had been able to claim as their exclusive domain almost the entire North American continent. In 1764, the British had wanted to guard against their expansion by "penning them as much as possible inside [their] Québec 'reserve.'" After the victory of the Québec Act in 1774, which granted them religious freedom, the French Canadians had nevertheless faced new obstacles. When the parliamentary government was installed in Lower Canada in 1791, the intent of the British authorities, Groulx deemed, was to "lower the status of the language of the majority to that of a vassal language, and thus, over time, to throw it out of parliament and the courts." The historian could rejoice in the victory that the first French-Canadian parliamentarians achieved the following year, when the French language was reinstated to its rightful place in the Legislative Assembly of Lower Canada. Thereafter, the clouds that hung over French Canada dissipated to make way for as many victories. First, the project of the fusion of the two Canadas was defeated in 1822–1823. Despite the Union of 1841 and its assimilating intentions—which had represented, Groulx admitted, a clear step backwards politically—the French language had recovered its rights by the end of the 1840s. Finally when responsible government was obtained shortly afterwards, the rights of French Canada in relation to British colonial power were officially established. The principal architect of the victory achieved under the Union was, in Groulx's opinion, Louis-Hippolyte La Fontaine. It was also to a large extent under pressure from this great politician that the educational rights granted to the Protestants of Lower Canada were extended to the Catholics of Upper Canada. Thanks to him, the efforts of the Grits and the Orangemen, who had sought to erase as completely as possible the Catholic influence from the schools of Upper Canada, had come to naught.

All of this, Groulx explained, had foreshadowed the 1867 "victory." Furthermore, it was on the origins of Confederation that Groulx focused his history

78. Lionel Groulx, *Nos Luttes constitutionnelles V*, p. 5.

courses in 1919.[79] He sought to demonstrate that the BNA Act, the result of victories accumulated by the French Canadians since the Conquest, rested on an immutable key notion: the existence of two nations, two "founding peoples" in Canada. In this, Groulx was making Henri Bourassa's argument his own. Still, his account also had as its fundamental premise the idea that the French Canadians were the first occupants of the land and the first to have brought European civilization and Christianity to it, and that they had already, thereby, acquired the right to exist everywhere in the new dominion. The negotiations involved in writing the BNA Act had therefore served only to have this reality recognized by legal and constitutional documents. Not that Groulx was unaware of how difficult it had been for the French-Canadian political class to achieve this recognition. On the contrary, he readily admitted that the provisions of the "pact" regarding the rights of religious minorities had been designed first and foremost to assuage the anxieties the Protestants had about the future of the province of Québec. However, it would be the Catholics of the other provinces who would eventually need to have recourse to these provisions before the courts.

The history professor was equally adamant that the Confederation of 1867 had been a solemn "pact" between two "founding peoples" who had equal rights throughout the country: the BNA Act—in particular, Sections 93 and 133—simultaneously protected Québec's autonomy within its own areas of jurisdiction and the educational, linguistic and religious rights of French Canadians in the provinces that had an Anglo-Protestant majority. He furthermore devoted an entire chapter of his *Confédération canadienne* to the study of these minority rights.[80] In his opinion, the constitutional documents committed the federal government, as well as the Senate, to intervene on behalf of the minorities whenever provincial governments adopted measures depriving them of their rights. We indicated in the previous chapter that certain historians believed there was a contradiction in Groulx's reasoning on this question. Jean-Pierre Gaboury, especially, goes so far as to state that the founding-peoples principle, as conceived by Groulx, involved a "dangerous inconsistency."[81] What would prevent the federal government, he wondered, armed with this principle, from ignoring the provincial autonomy of Québec, in order to intervene on behalf of its Anglo-Protestant minority? In the final analysis, Gaboury concludes that the provincial autonomy and founding-peoples principles were incompatible and that Groulx had not grasped this. However, this is far from true: actually, Groulx never deemed the principle of provincial autonomy an end in itself and always subordinated it to the Compact theory. If the provincial autonomy strategy fostered respect for the founding-peoples

79. Lionel Groulx, *La Confédération canadienne: Ses origines* (Montréal: Le Devoir, 1918), 265 p.

80. Lionel Groulx, "La Confédération et les minorités," in *La Confédération canadienne*, p. 137–192.

81. Jean-Pierre Gaboury, *Le Nationalisme de Lionel Groulx: Aspects idéologiques* (Ottawa: Presses de l'Université d'Ottawa, 1970), p. 154–155.

principle (as in the case of portfolios concerning strictly Québécois affairs), there was recourse without reserve. Otherwise, he did not hesitate to cast it aside. Such a hierarchy of ends and means is easily understood as long as the traditionalist dimension of Groulx's nationalism is not lost from view. The state (provincial or other) was only a tool to enable the French Canadian nation to flourish; the two entities covered different conceptual realities that were impossible to confuse. In his *Confédération canadienne*, Groulx wanted to warn the "fathers" of the dangers awaiting them if they made the principle of provincial autonomy into a dogma:

> Undoubtedly, the autonomy of the provinces demands that federal power be excluded from the provincial domain as much as possible. But we might have remembered that when a right dies, it doesn't die alone. To allow the rights of the minorities to be too easily violated is to start down the slippery slope of all kinds of justice being denied to our province.[82]

Groulx thus did not see any inconsistency in applying the Compact theory to defend not only the provincial autonomy of Québec but also the rights of the Franco-Catholic minorities. In both cases, the aim was to protect the higher interests of the French-Canadian nation, these interests being the same wherever the nation's members lived. His reasoning on this question evolved little. On the sixtieth anniversary of the BNA Act, some ten years later, he published in *L'Action française* a study entitled "Les Canadiens français et l'établissement de la Confédération," in which he pursued the same idea:

> French Canada likewise has the duty to draw up with its future partners a double political contract that will preserve all its provincial autonomy and carefully define federal and provincial jurisdictions; a contract, then, of a national and religious nature which, along with the rights of the French Canadian nationality, will establish the status of the religious minorities in the anglophone provinces.[83]

Groulx recognized that the "contractual" dimension of the BNA Act was twofold: it was "political" on the one hand, since it protected the autonomy of the Québec state in the face of infringements by the central government, and "national" on the other in that it defined the rights of the French Catholic minorities. He reiterated, therefore, the idea that the *national* existence of French Canadians did not depend in any way on the political structures within (or outside of) which

82. Lionel Groulx, *La Confédération canadienne*, p. 180.

83. Lionel Groulx, "Les Canadiens français et l'établissement de la Confédération," AF, May–June 1927, p. 282–301. See also Lionel Groulx, "Ce cinquantenaire (1867–1917)," AF, July 1917, p. 193–203; "La France d'outre-mer," *Notre Maître le passé, Tome II*, p. 289; "Le patriotisme des jeunes," *Notre Maître le passé, Tome I*, p. 17–18; "L'histoire et la vie nationale," *Dix ans d'Action française*, p. 248–252; "Nos responsabilités intellectuelles," *Orientations*, p. 33–34.

they evolved.[84] In 1937, at the Congrès de la langue française de Québec, he made the same distinction between the French-Canadian nation and the Québec state in a speech which, nevertheless, reignited the debate around his presumed "separatism": "Strange and flawed as the federative constitution may be, and confusing as they may wish to make the national ideology of the 'Fathers' of Confederation, the fact remains that 1867 once again established in our favour two vital principles: that of provincialism and that of nationality."[85]

The Minorities in the Anglo-Protestant World

Groulx's assessment of how things evolved subsequently, however, was decidedly less positive. He felt that everything necessary to ensure French Canada's freedom to develop culturally, politically and economically had been included in the Confederation "pact." Yet he believed that a slow national "decline" had begun as early as 1867. He attributed its cause directly to the intransigence of the Anglo-Protestant majority, certainly, but also to the slackness of the French-Canadian political class. The era of great parliamentarians of the stature of La Fontaine seemed to him, on the whole, a thing of the past. His historical studies led him to conclude that French Canada, in the absence of real national leaders, had too often become the prey of the more radical voices in the majority, voices seeking to suppress the nation's cultural and religious influence. The French-Canadian political class had neglected the higher interests of the nation by engaging in "fratricidal" partisan fights: instead of the nation, it was the party, red or blue, that received the unconditional allegiance of the vast majority of French-Canadian politicians. Abbé Groulx conceded that there were nonetheless some politicians who, since 1867, had succeeded in rising above what he considered the mediocrity of their colleagues, most notably Henri Bourassa and Franco-Ontarian senators Philippe Landry and Napoléon Belcourt, as we shall see further on. But, generally speaking, Groulx deplored the fact that, as new provinces were added and the French Canadians increasingly became minorities within Confederation, the political party had become for most leaders nothing more than an instrument of cultural assimilation. It was this spinelessness of the political class that the historian held responsible for having introduced into French Canada the alienating principle of "double nationality."

What ought in principle to have represented a victory for the French-Canadian nation had signalled instead the start of its decline. Let us state again that it was not the federal regime as such that Groulx was criticizing, but rather the partisan mentality of the French-Canadian politicians, which allowed English-Canadian and Protestant "persecutors" a free hand. This is why he spent his life trying to rebuild a "sense of nation" in his people, especially in the young, so that the

84. See also L'Action française, "Le problème national," *AF*, February 1927, p. 66-81; "La langue française," *AF*, March 1927, p. 130–151; "Les modes d'action nationale," *AF*, December 1927, p. 320–353.

85. Lionel Groulx, "L'histoire, gardienne des traditions vivantes," *Directives*, p. 219–220.

political elites of the future might rediscover the spirit that had animated the great parliamentarians who served before 1867. In his opinion, nothing revealed the shortcomings of the politicians more blatantly than the lamentable fate to which the French Catholic minorities were left after Confederation. In the next chapter, we shall take a close look at the way Groulx perceived the weaknesses of Québec's politicians vis-à-vis the minorities when he became leader of the nationalist movement around 1920. However, as a historian, he was aware that these weaknesses in the French-Canadian political class dated as far back as 1867. In a talk he gave in 1918, he said as much, without mincing words: "I see only two great national errors in our past: [one is Canada's participation in the Boer War and the other is] that we have betrayed our minorities, that is, the French Catholic schools, in all the provinces of Canada."[86] And of all the politicians he found guilty, it was George-Étienne Cartier who stood at the top of the list. On the one hand, Groulx admired his strength and determination, the national and religious conviction he displayed as the wording of the BNA Act was hammered out, especially during the Québec Conference of 1864. On the other hand, he often sharply condemned the cowardly behaviour he perceived after 1867. Cartier had fallen that much harder, in Groulx's opinion, for having been at one time the uncontested political leader of the French Canadians, imbued with the same courage that had animated the great La Fontaine before him. It was during the schools crisis in New Brunswick (1871–1875), the first of the great trials the young country would have to endure, that Cartier toppled from his pedestal. Groulx explained that the "pact" had, by rebuilding bridges with Québec, revived great hopes among the Acadians of New Brunswick: they had not guessed, however, that the new regime would mean the end of religious freedom in that province, or that Cartier would be complicit in this great "error." In a piece entitled "The Religious Ideas of Cartier," Groulx makes the following comments on Sir George's refusal to invoke the federal veto power to disallow the school law of 1871:

> History will henceforth answer him: Yes, my dear great man, a veto involves risks and will always involve risks. But to sanction iniquity, the denial of justice, does this not carry any risk and does this not in the end carry the greater risk? On that day, Sir George, you inaugurated, and it was not to your credit, the politics of short-sightedness, which many times since then has been thought capable of maintaining peace in our country through the sacrifice of rights, as if peace were not founded first of all on upholding rights.[87]

Cartier's logic, Groulx explains, had consisted of invoking the principle of provincial autonomy ahead of the federal government's veto power. This was

86. Lionel Groulx, "Pour l'Action française," *Dix ans d'Action française*, p. 268–269.
87. Lionel Groulx, "Les idées religieuses de Cartier," *Notre Maître le passé, Tome I*, p. 223–224.

why, he continued, Sir George had criticized the attitude of the Québec press and clergy, both of whom had demanded the intervention of the federal government in the schools crisis. According to Groulx, however, Cartier's reasoning did not hold water. When there was a conflict between the principle of provincial autonomy and that of the founding peoples, it was the latter that should indisputably outweigh the former. He was saying, in essence, that there was a great risk of confusing the end with the means.

The school problems experienced by the French minorities under Confederation arose frequently in Groulx's historical and polemical work. He even dedicated a lengthy study to these questions in 1935, the second volume of his *Enseignement français au Canada*. The first volume, which had appeared four years earlier, was an analysis of how the school system in Québec had evolved.[88] After a deliberate reminder that the Acadians and the French Canadians had been the first to arrive in all the country's provinces, Groulx studied each of the schools crises that had befallen them. His first chapter focused on the banning of Catholic teaching in the Acadian schools of Prince Edward Island. The second discussed the question of the separate schools of Manitoba, which, in 1890 were dealt the same fate, over the objections of the ecclesiastical hierarchy in the West. In the land of the Riels, the Langevins and the Tachés, it was Wilfrid Laurier that Groulx cast in the role of villain this time: like Cartier before him, the prime minister had shown a lack of courage when, by conspiring with his Manitoban counterpart, he imposed a solution which did nothing in fact but restore a few laughable crumbs to the "sons of the discoverers of the West." After an "epilogue" on the schools in the District of Keewatin, the next chapter analyzes the controversy surrounding the 1905 abolition of the rights to French language in the schools in the new provinces of Alberta and Saskatchewan. There too, the historian explained, the temerity of the "persecutors" was all the more immoral given that the French and the French Canadians had been the first to possess the land: "Arriving first, in the era of the La Vérendryes, the French took possession of the Canadian West. After the English Conquest, they would also be among the first to give this part of the continent the imprint of civilization." Next, he studied the controversy of the Franco-Ontarian schools, where, with a few exceptions, the French language had become outlawed between 1912 and 1927. As we shall see later in this study, the Regulation 17 crisis, the only one of the great school conflicts that Groulx was able to intervene in directly, had a major formative influence on his thinking. In any event, the historian of school conflict continued to appeal to the same

88. Lionel Groulx, *L'Enseignement français au Canada: Tome II: Les Écoles des minorités* (Montréal: Librairie Granger Frères, 1935), 271 p. An abridged version of the two volumes of this study had been published a few years earlier under the title *Le Français au Canada* by Libraire Delagrave in Paris in 1932 (234 p.). This book featured the course lectures that Groulx had given in 1931 and 1932 at the Sorbonne and the Institut catholique in Paris. It was likewise this lengthy study that earned him a doctorate in history from the Université de Montréal. See also Lionel Groulx, "Monseigneur Taché," AF, October 1923, p. 211–223.

arguments he had used in his early resistance days. To rob the first occupants of the land of their most fundamental rights was in his view an obscenity that could not be denied: "the French imprint is so deeply etched in the face of Ontario's landscapes that, in our time still, it remains there, in clear outline, created not just by the immortality of historic memories, but by the *survivance* of a French people."[89]

⋆ ⋆ ⋆

Groulx considered the infringement of the religious and language rights of the French Canadians and the Acadians to be the equivalent of a violation of constitutional law—which may at times have been unclear but was real all the same—and worse yet, natural law. That was the judgment he delivered at the end of this long analysis of the French minorities' schools crises. It was not just constitutional documents that served to justify the educational claims of the minorities. There was also the Compact theory, itself inspired by a concept of natural law that flowed from his traditionalist nationalism. The harshness with which the minorities' schools were persistently hounded drove Groulx to draw a number of conclusions. First, he thought to observe that French-Canadian politicians had not only failed to defend the rights of the French-Canadian nation, which were, after all, guaranteed by the BNA Act but they had time and again chosen to defend interests that were shamelessly partisan. While Groulx reserved this judgment for Québec politicians, he did not spare those in the provinces of the minorities either:

> What we say about the parliamentarians of the French race in Ottawa could just as easily be applied, need we say it, to the minority political groups in the various provinces of Canada. If the divisions among the former, in the federal parliament, seem difficult to justify, how can we excuse, in the other groups, which are so much smaller, the mad tendency to splinter? The minorities would not be entirely wrong to ask themselves whether one of their greatest misfortunes, one that seemingly caused them to lose at times their best power lever, was not their political divisions, the partisan mentality, to call it by its name, a sad inheritance brought with them from old Québec, or simply the bad habit of Latin temperament bickering.[90]

Another conclusion, this one slightly more encouraging, that Groulx drew from the schools crises, was that, confronted by the cowardice of the vast majority of their political leaders, the minorities had sounded the alarm. They had presented to typically lethargic Québec an example of heroism and dedication, which

89. Lionel Groulx, *L'Enseignement français au Canada: Tome II*, p. 123, 146, 195.
90. *Ibid.*, p. 253.

in every way appealed to him and contributed in a powerful way, in his opinion, to the nationalist "awakening" that took place at the turn of the twentieth century:

> The French Canadians themselves would not be among those who would benefit the least, over the last 60 years, from the persecution that befell them. Undeniably, the moral assets of the race are much indebted to the magnificent resistance of the minorities. While in the old province, the egotistical tendency to turn in on oneself and be lulled into a false sense of security was all too easy, the minorities, one after the other, went on guard to keep the ideal alive and foiled the numbness of sleep. One would even have to agree that the heroic attitude of the minorities in the face of persecution remains, in Canada, one of the most striking manifestations of French Catholic vitality.[91]

Throughout his entire career, Lionel Groulx sought to rekindle the spirit of national solidarity that had in his view taken root between Québec and the French minorities during the most epic moments of the schools crises. In the next chapter, we shall study some of the numerous measures he proposed to try to execute this great project of national rapprochement.

91. *Ibid.*, p. 241.

Chapter Three

Québec and Its Relationship to the French Minorities: The Ties That Bind

LIONEL GROULX regarded the French-Canadian nation as an organic entity or a "being" whose emergence, willed by Providence, dated back to the era of New France. As such, the national organism continued to evolve, grow and develop. Groulx's view was that the English Protestant majority had not been able to contain it, despite their repeated offensives against the two key foundations of the French "race" in America, namely, the Catholic faith and French culture. The schools crises in Acadia, in the Canadian West and in Ontario were eloquent testimonies to this. However, in the mind of Abbé Groulx, the legislative, juridical and institutional weaponry that had been unleashed against the French-Canadian people to thwart its expansion could never trump its apostolic mission or the designs of Providence. In his view, the French minorities had succeeded in overcoming their adversaries and surviving, more or less. But that didn't mean he believed their future was necessarily assured. He attributed the *survivance* of the minorities to their activism, certainly, but also to the support they received from Québec, in particular, from the clergy. On the other hand, Groulx often blamed Québec, and especially its political class, when the obstacles threatening the *survivance* of the minorities seemed to loom excessively large.

Some might think that this dualistic attitude, which both reprimanded and congratulated Québec for its behaviour towards the minorities, stemmed from a certain ambiguity in Groulx's thought. This is, however, not so. He was pleased about the contribution of the clergy historically to the cultural and institutional development of the French minorities. But it was his analysis of the damage done by partisan politics in French Canada since 1867 that led him to criticize the shortcomings of Québec politics. Let us be clear: although Groulx was sometimes wary of the principle of popular sovereignty, he did not reject the parliamentary system in effect in Canada as such. In fact, in his studies of the British government, the historian set out to show that the beginnings of parliamentary democracy in 1791 had ushered in a period of national "emancipation" that would culminate in 1867 with the adoption of the British North America Act, the only threat having been posed by the Union. But Groulx considered that the misdeeds of the regime of 1841 had been quickly overturned by the French-Canadian political class, led by the great Louis-Hippolyte La Fontaine, his all-time political hero, who had won for his people the restoration of French-language rights in the Assembly as well as responsible government. To Groulx, parliamentary democracy could therefore represent a powerful tool of national liberation. It is thus difficult to qualify his thought as "apolitical."[1]

What did sadden him, however, were the partisan divides which he felt had come to dominate French-Canadian political life after 1867. Partisan politics is often presented in his work as a pestilence or a fratricidal tug-of-war. Groulx had great difficulty accepting the idea of the political party as a place of compromise allowing for the integration of different ideological trends. His "organic" concept of nation ruled out any analysis that endorsed such a view and kept him from backing a system whose fundamental principle involved the division of the French-Canadian people. How can a person legitimately turn against himself, he was wont to repeat, without running the risk of the worst kind of psychological calamity? Nevertheless, this was exactly what Groulx believed he saw happening when he analyzed French-Canadian public life: forgetting its sense of duty and putting party loyalty ahead of national solidarity, the political class had drifted into a profound cultural anaemia, and, repeatedly, the nation lost out to the party, whether red or blue.

Groulx devoted much time to developing the theme of the "decline" of the French-Canadian political class during his career as a historian and polemicist. He also sought to demonstrate how the partisan mentality permeating a good part of Québec officialdom had resulted in a form of national paralysis that prevented it from supporting the French minorities in their numerous battles. As he understood it, this constituted a grave neglect of responsibilities that were incumbent upon Québec as the "ancestral home" of the French-Canadian nation. The minorities and the crises that had befallen them were serving, in Groulx's thought, as a wake-up call to the French-Canadian nation and, in particular, to Québec, revealing the magnitude of the threat looming over the preservation of French civilization in America. It was also true, he maintained, that Québec, the ancestral home, the metropolis, the beating heart of the nation, had the duty to intervene and to deploy all means available to defend the linguistic, cultural, educational and religious rights of the minorities, situated as they were, at the "outposts" of the Anglo-Protestant world. If Groulx held the opinion that all French Canadians, wherever they might be, were part of the nation, he nevertheless assigned a particular function to each of its various "members," extending in this way his organic analogy.

Groulx's nationalism thus assigned to Québec numerous responsibilities as the "ancestral home" and "cradle" of the French-Canadian nation. Given what he deemed to be a chronic inability on the part of the politicians to carry out their duties toward the minorities, he turned to other segments of French-Canadian

1. See especially André-J. Bélanger, "Lionel Groulx, une mystique québécoise," *L'Apolitisme des idéologies québécoises: Le grand tournant de 1934–1936* (Québec: Presses de l'Université Laval, 1974), p. 191–255.

society, in particular, the clergy, journalists and intellectuals, who seemed to him to be more imbued with the "national spirit." All means were acceptable, he felt, in the interest of building bridges between Québec and the French minorities. This was the cause to which he dedicated *L'Action française* from the moment he assumed its directorship in 1920.

Québec, the Metropolis of French Canada

The Citadel and the Vanguard

During his tenure at the helm of *L'Action française*, Lionel Groulx received this tribute from Joseph Hallé, Bishop of Hearst, in Northeastern Ontario: "May the Sacred Heart bless your works, your great apostolic works—you defend the cathedral! We are only in the vanguard. If the citadel and the rearguard . . . lose their strength, what will become of the vanguard?"[2] The terms "metropolis" and "hinterland" may not have been in Groulx's vocabulary, but the concepts they designate had a significant place in his thought. In his understanding of the French-Canadian nation, each member had a particular function. Historically, Québec, and in particular, the St. Lawrence Valley, had been the first swath of land in America, after Acadia, that the French, and subsequently the French Canadians, had evangelized, conquered and colonized. Demographically, Québec was the only province where French Canadians were the majority and where they possessed a full network of institutions, where they had, in fact, a state. In Groulx's opinion, Québec, as "cradle" and "ancestral home" of the French-Canadian people, enjoyed a special status within the nation. However, he assigned to the French minorities, immersed in an Anglo-Protestant world, the extremely important role of vanguard. This was a double role. On the one hand, they had to pursue, outside the "ancestral home of the nation," the civilizing and evangelizing mission that Providence had conferred on French Canada. On the other hand, the minorities, through their battles, were to sound the alarm and awaken Québec to the magnitude of the threat looming over the survival of French civilization in America. Groulx saw the minorities as "barometers," of a sort, that made it possible to keep a finger on the pulse of English Canada. The theme of the heroism of the minorities recurred often in his discourse and was meant to serve as an example to Québec, to shake them out of the complacency that beset them all too frequently, in his opinion. However, this distinction he made between the place of Québec and that of the minorities within the French-Canadian nation never translated into the establishment of a "national hierarchy" with Québec at the top looking down on the minorities. Individual French Canadians, wherever they lived, were all part of the French-Canadian nation and were all of equal status.

2. Letter from Joseph Hallé to Lionel Groulx, BAnQ, FLG, P1/A,1706, [no date].

They had simply inherited specific roles and missions according to whether they were situated in the "trenches" or in the "citadel" of the nation. In Groulx's opinion, then, Québec was the heart of the native land of all French Canadians, an idea he expressed in 1934 before a Trois-Rivières audience:

> For us French Canadians, there is a swath of this vast land which, before any other, deserves to be called the native land, the old Québec. Its historic role makes the cradle of New France, in certain respects, the most picturesque, the most cultured of all the provinces of Canada. . . . Very simple lessons, but which could convince our children forever, we believe, that while they are at home everywhere in Canada, they are especially so in that part of the country where every little space was conquered from the forest by their people.[3]

The heart of the native land does not, of course, cover the totality of it. As we saw in the second chapter, Groulx believed that Providence had called French Canadians to settle everywhere on the North American continent, including Ontario and the Western provinces. Therefore, we are still light years away from the idea of the Québec "reserve." *L'Action française*, for example, had no difficulty acknowledging, in 1921, that "we in Québec, ancestral home and principal nucleus, but not the majority of the race, are always aware that more than two and a half million men of our blood live away from here,"[4] a number that must have included the Franco-Americans. However, this expansion of the French-Canadian people, Groulx cautioned, had not always been smooth. The French minorities had to engage in countless fierce battles to have their educational and religious rights respected. As a historian, he often cited their struggles as examples of the heroism and dedication he would have liked to see emulated in Québec. In "Pour la neuvième croisade," an article he wrote for *Le Devoir* in 1914 to indicate his support for the cause of the French schools in Ontario, Groulx stated that Québec needed "frequent injections of heroism" and that, fortunately, the Franco-Ontarians were able to provide a copious supply.[5] In his estimation, Québec, "in offering assistance to its brothers dispersed across America, . . . g[a]ve less than it receive[d]."[6] He felt that the schools crises represented as many honourable battles fought for the benefit of the entire nation, especially Québec. To his friend Rodrigue Villeneuve, a Regulation 17 resistance sympathizer, he even confided that he envied him his "vanguard post": "You are involved in a tough battle. But at least you have the certainty of making your life count for something. You never

3. Lionel Groulx, "L'éducation nationale à l'école primaire," *Orientations* (Montréal: Éditions du Zodiaque, 1935), p. 135–136, 140–141.
4. L'Action française, "Pour la fraternité française," AF, February 1921, p. 65.
5. Lionel Groulx, "Pour la neuvième croisade," *Le Devoir*, May 12, 1914, p. 1.
6. Lionel Groulx, "L'Amitié française d'Amérique," *Dix ans d'Action française* (Montréal: Bibliothèque de l'Action française, 1926), p. 173.

have this horrible feeling of burning while being snuffed out like a candle under a glass."[7] Likewise, in the midst of the schools crisis, Groulx made the following remarks to the Franco-Ontarians, revealing the importance he placed on the consciousness-raising role he assigned to them:

> It is only right to declare that you have for fourteen years been the soldiers in the trenches while we of Québec were the civilians in the rear. In this battle, you were fighting as much for us as for yourselves. You in Ontario led the way and because you persevered, an even broader expansion, with our brothers in Manitoba and the West, was possible; had it not been for you, most certainly the French Canadians would have been forced back to the Québec reserve to await another 1760. Perhaps we could ignore these services you rendered, but only at the cost of our self-respect.
>
> As if it was not enough that you were saving us from outside danger, you were also saving us from ourselves.[8]

It is true that Groulx wanted the French minorities to use their French Catholic "civilization" to oust the "new barbarianism," by which was meant the insidious materialism of the dominant Anglo-Protestant society: "We also know that, in these battles and these efforts to resist absorption, during which our brothers demonstrated such admirable tenacity—affirming, in the face of peoples steeped in materialism, the predominance of moral assets—, there developed among them a distinctively French beauty that contributed to the enrichment of the communal soul."[9] Let us recognize, however, that the historian never had any illusions that the minorities would really be capable of imposing Catholic doctrine and French culture on the entire continent.

While Québec could indeed boast it was the "ancestral home" of the nation, this title was more onerous than honorific, according to Groulx's ideology. He systematically sought to remind the "old province" that, as the eldest in the family, it had duties toward the "brothers" beyond its borders. He developed the analogy of the ancestral home in great detail in a lecture he gave in 1922 at Lowell, Massachusetts. The purpose of this talk, given at the invitation of the Fédération catholique des Sociétés franco-américaines, was to stress the need for stronger ties between Québec and the French Canadians of New England. However, he used the opportunity to present ideas that concerned not only Franco-Americans but also all the French minorities on the continent. His speech, entitled "L'Amitié française d'Amérique," no doubt represents one of the most eloquent testimonies to national solidarity that Groulx ever delivered to French Canadians of the "diaspora." Pursuing the analogy of the family, he described relations between Québec

7. Letter from Lionel Groulx to Rodrigue Villeneuve, BAnQ, FLG, P1/A,3696, March 23, 1915.
8. Lionel Groulx, "Allocution pour le 'Grand Prix d'Action française,'" *Dix ans d'Action française*, p. 212.
9. Lionel Groulx, "L'Amitié française d'Amérique," *Dix ans d'Action française*, p. 174, 210.

and the minorities by calling the former the "eldest son who remained on the ancestral land to take over the work of his elderly parents after his younger brothers [had taken off] for distant parts to build other homes and cultivate other fields."[10]

Groulx was saddened by the indifference, even ignorance, that he witnessed at times among the French minorities, especially among the younger people, for whom the memory of Québec seemed almost as distant as that of France. Let us examine this excerpt from an article he published in *L'Action française* in 1918:

> We belong to a French brotherhood in America. It is not principally on France that the other French groups of the continent rely for their will to survive. For all of us, the province of Québec, heart of ancient New France, is the first native land in memory, the capital of French patriotism. It is because the Valley of the Saint Lawrence was the cradle of their race, the land where their ancestors sleep, the repository of the store of memories, customs and virtues that constitute the depth of their soul; it is because they feel a bond with all this history and all this nobility that our dispersed brothers want to perpetuate this heritage.[11]

For Groulx, the French Canadians differed from other cultural groups in the country in that they had been able, historically, to build a society, a distinct nation in America. They were therefore "founders," unlike, for example, the Italians, the Ukranians or the Germans who, when they immigrated to Canada, had no choice but to integrate into the society that received them. The memory of their country of origin was no doubt more vivid in the mind of those newcomers, having only just settled. However, Groulx believed that the French Canadians had a different relationship with their former mother country, France. Something existed, that had wedged itself between French Canada and France, something acting like a prism and playing on the way the latter would be remembered by the former: that "something" was New France. Far be it from Groulx to deny the French roots of the French-Canadian nation. As we noted in the previous chapter, being the francophile that he was, he saw a direct filial relationship between the French and French-Canadian peoples and made liberal use of the familial analogy to describe the relationship between them: French Canada was nothing less than the offspring of France. Although the umbilical cord had been cut prematurely, French Canada had managed, more or less successfully, to take flight on its own, without cutting itself off from the intellectual and cultural influence of France.

Clearly then, it was Abbé Groulx's wish that the memory of the former mother country never overshadow that of New France or Québec in the minds of the minorities: the unique place that the French-Canadian people occupied in America and, especially, in Canada, should have made it impossible for them to lapse into

10. *Ibid.*, p. 170.
11. Lionel Groulx, "Notre histoire," AF, August 1918, p. 355–356.

such an erroneous attitude. On occasion, he would reiterate this idea to the Franco-Americans, doing so first at Lowell in 1922, then at Manchester in 1935 during a Saint-Jean-Baptiste dinner organized by the Association canado-américaine:

> The fact that our common ancestors came from France does not in any way mean that six or seven generations of your fathers are not buried in the cemeteries of the country next door or that we in Québec are not your closest relatives in the French family. We have two hundred, perhaps three hundred, years of common history in the same country, in the same spiritual context; and neither can you pretend that of this history, which was not entirely disgraceful, there does not still linger in your souls some tiny spark. What therefore do you gain by renouncing this heritage and isolating yourselves from three million Frenchmen to whom you are related?[12]

Groulx felt he had good reason to be worried. Shortly after his visit to Manchester in 1935, he received word from Adolphe Robert of the Association canado-américaine about the breach that had been caused by this question of relations between the Franco-Americans, Québec and France. Robert explained to him that a rival Franco-American association, called l'Union Saint-Jean-Baptiste, had invited the French ambassador to Washington to be the speaker at another Saint-Jean-Baptiste Day dinner that had taken place at the same time as the one held by the Association canado-américaine. Robert viewed this gesture as an indication of the contempt with which the people of the Union viewed Québec and French Canada. "The organization," he concluded, had "turned its back on the province of Québec and asked France to come to its rescue. . . . I cannot bear," he added, "that the province of Québec should be seen as a poor relative by the Franco-Americans."[13]

Of all the French minorities, it was the Franco-Americans who, in Groulx's eyes, ran the greatest risk of forgetting their French-Canadian heritage. In his *Mémoires*, however, he shared his fear that the attitude of the Franco-Americans was one "that would become widespread among all our compatriots of the diaspora, as the memory of the old province, land of their immediate origin, began to fade irretrievably."[14] It was during a voyage he undertook in 1928 to visit the Franco-Manitobans that Groulx said he came to fully realize the importance of Québec's role for the French minorities. In his *Mémoires*, he recalled his stunned reaction to the French Canadians of Manitoba, especially the young people, whose sense of history appeared to go back little further than their immediate ancestors settling in the West. The result, he reported, was a deplorable feeling

12. Lionel Groulx, "Notre avenir en Amérique," *Orientations*, p. 306–307; Lionel Groulx, "L'Amitié française d'Amérique," *Dix ans d'Action française*, p. 181–183.
13. Letter from Adolphe Robert to Lionel Groulx, BAnQ, FLG, P1/A,3201, June 17, 1935.
14. Lionel Groulx, *Mes Mémoires, Tome I: 1878–1920* (Montréal: Éditions Fides, 1970), p. 328–329.

of "regionalism" which, although "legitimate," made Franco-Manitobans more sensitive on the delicate issue of Québec's support for their *survivance*, support that they sometimes interpreted as a form of meddling. Similarly, Groulx mentions in his *Mémoires* how the Franco-Manitoban nationalist leaders reprimanded Québec: "the apathetic attitude" of the old province, they said, had inflicted incalculable damage on them. That particular stay among the Franco-Manitobans left a lasting impression on his thought:

> That day, I became conscious of the poignant drama of all the minorities. Their need of Québec. Their vital need. The necessary connection to the cultural pole, as indispensable as the umbilical cord to the child in its mother's womb. For a French minority to survive in Canada without Québec is unthinkable. A tragic association of feelings is apparent in the soul of the dispersed brother or sister: a weakening of the emotional tie with the old province of origin, a weakening that becomes fatal after two or three generations, as it is followed by a weakening of the will to resist Anglo-Saxon assimilation. On the other hand, this inevitably gives birth to a certain regionalism, the beginnings of adult consciousness in those branches that have separated from the trunk and almost become autonomous cuttings.[15]

Groulx points out that the enormous cultural, economic and political assimilation pressures, being exerted by the dominant English-Canadian society on the Franco-Manitobans, threatened to sideline Québec's already very weak influence on their development. Consequently, for the French minorities to forget their origins represented a plague to be eradicated at all costs. Québec had a primary role to play, in this regard, by ensuring its cultural and intellectual influence on the "diaspora." We would be mistaken, however, if we interpreted Groulx's desire to intervene in the affairs of the French minorities as an expression of paternalism towards them or worse yet, of intellectual and cultural "imperialism." He was not trying to impose strictly "Québécois" cultural values on a people who did not share them. He was not talking about "Québécois" culture in the sense it is often used today: quite the opposite, this culture was about a heritage, a legacy belonging to all French Canadians, irrespective of where they lived. Abbé Groulx's goal was simply to lend assistance to the French minorities in their efforts to resist acculturation and retain their identity. And Québec had the tools needed for the job, while the minorities, by dint of circumstances, lacked them.

Groulx nevertheless feared that the minorities sometimes suspected Québec nationalists of having ulterior motives for the assistance they offered them. Accordingly, in "L'Amitié française d'Amérique," he wanted to reassure them by maintaining that Québec, "guardian of the ancestral homeland,"

15. Lionel Groulx, *Mes Mémoires, Tome III: 1926–1939*, p. 27.

> can claim nothing more over them than the honour of being the eldest, which gives it a certain aura, conferred on it by the old house itself. The family still remains connected by a powerful moral bond. There are areas where the old family unity pertains; there are others where each member has its own independence. When the common honour is at stake, when harm strikes one of its members, and mutual assistance is called for, the voice of blood and of charity demands that brothers help one another and defend their heritage. But in running their own home and conducting their personal affairs, each remains his own master and must not tolerate that counsel should become command.[16]

Groulx believed that national solidarity dictated that Québec had a duty to act on behalf of the French minorities and to come to their aid in their struggles, without such intervention translating in any way into a relationship of control. The French Canadians of Québec were, on the contrary, to take their cue from the minorities and adapt to the resistance strategies that only the latter were in a position to decide.

The French Minorities and the Ineffectualness of Québec

In Groulx's opinion, then, Québec had major responsibilities to assume toward the French minorities. This was to a very large extent a guiding principle of his analysis of the relationship between the "ancestral home" and the "vanguard" of the nation. However, in order for the French Canadians of Québec to be as effective as possible, it was important that they first of all gain their rightful place within their own province, the only one where French Canadians were in the majority and where political and economic power did not threaten to slip away from them completely. If Québec, as "ancestral home" of the nation, wanted to be of any help to the minorities, it would have to be an example of cultural, intellectual, political and even economic energy and vigour. Québec would have to act as a "beacon," lighting the way for the soldiers fighting their battles in the "trenches." However, Groulx was profoundly disappointed in the mediocrity that he felt had spread like a cancer in Québec's public life, preventing it from intervening effectively on behalf of the minorities. The "beacon" did not offer much light and was itself swallowed up by the darkness. If even within Québec, the "ancestral home" of the nation, French Canadians often seemed incapable of imposing their will and triumphing over injustice, how could the French minorities, who were even more deprived and wrestling with far more formidable adversaries, sustain any reason to hope? This is why the defence and reinforcement of the "citadel" was of benefit not just to those who lived there. On the contrary, Groulx considered this defence a *sine qua non* condition of minority resistance to assimilation.

16. Lionel Groulx, "L'Amitié française d'Amérique," *Dix ans d'Action française*, p. 170–171.

Abbé Groulx developed this idea quite frequently throughout his career as a historian and polemicist. In 1919, before he even became its director, he wrote in *L'Action française* that, as "ancestral home" and "base" of the French-Canadian nation, "our great duty is to accumulate enough material and moral power so that our dispersed brothers residing far away never look toward the province of Québec with anything other than confidence." Groulx pursued his line of reasoning by stating that embarrassment about their origins sometimes led the French minorities to yield more easily to the assimilating pressure exerted on them. For this, he blamed Québec, at least in part. He considered that it was the mother province's responsibility to prove to the minorities, even to the whole world, that "our French heritage" was in no way a condemnation to cultural or economic inferiority and that, on the contrary, they could "become the means to every kind of superiority." Too often, he added, it was instead the minorities who instructed Québec, demonstrating through their struggles a heroism that put the old province to shame.[17] Groulx frequently mobilized *L'Action française* to condemn, much of the time unabashedly, Québec's failings with respect to the minorities. For example, in 1923, the Congrès de l'Association catholique franco-canadienne de la Saskatchewan adopted resolutions which, according to the review, would "give the apathetic Québécois new heart": the French Canadians of the West provided an example of courage and tenacity that stood in singular contrast to the "notable indolence" of the old province. The minorities, the review went on, expected from the French Canadians of Québec more than sporadic succour in times of crisis: they demanded that the mother province truly embody French civilization with all its intellectual and moral qualities. Groulx spoke similarly in Trois-Rivières in 1934: "In summary, what they [the minorities] expect of us is the decisive and bold witness of a French people who can demonstrate that to live in French in North America represents neither a mirage nor resignation to mediocrity."[18]

Groulx found he often had to rise up against the spirit of "anglomania" he seemed to observe taking hold in Québec. While the Franco-Ontarians were fighting to keep the right to teach their own language, certain ill-advised individuals spat in their faces, he wrote in 1920, by endorsing the teaching of English in all the schools of Québec. Indeed it was difficult to justify the existence of French schools in Ontario when there were people in Québec who wished to impose English on the French-Canadian students under the pretext that teaching French alone was not enough. The French minorities, Groulx reported, "are begging us not to impose on ourselves a system against which they are defending themselves with all their might. Some of us are starting to feel that danger is lurking in the

17. Lionel Groulx, "Comment servir," AF, November 1919, p. 493–494.
18. L'Action française, "Le congrès de Prince-Albert," AF, March 1923, p. 187; Lionel Groulx, "L'éducation nationale à l'école primaire," *Orientations*, p. 124. See also Lionel Groulx, "Langue et survivance," AN, September 1934, p. 60.

old ancestral home." In *L'Action française*, Groulx often came back on the question of bilingual education in Québec and of the consequences such a system would have for the minorities:

> We are, in the eyes of our compatriots from the other provinces, the guardians of the French culture in Canada. Do we look as though we understand the dignity of this role and accept the duties it involves? There is between them and us that painful difference, which unfortunately they realize: subjected to full bilingualism, including practical equality of the two languages, they embrace first, and most passionately, the teaching of their mother tongue, while we, in Quebec, with a much more moderate form of bilingualism, appear to embrace especially the teaching of the second language.

This attitude from Québec "scandalized" the minority groups, he added. The "*Survivance française*" trips, that brought young French-Canadian delegations from the West to visit Québec, revealed to them a chronic lack of national will that was paralyzing the old homestead: Montréal, one of the great French cities of the world, was hiding its true identity behind Anglo-Saxon traits, while the city of Québec, "the capital of French Canada," was in many ways taking on the appearance of a "London suburb." Groulx, in conclusion, evoked this exhortation by Msgr. Élie-Anicet Latulipe, the first bishop of Haileybury, in Northeastern Ontario, who died in 1922: "We ask only one thing of our compatriots in the province of Québec: do not anglicize faster than we do."[19]

Similarly, Groulx and *L'Action française* made the 1921 census an issue of great importance for both Québec and the French minorities. French Canadians from all the provinces had the duty, according to the review, to oblige census takers to carry out their responsibilities "fairly" and not reduce numbers by relying on shameless manipulation. The census had significant implications, as it would determine the potential composition of representation in the House of Commons: "And since in this regard Québec is the pivot around which one of the essential elements of Confederation revolves, the French Canadians—who are the majority in this province—find here ample cause to scrutinize this decennial process closely."[20]

In Groulx's perception, there was in Québec a laxness that showed up as a form of "Anglomania," which posed a genuine threat to the viability of the minorities and their ability to resist assimilation. The discrepancy he noted between his idealized image of Québec and the much more disappointing reality troubled him deeply. But his voluntarism prevented him from lapsing into any kind of defeatism: the mother province could be transformed into a French-Canadian

19. Jacques Brassier [pseudonym of L. Groulx], "La vie de l'Action française," AF, November 1920, p. 527; "Nous faut-il plus d'anglais ?," AF, December 1927, p. 385, 386.
20. L'Action française, "Le recensement de 1921," AF, January 1921, p. 3

Jerusalem, if only its desire was strong enough. That was the message he delivered in 1935 to a Franco-American audience. Québec, he told them, was duty-bound to become a "pilgrimage destination for all the dispersed sons seeking a spiritual tonic, a tall transmission tower diffusing across French America the best of our thought and our triumphant faith in life."[21] The "intellectual influence" of Québec, which he considered indispensable to the *survivance* of the minorities, was a recurring theme with him, as attested in his correspondence with colleagues in the nationalist movement. In 1926, he complained to Abbé Henri Beaudé, alias Henri d'Arles, one of the most faithful Franco-American collaborators of *L'Action française*, that literary creation in French Canada made precious little use of what he saw as the ancient splendour of New France. The development of a truly "national" literature, that is, one that was respectful of the essential foundations of the French-Canadian people, could have, besides strengthening national sentiment within Québec itself, provided untold support to the minorities, by revealing to them the epic character of their own struggles. In this too, Groulx felt that Québec had failed in its responsibility:

> It seems to me that the intellectual influence of Québec, on our groups dispersed throughout other parts of Canada or the United States, is very weak. . . . These poor people die quietly in their French life. But so very little resuscitating breath has come to them from the heartland of the race. Our writers have not yet learned to exploit the moral and pictorial richness of our little French country. Can we say then that the picture of our early and deeper life has been painted in beauty, that the noble and seductive face of New France has been grasped and popularized so as to create a solid bond among all its sons? And yet, this work, this need, has become urgent for a dispersed nation such as ours![22]

Groulx shared this anxiety in 1937 with Jesuit priest Alexandre Dugré, a former professor at the *collège* in Edmonton and another collaborator at *L'Action française*. In the feverish atmosphere of nationalist groups preparing for the Deuxième Congrès de la langue française de Québec, Dugré wrote a brochure published as *Notre survivance française*, in which he lamented what he saw as a diminishing will to survive among the French minorities.[23] Groulx congratulated him on it, telling him these "stimulating pages" would achieve a lot of good. While conceding that Dugré was right to take a severe and demanding tone toward the minorities, he reproached him for being too indulgent with Québec. In his view, Québec was largely responsible for the problems experienced by the French Canadians in the other provinces and in the United States:

21. Lionel Groulx, "Notre avenir en Amérique," *Orientations*, p. 308.
22. Letter from Lionel Groulx to Henri d'Arles, BAnQ, FLG, P1/A,1786, September 23, 1926.
23. Alexandre Dugré, *Notre survivance française* (Montréal: Imprimerie du Messager, 1937), 15 p.

> But when are you going to spur the French Canadians of Quebec? Is it not true that if far away they are dying, it is because here we are not living passionately enough? If in New England, movements against the province of Québec have developed and these people prefer the bond with France, is it not our moral anaemia, our national indifferentism, that drove them to it? All our compatriots of the diaspora complain ceaselessly of the scandal we have brought upon them. The little French Canadians of Manitoba or Alberta no longer know what is meant by the old province of Québec because our intellectual and spiritual influence hardly extends beyond our borders.[24]

A few months later, Groulx gave his famous speech, "L'histoire, gardienne des traditions vivantes," at the Congrès de la langue française, a speech that contributed, in spite of its intended purpose, to reopening the debate on the "French state," which will be discussed further on. The orator pursued his criticism of Québec and its inability to fulfil its role toward the minorities. If the French Canadians of the mother province sometimes noted with sadness that their young compatriots in the West were not very familiar with the old homestead, and saw all the catastrophic consequences that Groulx attributed to this kind of national "amnesia," they had only themselves to blame:

> To avoid even here, in the heartland of the race, anything that might . . . scandalize [the French minorities], to conceal from the exiles our flabbiness, our divisions, our abdications; to keep the faith here so that they might keep it there; to create in the heart of New France a heartland of intense life, a heartland of civilization so that we might have influence, to accomplish a noble duty toward the French family of America, all of that, at least until recently, was for most of our people and most of our leaders, the least of their worries. But now, as I speak, mature boys and girls in Saskatchewan and in Alberta, children of our French race, ask their parents, "What is the province of Québec?" as if they were asking, "What is Greenland?" or "What is Cochinchina?" and that says a great deal about just how much influence we have.[25]

Thus, Abbé Groulx was extremely severe with Québec. He accused it of constantly ignoring its role as ancestral home of the nation for the French minorities. There was, however, a particular segment of the Québec population that managed to draw his strongest wrath. Groulx showed no mercy to the French-Canadian political class. Throughout his career, Groulx did his utmost to warn his contemporaries of the pernicious, and even lethal, consequences of partisan politics in French Canada. He maintained that the party system and the "partisan mentality"

24. Letter from Lionel Groulx to Alexandre Dugré, BAnQ, FLG, P1/A,1199, February 25, 1937.
25. Lionel Groulx, "L'histoire, gardienne des traditions vivantes," *Directives*, p. 227–228.

had increased the divisions within the French-Canadian people and in doing so had dealt what may have been a fatal blow to the national organism. We saw in the second chapter that Groulx conceived the nation as being outside the boundaries of geography or politics in the strict sense. Party politics, therefore, by pitting French Canadians against one another, directly challenged what he considered to be their deeper nature. Partisan fragmentation was totally unacceptable in Groulx's opinion by virtue of the fact that it placed the hunger for power, in other words, "electioneering," ahead of the higher and indivisible interests of the nation. The outcome was to him a disgraceful slide toward individualism and materialism, the worst pestilences on earth.

In his 1937 speech at the Congrès de la langue française, Groulx launched into a harsh criticism of the partisan mindset and its harmful repercussions. He drew a parallel between partisan politics and the "Marxist plague of class struggle," both of which he saw as responsible for "divisions, stupid hatred, distortions of conscience, and collective madness." We should not see in this comparison between Marxism and liberal democracy any lack of understanding on Groulx's part of the difference between the two systems. Groulx was only pointing out, rather, what he saw the two theories having in common, namely, a similar inclination toward materialism. As a man of faith, he could only feel concern in the face of the secularization of Western society that had been brought about by modernity and the great political, economic, ideological and cultural reforms of the previous one hundred and fifty years. Although Groulx refrained from condemning it outright, the modern principle of popular sovereignty, whether invoked by liberal democrats or Marxists, often struck him as suspect. There was nothing surprising in this: being so solidly grounded in the theory of the providential creation of nations, Abbé Groulx had difficulty accepting the removal of the religious element as the guiding and organizing principle of human societies. Party politics having been so instrumental in creating divisions, even within the collectivity of the nation, whose "organic" life had been willed by Providence, the highest of all authorities, it necessarily took on, in the eyes of Lionel Groulx, the form of a degenerative cancer: "*le parti* instead of *la patrie*," he said in 1937, "*le parti* instead of *la nation*, the party mystique instead of the national mystique, all this may well suffice to bring about death; but it can never sustain life."[26]

In the French-Canadian context, there were even greater dangers that Groulx attributed to the "partisan mentality." In Canada, the political party had so frequently served to gloss over differences that to him were fundamental, between the various cultural or religious groups that made up the country. The party could not tolerate that there should be differences over such questions and rather, transformed itself into a powerful agent of homogenization by incorporating minority

26. *Ibid.*, p. 228–229.

groups into the dominant majority. Let us examine this excerpt from a talk Groulx gave to a group of students in Montréal in March of 1941:

> Given the influence of the political party, the greatest concern of party leaders is to ensure the party's cohesion or unity. The instrument by which they reign must be solid. In the federal domain, leaders try therefore to suppress or mitigate clashes between ethnic groups, between provincial groups; they will apply themselves to minimizing opposition of any nature whatsoever: oppositions of faith, language, culture, irredentisms, provincial, cultural or otherwise. . . . Now, the French Canadians, being more different, oppose the others more vigorously. As a political group, they have higher interests to protect, constantly dealing in the cultural and moral order. Which is to say that the moral standards of Québec, higher than the others, will, more so than the others, be made to undergo erosion, in the name of the unity of the party, to the level of the lowest common denominator.

If Abbé Groulx believed the "moral standards" of Québec to be "higher" than those of the other provinces, it was because he believed that the French Canadians, a Catholic people, were less widely afflicted by the plague of materialism than the peoples who, by espousing the Protestant religion, had turned their backs on the Church. The main point to be retained from this passage is the negative judgment made by Groulx on the political party as an instrument of assimilation "winning us over bit by bit to the theories of the dominant race."[27]

It would be a useless exercise in meticulousness to do a complete inventory of the writings in which Groulx scolds French Canada's bourgeoisie and its political class for their weaknesses. This long digression has allowed us, however, to place his criticism of what he perceived as an inadequate response toward the minorities by the French-Canadian politicians of Québec within the general context of his thought. He lamented frequently and at length the fact that the Church had been, in his view, the only one to intervene on behalf of the minorities and in so doing to defend the national interest throughout Canada. He saw politicians as having shirked their duty and being largely responsible, on the one hand, for Québec's distancing from the minorities and on the other, for the fact that there were young French Canadians in the other provinces who did not really know their ancestral home. Groulx drew a parallel between the politicians' attitude toward their "dispersed brothers" and the way France abandoned the *Canadiens* after the Conquest of 1760. In 1933, in *L'Action nationale*, he reproached French-Canadian politicians for turning a deaf ear to the distress signals of the French

27. Lionel Groulx, "Le malaise canadien-français," *Paroles à des étudiants* (Montréal: Éditions de l'Action nationale, 1941), p. 20–21; "L'histoire et la vie nationale," *Dix ans d'Action française*, p. 255. See also "L'esprit estudiantin," *Orientations*, p. 187–200; "Pour qu'on vive," *Orientations*, p. 220–239; "La bourgeoisie et le national," AN, April 1939, p. 291–301; "L'an 1940," AN, August–September 1940, p. 5–21.

Catholic minorities while at the same time boasting that they had defended the rights and privileges of Québec's Anglo-Protestant minority:

> Everyone knows equally well that even the tiniest infringement on the right of an English or Protestant minority in this country has never been possible. But if we might be permitted to imagine the impossible just for a moment, what would have been, in such a situation, the behaviour of the French Canadians? Unable to reach unanimity when the worst denials of justice were being inflicted on their co-religionists and their own compatriots, is it not true that they would have reached, for the occasion and to avenge the rights of the oppressed, a most touching unanimity?[28]

In December 1927, Groulx's alter ego, Jean Tavernier, suggested, in the pages of *L'Action française*, that a new honour should be created: membership in "The Order of the Nose Ring," to be awarded for the most blatant folly committed by a French-Canadian public servant or politician. Tavernier wanted the first recipient of this dubious honour to be the speechwriter for the mayor of Montréal. This writer had added insult to injury by suggesting French Canadians in the West should show charity and tolerance toward the other groups around them (read: English Canadians). Why? So as not to provoke them unnecessarily. In his *Mémoires*, Groulx explains that this type of "cowardice" on the part of public figures made them "foolishly play into the hands of the adversary."[29] Groulx did not always, however, rely on a sardonic approach to criticize the official political world. In 1923, for example, *L'Action française* published an open letter addressed to French-Canadian federal MPs exhorting them specifically to see that the rights of their compatriots and co-religionists in all the Canadian provinces were respected.[30] In 1926, the review renewed its offensive:

> the French-Canadian MPs are the only ones who in the federal parliament have the duty to protect interests (the religious and educational rights of French Catholic minorities; their language rights; social legislation)—interests whose moral importance far exceeds any other political or economic interest.[31]

28. Lionel Groulx, "Pour qu'on vive . . . ," AN, June 1933, p. 362. See also "L'Amitié française d'Amérique," *Dix ans d'Action française*, p. 178.
29. Jean Tavernier [pseudonym of L. Groulx], "La vie de l'Action française," AF, December 1927, p. 393; Lionel Groulx, *Mes Mémoires, Tome II: 1920–1928*, p. 123.
30. Letter from Anatole Vanier, secretary of the Ligue d'Action française, to the representatives in the House of Commons, December 12, 1923, reproduced in Jacques Brassier [pseudonym of L. Groulx], "La vie de l'Action française," AF, December 1923, p. 379–380. Although this letter bears Vanier's signature, Groulx attributes the authorship to himself in *Mes Mémoires, Tome II*, p. 122.
31. "Le Québec à Ottawa," AF, August 1926, p. 96. Groulx made similar pronouncements in 1941 to Father Arthur Joyal, of *Le Droit*: "We, in our province, give you such a bad example. It has almost always been our minorities who have shaken us from our apathy" (Letter from Lionel Groulx to Arthur Joyal, BAnQ, FLG, P1/A,1862).

We have already studied Groulx's historical analysis of the unhelpful role played by Québec's politicians in the numerous religious and educational crises suffered by the French minorities immediately after the Confederation of 1867. Let us retain simply that Groulx, for all his admonishments, was, more often than not, disappointed in the behaviour of French-Canadian public figures toward the minorities. On the other hand, he was consoled by initiatives taken by other segments of Québec's French-Canadian population. Abbé Groulx often pointed to the efforts of the clergy and the nationalist movement which he perceived as offsetting the fatuousness of the formal political world. It was with them that the future of relations between Québec and the minorities lay, he thought. It is what he argued in November of 1944 before a group of Franco-Ontarians gathered in Sudbury: "Do not judge the old province by its politics or its politicians, any more than you would judge a man by the warts on his face. Québec lives and moves. Québec is full of signs of hope."[32]

National Solidarity At Work

L'Action française: Preaching by Example

In 1913, a group of nationalists, including Jesuit Joseph-Papin Archambault, Doctor Joseph Gauvreau and journalist Omer Héroux, founded the Ligue des droits du français in Montréal. Several nationalist institutions came into existence around that time. *Le Devoir* and the Association canadienne-française d'éducation d'Ontario, both founded in 1910, and *Le Droit*, launched by the Oblates of Ottawa three years later, were likewise part of this intellectual orientation. Nationalist circles, worried about the precariousness of the situation French Canadians were in throughout the country, were sounding the alarm. The outbreak of a new British imperial war, in which Canada would no doubt be called upon to participate, seemed increasingly likely. A renewal of the assault on the religious and linguistic rights of the French Catholic minorities, endured ever since Confederation, seemed likely as well. This time, it was in Ontario that the Orange and Irish-Catholic extremists' campaign would resume: in 1912, the Conservative government of James Whitney adopted its infamous Regulation 17, which, until 1927, would ban the French language from the province's schools beyond the first two years of instruction. In 1917, the Ligue, renamed the Ligue d'Action française, acquired a new mouthpiece, the monthly review, *L'Action française*, which Lionel Groulx came to direct in 1920 as successor to journalist Omer Héroux, editor of *Le Devoir*. Until it ceased publication in 1928, *L'Action française* was practically alone in occupying the vanguard of the French-Canadian nationalist movement.

32. Lionel Groulx, *Confiance et espoir* (Sudbury: Éditions de la Société historique du Nouvel-Ontario, 1945), p. 2.

The review led numerous battles to have the economic, political and cultural rights of French Canadians, wherever they were in America, respected. As far as the collaborators of *L'Action française* were concerned, these struggles, being fought by the minorities against the religious and cultural homogenization tactics of part of English Canada, constituted their central preoccupation, in accordance with the primary concern of their director. Groulx, in effect, saw his review as an ideal instrument through which to foster more and closer ties between Québec and the minorities and make the province aware of the sometimes difficult burden their dispersed brothers carried. *L'Action française* was to act as a counterweight to the deafening silence with which the French-Canadian political class met the cries for assistance coming from the minorities.

In the review's first issue, published under Groulx in October 1920, this desire to make *L'Action française* an instrument of national solidarity for all French Canadians, regardless of their province of origin, was unmistakably present: "With the utmost confidence, we ask . . . our friends to assist us in expanding our work. We address this call to all members of our race. We want this review to become, more than ever, *extra-québecoise*, the soldier of the French idea for all our groups in America." In that same issue, Groulx specified the manner in which he planned to set about achieving this objective: "We are in the process of selecting collaborators who are well placed to survey, each in their own part of the country, all of French life in Canada and the United States, and their regular columns will keep us informed." Groulx repeatedly stressed his desire that *L'Action française* should reach out to all the French groups on the continent. The review was to act as a "relay," so to speak, taking the nationalist movement from word to action: "We did not want to stop at words and advice. In order that mutual assistance might be supported by an intelligent empathy, we wanted the groups to get to know each other." This was the rationale behind the columns Groulx published regularly in *L'Action française* about the Franco-Ontarians, the French Canadians of the West and the Franco-Americans.[33] In March 1924, lawyer Antonio Perrault, one of the directors of the Ligue d'Action française, reaffirmed this desire to forge new ties between the minorities and Québec, during a formal luncheon held in honour of the Bishop of Prince-Albert and Saskatoon, Msgr. Joseph-Henri Prud'homme, who was visiting Montréal. In his account of the evening, which appeared in *L'Action française*, Groulx quoted Perrault's speech at length:

> No one has expressed the need for religious and national solidarity among all French Canadians, whether they live here in Québec, in the West or in the United

33. La Rédaction, "À nos lecteurs," AF, October 1920, p. 433–434; Jacques Brassier [pseudonym of L. Groulx], "La vie de l'Action française," AF, October 1920, p. 476; Lionel Groulx, *Mes Mémoires, Tome II*, p. 12; Lionel Groulx, "Pour l'Action française," *Dix ans d'Action française*, p. 46; Lionel Groulx, "Les Franco-Américains et nous," AF, June 1922, p. 363.

> States, more than *L'Action française*. No one has endeavoured to practise fraternity with the other groups of our race more than *L'Action française*.[34]

L'Action française often used the lecture format to spread its ideas. The invited speakers sometimes included members of the elite of the French minorities, such as Prud'homme, but also the Franco-Ontarian senator, Napoléon Belcourt, one of the leaders of the resistance against Regulation 17, and Msgr. Arthur Béliveau, Archbishop of Saint-Boniface. The collaborators of the review also pulled their weight, travelling across French America and giving numerous talks among the minorities. In this respect, however, no one could hold a candle to Groulx himself. His talks in Ontario, as we shall see in the following chapter, were numerous, but the director of *L'Action française* also appeared frequently in New England and in the Canadian West.[35] In 1928, while he was preparing his major study on the minority schools, he went to Saint-Boniface in order to consult Manitoba's provincial archives and give a few talks in that province. From there in Riel country, he sent *L'Action française* a lengthy travel account, in which he expressed his joy at the vitality manifested by his hosts:

> Of all the French groups in North America, the one in Manitoba is perhaps the one in which a Québécois can feel most at home. None has better maintained the spirit of the old province, its speech and its accent, the bonhomie, the bright, honest faces of our rural folk, the physical type of the race. . . . Here, one language has remained a living language, and it is the one that talks about French language, schools, national rights, the future; they discuss these important realities as current issues that affect the lives of everyone.

Groulx saw this dynamic spirit, which the Franco-Manitobans had despite the tremendous obstacles they encountered along the way, as being largely attributable to their clergy. The Manitoban clergy were "among the most active and respected in our country" and had the "rare good fortune of having been governed only by great bishops."[36]

L'Action française made numerous efforts to recruit collaborators from among all the French minorities in Canada and the United States. In his *Mémoires*, Groulx recounts how he wanted the review to be a "totally French-Canadian work, I mean belonging to all of French Canada. So I went in search of collaboration in every place where I hoped I might find it."[37] The goal he set for himself was to form a network of regular columnists extending as far as the West, Ontario, Acadia

34. Excerpt from a speech by Antonio Perrault, delivered March 10, 1924 to the Cercle universitaire de Montréal, cited in Jacques Brassier [pseudonym of L. Groulx], "La vie de l'Action française," AF, March 1924, p. 184.
35. Lionel Groulx, *Mes Mémoires, Tome II*, p. 62, 70–71, 75–76.
36. Lionel Groulx, "Lettre du Manitoba," AF, July 1928, p. 38, 39.
37. Lionel Groulx, *Mes Mémoires, Tome II*, p. 137.

and New England. In 1920, even before he had officially assumed directorship of the review, Groulx asked Jesuit Noël Bernier, of the *collège* in Saint-Boniface, whether Franco-Manitobans would be interested in contributing to a "Chronique de l'Ouest." Bernier, without however making any commitment, answered that it seemed to him a good idea: "We too feel it would be apt to have more frequent contact with the Province of Québec," he wrote. Groulx also won support in Saskatchewan, more precisely, in Prince Albert. Oblate Achille Auclair, of the newspaper *Le Patriote de l'Ouest*, responded favourably to Groulx's appeal by likewise agreeing to collaborate with *L'Action française*. "Your project to turn *L'Action française* more and more into a vehicle for all French groups," he wrote in May of 1920, "is such a logical aspect of the development of this work that it deserves everyone's approval."[38] (It should be noted that Auclair does not seem to have written anything for *L'Action française*, unless the pseudonym "Un Sauvage" was his, in which case he wrote, albeit on an irregular basis, a "Chronique de la Saskatchewan" beginning in March 1921.)

Groulx also wanted to get the pulse of Franco-Albertans by finding out where Jesuit priest Alexandre Dugré stood. Dugré, who had formerly been with Collège Sainte-Marie in Montréal, was a professor at the *collège* in Edmonton. Groulx invited him to write for *L'Action française* and then added, rather engimatically, "that only people from Québec were capable of sorting out what was going on in the West and to understand the development undergone there by the French-Canadian character." Dugré agreed to Groulx's request but told him he was pessimistic about French-Canadian *survivance* in his part of the country, especially when it came to the younger generation: "*Monsieur l'abbé*, I am not a 'man of the West.' It is in the East that we will form a people. Here, we are swallowed up; you have to hear the children talk to know what it is like around here: the grown-ups were born and raised in Québec, but they are not Alberta!"[39]

These rather fatalistic remarks were, however, powerless to deter Groulx, who furthermore did not limit his recruitment efforts to the West. Several times he relied on the services of his friend and confidant, Oblate Rodrigue Villeneuve of Ottawa, when he sought to reserve a few pages of his review for French Canadians from the West. In 1923, for example, he asked Villeneuve to suggest a collaborator who could study the contribution of Msgr. Taché to the colonization and evangelization of the West in the nineteenth century. He called Taché "a great Oblate to whom *L'Action française* would like to pay tribute." A few weeks earlier, however, the Bishop of Prince Albert and Saskatoon, Joseph-Henri Prud'homme, had agreed to write this article about Taché, referring to him as "the greatest

38. Letters from Noël Bernier to Lionel Groulx, BAnQ, FLG, P1/A,346, May 17, 1920; from Achille Auclair to Lionel Groulx, BAnQ, FLG, P1/A,110, October 28, 1920.

39. Letters from Lionel Groulx to Alexandre Dugré, BAnQ, FLG, P1/A,1199, July 4, 1925; from Alexandre Dugré to Lionel Groulx, BAnQ, FLG, P1/A,1199, July 20, 1925.

figure in the episcopacy of the West." We do not know what prevented the prelate from following through on his commitment. In the end, it was Groulx who had to write the article even though a few weeks earlier, he had said he was "too swamped" to take it on.[40] Around the same time, Villeneuve suggested he should entrust his colleague, Oblate Georges Simard, with writing a piece on Msgr. Louis Rhéaume to mark his installation as Bishop of Haileybury.[41] We should mention that Prud'homme was not the only prelate working among the minorities who was pressed into service by Groulx. In 1920, the Bishop of Haileybury, Msgr. Élie-Anicet Latulipe, provided an article for the review, as did the Archbishop of Saint-Boniface, Msgr. Arthur Béliveau, a few years later.[42]

L'Action française was also able to benefit from contributions by a Franco-American collaborator, Abbé Adélard Duplessis, who went by the pen name of Charles Dollard. And the Franco-Ontarians had their regular columnist too: Aurèle Gauthier, the pseudonym used by Oblate priest Georges Simard, took on this role when Groulx became director of the review.[43] In the midst of the Regulation 17 crisis, the Franco-Ontarians had no problem finding more than a few champions in the nationalist circles of Ontario and Québec who were ready to cross swords with the Orangemen and the Irish Catholics. However, the review seems to have had greater difficulty recruiting regular collaborators among the Acadians and only published about ten pieces dealing specifically with that community, the remarks being limited, in general, to a lament on the injustice of the Deportation of 1755.[44] This relative absence of the Acadians in the pages of *L'Action française* did not go unnoticed. In 1924, René Chaloult, future politician and activist in the Bloc populaire canadien, a law student in Québec at the time, offered to write an article on the Acadians in order to fill what he perceived as a deficiency in *L'Action française*. He complained to Groulx that the review had "hardly mentioned the Acadian group that year. . . . On the other hand, it has on several occasions discussed the Franco-Americans and the Ontarians." Chaloult explained that his interest in the Acadians had been stimulated during his travels among them the previous summer. Groulx greeted his proposal for an article with enthusiasm.[45]

---

40. See Lionel Groulx, "Monseigneur Taché," AF, October 1923, p. 211.
41. Letters from Lionel Groulx to Rodrigue Villeneuve, BAnQ, FLG, P1/A,3696, September 21, 1923; from Joseph-Henri Prud'homme to Lionel Groulx, BAnQ, FLG, P1/A,3102, August 14, 1923; from Lionel Groulx to Rodrigue Villeneuve, BAnQ, FLG, P1/A,3696; from Rodrigue Villeneuve to Lionel Groulx, BAnQ, FLG, P1/A,3696, October 4, 1923. (The article on Rhéaume, however, was published without a signature. See "Monseigneur Rhéaume," AF, October 1923, p. 204–207.)
42. Letter from Élie-Anicet Latulipe to Lionel Groulx, BAnQ, FLG, P1/A,2137, October 7, 1920. The article was published the following month: Élie-Anicet Latulipe, "Nos traditions," AF, November 1920, p. 492–498. See also Arthur Béliveau, "Les Canadiens français et le rôle de l'Église catholique dans l'Ouest," AF, May–June 1927, p. 357–365; Joseph-Henri Prud'homme, "L'apostolat catholique dans l'Ouest," AF, March 1924, p. 146–154.
43. Letter from Georges Simard to Lionel Groulx, BAnQ, FLG, P1/A,3453, November 11, 1920.
44. See, for example, Émile Chartier, "La tragique histoire d'un peuple," AF, June 1923, p. 345–350; Henri d'Arles [pseudonym of Henri Beaudé], "*Innocens Ego Sum*," AF, July 1919, p. 306–316; Henri d'Arles, "Choses acadiennes," AF, January 1917, p. 18–19.
45. See René Chaloult, "Les Acadiens et nous," AF, July 1924, p. 40–46.

The director of *L'Action française* held his young collaborator in sufficiently high esteem to entrust him with the column, "A travers la vie courante" [Through the lens of everyday life], two years later. He suggested he use this "to highlight the best examples or manifestations of French life in groups outside Québec," but at the same time he advised him to adopt a pseudonym—"Veilleur"—to shield him against the "narrow-minded" response his "forthright comments" might elicit from certain circles. Chaloult accepted responsibility for the column and took the pseudonym. Groulx, in the months that followed, regularly fed the *Veilleur*'s column by directing him to interesting content being published in Moncton's *L'Évangéline* and Winnipeg's *La Liberté*.[46]

Chaloult's criticism of the limited space the Acadians occupied in the review earned him a lengthy explanation from Lionel Groulx. "The Acadians may not be featured often in the review," he admitted, "but I entreat you to believe that it is hardly through any fault of mine." He claimed that he had "tried the impossible" to have his review feature a "regular" Acadian column, approaching specifically one of his Acadian acquaintances, Msgr. Patrice-Alexandre Chiasson, Bishop of Chatham. Chiasson, he confided to Chaloult, "was keen on my idea and gave me an address to write to. But just like what happened four years ago, I came up against a brick wall." Indeed, a few months earlier, Groulx had written to Chiasson to try to obtain his support for a possible Acadian collaboration with *L'Action française*, and the prelate had shown great enthusiasm:

> Like you, I believe that closer ties between the French Canadians and the Acadians can only do a lot of good. They are like twin brothers, one of whom, however, through circumstances we are well aware of, matured faster than the other. A greater and more intimate bond between them will certainly foster the development of the French language, customs and habits in Canada. You are right to wish each of these brothers, however, to maintain their distinctive characteristics. Therefore, I have no objection to our people writing in *L'Action Française*; quite the contrary, and I hope this project will come to fruition.

As Groulx would tell René Chaloult later, Chiasson proposed the name of a possible collaborator for *L'Action française*, namely, Alfred Roy, a writer for *L'Évangéline* in Moncton. Groulx called on Roy's help but the latter refused, citing poor health.[47] The door indeed seemed closed.

In his correspondence with René Chaloult, Groulx identified three reasons why, in his view, the Acadians demonstrated such "extraordinary mistrust toward

46. Exchange of correspondence between Lionel Groulx and René Chaloult, BAnQ, FLG, P1/A,704, February 7, 1924 to October 17, 1927.

47. Letters from Lionel Groulx to René Chaloult, BAnQ, FLG, P1/A,704, February 10, 1924; from Patrice-Alexandre Chiasson to Lionel Groulx, BAnQ, FLG, P1/A,795, October 6, 1923; from Alfred Roy to Lionel Groulx, BAnQ, FLG, P1/A,3261, November 15, 1923.

the French Canadians," some "extremists mistrusting them even more than they did the Irish." First of all, he explained, certain Acadians, even some of the most educated ones, lacked confidence in their own abilities and let themselves be too easily intimidated by their journalist colleagues or writer friends in Québec. There were others who were suspicious of the real intentions of the French Canadians, whom they accused of wanting to "swallow them up." Lastly, Groulx mentioned the dearth of writers left in Acadia: the few who were talented often preferred to dedicate themselves entirely to strictly Acadian works. The director of *L'Action française* advised Chaloult to appear extremely prudent in his articles on the Acadians, so as to guarantee that their sensibilities would not be offended. Unfortunately, French Canadians of previous generations had behaved irresponsibly toward the Acadians, making fun of their unique traits and thereby exacerbating their distrustful attitude toward them:

> It must be said that the *Canadiens* of the old generation did not refrain from making gaffes of all kinds in Acadia and are to a large extent responsible for the prejudices held there against us. For some twenty years now, we have fortunately adopted wiser attitudes. At *L'Action française* we have never lost an opportunity to show our respect for the rights of the Acadian nationality. It is a nationality different from ours, with its own customs, history, traditions and flag, we must have the good sense to recognize this. . . . A *Canadien* who writes about the things of Acadia is a little like a Frenchman who writes about Canada: he must be careful and measure his words.[48]

It did not take long for Groulx's influence to rub off on the young Chaloult. He took two more trips to Acadia, in 1924 and in 1926, with student colleagues from Québec. Chaloult made sure not to offend his hosts, in accordance with Groulx's lavish advice, and said nothing that would induce them to doubt his good faith: "We always took care not to offend the national susceptibility of our listeners. In contrast to what some *Canadiens* of old did, and following your advice, we lost no opportunity to acknowledge the Acadian nationality as being distinct from our own." Chaloult returned to Québec very satisfied with his 1924 tour of Acadia and confident that it "had contributed to dissipating many prejudices among the people there." Upon returning from his 1926 trip, he commented similarly to Groulx and mentioned at the same time the numerous merits of the Acadian clergy, who seemed to him markedly "superior to ours from a national perspective."[49]

In Groulx's mind, the Acadians constituted an exceptional case among the French minorities. He saw them as a group that possessed particularities, and jealously sought to preserve them. Groulx never reproached them for their

48. Letter from Lionel Groulx to René Chaloult, BAnQ, FLG, P1/A,704, February 10, 1924.
49. Letters from René Chaloult to Lionel Groulx, BAnQ, FLG, P1/A,704, September 25, 1924 and September 20, 1926.

sensitivity, which sometimes made them easily offended when it came to their "national" identity: on the contrary, he felt it was best to acknowledge and respect the uniqueness of the Acadians in order to placate them, so to speak, and foster cooperation between the "two twin brothers." One cannot help but notice, moreover, that Groulx never established a similar distinction between the French Canadians from Québec and, for example, the Franco-Ontarians or the Franco-Manitobans. The prudent attitude he displayed toward the Acadians did not, it seemed to him, need to be applied in the same measure in his relations with the other minorities. He saw them as belonging to the French-Canadian nation, clearly and unequivocally, in the same way as their Québec compatriots. The obstacles Groulx sometimes encountered in his efforts to recruit Acadian collaborators never diminished his conviction that *L'Action française* should serve to forge closer ties among all the French groups on the continent, including Acadia.

Whenever the review made a breakthrough among the minorities, Groulx celebrated the occasion as a victory in the struggle for the *survivance* of French civilization in America. Just a few weeks after he took over *L'Action française*, the new director shared with his readers the congratulatory remarks he had received from Archbishop Béliveau of Saint-Boniface:

> His Excellency blesses *L'Action française* once more and finds the new column on our guiding principles [a short editorial that *L'Action française* published at the beginning of each issue] to be 'superb.' His Excellency sends us substantial gifts and, moreover—given the eminent source, we cannot fail to mention this—is taking out a new subscription for one of the priests in his diocese.

"Let us spread *L'Action française* always and everywhere," wrote Doctor Damien Saint-Pierre in 1923. Saint-Pierre was a faithful reader from Ford City in Southwestern Ontario. In 1924, upon returning from a speaking tour in the counties of Kent and Essex, Groulx, writing under the pen name Nicolas Tillemont, reported the warm comments made to him by the Franco-Ontarians of the South:

> I wish simply to say here what a surprise and what a good feeling it was for Abbé Groulx to see how much, in this southernmost part of Ontario, our work is known and sometimes passionately pursued. In this region, our advice is attentively read and often followed. All the leaders of the resistance [to Regulation 17] are faithful readers of *L'Action française*; in all the centres where he spoke, our director heard the modest task we perform being praised enthusiastically, sometimes too enthusiastically.

In his *Mémoires*, Groulx points out with satisfaction the connections the review managed to build with the different communities of the French minorities and he lists some of the positive comments he received, at the time, from *Le Droit* in Ottawa, *La Liberté* in Winnipeg and *L'Indépendant* in Fall River, Massachusetts, to name just a few. Oblate Father Charles Charlebois, publisher and founder of *Le Droit*, was, for his part, one of the fervent promoters of *L'Action française* in the federal capital. In 1925, he confided to Groulx that he had been "obsessed" for a long time "by the desire to found a cercle d'action française that would operate in collaboration with l'Association [canadienne-française] d'éducation [d'Ontario] and *le* '*Droit*'." "Your ideas make an impact," he added; "and they are heartening." Groulx immediately conveyed to him his enthusiasm for the project. He too had dreamed of one like it for some time: "If we had a group of friends like that in every city or large centre, what strength we could develop in a short time."[50]

Building Bridges: La Fête de Dollard, *the "Saving Organization" and Other Measures*

During the 1920s, *L'Action française* embodied the same national solidarity that Abbé Groulx hoped all of Québec would demonstrate toward the French minorities. Groulx launched a number of campaigns in his review, aimed at bringing Québec and the minorities closer together. Some of them he pursued right into the 1930s. For example, in 1922, Groulx wanted ACFEO to back a report he was preparing to submit to l'Internationale catholique to raise awareness about the situation of the Catholic minorities in Canada. He succeeded in getting the president of ACFEO, Senator Napoléon Belcourt, to draw up a memorandum showing "that the suppression of a *French* school is the suppression of a *Catholic* school." Groulx also asked him to sign, on behalf of ACFEO, a message of support that the Société Saint-Jean-Baptiste of Montréal was sending to General de Castelnau, founder of the Fédération nationale catholique de France.[51]

According to Abbé Groulx, one of the reasons why Québec sometimes fell short in its duties toward the minorities was that Québec was kept in the dark so much of the time about the battles French Canadians were courageously fighting elsewhere in the country. In 1933, Groulx thought he had found the way to remedy this situation, at least in part. In a speech on the concerns of the nation's youth and national education, which he delivered at the Palais Montcalm in Québec, he suggested religious communities organize exchange programs between

50. Jacques Brassier [pseudonym of L. Groulx], "La vie de l'Action française," AF, January 1921, p. 63–64. See also Jacques Brassier, "La vie de l'Action française," AF, November 1920, p. 524–527; Nicolas Tillemont [pseudonym of L. Groulx], "La vie de l'Action française," AF, June 1923, p. 383; Jacques Brassier [pseudonym of L. Groulx], "La vie de l'Action française," AF, March 1923, p. 191; Nicolas Tillemont [pseudonym of L. Groulx], "La vie de l'Action française," AF, May 1924, p. 315; Lionel Groulx, *Mes Mémoires, Tome II*, p. 12, 113, 116, 279, 352–353; Letters from Charles Charlebois to Lionel Groulx, BAnQ, FLG, P1/A,746, August 20, 1925; from Lionel Groulx to Charles Charlebois, BAnQ, FLG, P1/A,746, September 6, 1925 and September 19, 1925.

51. Letters from Lionel Groulx to Charles Charlebois, BAnQ, FLG, P1/A,746, [no date]; from Rodrigue Villeneuve to Lionel Groulx, BAnQ, FLG, P1/A,3696, June 3, 1922; from Lionel Groulx to Napoléon Belcourt, BAnQ, FLG, P1/A,283, [no date].

French-Canadian students from Québec and those from the other provinces, and see that they were followed up by correspondence. Being an educator, Groulx found it "inconceivable" that an initiative "of such moral benefit" had not been thought of before:

> The school children of Québec could in this way become well informed about the educational adversities and other problems faced by each of the French groups in North America; they would learn of the heroism with which French Catholic life is being defended in difficult conditions in other regions, what ideals and what hopes nourish the youth of the minorities; being better educated about the nation, the children who attend Québec schools could offer solace to their faraway young brothers by sharing their patriotic faith and their steadfast spirit.

At the same time, the speaker criticized in no uncertain terms similar projects that had already been created, especially at the university level, but which were geared rather to increasing the contact between French-Canadian and English-Canadian students. While he did not see this practice as harmful in itself, Groulx felt it scattered the energies that would have been put to better use in redressing the sometimes woeful state of relations between Québec and the French minorities. That was what people should be devoting themselves to, first and foremost: "Ha[d] it occurred to very many," he wondered, "that ties should be forged first between brothers?"[52]

In 1922, in his talk, "L'Amitié française d'Amérique," given at Lowell, Abbé Groulx suggested other initiatives along the same lines. He may have been addressing a Franco-American audience, but the vision he presented to them was meant for all French minorities living on the continent. He stressed the importance of starting to read each other's newspapers, with the Catholic and nationalist press constituting, in his mind, a powerful tool for bringing about unity. The struggle to maintain French civilization was the same everywhere on the North American continent. French-Canadian groups should, he felt, come to one another's assistance. However, they had to get to know each other: "If we are to have a common way of thinking as the sign and the bond that unites us, the newspapers of French America will have to show a bit of concern for all of French America!"[53] As a historian, he likewise assigned an important role to the development of what he called "the teaching of [national] history," and wanted to see it

52. Lionel Groulx, "L'inquiétude de la jeunesse et l'éducation nationale," *Orientations*, p. 125.

53. Lionel Groulx, "L'Amitié française d'Amérique," Dix ans d'Action française, p. 190-191; L'Action française, "Pour la fraternité française," AF, February 1921, p. 65; Lionel Groulx, "L'Amitié française d'Amérique," *Dix ans d'Action française*, p. 192; Jacques Brassier [pseudonym of L. Groulx], "La vie de l'Action française," AF, December 1922, p. 381; Jacques Brassier, "La vie de l'Action française," AF, October 1922, p. 252, 253; Jacques Brassier, "La vie de l'Action française," AF, November 1922, p. 319; Jacques Brassier; "La vie de l'Action française," AF, January 1923, p. 62.

made mandatory in all the French schools of the continent: "For a fragmented and scattered race, like the French race of America, it is still history, connecting us to the same memories, instilling in us the ideal of the same forefathers, which, despite the distances, preserves the essential fraternity." At *L'Action française*, the talk at Lowell quickly took on the character of a "rallying cry." Jacques Brassier missed no opportunity to promote "L'Amitié française d'Amérique" once it was published as a brochure: "The French groups in Canada and the United States do not have the cohesion they ought to have. They are weak because they are too dispersed. The time has come for us to unite in order to be strong. *Amitié française d'Amérique* is our first rallying cry." Groulx was delighted that the Franco-Americans decided to run off ten thousand copies of the brochure and proudly noted how well it was received by the French minority press in Canada. "Those who need to be convinced of our magnificent role toward our dispersed brothers," he added, "will do well to read these pages by Abbé Groulx."

The director of *L'Action française* also praised the efforts of institutions that, in his view, had never failed in their duty of national solidarity toward the minorities. The Association catholique de la jeunesse canadienne topped the list: "Even if, nationally speaking, it had only held two fundraisers in aid of the French schools in Ontario, these were a testimony to its generosity and its strength."[54] Such fundraisers, he explained, stood in singular contrast to the "lukewarm attitude" displayed toward the minorities, more often than not, by the people of Québec. In 1924, during a Société Saint-Jean-Baptiste de Montréal conference, he expressed bitter disappointment in the lethargy of his fellow Québécois:

> Are we appalled at our great indifference toward the French groups of America, at our lukewarm attitude, all too real, toward the fate of the French minorities in Canada? Have we noticed that, to help them out with a puny offering of a few thousand dollars, it takes months of hype, a degrading propaganda campaign, in competition with the popularity of boxers and criminals? We see in this a lack of a sense of nationhood.[55]

Abbé Groulx thought that one of the most effective ways to create this sense of national solidarity was to help increase the number of national events and celebrations. There was the *fête Saint-Jean-Baptiste*, but also and especially, the *fête de Dollard des Ormeaux*. The *fête nationale* had an important symbolic function in Groulxist nationalism because, by establishing the parameters of the French-Canadian nation, it made it possible to clearly identify those who belonged to it and those who didn't. Groulx and *L'Action française* became ardent promoters of the celebration of the hero from Long Sault. All French Canadians, he insisted,

54. Lionel Groulx, "Les vingt ans de l'A.C.J.C.," AF, June 1924, p. 367–368.
55. Lionel Groulx, "Nos devoirs envers la race," *Dix ans d'Action française*, p. 219.

from Québec and elsewhere, could claim Dollard, "the hero who belong[ed] to the entire French family of America."[56] In 1919, Groulx gave a speech on the occasion of the unveiling at Long Sault of a monument honouring the memory of Dollard. Powerfully emotive and waxing lyrical, to say the least, he used the opportunity to present the national hero as a rallying symbol for the entire French-Canadian nation. The memory of his deed would allow all French groups on the continent to be inspired by the ideal of New France:

> From this trench, covered over two and a half centuries ago, a prayer rises up that is still ours, a prayer ascends in the same language and in the same accent. Let us know how to hear it, how to respond to it; let us know also how to hear the French and Christian prayer that rises from the Ontario marches, from our marches in the West, those in Acadia and those beyond the [American] border; let us send up, over the trenches that separate us, the hymn of our unshakeable and fraternal faith and may the unity of New France last forever.[57]

Groulx wanted the holiday celebrating the hero from Long Sault to "become universal, to become such an integral part of our customs and our traditions that, in French America, May 24 would henceforth only be called '*la fête de Dollard*'."[58] The director of *L'Action française* was delighted at the success the campaign enjoyed everywhere in French America. Year after year, Jacques Brassier gave an account of the festivities organized by the French minorities to celebrate Dollard in the United States and Canada alike. Gatherings held in Ottawa, Saint-Boniface, Edmonton, Gravelbourg, Prince Albert, Sudbury, Sturgeon Falls, Woonsocket, Morinville and Windsor, among other places, elicited the enthusiasm of both Groulx and his collaborators.[59] "This *fête de Dollard* is truly taking on the proportions of a phenomenon in our national life," he declared with great satisfaction in 1924. "With almost no directives given, with little or no advertising, it goes ahead all the same, with more solemnity and greater emotion each time."[60]

From time to time, Groulx approached some of his colleagues and friends among the minorities personally to get them to participate in the festivities he wanted to see everywhere in French America. In May of 1920, he wrote Father

56. L'Action française, "Pour Dollard," AF, April 1923, p. 193. See also Lionel Groulx, "L'Amitié française d'Amérique," *Dix ans d'Action française*, p. 188–189.
57. [Lionel Groulx], "Le discours de M. l'abbé Groulx au Long-Sault," AF, June 1919, p. 288.
58. L'Action française, "La fête de Dollard," AF, April 1920, p. 168.
59. Jacques Brassier [pseudonym of L. Groulx], "La vie de l'Action française," AF, June 1921, p. 380–381; Lionel Groulx, "Pour la fête de Dollard," AF, April 1922, p. 217; Jacques Brassier, "La vie de l'Action française," AF, July 1922, p. 54-55; Jacques Brassier, "La vie de l'Action française," AF, March 1923, p. 189–192; Jean Tillemont [pseudonym of Hermas Bastien], "La vie de l'Action française," AF, March 1923, p. 190–191; Jean Tillemont, "La vie de l'Action française," AF, May 1923, p. 320; Jacques Brassier, "La vie de l'Action française," AF, June 1924, p. 377.
60. Ibid., p. 376. See also *Mes Mémoires, Tome II*, p. 55–56.

Charles Charlebois, publisher of *Le Droit* in Ottawa, to ask the Franco-Ontarian daily to lend "a helping hand," just as ACFEO was doing, to *L'Action française*, in its work to help organize a celebration in Carillon. Charlebois answered that he would do his best but, with May 24 only three days away, could do only so much. Groulx made a point, the following year, of starting at the beginning of April. This time, he was asking the Franco-Ontarians to join a gathering to take place at Long Sault. He wrote Charlebois, "we would be very pleased if this could be an opportunity for the Ontario and Québec groups to meet." He further asked the publisher of *Le Droit* to do his part in distributing the *rose de Dollard* to the general public: "We are insisting on the rose because, for most of the crowd, displaying this symbol on their lapel will be their only way of celebrating." The rose, Groulx hoped, would spread throughout French Canada like the shamrock among the Irish.[61]

In his view, the *fête de Dollard* furthermore provided Québec with an excellent opportunity to show its support for the resistance to Regulation 17 by Franco-Ontarians, "who more spontaneously than any other group joined in celebrating the hero who had fallen near the marches of Ontario."[62] At least this is what he said in 1924 to Edmond Cloutier, secretary of ACFEO. That year, *L'Action française* sought to get participation in the *fête de Dollard* from business leaders, senators and Québec federal MPs: "We would like the holiday to have a truly official character, in order to get everyone involved in this Ontario affair and the *fête de Dollard*."[63] Groulx even entertained the hope that Premier Taschereau would take part. He told Cloutier that senators Beaubien and Dandurand had already promised to attend the event, but asked him to approach Rodolphe Lemieux, Speaker of the House of Commons at the time, who had refused the initial invitation by *L'Action française*.

The reaction from the minorities to the Dollard campaign was extremely enthusiastic. In 1922, Rodrigue Villeneuve informed Groulx that the *fête de Dollard* had "become part of the common culture" and "that *Empire Day* [was] dead here," that is, in Ottawa.[64] Groulx himself regularly received invitations to take part in May 24 celebrations organized by the minorities throughout the country. In 1924, Abbé Antoine d'Eschambault of Saint-Boniface tried everything to get him to participate in the festivities being planned in his part of the country: "You will be fêted, spoiled and admired by your friends! Above all, your visit will buoy up our spirits! We need that!" Later, in 1934, Groulx received a similar invitation

61. Exchange of correspondence between Lionel Groulx and Charles Charleboix, BAnQ, FLG, P1/A,746, [May 1920] to April 7, 1921.
62. Lionel Groulx, "Pour la fête de Dollard," *AF*, April 1922, p. 217.
63. Letter from Lionel Groulx to Edmond Cloutier, BAnQ, FLG, P1/A, May 12, 1924.
64. Letter from Rodrigue Villeneuve to Lionel Groulx, BAnQ, FLG, P1/A,3696, June 3, 1922. Empire Day was held on the last working day before May 24, the birthday of Queen Victoria. During the first half of the twentieth century, this was marked by a major patriotic celebration in English Canada.

from Paul Chartiez, of the Jesuit *collège* in Sudbury. He also wanted Groulx to give a talk, while he was there, on "reasons for keeping the bond with our race and being proud of our ancestors."[65] At Gravelbourg, in Saskatchewan, Oblate Georges Boileau ascribed the success of the 1923 celebrations directly to Groulx:

> Our *fête de Dollard*, dear Monsieur Groulx, enjoyed incomparable success and exceeded all our hopes. We refer to the beautiful religious and patriotic displays as well as the considerable crowds. Our compatriots came from all the surrounding parishes to watch the impressive ceremonies. We give thanks to God! It is your passionately patriotic spirit and the evocative clamour of your emotional speeches about Dollard des Ormeaux that have moved us, and have stirred the French race, even as far away as the broad plains of Saskatchewan.[66]

Groulx knew that to bring together all French Canadians from one end of the country to the other, if not from the whole continent, was a very tall order, considering how fragmented and scattered they were. Already in 1922, he proposed a means of counteracting this dispersal: a central organization should be created that would serve as an umbrella for all the *sociétés nationales* of French Canada and the United States. The next best thing to being able to bring all French Canadians together within one state would be to offer them the benefits of a permanent administrative structure that would have the power to follow through on their projects and to put them in regular communication with each other. That was his proposal in his speech, "L'Amitié française d'Amérique." In that speech, Groulx compared the situation of the French Canadians to that of the Irish and the Polish, for they too knew what it meant to be "a fragmented and scattered race" suffering a "terrible disintegration." But in the case of the Polish, "the fragmentation was not a dispersal." It seemed the "roots" of French Canada had been "broken up." To remedy this lamentable state of affairs, Groulx hoped and prayed that "an organization might be created that would undertake and facilitate official exchanges." He felt that by fostering assembly and cohesion, such a structure would allow the French-Canadian spirit of solidarity to develop throughout America: "no longer will any of our groups be attacked, without a wave of sympathy immediately passing through all of French America."[67]

This was a campaign that Groulx likewise pursued in his private correspondence with the various representatives of the French minorities, including Senator Napoléon Belcourt, President of ACFEO. But he especially did so, during the 1920s, in the pages of *L'Action française*, so instrumental in all his battles. In 1925,

65. Letters from Antoine d'Eschambault to Lionel Groulx, BAnQ, FLG, P1/A,1297, April 29, 1924; from Paul Chartiez to Lionel Groulx, BAnQ, FLG, P1/A,766, April 7, 1934.
66. Letter from Georges Boileau to Lionel Groulx, BAnQ, FLG, P1/A,427, June 5, 1923.
67. Lionel Groulx, "L'Amitié française d'Amérique," *Dix ans d'Action française*, p. 167, 189, 200.

as a group of French Canadians from Saskatchewan was visiting Montréal, the review again promoted the cause:

> Groups of French origin in America must defend and promote moral interests whose importance is to be placed above all else. Being dispersed minorities, they can only be strong if they are united, through an effective agreement whereby the independence of the groups will be preserved but all will form a coalition for the common defence.
>
> It is this deep concern that leads the pilgrims of the French-Canadian *survivance* to come to us. Let us offer a warm welcome. But let us not forget that this meeting must also have a tomorrow. Let us unite. Let us create the organization that will build this unity and make it effective. We have been saying it for a long time here: Québec has the cure of souls.[68]

Another trip made by "our brothers from the West" two years later gave rise to similar remarks: "May heaven show us how to finally found that saving organization that will gather and harness all the energies." Groulx received support from some of the representatives of the French minorities, including Raymond Denis, of the Association catholique franco-canadienne de la Saskatchewan. Denis told Groulx that he too wanted to establish a more active union between the various organizations across Canada that were experiencing the same problems. Groulx reiterated this desire to see the birth of a "saving organization," even following his tenure as director of *L'Action française*. In 1935, during a presentation to the *jeune barreau de Québec* (young lawyers' association), he lamented the "deplorable fact" that "threatened as we are, persecuted as our brothers have been, from one end of Canada to the other, we have not yet been able to establish an effective organization through which we can support one another." On the contrary, he continued, the only officially established organization in French Canada was the political party, instrument of the most unfortunate divisions.[69]

Shortly afterwards, during the Deuxième Congrès de la langue française in 1937, Groulx's wish was finally granted. The Comité permanent de la survivance française, which would become the Conseil de la vie française en Amérique in 1952, was created. The importance given by Groulx to the founding of such an organization attests to the indissolubility of the ties that, in his view, must bind Québec to the French minorities. After helping to organize the founding conference, he also sat on the Comité permanent for two years, from 1937 to 1939,

68. L'Action française, "L'union dans la race," AF, November 1925, p. 265.
69. L'Action française, "À la 'survivance française,'" AF, December 1927, p. 319; "Vers l''union dans la race,'" AF, October 1924, p. 245; "Le voyage de la survivance française," AF, October 1926, p. 209; Jacques Brassier [pseudonym of L. Groulx], "La vie de l'Action française," AF, November 1926, p. 316–317; Letter from Raymond Denis to Lionel Groulx, BAnQ, FLG, P1/A,1025, January 22, 1927; Lionel Groulx, "Nos positions," *Orientations*, p. 258.

and would continue subsequently to take part in its activities.[70] In 1943, Raymond Denis invited him to sponsor a fundraising campaign to found an Acadian daily. We do not know how Groulx responded to the request, but everything leads us to believe that he accepted the honour. Denis, for his part, by all accounts, expected a positive reply: "If we do not hear from you within a few days, allow us to conclude that you agree to join all of us in ensuring the success of our campaign and we will take the liberty of including your name on the list of honorary members." Soon afterwards, Denis approached Groulx again to offer him the chance to sponsor a campaign to establish a French language radio station in the West. These two fundraising campaigns enjoyed remarkable success, raising nearly $300,000 for the Acadians and the French Canadians of the West.[71]

Groulx also approached the Secretary General of the Comité permanent de la survivance, Abbé Paul-Émile Gosselin, when he had the idea of organizing a *Saint-Jean-Baptiste de la jeunesse* all across French Canada. This would be another way to awaken in them that "sense" of the people to which they belonged. Groulx said he was giving up "on shaking the older generations out of their torpor" and wanted to dedicate the better part of his energy to educating the youth about the nation. The festivities, he explained, would be organized entirely by young people throughout the country and would include both a mass and a secular celebration. Groulx did not exclude the possibility that some *sociétés* Saint-Jean-Baptiste might participate in the project but it was first to the Comité de la survivance that he wanted to entrust responsibility for it: "It seems to me," he wrote to Gosselin, "that the Comité de la survivance française is ideally suited to send out this directive all across French Canada, from one end to the other, indeed, to all of French America." Gosselin in reply conveyed his enthusiasm for the project and promised that the Comité "would begin without delay to see to its implementation" upon securing the participation of the clergy, the media and the other patriotic associations. However, the *Saint-Jean-Baptiste de la jeunesse* never took place. A few months later, Gosselin admitted to Groulx that the project had "got stuck at the general planning stage," the campaign for the Acadian paper having taken up all his energy." He said he hoped, however, that the following year, "Acadia would leave him free to pursue other matters."[72] Whatever the case, it is easy to see how important a role Lionel Groulx envisioned for the Comité permanent, the organization he had been clamouring for since the beginning of the 1920s to foster the rapprochement of all the French groups in Canada.

70. Marcel Martel, *Le Deuil d'un pays imaginé: Rêves, luttes et déroute du Canada français* (Ottawa: Presses de l'Université d'Ottawa, 1997), p. 58, 181. It may be that it was distance that prevented Groulx from extending his participation on the committee, its headquarters being in Quebec City.

71. Letters from Raymond Denis to Lionel Groulx, BAnQ, FLG, P1/A,1025, May 19, 1943 and [no date]; Marcel Martel, *Le Deuil*, p. 46–55.

72. Exchange of correspondence between Lionel Groulx and Paul-Émile Gosselin, BAnQ, FLG, P1/A,1604, October 15, 1942 to July 2, 1943.

* * *

We have noted that Lionel Groulx was saddened by Quebec's failure to properly carry out its duty, as "the eldest son," towards the French minorities of the other provinces. The "national solidarity" that he longed for was regularly obliterated by what he saw as a lack of backbone on the part of the French-Canadian political class, whose partisan mentality won out, generally speaking, over its sense of nationhood. Groulx therefore turned to other segments of the French-Canadian population, among them the clergy, who had always constituted the principal source of support for the minorities, providing them with many colonist missionaries and teachers. He furthermore considered that *L'Action française* likewise represented a powerful instrument of national solidarity, as confirmed by the numerous campaigns it led to defend the rights of the minorities and unite all the French communities in the country with one another.

> There was not one of these minorities, he wrote later in his *Mémoires*, that it [*L'Action française*] did not defend and encourage, whose resistance it did not proclaim far and wide. Acadians, French Canadians of the West and of Ontario, Franco-Americans of New England, these will some day come and seek, in the twenty volumes of *L'Action française*—and that will be our most valuable achievement—large segments of their history.[73]

In spite of the debate over the "French state," which we will discuss later, the minorities saw in *L'Action française* and, more generally, in Groulx's work, an eloquent expression of the support and national solidarity they wished to have from their compatriots in Québec. During the interwar period, Groulx had become a figure who was regarded as the intellectual leader of the nationalist movement. It is hardly surprising that the minorities frequently turned to him to draw his attention to their activities and thank him for his numerous interventions on their behalf. The influence he had on them, at least on their elites, had become considerable. Let us take as evidence the words of Georges Boileau, who wrote to him in 1924:

> The echo of your salutary lessons in history and pride is heard and resonates magnificently even as far away as the broad plains of Saskatchewan and all of the Canadian West. The humble Collège de Gravelbourg, for its part, has greatly benefited from the salutary tone of your saving guidelines, and we are deeply grateful to you.

73. Lionel Groulx, *Mes Mémoires, Tome II . . .*, p. 317–318.

In 1926, Georges Bugnet, of *L'Union* of Edmonton, informed Groulx that "the press, in the province of Québec, is starting to show fairness toward the French Canadians of the Northwest in general and of Alberta in particular," implying in the same writing that Groulx's efforts had a lot to do with it. Donatien Frémont, of *La Liberté* of Winnipeg, even compared him to Taine after once again giving him a free subscription to his newspaper, a gesture, he explained to him, which was "entirely to the advantage of French Manitoba, which strongly wishes to see its activities become part of your field of observation." In October of 1937, a student at the Jesuit *collège* in Edmonton, who had previously been indifferent to the controversy surrounding the Congrès de la langue française, asked Groulx for a large photograph of himself as a way to sustain the sense of nation among his fellow students. Another Edmontonian, Gérard Le Moyne, of the newspaper *La Survivance des Jeunes*, told him of the deep influence he exercised among the young Franco-Albertans. These youth, he told him, "gear themselves toward the ideal that you advocate and they know you very well. They read; and they read Groulx. Our libraries . . . are full of your writing. School principals . . . acquaint the children with you, as the Leader who will take us to victory." In 1939, another collaborator of *La Survivance des Jeunes*, Oblate Jean Patoine, sent Groulx a collection of letters written to him by some young French Canadians in the West to express their gratitude for his commitment. Raymond Denis, President of the Association catholique franco-canadienne de la Saskatchewan, told him about the impact of a talk he had given on his behalf at a conference of the Association in Gravelbourg. He contritely admitted that he had composed the message himself, but added that it had nevertheless "given new courage." Abbé Groulx, moreover, regularly received invitations to take part in the social, cultural and political activities of the minority communities.[74]

In 1937–1938, the national societies of French Canada, at the instigation of the *sociétés* Saint-Jean-Baptiste and the Ordre de Jacques-Cartier, conducted a huge fundraising campaign, which they christened *Les amis de l'abbé Groulx*, in order to provide him with the financial means to hire a secretary. The $8,000 that was raised served instead to provide him with a house in Outremont, where he would end his days some thirty years later.[75] It had been a truly national campaign: even the French Canadians' children of the West had been recruited to it. In Edmonton, Gérard Le Moyne took charge of promoting it with the school children. In his

74. Letters to Lionel Groulx from Georges Boileau, BAnQ, FLG, P1/A,42, December 30 1924; from Georges Bugnet, BAnQ, FLG, P1/A,603, August 3, 1926; from Donatien Frémont, BAnQ, FLG, P1/A,1426, May 1, 1929 and March 6, 1932; from Armand Saint-Pierre, BAnQ, FLG, P1/A,3344, October 17, 1937; from Gérard Le Moyne, BAnQ, FLG, P1/A,2310, February 29, 1936; from Jean Patoine, BAnQ, FLG, P1/A,2906, October 9, 1939; from Raymond Denis, BAnQ, FLG, P1/A,1025, July 22, 1939; from Noël Bernier, BAnQ, FLG, P1/A,346, June 6 [no year]; from Anatole Vanier, BAnQ, FLG, P1/A,3646, July 18, 1924; from Paul-Émile Breton, BAnQ, FLG, P1/A,551, September 18, 1939; from Rodolphe Tanguay, BAnQ, FLG, P1/A,3504, August 15, 1933 and March 23, 1934; from Oscar Racette, BAnQ, FLG, P1/A,3117, June 11, 1938.

75. Letter from J.A.S. Plouffe to Lionel Groulx, BAnQ, FLG, P1/A,3029, February 4, 1942.

Mémoires, Groulx recalls the emotion he felt at this sign of affection from the little Franco-Albertans:

> The appeal is going out even as far as in the schools of Alberta, to groups of children called *avant-gardistes*. They are being asked to make a small offering, even if it is just a penny. A penny is not much, Uncle Gérard Le Moyne wrote to them in *La Survivance* of Edmonton: "But don't you see that Abbé Groulx would weep for joy just to see that there is in the West and in all of Canada a real crusade of children who are paying from their own pockets to help him make them 'the generation of the living?'" Indeed, pennies are being sent to me, along with lists of the names of children who have contributed and a bundle of kind letters. One little girl writes me saying, among other things, "We will never be able to repay you what we truly owe you in gratitude or appreciation." Greetings from the little Albertans! It went straight to my heart. Even today, I cannot bring back this memory without a shiver running through me.[76]

Testimonies of this kind abound in Groulx's correspondence and it would be sheer fastidiousness to undertake a complete inventory of them. However, we can already observe the profound influence he exercised among the French minorities, who saw in him an unconditional ally.

76. Lionel Groulx, *Mes Mémoires, Tome III*, p. 353–354.

Chapter Four

The Franco-Ontarians and Regulation 17: The Awakening of the Nation

THE REGULATION 17 CRISIS (1912–1927) is considered even today as a foundational event for the Franco-Ontarian[1] identity. In fact, it was during those years of conflict that some of the most important Franco-Ontarian institutions were born, the Association canadienne-française d'éducation d'Ontario (ACFEO) and the daily, *Le Droit*, among them. The French Canadians of Ontario thus provided themselves with a common voice for their struggle against the assimilating policies of the Ontario government. By virtually prohibiting the use of French in the schools, the provincial government was able to garner the support of the Anglo-Protestant extremists (found principally in the Orange Lodges) and the anglophone Catholics (for whom certain Irish bishops had become the spokesmen).

According to René Dionne, the schools conflict allowed Franco-Ontarians "to forcefully affirm their collective identity."[2] However, this episode, which at times came to resemble an epic battle, did not affect only the Franco-Ontarians. It belongs, rather, to the larger history of all of French Canada. Indeed, several French-Canadian nationalist groups, both inside and outside Ontario, became involved, or at least interested, in the Regulation 17 crisis. As far as Québec was concerned, it did not stay out of the schools conflict either. Far from it. Many came to the defence of the Franco-Ontarians in their fight against adversaries who were as numerous as they were intractable. In Québec, prelates, journalists and politicians sought in various ways to lend a hand to their "oppressed brothers" in Ontario. Several famous names can be recognized among them: Cardinal Bégin of Québec City, Archbishop Bruchési of Montréal, Henri Bourassa, politician and founder of *Le Devoir*, as well as Olivar Asselin, journalist, president of the Société Saint-Jean-Baptiste de Montréal and militant in every cause.

1. The terms "Franco-Ontarian" and "French Canadian from/in Ontario" are interchangeable in the context of this chapter.
2. René Dionne, "La littérature franco-ontarienne: esquisse historique," in Cornelius J. Jaenen, ed., *Les Franco-Ontariens* (Ottawa: Presses de l'Université d'Ottawa, 1993), p. 357. See also René Dionne, "1910: Une première prise de parole collective en Ontario français," in *Cahiers Charlevoix 1: Études franco-ontariennes* (Sudbury: Société Charlevoix and Prise de parole, 1995), p. 15–124; David Welch, "Early Franco-Ontarian Schooling as a Reflection and Creator of Community Identity," *Ontario History*, Vol. 85, No. 4 (December 1993), p. 321–347. For a complete history tracing the development of the Franco-Ontarian schools crisis, consult the following titles: Gaétan Gervais, "Le Règlement XVII (1912–1927)," *Revue du Nouvel-Ontario*, No. 18 (1996), p. 123–192; Robert Choquette, *Langue et religion: Histoire des conflits anglo-français en Ontario* (Ottawa: Éditions de l'Université d'Ottawa, 1977), 268 p.; Victor Simon, Le Règlement XVII: sa mise en vigueur à travers l'Ontario, 1912–1927 (Sudbury: Société historique du Nouvel-Ontario, Documents historiques No. 78, 1983), 58 p.

Sometimes the gestures of sympathy came from the highest political spheres: even the Premier of Québec, Lomer Gouin, intervened in the crisis to try to make his Ontario counterpart back down. The Franco-Ontarians would of course also receive the indefatigable support of Lionel Groulx, the rising star of the French-Canadian nationalist movement who would soon be at its helm, succeeding none other than Bourassa himself.

In 1912, when the schools conflict broke out, Groulx was a teacher at the *collège* in Valleyfield. He was not very well known at that time, but within fifteen years, owing to his appointment as the first Chair of Canadian History at Université Laval de Montréal, his taking on the directorship of *L'Action française* and his numerous interventions on behalf of the Franco-Ontarian resistance, he stood at the forefront of French-Canadian intellectual life. During those years of doing battle, he developed an important social network in French Ontario and communicated regularly with the principal leaders of the resistance to Regulation 17. Groulx saw himself as a sort of intermediary between the nationalist militants of Québec and those of Ontario. These contacts allowed him to deepen his understanding of French Ontario and, at the same time, increase his influence with some of its elites.

Abbé Groulx saw the schools crisis as a catalyst for what he considered to be an "awakening" of the French-Canadian nation. The Franco-Ontarian struggle was part of a series of events that, starting with the Boer War of 1899, had triggered the rebirth of the nationalist movement. Unlike the other schools conflicts that the French minorities had experienced in the period following 1867, the Regulation 17 crisis took place just when Groulx was starting to hold an increasingly important position in the nationalist movement. The crisis afforded him the opportunity to manifest, for one of the first times ever, the multi-faceted nature of his public persona: on the one hand, immediately after the resolution of the conflict, Groulx, became one of the earliest historians of Regulation 17, dedicating an entire chapter in the second volume of his *Enseignement français au Canada*[3] to it; on the other hand, he was for many years a strongly committed participant in the resistance movement itself. The schools crisis allowed Groulx to play, no doubt, for the first time, a polemicist role he would subsequently never abandon. He charged himself with the mission of alerting Québec opinion—through the skilful use of lectures, newspapers, reviews and even literature—to the tragic element in the Franco-Ontarian situation and compelling Quebecers to display greater national solidarity toward their "oppressed brothers."

During this tumultuous second decade of the twentieth century, Regulation 17, together with the Conscription Crisis of 1917–1918, played a determining role in the development and refinement of Lionel Groulx's nationalist ideology. He believed he was witnessing before his very eyes the playing out of a critical

3. Lionel Groulx, *Enseignement français au Canada, Tome II: Les Écoles des minorités* (Montréal: Éditions Granger Frères, 1935), 272 p.

episode in the epic struggle for *survivance*, which the French Canadians had been leading since the Conquest of 1760. At the same time, he assigned to Franco-Ontarians the responsibility of raising awareness throughout the entire French-Canadian nation. Naturally, Groulx did not delight in the "persecution" engaged in by the Ontario government. However, he felt that the schools conflict could convey to French-Canadian opinion, unresponsive and even indifferent for far too long, the true measure of the threat hanging over the future of French civilization in America. Thus, Groulx considered Regulation 17 a strangely salutary crisis, willed by Providence and meant to impel French Canadians all across the country toward greater national solidarity.

Groulx and French Ontario: Contacts and Connections

In Ottawa

The contacts Groulx maintained in Franco-Ontarian nationalist groups were many and, sometimes, very personal. Starting in 1913, he undertook a long series of research trips to the public archives in Ottawa for the purposes of his historical work. During these trips, he had many decisive encounters. His first stay in the capital, furthermore, did not go unnoticed. His *Croisade d'adolescents*, a book about the beginnings of the Association catholique de la jeunesse canadienne (ACJC) in Valleyfield at the turn of the century, had been published the previous year and was already starting to earn him a certain popularity in nationalist circles.[4] The ACJC groups in the Ottawa region took advantage of his first visit to the capital by inviting him to speak, to a very small gathering, he explained later in his *Mémoires*, on the origins of the association.[5] It was also during this trip that he began a deep and long-lasting friendship with a young Oblate destined to become a cardinal in Québec, Rodrigue Villeneuve. During the 1910s and 1920s, the future primate of the Canadian church, affectionately dubbed le *petit père Villeneuve* by Groulx, remained among his principal "informers," so to speak, providing him with numerous details on the various incidents of the Franco-Ontarian crisis, as experienced in the federal capital. Villeneuve had a lengthy acquaintance with the French minorities. After spending many years among the Oblates in Ottawa, he became the first bishop of the new diocese of Gravelbourg, Saskatchewan in 1930, before being promoted to archbishop of Québec the following year and cardinal in 1933. Groulx's admiration for Villeneuve remained constant up until the Second World War, when a strong divergence of opinion over Canada's participation in the war provoked an irreparable rift between the two former comrades-in-arms.[6] The

4. Lionel Groulx, *Une Croisade d'adolescents* (Québec: Imprimerie de l'Action sociale, 1912), 264 p.
5. Lionel Groulx, *Mes Mémoires, Tome I: 1878–1920* (Montréal: Éditions Fides, 1970), p. 215–216.
6. See Lionel Groulx, *Mes Mémoires, Tome I*, p. 216–217, 240; Lionel Groulx, *Mes Mémoires, Tome IV: 1940–1967*, p. 221–232.

close relationship that had formed between the two men even prompted them, in 1915, to make a long journey together to Acadia, which left a deep impression on Groulx's mind. Villeneuve then became, under Groulx's direction, one of *L'Action française*'s most faithful collaborators. From his post in Ottawa, the Oblate joined the many defenders of the Franco-Ontarian minorities who wrote in its pages.

Of all Groulx's Franco-Ontarian connections, Villeneuve was without a doubt the one who supplied him with the most information (and opinions) on the development of the Regulation 17 crisis in Ottawa. Indeed, Villeneuve sent Groulx a veritable saga of the most decisive episodes in the schools tragedy. For example, in a long missive of sixteen pages that spared no details, he recounted the famous "hatpin affair." In January 1916, several women, mothers of families, armed with their hatpins, surrounded École Guigues in Ottawa in order to prevent the president of the "Petite Commission," Arthur Charbonneau, from taking possession of it. This "Petite Commission," appointed by the provincial government in 1915, had received a mandate to replace the duly elected—and, for the most part, French-Canadian—Commission des écoles catholiques, which, for its part, was refusing to comply with Regulation 17. The Franco-Ontarian resistance shouted down the "usurper" school board, whose legitimacy it did not recognize. The mothers had mobilized to come to the defence of the two teachers at École Guigues, Béatrice and Diane Desloges, who had decided to defy a court order that prohibited them from setting foot in the school. The "siege of École Guigues" concluded with the stunning victory of these women, who forced Charbonneau, and the police who had come to back him up, to beat a retreat.

In describing this colourful episode to Groulx, Father Villeneuve did not hide his admiration for the coup achieved by the "amazons" of École Guigues, as he called them. His reports were almost blow-by-blow accounts, sent barely a few days after each event:

> I have to write and tell you something of the deeds and actions of the race in Ottawa. We are truly living epic days! You *write* history; here, people are *making* history! This siege of École Guigues is at the same time high comedy and most admirable heroism. One would want to write a book about it.[7]

At the same time, Villeneuve confided that he did not hold the president of the "Petite Commission" in very high esteem: Charbonneau was, in his opinion, an "absolute viper," whose conduct resembled that of "a base character, by virtue of his language and his lack of honour."

In another letter, more than twenty pages in length, the Oblate described to Groulx the debate sparked by the intervention of the Archbishop of Montréal, Paul

7. Letter from Rodrigue Villeneuve to Lionel Groulx, BAnQ, FLG, P1/A,3696, January [6, 7 or 8], 1916.

Bruchési, in the Franco-Ontarian crisis.[8] In September of 1915, at the request of Charles-Hugues Gauthier, Archbishop of Ottawa, Msgr. Bruchési had gone to the federal capital to negotiate a compromise on the schools question with the provincial government. According to Villeneuve, Gauthier had appealed to his Montréal counterpart in order to avoid having to commit himself on the schools crisis. Bruchési had then tried to have the agreement accepted by the Franco-Ontarians. But Villeneuve pointed out that the means the prelate had used to achieve this were not very edifying: claiming that the government had refused all dialogue with ACFEO, Bruchési, unbeknownst to the Association, had spoken directly to a group of parish priests in the capital, threatening to withdraw the support they received from the Québec bishops if they rejected the proposed agreement. The Ottawa clergy, refusing to act behind ACFEO's back, had opted instead to despatch two representatives to the Québec episcopate to find out from a reliable source its position on Bruchési's compromise. When Bruschési learned of the Franco-Ontarian delegation's purpose in Québec, he was livid. Obviously needing to salvage something from the wreckage, the Archbishop agreed to meet with Napoléon Belcourt, one of ACFEO's directors. Belcourt, who rejected the government agreement, asked him, with all the respect due his ecclesiastic rank, to kindly mind his own business (Villeneuve expressed some doubt here as to the reliability of his sources). By this point, the representatives of the Ottawa clergy, having conferred with the Auxiliary Bishop of Québec, Msgr. Roy, were back in the capital. Roy had advised them not to capitulate and to reject the provincial government's agreement, thus dealing a severe blow to the credibility of Archbishop Bruchési, who had claimed he was speaking on behalf of the entire Québec episcopate.

Unfortunately, Villeneuve does not provide Groulx with any details describing the nature of the compromise. There is, however, a reference to it in the second report on the Franco-Ontarian schools crisis, drawn up for the benefit of Rome by the Apostolic Nuncio to Canada, Msgr. Pellegrino Stagni, in December of 1915. It states that Bruchési had advised the priests to put up with the "Petite Commission" until such time as the courts ruled on its legitimacy. (The Privy Council in London endorsed the elected Commission the following year, and the "Petite Commission" was abolished.) In return for the clergy's support, the Ontario government had reportedly promised to assume all the court costs incurred by the two parties.[9] Villeneuve indicated that ACFEO had in fact rejected this compromise because the *modus vivendi* proposal had only been made on the good faith of a civil servant. The government had never made a formal commitment. (Stagni was, moreover, dismayed that Bruchési's "wise counsel" had been rejected.) Basically, Villeneuve added, no real solution had been put forward to

8. Letter from Rodrigue Villeneuve to Lionel Groulx, BAnQ, FLG, P1/A,3696, November 1915.
9. Pellegrino Stagni, *The View from Rome: Archbishop Stagni's 1915 Reports on the Ontario Bilingual Schools Question*, translated from the Italian by John Zucchi (Montréal and Kingston: McGill-Queen's University Press, 2002), p. 100.

deal with the problem of the Anglo-Protestant inspectors. They had to continue to be admitted into the Franco-Catholic schools.

Villeneuve had not witnessed these events, but still claimed he could guarantee the accuracy of the story, "having received it from various individuals who were involved." Groulx, from his side, replied that on this matter he had received "a version from another individual, an important player, perhaps the principal one in the little melodrama that had been acted out in Ottawa." Was it Bruchési? Groulx was not so indiscreet as to reveal the identity of this "important player." He did claim, however, that this other version of the facts did not in the least correspond to the one given by Villeneuve. In closing, he in turn acknowledged the wisdom of rejecting Bruchési's compromise.[10]

Groulx and Villeneuve also had occasion to commiserate at length about the setbacks suffered by the representatives of the Franco-Ontarian cause in Rome, setbacks largely due, in their view, to the damaging intervention of the Irish lobby with the Holy See. Villeneuve told Groulx how, for example, Father M.J. Whelan, one of the spokespersons for the Irish group in Ottawa, had pressed for the Catholic School Board to be separated into its two linguistic components and for the same to be done with the University of Ottawa. The hitch was that the Irish demanded an equal share of the resources, even though both institutions were dominated mainly by French Canadians.[11]

In September of 1916, Benedict XV sent a letter to the Bishops of Canada, entitled *Commisso divinitus*, in which he asked the Ontario clergy to put an end to the language conflict that was dividing them. Even as he acknowledged the right of French Catholics to be taught in their own language, the Pope nevertheless concluded that the Ontario government had the authority to require all the students in the province to learn English. What mattered more than anything, he insisted, was that nothing should happen to jeopardize the existence of the separate schools in Ontario.[12] This pontifical missive, which did not side clearly with either the French Canadians or the Irish, sowed consternation, indeed, disillusionment, among the Franco-Ontarians. At least, that is the impression that emerges from Villeneuve's analysis of it:

> The people at ACFEO still don't know what to do . . . The letter from the Holy See [seems] to condemn all that we have done [and] blocks a good many courses of action.

10. Letters from Rodrigue Villeneuve to Lionel Groulx, BAnQ, FLG, P1/A,3696, October 24, 1915; from Lionel Groulx to Rodrigue Villeneuve, BAnQ, FLG, P1/A,3696, November 5, 1915.
11. Letters from Rodrigue Villeneuve to Lionel Groulx, BAnQ, FLG, P1/A,3696, February 24, 1915, January 13, 1917. See also Robert Choquette, *La Foi gardienne de la langue en Ontario, 1900–1950* (Montréal: Bellarmin, 1987), p. 123.
12. This letter is reproduced in Pellegrino Stagni, *The View from Rome*, p. 109–114. On the confrontations between French-Canadian and Irish Catholics in Rome, consult Yvan Lamonde, "Rome et le Vatican: La vocation catholique de l'Amérique française ou de l'Amérique anglaise?" in Jean-Pierre Wallot, ed., with collaboration by Pierre Lanthier and Hubert Watelet, *Constructions identitaires et pratiques sociales* (Ottawa: Presses de l'Université d'Ottawa and Centre de recherche en civilisation canadienne-française, 2002), p. 324–343.

> May it please heaven to spare this unfortunate people of ours from being greatly affected in its faith. What an abyss we have been thrown into . . . I have to admit that here, no matter how we try to console one another or to retrieve all the principles that faith, history and reason can offer, dark clouds still gather on our horizon.[13]

At least, Villeneuve added, the Irish did not seem any more satisfied with the Pope's directive than the Franco-Ontarians, although that was little consolation. Groulx, in his reply to Villeneuve, concurred. The Holy See's intervention in the schools crisis, rather than rekindling hope, had left them feeling totally let down in Montréal. He did not conceal from his friend that he was finding the pontifical pill extremely difficult to swallow:

> I did not think it could be that hard to obey the Pope's word. This whole venture has made me almost charitably inclined toward those Catholics in other countries whom I sometimes considered quite insubordinate and quite arrogant. It is hard to exaggerate the regrettable impression this document has created among the laity. Their disaffection with Rome and with the Pope has unfortunately increased significantly. I know there was very negative talk, on the day itself and on the days following, in the offices and in the restaurants. People did not hesitate to accuse the Roman court of deferring totally to Anglo-Saxon influence.[14]

Like a good ultramontane priest, Groulx tried to defend the sovereign pontiff against the bitterness of his lay detractors, including, among others, Édouard Montpetit of Hautes Études commerciales. He tried to show them that the Pope's letter was only advising moderation among Catholics themselves, and that nothing obliged French Canadians to be more lenient with the Ontario government; that Franco-Ontarians could only maintain peace if their adversaries did as much; and that "Rome would not impose on us this immoral thing of going like lambs to the slaughter." He admitted, however, that he was having a hard time persuading himself to believe his own words: "My God! It was not very forceful or convincing. But, anyway, I did my best."

Lionel Groulx's contacts in the federal capital were not limited, however, to Rodrigue Villeneuve. His network of acquaintances in Ottawa was broad and included some regular and some occasional correspondents, such as Oblate Georges Simard of the University of Ottawa. At Groulx's request, Simard accepted responsibility for the Franco-Ontarian column in *L'Action française* in 1920, using the pseudonym Aurèle Gauthier. Furthermore, during each of his visits to Ottawa, Groulx was hosted by Joseph-Alfred Myrand, pastor of Paroisse Sainte-Anne,

13. Letter from Rodrigue Villeneuve to Lionel Groulx, BAnQ, FLG, P1/A,3696, November 4, 1916.
14. Letter from Lionel Groulx to Rodrigue Villeneuve, BAnQ, FLG, P1/A,3696, November 20, 1916. See also Lionel Groulx, *Mes Mémoires, Tome 3: 1926–1939*, p. 132.

whom he described in his *Mémoires* as "the echo chamber where all the political and ecclesiastical news reverberated." It is noteworthy also that whenever he visited the capital region, he rarely missed an opportunity to pay a visit to his former spiritual director, Sylvio Corbeil, who had been appointed principal at the École normale (teachers' college) in Hull in 1909.[15]

Abbé Groulx also socialized with journalists like Jules Tremblay, the founder in 1912 of Ottawa's short-lived *La Justice* whose sole objective was to combat the authors of Regulation 17.[16] This feisty newspaper disappeared in 1914, a year after the daily *Le Droit* was founded, as it seemed nationalist circles in Ottawa did not want to spread their energies too thin. Groulx furthermore developed numerous allies at *Le Droit*, one being Fulgence Charpentier,[17] but also—and especially—Oblate Charles Charlebois, publisher and founder of the new Franco-Ontarian daily. Often described as the mainspring of the resistance to Regulation 17, Father Charlebois continued to run the paper throughout the entire duration of the schools crisis and led the fight with uncommon tenacity. In his earlier years at the helm of *Le Droit*, he befriended Abbé Groulx and began a long relationship of correspondence with him. It appears that the first letters they exchanged were written shortly before Groulx became director of *L'Action française* in 1920. Like Villeneuve, the publisher of *Le Droit* kept his correspondent informed about the political situation in Ottawa, describing for him in particular what he saw as the "Irish peril":

> The Irish peril is more serious than most of our compatriots seem to think. These people stop at nothing in order to take over dioceses and parishes and communities. They are brazen in the pursuit of their goals.
>
> . . . And to think the Irish episcopate has more bishops than any other in the world. They work with one accord to have their views accepted in the Church through the influence they exert in Rome. They deride the submission made by the "French Catholics of Québec" under the leadership of their bishops to the Roman curia.[18]

The confidence Charlebois placed in Groulx's judgment was such that in 1928, he consulted him about hiring a replacement for Edmond Cloutier, Secretary of ACFEO, who was resigning that year and was another of Abbé Groulx's frequent correspondents.[19]

15. Letter from Georges Simard to Lionel Groulx, BAnQ, FLG, P1/A,3453, November 11, 1920; Lionel Groulx, *Mes Mémoires, Tome IV*, p. 252.
16. Correspondence between Lionel Groulx and Jules Tremblay, BAnQ, FLG, P1/A,3587, May 17, 1925 to May 23, 1927, 14 items.
17. Correspondence between Lionel Groulx and Fulgence Charpentier, BAnQ, FLG, P1/A,755, January 8, 1923 to May 31, 1952, 23 items.
18. Letter from Charlebois to Lionel Groulx, BAnQ, FLG, P1/A,746, January 15, 1928.
19. Exchange of correspondence between Charles Charlebois and Lionel Groulx, BAnQ, FLG, P1/A,746, January 15, 1928; between Lionel Groulx and Edmond Cloutier, BAnQ, FLG, P1/A,818, November 29, 1920 to November 2, 1934.

In Southern Ontario

During the schools crisis, Abbé Groulx still had relatively few contacts among the Franco-Ontarians in the northern part of the province. He corresponded briefly with the Bishop of Hailebury, Msgr. Élie-Anicet Latulipe, and with the apostolic vicar of Northern Ontario (Hearst), Msgr. Joseph Hallé.[20] Groulx's connections in the northern Franco-Ontarian communities were still few and far between during the 1910s and 1920s, although they did increase after the Second World War. However, by the early 1900s, Groulx had already developed numerous relationships with the activists in Kent and Essex counties, in the southern part of the province. These counties were situated in the diocese of London, which was ruled with an iron fist by Bishop Michael Francis Fallon, one of the most ardent supporters of Regulation 17 and one of the most vocal spokespersons of the Irish Catholic lobby with the Ontario government. One of Groulx's connections in Southern Ontario was none other than his old friend from the *collège* in Sainte-Thérèse, Alfred (*le Gros Fred*) Émery, a parish priest in Paincourt throughout the entire schools crisis.[21] Abbé Émery recounted to him in great detail the frequent and sometimes heated arguments he had with his implacable bishop. Through this source, Groulx discovered yet another dimension of the Franco-Ontarian battle for *survivance*. He learned, specifically, about how Bishop Fallon, one of the main protagonists in the schools crisis, behaved toward his French-Canadian priests and parishioners.

Relations between Émery and the combative bishop of London began to grow tense in 1912, when the pastor of Paincourt rallied to the support of a number of his colleagues who had addressed a petition to the Sacred Congregation of the Consistory to protest the excessive taxes Fallon was imposing on the parishes in his diocese. The following year, Émery came to Abbé Beaudoin's defence in a matter placed before the Sacred Roman Rota. Beaudoin had been trying to prevent Fallon from splitting his Ford City parish, Notre-Dame-du-Lac, by adding a parish in Walkerville. When the prelate fired back by depicting Beaudoin as an incompetent administrator and an agitator who had no respect for episcopal authority, Émery immediately came to the aid of his maligned colleague by praising his numerous pastoral qualities.

All these intrigues, along with Émery's fierce determination to openly denounce both Regulation 17 and its zealous Irish lobby, finally got the better of Fallon's sangfroid: he could tolerate the insolence of his subordinate no longer. In 1914, in a letter to the Apostolic Nuncio, Msgr. Stagni, he listed Émery among the nine "key agitators" in his diocese whom he accused of systematically seeking to undermine his authority. From that point onwards, Fallon hounded Émery with exceptional persistence. In 1917, the diocesan tribunal he had convened to

20. Letters from Élie-Anicet Latulipe to Lionel Groulx, BAnQ, FLG, P1/A,2137, October 7, 1920; letters from Joseph Hallé to Lionel Groulx, BAnQ, FLG, P1/A,1706, October 26, 1912 and undated letter.
21. Lionel Groulx, *Mes Mémoires, Tome II*: 1920–1928, p. 76.

re-establish order among his clergy ordered the dissident priest to apologize. Fallon went so far in his resentment as to accuse Émery of having called him simply by his first name, "Frank."[22] Groulx, in his *Mémoires*, records another episode that perhaps marked the apex of the conflict between these two bitter antagonists. One Sunday morning, during mass, Fallon stormed Émery's church. Émery, who had already ascended the pulpit, had to suffer a stream of insults from his bishop. Fallon then ordered the parishioners to bring their pastor back from the rectory, where he had in the meantime taken refuge. Groulx concluded his account by explaining that the Bishop had to "leave empty-handed in order to escape the worst," thereby implying that Émery's parishioners, or at least some of them, had decided they would rather disobey Fallon and defend their pastor.[23]

Abbé Émery made no effort at restraint when enumerating Fallon's character flaws to his friend Groulx: in his correspondence, he described his episcopal superior as a "Nero" of modern times, a "mortal demon," a "priest killer" who should be held responsible for having provoked in Ontario a conflict comparable to the war then raging in Europe! In Émery's mind, the Franco-Ontarian resistance took on the proportions of an epic struggle waged against a "tyrannical" adversary. Let us examine this excerpt from a letter he dispatched to Groulx shortly before appearing before Fallon's diocesan tribunal:

> We are still in the midst of the Fallonic wars; the persecution is starting up again like in the past. Kaiser Number Two [Fallon] has just set in motion the wheel of his tribunal which has only one purpose: suspension. I have been summoned to appear before the Sanhedrin on February 10 in order to come away more wounded than ever. Far less is known about the cause of the mortally wounded than about the cause of those who are less wounded: we do not have the same freedom to make our cause known. I am quite determined to allow myself to be suspended, for by acting thus, I am following the rules of canon law. . . . Msgr. Fallon, on that score, shows himself to be *profoundly ignorant*, you can see I'm not being flattering. He has the power and he wants to use it, at any cost. You haven't the least idea of this man; he is the most tyrannical person I have ever met in my life. You have only to be a French-Canadian priest to be an object of horror to him, deserving of the greatest torments of hell.[24]

Émery also confided to Groulx that he was not far from considering himself "[Fallon's] greatest enemy in the current battle."[25] Still in Kent and Essex

22. These episodes are recounted in Robert Choquette, *Langue et religion*, p. 142–155. See also Jack Cecillion, "Turbulent Times in the Diocese of London: Bishop Fallon and the French-language controversy, 1910–1918," *Ontario History*, Vol. 87, No. 4 (December 1995), p. 369–395.
23. Lionel Groulx, *Mes Mémoires, Tome III*, p. 173.
24. Letter from Alfred Émery to Lionel Groulx, BAnQ, FLG, P1/A,1270, February 1, 1915.
25. Letter from Alfred Émery to Lionel Groulx, BAnQ, FLG, P1/A,1270, May 4, 1914 to October 6, 1924.

counties, Abbé Groulx also corresponded with François-Xavier Laurendeau, the new pastor of the Ford City parish, a man who, however, shared neither the temperament nor the convictions of Émery. In 1917, Laurendeau found himself at the centre of the famous "Ford City affair," which arose when several of his parishioners decided to bar him from access to his own church. Laurendeau, we should explain, was one of the dozen priests whom Fallon considered loyal and who had managed to raise the ire of the strongest nationalist elements in the French-Canadian community of Southern Ontario.[26] Irony of ironies, the Ford City pastor was another of Groulx's old *collège* friends. He, along with Alfred Émery, had even given him, in 1906, a portion of his mass stipends to help pay for his first study trip to Europe. That Groulx had ties of friendship with two such opposite minds, ideologically speaking, must surely have caused him much heartbreak. Also, although it saddened Groulx that Laurendeau seemed to pledge Fallon his loyalty, albeit perhaps a somewhat faint-hearted loyalty, he never reproached him for it, as far as we know.[27] Even during the worst of the Regulation 17 crisis, their correspondence (at least the portions of it that remain extant) barely touched on the schools conflict.

Laurendeau invited Groulx, all the same, to address his parishioners while on a speaking tour in Kent and Essex counties in 1924.[28] Abbé Émery, on the other hand, was far less indulgent toward Laurendeau and did not refrain from letting Groulx know what he really thought about the conduct of their former classmate. It should be pointed out that Laurendeau was also the secretary of the diocesan tribunal Fallon had set up to discipline Émery and the other dissident priests who persisted in accusing him of intolerance toward the Franco-Ontarians in educational and religious matters. In this regard, Laurendeau's conduct left Émery totally baffled:

> With respect to our friend Frank, you could say he's an unusual fellow; alone in his class, he is neither for the French Canadians nor against them, neither for or against anyone, everyone is in the wrong. He is the only one following the right path. He doesn't listen to reason, condemns all French-Canadian newspapers and does not endorse the English[-language ones]; furthermore, he only reads the *London Free Press*, which never deals with any serious questions, so it is a safe bet for avoiding controversy.
>
> He is one of the judges who condemned the French-Canadian priests suspended last summer, he is one of our judges. How edifying. Come and be judged by Frank if you wish or come and ask him for guidance on the current issue if you

26. Robert Choquette, *Langue et religion*, p. 147.
27. Lionel Groulx, *Mes Mémoires*, *Tome II*, p. 75–76.
28. Letters from François-Xavier Laurendeau to Lionel Groulx, BAnQ, FLG, P1/A,2147, [no date] and February 19, 1924. It should be noted, however, that this file does not contain a single letter from Groulx to Laurendeau.

> want a fair and definite answer. No need to tell you he doesn't set foot on our turf; he would like to stay neutral from start to finish.[29]

Although Groulx did not go as far in his criticism of Laurendeau, the *maquis* temperament of his friend Émery in no way lessened his admiration for him. When a brain hemorrhage took his life in 1932, Groulx made a point of rendering him a final tribute by publishing his eulogy in *Le Devoir*. He portrayed him as a man of valour, whose courage had cost him more than his fair share of trials and sorrows:

> One can imagine the emotion felt by the patriotic pastor when the bilingual schools dispute broke out in French Ontario. A terrible tempest threatened to knock down what appeared to him as the indispensable bulwark of the faith of his people. . . . He was not a man to back down from resistance. As the struggle got under way, he very soon took on a kind of leadership role. He was perhaps too loyal and too spontaneous to be able to avoid all imprudence. He brought upon himself grave and difficult trials, which caused him dreadful suffering. Providence, it is true, saw fit to vindicate him at times and even to grant him triumphs. This colossus, still young and nurturing a vision of action, nevertheless came away from the melee broken and mortally wounded.[30]

Besides keeping up correspondence with Émery and Laurendeau, Abbé Groulx communicated regularly with Doctor Damien Saint-Pierre, one of the organizers of the Ford City demonstration in 1917 and founder, in 1923, of Club Lasalle. Their first exchanges by letter seem to date back to the beginning of the 1920s, when Groulx took over the directorship of *L'Action française*. Saint-Pierre was one of the review's most faithful readers and had taken it upon himself to see to its circulation in his neck of the woods. He constantly sent Groulx subscriptions and congratulatory and encouraging messages.[31] But he was not unaware that his own pastor, François-Xavier Laurendeau, the same whom he himself had fought against a few years earlier, was an old classmate of Groulx's. When he chatted about this with the director of *L'Action française*, his tone remained generally respectful, sometimes even forgiving. Was it to avoid offending the review's director that he showed such moderation? Or was it rather that Laurendeau had finally found the road to Damascus and had rallied to the nationalist cause? At times Saint-Pierre seemed to feel genuine sympathy for his pastor, who constantly had to deal with a superior as irascible as Bishop Fallon: "I know that the *Dictatorship*,

29. Letter from Alfred Émery to Lionel Groulx, BAnQ, FLG, P1/A,1270, January 5, 1915.
30. This text, appearing originally in the February 2, 1932 issue of *Le Devoir*, was reproduced in Lionel Groulx, *Mes Mémoires, Tome III*, p. 174–179.
31. Letters from Damien Saint-Pierre to Lionel Groulx, BAnQ, FLG, P1/A,3346, April 20, 1923, May 22, 1923, December 9, 1923, January 7, 1925.

the reign of TERROR, weighs heavily on his shoulders. The current administration causes him much mental anguish."[32] At other times, he had difficulty concealing a point of irony when describing what he perceived as Laurendeau's new attitude toward the Franco-Ontarian resistance:

> People like your classmate . . . fought us fiercely in the old days . . . They saw in those combatants, imported from Québec, protagonists on our shores bringing those "damned nationalist ideas."
>
> These same individuals declare [today] that we will not have peace in our sad diocese until the day when the great persecutor of our people [obviously, Fallon], has left us for a better place.[33]

Saint-Pierre added that the antagonists of yesterday asked nothing more now than to renew their bond with the "luminous beacon of the old province of Québec" by inviting speakers from the metropolis who could come and offer Franco-Ontarians in the southern part of the province "moral and intellectual support."

Just a few months after these exchanges, in the spring of 1924, Abbé Groulx travelled to Southern Ontario to offer a series of talks—at the requests of Laurendeau and Émery, no less. During this stay, Groulx was, quite in spite of himself, thrust into the middle of a dispute that was threatening to split the Franco-Ontarian resistance in Kent and Essex. It is difficult to determine the origin of it, or even its exact nature, but it seems the two main opponents were Damien Saint-Pierre and Joseph de Grandpré. The latter was secretary of the Ligue des Patriotes, founded in 1922 for the purpose of establishing an independent French school in Windsor, École Jeanne-d'Arc (not to be confused with the famous École Jeanne-d'Arc in Pembroke). In a letter to Groulx, Saint-Pierre lamented the fact that his former comrade-in-arms insisted on harbouring a grudge. Grandpré had become "intransigent to the extreme," he said, and could not accept that adversaries of the nationalists (like Abbé Laurendeau, apparently) could change course and "evolve quickly toward the cradle of their origins." For his part, Grandpré, who was also corresponding with Groulx, accused Saint-Pierre and the Club Lasalle of knowingly and systematically sabotaging École Jeanne-d'Arc's efforts, under the pretext that it had not obtained the support of ACFEO. Club Lasalle, furthermore, he reported, had appropriated the right to receive most of the guests of note from Québec, who were unaware that the school even existed. According to Grandpré, there was a great deal at stake:

> Given the particular nature of the campaign of lies and calumny that a small group is mounting against the school, each time our friends from the East [i.e., from

32. Letter from Damien Saint-Pierre to Lionel Groulx, BAnQ, FLG, P1/A,3346, October 29, 1923 (underlined in the original; the capital letters are the author's).
33. Letter from Damien Saint-Pierre to Lionel Groulx, BAnQ, FLG, P1/A,3346, December 8, 1923.

> Québec] come here to speak to us about French and refrain from speaking about École Jeanne-d'Arc, founded for the survival of the French language in Windsor, it is a step backwards for the school, in the eyes of our people, and it becomes an uphill battle.

Joseph de Grandpré therefore invited Lionel Groulx to visit École Jeanne-d'Arc and asked him to use the opportunity of his stay in Kent and Essex to sensitize Québec opinion to his work.[34]

It is difficult to determine exactly how this conflict began, which may explain why Groulx hesitated to get involved despite exhortations from various quarters. Did he agree to visit École Jeanne-d'Arc? We don't know. We do know that he spoke at Club Lasalle. In the account of the trip, which he published in *L'Action française* shortly after getting back to Montréal, he tried, however, to remain above the fray. While mentioning Club Lasalle, he praised the patriotic work of École Jeanne-d'Arc in a passage no doubt intended to tread carefully on the sensibilities of Grandpré and his acolytes:

> There is also a concern among this people, that it receive instruction and be convinced of its duty. Proof lies in the founding of this school, École Jeanne d'Arc, an independent school, established in the city of Windsor. The fruit of much labour, this school has existed for only one year. But it is attended by more than one hundred students and already the demand from parents exceeds what the size of the school can accommodate; and it should especially be noted that it is heroically supported by ordinary people who must pay double the tax.[35]

⋆⋆⋆

These are just some of the Franco-Ontarian visits made by Groulx, who clearly sought to keep abreast of all the dealings and developments regarding the Regulation 17 crisis. The schools crisis was, furthermore, one of the most frequently discussed subjects at the rectory of Philippe Perrier, pastor of Paroisse Saint-Enfant-Jésus-du-Mile-End, in Montréal, where Groulx moved in 1917. A veritable den of nationalists, the Mile End rectory was a regular port of call for several of the star players in the movement from all across French Canada when they were passing through Montréal. Besides Henri Bourassa, who was one of Perrier's parishioners, activist nationalists like Omer Héroux, of *Le Devoir*, Antonio Perrault, of the Ligue d'Action française, Fathers Charlebois and Villeneuve of

34. Letters from Damien Saint-Pierre to Lionel Groulx, BAnQ, FLG, P1/A,3346, December 8, 1923; from Joseph de Grandpré to Lionel Groulx, BAnQ, FLG, P1/A,1623, March 30, 1924. Unfortunately, none of the letters Saint-Pierre and Grandpré received from Groulx have been preserved.

35. Jacques Brassier [pseudonym of Lionel Groulx], "Dans Kent et Essex," AF, May 1924, p. 297–309.

Ottawa, and the Archbishop of Saint-Boniface, Arthur Béliveau, were known to spend time there. The exchanges that took place at the rectory were exceptionally formative for Groulx and allowed him to fine-tune his nationalist ideology.[36]

In the eyes of the French-Canadian elites of Ontario, Abbé Groulx had become an influential figure whom they would do well to invite into their circles. In him they had found a faithful ally and an enthusiastic propagandist for their movement. In return, the field education Groulx received from the Franco-Ontarians with respect to French-English relations contributed enormously to the development of his own nationalist ideology. Very quickly, the rising star of the nationalist movement saw in the educational crisis the "shot in the arm" with which he hoped to draw French Canada out of its intellectual and national torpor.

The French-Canadian Nationalist Movement and the Catalyzing Role of Regulation 17

"It is therefore the solidarity of a whole race that affirmed itself around the [Franco-Ontarian] minority and its superb resistance. We were able to say, 'all of French America, at one point or another, was moved by this magnificent spectacle.'"[37] In 1935, that was how Lionel Groulx, in his major study of the French minority schools conflicts, described the intense feeling of national solidarity that, in his view, had been generated all across French Canada through the resistance to Regulation 17. He traced the rebirth of the nationalist movement back to the controversy surrounding Canada's participation in the Boer War in 1899, but there was another event, which occurred ten years later, that had taken the movement to a whole new level. It was the famous speech given by Henri Bourassa at the Notre-Dame Basilica in Montréal during the international Eucharistic Congress of 1910. Let us recall the context. Internationally, the hotly debated question of Canada's participation in a possible British war was making the news more and more frequently and was sowing division between the two "founding peoples" of the country. In 1896, in Manitoba, and in 1905, in Alberta and Saskatchewan, the educational rights of French Canadians had been considerably curbed. A renewed offensive could be imminent, this time in Ontario: for several years already, Bishop Fallon and certain members of the Irish Catholic clergy had been waging silent warfare on the Franco-Ontarians by seeking to establish the supremacy of the English language within the Ontario Church.

The situation of the French Canadians, especially of the French minorities, therefore seemed increasingly precarious. It was in this context that the

36. On the importance of the rectory at Mile End in Groulx's intellectual development, consult first Lionel Groulx, *Mes Mémoires, Tome II*, p. 201–207. Read also Georges-Émile Giguère, *Lionel Groulx: Biographie, "Notre État français, nous l'aurons!"* (Montréal: Bellarmin, 1978), 159 p.; Guy Frégault, *Lionel Groulx tel qu'en lui-même* (Montréal: Leméac, 1978), 237 p.; Susan Mann Trofimenkoff, *Action française: French Canadian Nationalism in the Twenties* (Toronto: University of Toronto Press, 1975), 157 p.

37. Lionel Groulx, *L'Enseignement français au Canada, Tome II*, p. 232.

Eucharistic Congress took place in 1910. During the Congress, the Archbishop of Westminster, Francis Bourne, gave a speech that appeared to endorse the assimilationist ideas of the most radical faction in the Anglo-Ontarian clergy. And he was bold enough to maintain that in America, in order to foster the spread of the Church, the language of Catholicism should be English. It was Bourassa who took on the responsibility of offering Bourne a rebuttal, denouncing this "argument of religious imperialism,"[38] to use Groulx's words. Providence, Bourassa stated, had mandated French Canada with a civilizing mission, that of propagating the Catholic faith in America. The French Canadians were, he maintained, the first apostles of Christianity on this continent; the vast majority of Catholic missionaries working throughout America had come from among the French-Canadian clergy. French Canadians, Bourassa argued, had an inalienable right to survive without assimilating to the Anglo-Saxon majority, without having to feign a different identity: if the Church wanted to foster its expansion, it ought to respect the customs and traditions of its people.[39]

The nationalist groups of Québec would probably have become involved in the Franco-Ontarian schools conflict whether Bourne had given his speech or not, but it would not be wrong to suggest that the Eucharistic Congress of 1910 provided an opportunity to galvanize energies and stimulate nationalist resolve all across French Canada. The remarks exchanged between Bourne and Bourassa did not go unnoticed in Ontario, particularly in the Irish episcopate. Bishop Fallon, after reading the reports on the Congress, accused the founder of *Le Devoir* of having "triggered a brutal attack" against Cardinal Bourne, with whose sentiments he said he was, incidentally, in perfect agreement:

> His Grace presented the only line of conduct according to which the Catholic Church can succeed in winning Canada's influential classes . . . and as I wholeheartedly approve of Archbishop Bourne's attitude, I just as wholeheartedly reprove the conduct and the principles of Mr. Bourassa. I see him as the most dangerous influence in Canada today jeopardizing the best interests of the Catholic Church across the country.[40]

Emboldened by an endorsement from the hierarchy, Fallon redoubled the fervour of his crusade against the French schools of his diocese, indeed of the entire province. In the opposite camp, however, Bourassa was praised to the skies by the French-Canadian nationalist groups. In the Notre-Dame Basilica, Bourassa had in his large and spellbound audience, a thirty-two-year-old priest, Lionel Groulx,

38. Lionel Groulx, *Mes Mémoires, Tome II*, p. 198.
39. Henri Bourassa, *Religion, langue, nationalité: Discours prononcé à la séance de clôture du XXIe Congrès eucharistique à Montréal, le 10 September 1910* (Montréal: Le Devoir, 1910), 30 p.
40. Michael Francis Fallon, cited in Robert Choquette, *Langue et religion*, p. 100.

who was deeply impressed by this speech. In his mind, Bourassa had at that moment reached the pinnacle of his glory: he represented the leader, the great man who would be able to inspire his compatriots and bring about the long-awaited awakening of the French-Canadian nation. Here is how Groulx, several decades later, described what had been at stake in Bourassa's intervention and recalled what, for him, had been a great day:

> The Ontario schools battle is beginning. The Episcopal See of Ottawa is at stake, vigorously disputed by the Irish. Led and spurred by the pugilistic bishop of London (Ont.), Msgr. Fallon, these coreligionists are, everywhere in Canada and even as far away as in Rome, waging a silent but determined war on French-Canadian influence. Would it not be time now to bring to the attention of an exceptional public a debate that is contaminating the life of the Canadian Church? . . . Bourassa is making his way to the stand. In one smooth motion, the assistants rise. The people want to see, to hear. The police barrier is broken; there is general pushing in the nave, in the galleries. People leave their pews to press in as closely as possible to the choir. Those who have kept their places have only one choice now: to stand on their seats. I climb onto mine. The orator is there, on a rather wide platform surrounded by a gilded copper railing. He seems emotional, nervous. But his deep voice easily reaches the audience, now gathered round. And suddenly, a shiver runs through the crowd. Bourassa launches an attack against an argument, the one made by Archbishop Bourne. And this argument, barely understood, if at all, a few moments ago, strikes deeply at the passions dividing Irish and French-Canadian Catholics. An argument of religious imperialism that can be summarized in this master plan: make the English language, in an English-speaking country, the official and common language in which the Gospel will be preached. Bourassa has the topic he was looking for. His speech immediately gains momentum, and solemnity.[41]

Groulx then described the hero's welcome the crowd gave Bourassa. The founder of *Le Devoir* may have been speaking in defence of all French Canadians, but his remarks were naturally of particular interest to Franco-Ontarians. Here, Groulx places the Notre-Dame speech in the context of the hostilities that would soon break out in Ontario. In his opinion, the Regulation 17 crisis even had a salutary aspect since it made Québec aware of its responsibilities toward the French minorities. In the schools crisis, he saw nothing less than the hand of Providence. To his friend, Rodrigue Villeneuve, he even said he feared that a resolution of the conflict would come too quickly. He felt this would have risked destroying in its infancy the nationalist renaissance that French Canada was finally undergoing:

41. Lionel Groulx, *Mes Mémoires, Tome II*, p. 197, 198–199.

> Don't you find that the recovery is still going marvellously well in Québec? What services you rendered to us, you, our Ontario friends! When I look at the thing from that angle, this may be a bit arbitrary, but do you know that I would hardly count on a victory for you very soon? It seems to me this struggle has too much of a providential character. It is obvious that it is the shot in the arm meant to keep us awake, make us gather up our strength and once again set our sights on the future more resolutely. Now, Providence has not completed its work. If we are to see in this trial a force of salvation, it is quite possible that the blessing of persecution will be upon us for another twenty-five years.[42]

The Franco-Ontarian crisis, Groulx went even further in saying, was part of the "designs of Providence" and had the "purpose of drawing us out of our lethargy and saving our French soul from being absorbed."[43] Villeneuve, for his part, agreed with this analysis by Groulx:

> Dear old Québec has finally been shaken. A serious and heartfelt shift. It makes one cry for joy to finally see that it is no longer just individuals, but the whole mother Province who understands us and is starting to act. Perhaps we are inclined to be severe—as New France must have been in 1760 toward Old France—but the wounded heart loses patience more easily. Nevertheless, it is certain that what has happened chases all clouds away and softens the bitterness.[44]

Groulx was accordingly delighted with all the initiatives that showed the nationalist leaders of Québec to be in solidarity with the minorities. Naturally, Bourassa, "champion of the Franco-Ontarian minorities," earned the unconditional admiration of the young priest. Relations between Groulx and Bourassa became tense, however, at the start of the 1920s, the former espousing ideas that were deemed, in the eyes of the latter, to be too "separatist." It remains nevertheless true that for many years, Groulx considered Bourassa "the strongest and most eloquent leader of French Canada that the race had ever produced." *Le Devoir*, which the nationalist leader founded in 1910, represented, in his opinion, an indispensable contribution to the defence of the French-Canadian nation from one end of the country to the other.[45] In 1920, he praised the daily in *L'Action française*, emphasizing, among other things, the abundant efforts Bourassa had made to defend the French minorities:

> In 1910, it was . . . political education and a concern for the defence of French culture that prompted the founding of *Le Devoir*. The enemy is within and without.

42. Letter from Lionel Groulx to Rodrigue Villeneuve, BAnq, FLG, P1/A,3696, March 23, 1915.
43. Letter from Lionel Groulx to Rodrigue Villeneuve, BAnQ, FLG, P1/A,3696, December 30, 1916.
44. Letter from Rodrigue Villeneuve to Lionel Groulx, P1/A,3696, February 24, 1915.
45. Lionel Groulx, *Mes Mémoires, Tome II*, p. 206.

> Against us and against our minorities, attacks by the Anglo-Saxon majority are on the rise. All our constitutional rights are being questioned. We ourselves are seriously afflicted by national indifferentism. . . . *Le Devoir* has been a magnificent labourer for the nation's salvation. Once it existed, it was no longer possible to bleed the French minorities or to violate any of our rights in silent complicity. Anglo-Saxon imperialism saw a man rise up against its doctrines, a fighter of extraordinary energy, with ideas and with words; it found in Mr. Henri Bourassa its most formidable opponent.[46]

Bourassa was not the only one to receive congratulations from Groulx. Other militants sympathetic to the Franco-Ontarian cause, such as theologian Louis-Adolphe Pâquet and economist Édouard Montpetit, came to symbolize, in his mind, the awakening of the French-Canadian people.[47] In *L'Action française*, Groulx recalled as well the numerous fundraising campaigns led by the Association catholique de la jeunesse canadienne-française (ACJC) to come to the aid of the Franco-Ontarian schools.[48]

These are just some of the manifestations of the national "awakening" that Lionel Groulx attributed at least in part to the Regulation 17 crisis. The schools conflict was not, in his opinion, just the business of Franco-Ontarians. On the contrary, it was a determining episode in the history of the whole of French Canada. The French-Canadian nation being an "organic" entity in his mind, Groulx believed that the desecration of the educational rights of the minorities invariably constituted an attack on Québec, that is to say, on the ancestral home of the nation.

Groulx Intervenes in the Franco-Ontarian Crisis

The Franco-Ontarian School Penny

Groulx was not content to sit back and take note of the militant activity of his nationalist contemporaries. Far from it. Unlike the other schools conflicts, which the French minorities experienced in the nineteenth century and at the start of the twentieth, the Regulation 17 crisis provided Groulx with the opportunity to play a double role: besides being one of the first historians of the Franco-Ontarian crisis, he became a deeply involved participant in it. He may even be considered, without risk of exaggeration, the embodiment, as it were, of the national solidarity he wanted all of Québec to show to the Franco-Ontarians. Besides offering

46. Lionel Groulx, "Notre hommage au 'Devoir'," AF, January 1920, p. 30, 31.
47. See Lionel Groulx, *Mes Mémoires, Tome II*, p. 173–174, 180–181.
48. Lionel Groulx, "Les vingt ans de l'A.C.J.C.," AF, June 1924, p. 360–372; L'Action française, "Pour qu'on s'entr'aide," AF, December 1923, p. 321; Jacques Brassier [pseudonym of L. Groulx], "La vie de l'Action française: Nos groupes d'Action française et les persécutés," AF, November 1923, p. 311–312. See also Lionel Groulx, *L'Enseignement français au Canada, Tome II*, p. 230–231.

his debating, writing and speaking skills to the Franco-Ontarian resistance, Groulx sought at the same time to awaken the French Canadians of Québec to the enormity of the schools crisis and their responsibilities toward their "oppressed brothers."

In 1913, the Société Saint-Jean-Baptiste de Montréal, under the direction of Olivar Asselin, launched the *Sou de la pensée française* campaign. The project would raise funds to assist the daily, *Le Droit*, which the Oblates of Ottawa had just founded as a mouthpiece for the Franco-Ontarian resistance to Regulation 17.[49] A year earlier, Lionel Groulx, at that time a professor at the Valleyfield *collège*, had tried to launch a similar project, called the *Sou scolaire*. Rather than support the big Franco-Ontarian institutions, Groulx preferred instead to gather funds that would be handed over directly to the dissident Franco-Ontarian schools. He wanted all the children in the French schools in Quebec to make their contribution to the fund in the symbolic amount of one penny. It is hard to measure how successful this initiative actually was or to calculate the sums that were raised. But there is another reason why we should be interested in the campaign. What it shows us is the importance of the Franco-Ontarian crisis in the development of Groulx's nationalist ideology.

Groulx wanted to capitalize on the enthusiasm that was sweeping through nationalist groups across French Canada as the date of the Congrès de la langue française approached. It would take place in Québec in June of 1912. A few months earlier in March, he launched his project by publishing a long article in *Le Devoir* entitled "Le congrès de la langue française et le sou des tout petits."[50] It was in fact a fictional account in which the pupils of school Three in the parish of St. G in Québec received a "lesson in patriotism," their teacher encouraging them to contribute, through their offering, to the cause of the French minority schools.[51] In the preamble, Groulx wrote that "nothing could now prevent the 1912 Congrès from becoming the most magnificent awakening of our people ever to take place in our history." The success of the gathering would result, in his view, from "the sense of belonging that all of the French groups shared." It was not enough, Groulx believed, to make this "awakening" the business of the elites alone. All layers of the population, including children, should take part in it. We can observe here the pedagogical concern that motivated Groulx the educator at the time: "We seek a way to reach everyone, to bring the question of French even into the humblest home. Is there a surer way than to appeal to the children? If all

49. See Gaétan Gervais, "Le Règlement XVII"; Hélène Pelletier-Baillargeon, *Olivar Asselin et son temps: Le Militant* (Montréal: Fides, 1996), 780 p.

50. Lionel Groulx, "Le congrès de [la] langue française et le sou des tout petits," *Le Devoir*, March 2, 1912, p. 1.

51. Groulx reproduced part of this text, under the title, "Une leçon de patriotisme," in *Les Rapaillages*, a collection of stories which he published in 1916 (see Lionel Groulx, *Les Rapaillages* (Montréal : Le Devoir, 1916), 159 p.). It should be noted that the 1935 re-issue has a different title, "Le 'sou' des écoles ontariennes" (Lionel Groulx, *Les Rapaillages* (Montréal: Éditions Albert Lévesque, 1935), 139 p.).

that is needed is a little babble, we cannot deny that the little ones could become marvellous propagandists."

A few days after the article was published, Groulx received a letter from Abbé Émile Chartier, of the *collège* of Saint-Hyacinthe, with whom he had founded the ACJC some ten years earlier. "Bravo for your article in Saturday's paper!" he wrote. "Several of us here were moved to tears. I am recommending to the parish priests that they organize the school penny."[52] On what kind of scale was this project carried out in Québec? In his major study on the minority schools, Groulx did not hazard an evaluation of the amounts raised but said that several Québec bishops had recommended the "school denarius" to their flocks.[53] Apart from the amounts collected, however, it is the symbolic importance of this episode that should be retained. The *Sou scolaire* campaign was an eloquent demonstration of the national solidarity that, according to Groulx, ought to set the tone for Québec's attitude to Franco-Ontarians.

The Ninth Crusade

Robert Choquette has written that the French-Canadian nationalists of the start of the twentieth century were not "revolutionaries," but rather "crusaders."[54] In his view, the philosophy that drove them owed nothing to the modern concept of the sovereignty of the people. As we have already pointed out, in defending the Franco-Ontarians, Groulx and his contemporaries were adhering to an older, or at least more "traditionalist," understanding of the world, by virtue of which power and authority originated with a superior or "providential" entity. The metaphysical implications of such a premise are clear: French Canada was a nation whose existence had been willed by Providence. To try to assimilate Franco-Ontarians into the Anglo-Saxon majority represented, for these militant nationalists, an offence against natural law. The term "crusade" applies very well therefore to their campaigns. Groulx himself used the term liberally, as shown by the *Neuvième croisade* campaign, which he launched in 1914. Here is what he had to say about it several years later, in his *Enseignement français au Canada*:

> The appeal to the supernatural would take . . . forms that were even more poignant and perhaps more solemn. In 1914, on the morning of the day that a conference of the Association [canadienne-française] d'éducation [d'Ontario] was opening in Ottawa, the children from the parish in Walkerville [in Southern Ontario] went as one group to receive communion together. Soon afterwards, someone wrote in the Montréal paper, *Le Devoir*, "I wondered the other day whether this happening was not some kind of indication of the battlefield toward which all children in the

52. Letter from Émile Chartier to Lionel Groulx, BAnQ, FLG, P1/A,764, March 7, 1912.
53. Lionel Groulx, *L'Enseignement français au Canada, Tome II*, p. 231.
54. Robert Choquette, *La Foi gardienne*, p. 226.

> oppressed province should be directed. I began to dream of an annual communion, made on the same day, by all the little heroes who want to continue to protect their schools . . ."[55]

That "someone" who had written in *Le Devoir* was Groulx himself. The article, entitled "Pour la neuvième croisade," was published on May 12, 1914. The expression, which Groulx borrowed from René Bazin, communicated clearly the mystical character he wanted to confer on this initiative. The idea was to urge all the pupils in French Canada to take part in a general communion at the same time and on the same day, in order to "attempt a supreme intercession before God" in support of the Franco-Ontarian cause. The event was set for June 19, 1914, the feast of the Sacred Heart. Groulx sustained the hope that this communion would serve as a way to strengthen the bonds uniting all the French groups in the country, indeed, on the continent, and encourage Québec to become aware of its responsibilities toward the minorities:

> Who knows? I said to myself, that over there in the West, and closer to us in Acadia, where there are small, wounded peoples, where the same strength is needed because they must suffer the same pains, I said to myself that in these *petites patries* where loyalty to higher values is still a common virtue, the Ontario gesture will naturally find imitators. I said to myself that Québec, Québec which is the heart of the race and which seems to remember this a little better each day, Québec, where all French suffering will now resonate, Québec will without a doubt want to walk with the others and once more tighten the unbreakable bond of national solidarity.[56]

Actually it was Rodrigue Villeneuve who, from his post in Ottawa, had asked Groulx to draft this article for *Le Devoir*. If the goal of the *croisade* was to support the Franco-Ontarian cause in general, Villeneuve had a more specific objective in mind: to implore Providence to reverse the Mackell injunction prohibiting the Ottawa Catholic school board, largely dominated by French Canadians and an opponent of Regulation 17, from offsetting the decrease in government subsidies by borrowing on the financial markets. The day after the publication of the article in *Le Devoir*, Villeneuve shared with Groulx the favourable reactions it had elicited in the capital.[57] He furthermore let him know that ACFEO had promised to promote the *Neuvième croisade* throughout Ontario, especially among the parish priests. In the letter they addressed to the clergy shortly thereafter, the directors of the Association made it clear who the author of the project was, saying they

55. Lionel Groulx, *L'Enseignement français au Canada, Tome II*, p. 230.
56. Lionel Groulx, "Pour la neuvième croisade," *Le Devoir*, May 12, 1914, p. 1. The article would be reprinted a few days later in the Ottawa paper *Le Droit* (Lionel Groulx, "La neuvième croisade," *Le Droit*, May 2, 1914, p. 2) and in *Dix ans d'Action française* (Montréal: Bibliothèque de l'Action française, 1926), p. 22–28.
57. Letters from Rodrigue Villeneuve to Lionel Groulx, BAnQ, FLG, P1/A,3696, May 6, 1914 et May 18, 1914.

were "happy to respond to the sensitive suggestion that had been made . . . in *Le Devoir* on the previous May 12 by *M. l'abbé* L. A. Groulx."[58] After asking Groulx to persuade the educational institutions in Québec to follow in ACFEO's footsteps, Villeneuve himself became an ardent promoter of the crusade and was pleased with the numerous participants it gained in Ontario, Québec and elsewhere.[59]

Groulx saw himself increasingly as an intermediary between the nationalist circles in Québec and those in Ontario. To Abbé Chartier, he wrote, "We would really like to see the schools and *collèges* in Québec get involved in the movement and I am asked to promote it among my friends. Perhaps you will be able to do something in your area and then let Ottawa know you are joining." Chartier answered him almost right away that his superiors at the *collège* of Saint-Hyacinthe had entirely approved the general communion project, and asked him to convey their membership to ACFEO, which Groulx did without delay. He pointed out to Rodrigue Villeneuve that several individuals and institutions, in Québec, had rallied behind the Franco-Ontarians, including his students in Valleyfield and those of the *collège* of Saint-Hyacinthe. (It is worth noting, however, that Groulx asked Villeneuve not to mention the name of the *collège* in Valleyfield: "Here, any national question is suspect," he explained, "and I have not dared to attempt a general communion.") Even the review *L'Ami des sourds-muets* [Friend of the deaf and mute] in Montréal had got caught up in the enthusiasm of the campaign. Groulx asked Villeneuve to convey these details to *Le Droit*, and expressed his desire to see French Canadians in the Western provinces take part in the campaign as well.[60]

How many communicants participated in the *Neuvième croisade*? It is hard to say with any precision. In his *Mémoires*, Groulx referred to it as a mass movement: "Throughout French America," he wrote, "long lines of little communicants offered their solidarity to their little compatriots in distress."[61] One thing is certain: this episode allowed Lionel Groulx to carve out a significant place for himself among the French-Canadian nationalist elites and thereby to increase his own profile. Omer Héroux of *Le Devoir* even made Groulx one of his "sources," so to speak, asking him to keep him up to date on campaign developments, which is an indication of the importance of the intermediary role Groulx had started to play.

58. Alex. Grenon [secretary of the executive committee of ACFEO], "La Croisade Eucharistique," *Le Droit*, June 2, 1914, p. 2. Omer Héroux, of *Le Devoir*, after consulting Father Charlebois, of *Le Droit*, indicated to Groulx that the appeal to the Ontario pastors "had already provoked a warm response" (letter from Omer Héroux to Lionel Groulx, BAnQ, FLG, P1/A,1758, June 6, 1914).

59. Letter from Rodrigue Villeneuve to Lionel Groulx, BAnQ, FLG, P1/A,3696, May 18, 1914. See Rodrigue Villeneuve, "Croisade eucharistique," *Le Droit*, May 28, 1914, p. 1–2; Rodrigue Villeneuve, "Pour la neuvième croisade. L'article de M. l'abbé Groulx commenté à Ottawa – Une proposition du R.P. Villeneuve," *Le Devoir*, May 30, 1914, p. 11; Rodrigue Villeneuve, "La croisade eucharistique," *Le Droit*, June 18, 1914, p. 1.

60. Exchange of correspondence between Lionel Groulx and Émile Chartier, BAnQ, FLG, P1/A,764, June 1, 1914 to June 7, 1914; letter from Lionel Groulx to Rodrigue Villeneuve, BAnQ, FLG, P1/A,3696, June 5, 1914.

61. Lionel Groulx, *Mes Mémoires, Tome I*, p. 219.

Groulx sought by every means possible to strengthen the ties between French Canadians on either side of the Ottawa River.[62] The Valleyfield teacher had already become a full-fledged member of the resistance to Regulation 17 and had made a powerful contribution to awakening Québec to the scale of the crisis.

The Lecture: Another Means of Action

Groulx's growing reputation meant that he was increasingly sought after by activists in the French-Canadian cause. Following on the school-penny and ninth-crusade campaigns, Groulx was invited more and more frequently to give lectures in Ottawa on various subjects. From 1914 to 1926, Groulx spoke several times before the ACJC, the French-Canadian Institute and the Cercle littéraire of the University of Ottawa and at the Eastern Ontario teachers' conference. In the fall of 1916, the Fédération des femmes canadiennes-françaises invited him to make a presentation at a fundraiser event. The proceeds of the evening would be used to heat Ottawa's dissident French schools. Groulx accepted and gave a talk entitled, "L'éducation du patriotisme par l'Histoire." "Coal Evening," as the event was later dubbed, took place on October 15, 1916 and raised over $800. The speaker was flanked by two distinguished guests: to introduce him, Senator Philippe Landry, the president of ACFEO, and, to thank him, none other than the former prime minister Wilfrid Laurier, who was at the time the leader of the Opposition in the House of Commons.[63]

Groulx did not, however, limit his efforts to Ontario: he also kept the public in Québec informed about the schools crisis. He spoke in Vaudreuil, for example, in May of 1917. The conscription crisis, which was happening at the same time, coloured his remarks in a singular way and made him draw a comparison between what he saw as two simultaneous offensives against the rights of the French-Canadian people. Only a handwritten draft, with a great many corrections, survives. Groulx saved his harshest words to attack those French Canadians who were, in his view, so "hateful" as to encourage the Franco-Ontarians to suspend their cause until the end of hostilities in Europe: "It is appalling that these lackeys of politics and enlistment should come and tell us, don't make waves, it's the wrong time, wait 'til after the war . . . They advise moderation? Well then, let the gullible fools and hypocrites go and tell that to the murderers and get the murderers to take their advice first." After providing a background to the schools conflict and demonstrating the injustice of it, Groulx, by way of conclusion, entreated his

62. Letter from Lionel Groulx to Rodrigue Villeneuve, BAnQ, FLG, P1/A,3696, June 5, 1914.

63. See [Juliette Rémillard and Madeleine Dionne], *L'œuvre du chanoine Lionel Groulx. Témoignages: Bio-bibliographie* (Montréal: Publications de l'Académie canadienne-française, 1964), p. 141–145; letter from Amanda Walker-Marchand to Lionel Groulx, BAnQ, FLG, P1/A,2462, September 21, 1916; Gaétan Gervais, "Le Règlement XVII," p. 161; Lionel Groulx, *Mes Mémoires, Tome I*, p. 314–316, 323. A handwritten version of this talk has been preserved: Lionel Groulx, "Conférence de l'automne de 1916 pour le charbon des écoles d'Ottawa," BAnQ, FLG, P1/13, 06.

listeners to support the Franco-Ontarian resistance by reading their newspapers and contributing generously to their works.[64]

In January of 1924, at the request of the ACJC, he agreed to speak at Université Laval, the proceeds of the event going once again to the Franco-Ontarian schools. *Le Canada français*, published by the Société du parler français, reported the enthusiasm and warm welcome with which the audience greeted the speaker:

> The members of the cercle Casault of the A.C.J.C. had the happy idea of holding an evening for the benefit of the schools in Ontario. Thanks to the kind of impeccable organization that young people, when they put their mind to it, are always capable of, they succeeded in attracting a full house. It was a success on which they deserve to be congratulated. And, for a full hour, interrupted only by frequent applause, the speaker, with warm and contagious conviction and great mastery, and in a language full of charm and poetry, spoke of our homes, those *sacred stones* that are the increasingly necessary solid foundations of our entire social structure.[65]

A few months later, in April, Groulx went on a speaking tour in Kent and Essex counties in Southern Ontario, Bishop Michael Francis Fallon's fiefdom. We have already mentioned that this was in response to an invitation from his former classmates, Abbés Alfred Émery and François-Xavier Laurendeau. He spoke before crowds gathered at Windsor, Tilbury, Chatham, Belle-Rivière, Pointe-aux-Roches, Pointe-aux-Bouleaux, Paincourt and Rivière-aux-Canards. Father Charlebois of *Le Droit* said he was "overjoyed at the thought of the good this visit [would do] our compatriots who are so sorely tested in that part of Ontario."[66] Back in Montréal, Groulx published an account of the trip in *L'Action française*, expressing his dismay at the lack of interest Québec showed in the plight of French Canadians in the southern part of the province. The threat weighing on them, he wrote, was not just the result of their proximity to the United States, or even the assimilating policies of the English-language clergy and the provincial government: it was caused, at least in part, by the indifference of Québec, especially of its political class.

> Among the motives that have spurred this French people to remain so marvellously steadfast, we seek in vain the part played by intellectual or political Québec. . . . For too long we have abandoned to the Church alone the duty of remembering and helping. For too long, the province of Québec has behaved irresponsibly and

64. Lionel Groulx, "Causerie sur la question ontarienne," BAnQ, FLG, P1/13, 17; See [Juliette Rémillard and Madeleine Dionne], *L'œuvre du chanoine*, p. 143.
65. Laval, "Chronique de l'Université," *Le Canada français*, February 1924, p. 467. See also Nicolas Tillemont [pseudonym of L. Groulx], "La vie de l'Action française," AF, February 1924, p. 125.
66. Lionel Groulx, *Mes Mémoires, Tome II*, p. 75; letter from Charles Charlebois to Lionel Groulx, BAnQ, FLG, P1/A,746, April 16, 1924.

> turned in on itself, a stranger to ethnic solidarity, more caught up in its own rights than in its duty as the eldest son.[67]

From the beginning of the schools conflict, the Franco-Ontarian resistance could see that in Groulx they had a major ally. At the same time, Groulx, thrust into the leadership of the French-Canadian nationalist movement during the early years of the crisis, was frequently given the opportunity to showcase his speaking and debating talents. He had not yet, however, reached the height of his prominence. In addition to his historical works, which contributed to his renown, it was his tenure as director of *L'Action française*, from 1920 to 1928, that enabled him to make his mark as one of the key intellectual leaders of the nationalist movement. Groulx brought to that role his concern for French Ontario and made the schools crisis one of the principal dossiers chronicled by the review.

Lionel Groulx, *L'Action française* and the Franco-Ontarian Crisis

The Schools Conflict as Represented in the Review

In 1917, as we have already seen, the Ligue d'Action française created a monthly publication, *L'Action française*. Very quickly, under Lionel Groulx's direction, the review became one of the main voices in the French-Canadian nationalist movement.[68] The defence of the religious and educational rights of the French minorities, furthermore, occupied a place of privilege in its discourse. While Regulation 17 was in effect, the battle waged by the Franco-Ontarian resistance against the government in Toronto remained at the centre of the review's coverage of minority concerns. Strongly influenced by the thinking of its director, *L'Action française* developed a specific line of reasoning to justify the right of the minorities to *survivance*. It was founded on the notion that the ancestors of those living in the provinces with an English majority had belonged to the great "French Empire of America." French Canada, in the mind of Groulx and his collaborators, was a nation begotten by Providence and invested with an apostolic mission—namely, to keep the flame of Catholicism and French civilization alive in America. According to this reasoning, any effort to assimilate the descendants of the first apostles of Christianity in Ontario constituted nothing less than an affront to the divine plan.[69]

L'Action française, then, followed the development of the Regulation 17 crisis very closely and brought its unfailing support to the Franco-Ontarian resistance. The review repeatedly highlighted the activities of the institutions and major actors in the schools crisis. In 1923, a member of the Ligue d'Action française,

67. Jacques Brassier [pseudonym of L. Groulx], "Dans Kent et Essex," AF, May 1924, p. 298–299, 309.
68. On the origins and founding of *L'Action française*, consult Susan Mann Trofimenkoff, *Action Française*, p. 29–35.
69. See Michel Bock, "'Le Québec a charge d'âmes': *L'Action française* de Montréal et les minorités françaises (1917–1928)," RHAF, Vol. 54, No. 3 (Winter 2001), p. 345–384.

lawyer Antonio Perrault, was speaking at a banquet celebrating *Le Droit*'s tenth anniversary when he said of the Franco-Ontarian daily that it was the "comrade-in-arms of a review like *L'Action française*" and "was strengthening the French soul throughout Canada." The review frequently compared senators Philippe Landry and Napoléon Belcourt, past presidents of ACFEO, to the greatest political heroes of the French-Canadian nation, in particular, to Louis-Hippolyte La Fontaine, who had succeeded in defeating the assimilating aims of the 1841 Union. The review regularly offered its pages to the leaders of the Regulation 17 resistance, who used the opportunity to comment on the schools crisis and to expound on the justice of their cause. Lionel Groulx, believing that "the Ontario question could not help but gain from this," personally asked Senator Belcourt to contribute. In 1925, Belcourt provided an article on "La part réservée au bilinguisme dans l'Ontario." Two years earlier, Edmond Cloutier, secretary of ACFEO, recognizing the importance of sensitizing Québec opinion to the Franco-Ontarian situation, had offered a similar article. Groulx, for his part, had only been too happy to publish it.[70]

Nor did *L'Action française* fail to highlight the heroism of Jeanne Lajoie, a young teacher in Eastern Ontario, affectionately called the "Maid of Pembroke."[71] She had defied the authority of the bishop and the local school board by keeping École Jeanne-d'Arc open in contempt of Regulation 17. In the eyes of Lionel Groulx, Pembroke had become the symbol par excellence of the battle for *survivance* that all French Canadians had been waging since the Conquest:

> Pembroke! A name that will henceforth in our history stand for one of the many calvaries where our race has suffered. Pembroke will also be one of the places where the bold French-Canadian spirit will have rediscovered itself in order to shake off the yoke of its persecutors. [These persecutors] will see how separate school board trustees, all of them Knights of Columbus, tried to suppress the teaching of French by a coup. They will also see how the resistance was embodied in a heroic little teacher, *Mademoiselle* Jeanne Lajoie, and an honest worker, *Monsieur* Alfred Longpré, president of the Cercle Lorrain of Pembroke, whose infectious faith set the stage for this awakening.[72]

70. Antonio Perrault, "Pour "Le Droit"," AF, December 1923, p. 338. The review also celebrated *Le Droit*'s fifteenth anniversary, in 1928. See Jean Beauchemin, "Sur un anniversaire," *L'Action canadienne-française* (hereinafter ACF), April 1928, p. 247–249; Joseph Gauvreau, "Pour La Fontaine," AF, September 1917, p. 278; letter from Lionel Groulx to Napoléon Belcourt, BAnQ, FLG, P1/A,283, January 15, 1925; Napoléon Belcourt, "La part réservée au bilinguisme dans l'Ontario," AF, April 1925, p. 204-221; letter from Edmond Cloutier to Lionel Groulx, BAnQ, FLG, P1/A,818, 17 October 1923. See Edmond Cloutier, "Le bilinguisme dans l'Ontario," AF, November 1923, p. 286–287.
71. Translator's Note: Naming Jeanne Lajoie the "Maid of Pembroke" (in French, *la pucelle de Pembroke*) was an explicit reference to the title given to Joan of Arc: "Maid of Orleans" (in French, *Jeanne d'Arc, la pucelle d'Orléans*). Hence, also, the decision to name Pembroke's independent school École Jeanne d'Arc.
72. Jacques Brassier [pseudonym of L. Groulx], "La vie de l'Action française," AF, November 1923, p. 310.

The review also took part in a fundraiser to support the "independent school" in Pembroke. Groulx was pleased with the numerous groups who joined in this endeavour, especially the young people and students at Université de Montréal. The emerging consensus, as he saw it, around the need to rally behind the resistors in Pembroke, represented an excellent way of bringing together all young French-Canadian students:

> [Let young people] dream first of a federation that would unite the strength of all the French youth; let them connect with the young university crowd in Québec City and in Ottawa, with the Franco-American student circle in Boston. Running this federation should come before organizing any other groups and they themselves will be surprised at the positive energies it will be able to generate.[73]

ACFEO made a point of thanking *L'Action française* for its support in the defence of the "Maid of Pembroke." Moreover, École Jeanne-d'Arc became the subject of a great deal of negotiation between the Association and the Comité catholique du Conseil de l'instruction publique du Québec, negotiations whose developments Groulx could follow thanks to the information provided to him by Edmond Cloutier. ACFEO was of the opinion that the sorry state of the teaching of French in Pontiac, a predominantly English county in Québec, brought considerable harm to the cause of the militants in Pembroke. The two counties, although situated on either side of the interprovincial border, were nevertheless grouped together in one diocese. ACFEO feared that the problems faced by the teaching of French in Pontiac would serve to back the detractors of École Jeanne-d'Arc, especially as the Bishop of Pembroke, Msgr. Ryan, had recommended to his Franco-Ontarian flock that they should tolerate Regulation 17. ACFEO turned to the superintendant of public education for the province of Québec, Cyrille Delâge, in the hope that he would intervene to set an example by improving the situation of French in the schools in Pontiac. Edmond Cloutier, who recognized in this matter an excellent opportunity for Québec to lend a hand to the Franco-Ontarians, forwarded to Groulx all correspondence that had been exchanged between ACFEO and Delâge's office.[74] Now, the director of *L'Action française*, not wanting to attack the authority of the Bishop of Pembroke directly, showed great prudence in this matter. However, he recommended to ACFEO that they approach bishops François-Xavier Léonard of Rimouski and Joseph-Romuald Ross of Gaspé: "These are pretty much the bishops we can absolutely count on. And if the matter is to be brought before the Comité catholique du Conseil de l'instruction publique, it is urgent that these bishops be informed."[75]

73. *Ibid.*, p. 312. See also L'Action française, "L'affaire de Pembroke," AF, February 1923, p. 65.
74. Letter (and documents inserted as an appendix) from Edmond Cloutier to Lionel Groulx, BAnQ, FLG, P1/A,818, March 2, 1923.
75. Letter from Lionel Groulx to Edmond Cloutier, BAnQ, FLG, P1/A,818, March 8, 1923.

There was yet another battle *L'Action française* fought in defence of the educational rights of Franco-Ontarians, this one over numbers. The review wanted Franco-Ontarians to make use of the federal census of 1921 to proclaim loud and clear their presence in the province. French-Canadian nationalist circles throughout Ontario were worried about the formulation of the question regarding the "language commonly spoken." "Many French Canadians in the province," Charles Charlebois wrote to Groulx, "could be led into error by that question because, constantly mingling with an anglophone population, they do commonly speak English outside the home."[76] In the context of the fight against Regulation 17, the Franco-Ontarians could not afford to let their demographic weight be minimized.

Groulx agreed one hundred percent. In April 1921, he announced to Charlebois that he would come to Ottawa with Omer Héroux of *Le Devoir* to discuss the census question with him. The two Montrealers also took advantage of their stay in the capital to meet with a federal civil servant on this matter, "a French Canadian who was well disposed," to quote Héroux.[77] The pages of *L'Action française* highlighted the importance of the census for all French Canadians and especially for the French minorities. In their capacity as "one of the two races that sealed the federation pact of 1867," the French Canadians were to monitor the census not only in Québec, "but also in the other eight provinces they had spread to." The minorities had to be even more wary than their compatriots in Québec of the tactics of the "foreign census-takers . . . liable to lower [their numbers]."[78]

The Grand Prix d'Action française

One of the most significant displays of national solidarity made by *L'Action française* toward the Franco-Ontarians took place in 1924, when the directors of the review awarded Napoléon Belcourt with their first—and only—*Grand Prix d'Action française*. A few months before the award was given, *L'Action française* had already published a very flattering portrait of the Senator, written, at Groulx's request, by Fulgence Charpentier, a journalist with *Le Droit*.[79] The Senator had been described as an "indefatigable apostle of French irredentism in his province." The *Grand Prix d'Action française* was intended in this instance to reward "the most meritorious and fruitful deed carried out in defence of the French soul of America."[80] The idea had first come to the directors of the Ligue d'Action française in 1922. The review

76. Letter from Charles Charlebois to Lionel Groulx, BAnQ, FLG, P1/A,746, November 3, 1920.
77. Letters from Lionel Groulx to Charles Charlebois, BAnQ, FLG, P1/A,746, April 7, 1921; from Edmond Cloutier to Lionel Groulx, BAnQ, FLG, P1/A,818, May 11, 1921 and May 20, 1921; d'Omer Héroux to Lionel Groulx, BAnQ, FLG, P1/A,1758, April 5, 1921.
78. L'Action française, "Le recensement de 1921," AF, January 1921, p. 3; Joseph Bruchard, "Préparons le recensement," AF, March 1921, p. 152.
79. Letters from Fulgence Charpentier to Lionel Groulx, BAnQ, FLG, P1/A,755, January 8, 1924, March 29, 1924; "Le sénateur Belcourt," AF, March 1924, p. 142.
80. Anatole Vanier, "Notre premier grand prix," AF, June 1924, p. 357.

then proposed a general consultation, a "plebiscite," as Groulx called it, among the readers and the national societies of all of French America.[81] The prize was awarded on May 24, the day of the *fête de Dollard des Ormeaux*, in the parish hall of Paroisse de l'Immaculée-Conception in Montréal. Inclement weather had obliged organizers to hold the ceremony that was to have taken place in Parc La Fontaine indoors. In a speech that preceded the presentation to Belcourt of a bronze medal bearing his image,[82] the director of *L'Action française* first highlighted the numerous leadership qualities of the award winner. He then went on to describe the Franco-Ontarian crisis. It was an attack "whose gravity exceeded all those we have suffered since Confederation. This time it was affecting more than 200,000 of our people, even at the very doorstep of Québec; although the assault was on their language, a threat against the Catholic separate schools could be detected in it as well." Groulx also explained that the choice of *la fête de Dollard* as the day to honour Belcourt was in no way a coincidence and he did not hesitate to draw a parallel between the exploits of the hero from New France and those of the Senator: "If you feel a quiver of excitement in your breast," he told his guest, in a flight of lyricism, to say the least, "do not be too surprised, you inherited it somewhere near Long-Sault." Like Dollard, Belcourt helped spare French civilization from the fate of being limited to the confines of a "Québéc reserve." Groulx reiterated one of his deepest convictions—namely, that the Franco-Ontarian crisis extended far beyond the borders of Ontario and that it was making a powerful contribution toward bringing about the long-awaited "awakening" of the French-Canadian nation:

> This evening, around this platform, if the voice of all the French groups of America echo our voice, and if, perhaps for the first time ever, we unite to claim the same right, is it not around the Ontario minority that this miracle is being worked?
> All of you, persecuted heroes, you are even teaching us all over again some of our most necessary virtues.

Groulx wanted the May 24 ceremony to serve as an opportunity for all of French America to demonstrate symbolically its support for the Franco-Ontarian cause. "What should be noted," he wrote later, in *L'Action française*, "and what serves as a sign of a new era, is the unanimous tribute paid by the race that day to the leader of the Ontario minority. We believe this is the first time there is unanimity around a national claim."[83] Groulx, needless to say, had invited all the regional vice presidents of ACFEO, as well as a representative from "each of the national societies of French America" to the ceremony. And it will come as no surprise that this

81. Lionel Groulx, *Mes Mémoires, Tome II*, p. 349–351.
82. Lionel Groulx, "Allocution pour le 'Grand Prix d'Action française,'" in *Dix ans d'Action française*, p. 207–216.
83. Jacques Brassier [pseudonym of L. Groulx], "La vie de l'Action française," AF, June 1924, p. 377.

gesture by *L'Action française* was much appreciated by the leaders of the resistance to Regulation 17. A few days after the ceremony, Edmond Cloutier, speaking on behalf of the executive committee of ACFEO, expressed to Groulx his gratitude for "the happy initiative taken by *L'Action française*," which "assuredly marked an important stage in the uniting of our forces and the development of national solidarity."[84]

However, unanimity around the honour conferred on Belcourt was not total. In fact, by raising the Senator to the rank of hero, Groulx attracted the ire of his former spiritual director, Abbé Sylvio Corbeil, then principal of the École normale in Hull. Groulx was frequently and severely reproached by Corbeil, in whose opinion Belcourt was just a "harmful character," and the *Grand Prix d'Action française*, nothing less than a "historical lie." What could Belcourt have done to deserve such opprobrium from Corbeil?

Corbeil drew up a long list of the Senator's faults for Groulx: he was a Liberal, who had supported Laurier in 1896 and in 1905, when the federal government allowed the abolition of the educational rights of the French minorities in the Western provinces; as a lawyer, he had taken advantage of the Commission scolaire catholique d'Ottawa which he represented in the courts (incompetently, besides); hypocritically, he married two English Canadians and consecutively founded two English families; finally, although he had never hesitated to come down on the Conservative government in Toronto, his partisan spirit had repeatedly shown excessive indulgence toward the Liberals in power in Ottawa, a party that had always refused to intervene in the Franco-Ontarian schools crisis. Corbeil repeatedly criticized his former student on this question, first in 1927, after he had read the "speech for the *Grand Prix d'Action française*" that Groulx published in his *Dix ans d'Action française* and, stubbornly, again, for what he considered to be the excessive praise heaped on Belcourt by Groulx in the second tome of his *Enseignement français au Canada*, which appeared in 1935.[85]

Groulx, for his part, did not offer Corbeil any justification that we have on record. However, in his *Mémoires*, he explained his former teacher's attitude by invoking, in turn, what he considered his own partisan mindset: "Old-school blue, [Corbeil] had been unable to tolerate this praise for the red senator."[86] This quarrel with Corbeil contributed, moreover, to showing Groulx the pitfalls that the partisan mentality could create for even the noblest of causes. Notwithstanding his personal and professional path, Belcourt, in Groulx's opinion, had devoted himself fully to the Franco-Ontarian cause, which he had indeed inspired. No matter how disdainfully the Senator was viewed by Corbeil, he had the singular

84. Letters from Lionel Groulx to Edmond Cloutier, BAnQ, FLG, P1/A,818, May 7, 1924; from Edmond Cloutier to Lionel Groulx, BAnQ, FLG, P1/A,818, June 11, 1924.

85. Letters from Sylvio Corbeil to Lionel Groulx, BAnQ, FLG, P1/A,849, May 17, 1924, December 29, 1927, [January 1,] 1934.

86. Lionel Groulx, *Mes Mémoires, Tome I*, p. 363.

distinction all the same of embodying an entire people and symbolizing their cause. In honouring him, it was the courage of the whole Franco-Ontarian resistance movement that *L'Action française* sought to celebrate, a point that Groulx did not fail to raise in his speech on May 24: "We do not forget, . . . M. *le sénateur*, that your main honour, one of the highest anyone can claim, is that of being . . . the personification of a *petit peuple*. For this reason, our tribute to you goes, through you, to all of the Ontarian minority."[87]

Spurred on by its director, *L'Action française* ranked among the most loyal friends of the Franco-Ontarian resistance. Groulx, however, made use of yet another instrument, during the 1920s, to come to the defence of the French Canadians of Ontario, and that instrument was literature.

Alonié de Lestres and *L'Appel de la race*

The Novel and its Reception by Franco-Ontarians

In 1916, as we have seen, Groulx made his initial foray into the world of literature with the publication of a short story collection called *Les Rapaillages*. The collection included the story that had launched the *sou* campaign for the Franco-Ontarian schools a few years earlier. In September 1922, he returned to the task, this time under the pseudonym of Alonié de Lestres, and published his first novel *L'Appel de la race*, which some would say ranks among the first best-sellers of French-Canadian literature.[88] For Groulx, literary expression was transformed into another means of action and offered him new ammunition in his fight against the unjust educational laws in Ontario. The writer in fact chose to set his story and his characters in Ottawa at the height of the language crisis. His hero, Jules de Lantagnac, is a lawyer and federal member of Parliament and very friendly with the English bourgeois circles in the capital. Although he recognizes that the cause of the Franco-Ontarian militants is just, he hesitates to intervene on behalf of his people in the House of Commons: neither his wife, Maud Fletcher, a Catholic English Canadian, nor her family, would tolerate it. Lantagnac therefore faces a double dilemma. If he chooses to support the Franco-Ontarian resistance and rediscover his French roots, left buried for too long, he risks alienating his business relations and jeopardizes his political future. Furthermore, denouncing Regulation 17 would in all likelihood bring about the breakup of his marriage, which would represent an even greater upheaval for a man of faith like him. Yet, on the advice of a respected priest, Father Fabien, Lantagnac chooses to respond in the affirmative to the "call of the race" and to rally to the French-Canadian cause: he becomes one of the principal leaders of the Franco-Ontarian resistance. The inevitable collapse of his household

87. Lionel Groulx, "Allocution pour le 'Grand Prix d'Action française,'" *Dix ans d'Action française*, p. 211.
88. Alonié de Lestres [pseudonym of L. Groulx], *L'Appel de la race* (Montréal: Bibliothèque de l'Action française, 1922), 279 p.

follows. Maud leaves him, taking with her the two most anglicized of their four children, who choose to follow their mother.

In his *Mémoires*, Groulx indicated that when the idea of writing *L'Appel de la race* first came to him, it was to be purely for his own "relaxation."[89] Very quickly, though, he recognized the service the novel could render to the activists of French Ontario. The author told Rodrigue Villeneuve, who was still living in Ottawa, that he planned to provide "'backing' . . . for the defenders of bilingual schools" and that he hoped Franco-Ontarians would respond favourably: "Ask the good Lord to enlighten me, if this book is to do a little good. I would not have written even ten lines if I had not felt a driving force that was stronger than all my aversions."[90] Villeneuve, for his part, took it upon himself to send Groulx some of the very positive reactions that the novel had received in nationalist circles in the capital and elsewhere. He also told him he planned to have it read "in community with commentary" by the Oblates in Ottawa.[91] Groulx received congratulations from every quarter in French Canada for *L'Appel de la race*, since the real identity of Alonié de Lestres was an open secret, at least among the main actors of the French-Canadian nationalist movement. For example, Groulx received praise from the Bishop of Prince Albert and Saskatoon, Joseph-Henri Prud'homme; the publisher of *La Survivance* in Edmonton, Rodolphe Laplante; Georges Bugnet of *L'Union* in Edmonton; Ceslas Forest of the Dominican *collège* in Ottawa; Antoine Bernard, studying in Europe at the time and future professor of Acadian history at Université de Montréal; Georges Boileau, professor at the *collège* in Gravelbourg and others. Laplante and Bugnet even asked Groulx for permission to reproduce *L'Appel de la race* in their newspaper in a series format. The editor-in-chief of *Le Droit*, Charles Gautier, likewise gave a flattering critique of the novel in his newspaper.[92]

Naturally, Groulx's colleagues at *L'Action française* were the first to congratulate Alonié de Lestres on his novel. The review did, in fact, do a lot of promotion for *L'Appel de la race*, highlighting especially all the ways the book would no doubt benefit the cause of the French schools in Ontario. It was Oblate Georges Simard in Ottawa whom Groulx and Villeneuve designated to review the novel, on behalf of Franco-Ontarians, in *L'Action française*.[93] In Simard's estimation, *L'Appel de la race* offered invaluable support to the Franco-Ontarian cause:

89. Lionel Groulx, *Mes Mémoires, Tome I*, p. 368–370.
90. Letters from Lionel Groulx to Rodrigue Villeneuve, BAnQ, FLG, P1/A,3696, April 3, 1922, June 18, 1922.
91. Letters from Rodrigue Villeneuve to Lionel Groulx, BAnQ, FLG, P1/A,3696, June 16, 1922, October 8, 1922, [January 6, 1923], August 14, 1922.
92. Letters to Lionel Groulx from Joseph-Henri Prud'homme, BAnQ, FLG, P1/A,3102, December 14, 1922; from Rodolphe Laplante, BAnQ, FLG, P1/A,2096, May 17, 1930; from Georges Bugnet, CRLG, FLG, P1/A,603, August 3, 1926; from Ceslas Forest, BAnQ, FLG, P1/A,1369, [no date]; from Antoine Bernard, BAnQ, FLG, P1/A,326, November 4, 1922; from Georges Boileau, BAnQ, FLG, P1/A,427, October 23, 1922; Charles Gautier, "*L'Appel de la race*", *Le Droit*, October 14, 1922, p. 3.
93. Letters to Lionel Groulx from Rodrigue Villeneuve, CRLG, FLG, P1/A,3696, August 14, 1922; from Georges Simard, BAnQ, FLG, P1/A,3453, September 22, 1922.

> Where Alonié de Lestres excels is in the exposition of his ideas. For his book contains a doctrine—let's not mince words here: full nationalism. While he deals with many other issues besides those concerning Ontario, to us he brings precious encouragement, whose impact we will only know in a more-or-less distant future . . . For us, who live, feel and think with the Franco-Ontarians, we want only to consider in *L'Appel de la Race* the "moral support" of which we are in such great need.[94]

Groulx was not averse to commenting personally on the work of his alter ego, even though, for reasons of propriety, he relied on another of his favourite pseudonyms, Jacques Brassier.[95] In "La vie de *L'Action française*," his monthly column, his alter ego followed closely the kind of reception *L'Appel de la race* was getting throughout French Canada and delighted in the good the novel appeared to be accomplishing among the French minorities. The most touching expressions of gratitude that Alonié de Lestres received, wrote Brassier, "were from our brothers living outside Québec, to whom *L'Appel de la race* had brought solace. Now this gratitude was being heard, expressed in so many different ways."[96]

When the novel was attacked, the Franco-Ontarians were the first to flock to its author's defence. In November 1922, Edgar Boutet and Louis-Joseph de la Durantaye published a scathing critique of the book in *Les Annales* of the French Canadian Institute of Ottawa, deploring its lack of imagination. Too wooden, too imbued with rhetoric, the novel showed no understanding of psychology or of the genuine emotions experienced by its characters, who were mere mouthpieces for "thoughts," intellectual abstractions:

> It is time to teach Canadian intellectuals to have emotions and to observe. Leave less room for rhetoric and scholastic talk. Inaugurate the era of experimental psychology, which does not yet seem to have crossed the Atlantic. We want to see realities, life, *images and sensations* in our literature. We are finally fed up with abstract ideas and general feelings. The idea of fatherland remains for us the least fruitful of all lyrical themes. We want to see, etched in the face of our landscapes and in the soul of our people, the original, human, timeless feelings, resembling nature, love and death.[97]

Rodrigue Villeneuve advised Groulx not to take offence at this criticism from Boutet and de la Durantaye, whom he wrote off as "puffed-up little roosters."

94. Georges Simard, "Un épaulement moral," AF, October 1922, p. 210–215.
95. See Marie-Pier Luneau, Lionel Groulx. *Le mythe du berger* (Montréal: Leméac, 2003), 226 p.
96. Jacques Brassier [pseudonym of L. Groulx], "*L'Appel de la race*", AF, February 1923, p. 119. See also Jacques Brassier, "La vie de l'Action française," AF, February 1923 (p. 118–123); November 1922 (p. 318–320); December 1922 (p. 379–382); January 1923 (p. 60–64).
97. Edgar Boutet and Louis-Joseph de la Durantaye, "*L'Appel de la race*," *Les Annales: Lettres, histoire, sciences, arts*, November 1922, p. 1.

He even reported to him, a few weeks later, that Boutet, "was overcome with remorse," and that he had shown Father Charlebois, his employer at *Le Droit*, "as proof of his regret, a most appropriate letter,"[98] which he was sending to Alonié de Lestres. Boutet had, in fact, sent Groulx a letter in which he almost apologized for having published such a negative review of *L'Appel de la race*. In it, he explained that his "superiors" and his "friends at *Le Droit*" (including Charlebois, no doubt) had urged him to explain himself to the novelist:

> Please, *Monsieur l'abbé*, do not judge me by those remarks: they express in a very incomplete manner my humble opinions on the novel. If I had expressed them more fully and, above all, developed them better, they would definitely have placed me with my superiors, who greeted its appearance with enthusiasm. Looking back with a critical mind, I regret having written a review that gives the impression that I share the opinions presented in it. We deliberately strayed from the purely literary debate in order to thwart, via an ill-considered critique, a work that deserves the support of all who believe in our *survivance*. And I sincerely beg you to believe that if I had realized the false impression I may have given through this review, I would, you may be sure, not have written what the *Annales* published.[99]

Actually, the tone of the article by Boutet, which went so far as to denounce Groulx's nationalist "paganism," was much more virulent than he implies in this letter. Given the importance and urgency of the cause that *L'Appel de la race* was defending, it seemed important to relegate to second place any purely aesthetic or literary criticism of it and to highlight, rather, its ability to strengthen resolve, from one end of French Canada to the other.

Literature and Theology

With a print run of several thousand copies, the novel was clearly a hit.[100] However, it did not just earn adulation for its author. Boutet and de la Durantaye were neither the sole nor the first critical voice. In fact, *L'Appel de la race* found itself at the heart of two major debates that stirred up the French-Canadian literary and intellectual world for several months. Groulx had anticipated the first one before the novel was even published. To Rodrigue Villeneuve he had confided that he had "always been a bit worried with respect to the theological discussion."[101] An utramontane priest writes a novel that ends with a marriage breakup. This would

98. Letters from Rodrigue Villeneuve to Lionel Groulx, BAnQ, FLG, P1/A,3696, December 16, 1922 and January 20, 1923.
99. Letter from Edgar Boutet to Lionel Groulx, BAnQ, FLG, P1/A,524, December 24, 1922.
100. See Pierre Hébert, in collaboration with Marie-Pier Luneau, *Lionel Groulx et* L'Appel de la race (Montréal: Fides, 1996), 204 p.; Yves Saint-Denis, *Une Édition critique de* L'Appel de la race *de Lionel Groulx*, doctoral thesis (lettres françaises), University of Ottawa, 1991, 1422 p.
101. Letter from Lionel Groulx to Rodrigue Villeneuve, BAnQ, FLG, P1/A,3696, June 18, 1922.

inevitably set tongues wagging in the French-Canadian intellectual context of the time. It was, in effect, on the matter of Alonié de Lestres' theological orthodoxy that certain individuals, such as Abbé Camille Roy, took him to task. While acknowledging the novel's numerous qualities, Québec's influential literary critic wrote in *Le Canada français* that he was alarmed that the author had placed a higher value on the national interest than on the marital interest, thus placing the profane ahead of the sacred:

> If there are cases of necessity where the family must be sacrificed for one's native land, the case of Jules [de] Lantagnac is not one of them. When one has been what he was, and when one has "embarked" on founding a family as he did, one no longer has the option, nor does one have the patriotic obligation, to serve one's race at any cost, even by honest means.
>
> He is the one who has backed himself into a corner: too bad for him and too bad for the causes he wants to serve! And we think the theology of Father Fabien is ill-advised when it calls it a duty to go all the way, to take the step that will destroy his household.[102]

Abbé Roy even labelled as "repugnant" the absolution Fabien gives Lantagnac when the latter decides, at the risk of destroying his marriage, to rally to the Franco-Ontarian resistance. Obviously, Groulx was shaken by this accusation, though he denied it to others. In fact, his friend Villeneuve sought time and again to reassure him by playing down the impact of Abbé Roy's review. He reported to him that even the dean of the Faculty of Theology at Université Laval, Msgr. Louis-Adolphe Pâquet, had endorsed his novel and characterized Roy's argument as "untenable" during a conversation with the publisher of *Le Droit*, Charles Charlebois.[103]

Villeneuve felt that it was primarily up to Franco-Ontarians to defend Groulx against the accusations of Camille Roy: "They tell me here, in fact, that since the book was written to serve us, it's up to us to defend it."[104] It was Villeneuve himself who, after asking Groulx's advice, provided the official reply from *L'Action française* to Camille Roy in a long text showing the theological orthodoxy of *L'Appel de la race*.[105] The apologist for Alonié de Lestres helped him out of the awkward position he was in by producing a clever reflection on intended and unintended consequences, concepts he borrowed from moral theology. Camille Roy, who had also taken these arguments into account, had condemned Lantagnac's behaviour all the same. Villeneuve, on the other hand, came to a different conclusion. Yes, he wrote, Lantagnac's actions triggered the breakup of his marriage, but the

102. Camille Roy, "*L'Appel de la race*: Un roman canadien," *Le Canada français*, December 1922, p. 308–309.
103. Letter from Rodrigue Villeneuve to Lionel Groulx, BAnQ, FLG, P1/A,3696, January 20, 1923.
104. Letter from Rodrigue Villeneuve to Lionel Groulx, BAnQ, FLG, P1/A,3696, December 16, 1922.
105. J.-M.-Rodrigue Villeneuve, "*L'Appel de la race* et la théologie du père Fabien," AF, February 1923, p. 82–103.

blame for this fell, rather, on Maud's shoulders. Her intransigence prevented her from recognizing the justness of the cause defended by her husband. By virtue of the principle of "unintended consequence," Lantagnac could, with a clear conscience, rally to the Franco-Ontarian cause, a basically "honest" act, even as he realized it would, in all likelihood, bring about the division of his family. The "accidental" evil did not result from his national convictions but rather from Maud's lack of tolerance.

Jules de Lantagnac and Napoléon Belcourt

The second debate sparked by *L'Appel de la race* revolved around a question that, although less compromising theologically, caused Groulx the kind of grief he would gladly have done without. In a devastating article published in the December 1922 issue of *La Revue moderne*, McGill literature professor René du Roure accused Alonié de Lestres of having written a novel of unjustifiable hostility, whose only objective was to attack and condemn English Canada. Du Roure, furthermore, abhorred the author's style and dismissed his effort as "juvenile." "Had it been better composed and better written, *L'Appel de la race*, inspired by passion and hatred, could have been a dangerous work. As it is, I think it harmless."[106] However, what caused Groulx the most distress in du Roure's article was the insinuation that Alonié de Lestres had written a *roman à clé*, that is to say, had infringed on the personal life of a public figure in the schools crisis in creating his hero Lantagnac. The alleged victim was Senator Napoléon Belcourt, although du Roure took great care not to name him:

> Let us draw attention first of all to the deplorable method, which consists of suggesting, through physical resemblances, situational analogies and similar nomenclature in his character portrayals, inevitable parallels with public figures living and acting today. Let us hasten to add that his pitiful hero, fretful and unsure of himself, is but a pale caricature of the courteous gentleman, whose constant energy, upright character and intelligent and moderate action arouse so much sympathy and prove to be so fruitful . . .

Starting the previous fall, there were rumours in the capital that the novel had shamefully exploited the family problems of the Senator and Franco-Ontarian leader by bringing them, without authorization, to the general public's awareness. And this was not the worst of Groulx's tribulations. In the following issue of *La Revue moderne*, Louvigny de Montigny, a translator in the Senate at the time, made similar comments to those of du Roure, denouncing the "intransigence" of Alonié de Lestres, as well as his "racial prejudices." De Montigny, too, believed he

106. René du Roure, "*L'appel de la Race*: Critique littéraire," *La Revue moderne*, December 1922, p. 9.

had solved the mystery of Lantagnac's identity, which the author had borrowed directly, in his opinion, from a "real-life person" (read: Belcourt). The critique stated that the author had understood nothing of the Senator's true motives in his campaign against Regulation 17 and that he had sought only to foster harmony between French Canadians and English Canadians. However, in de Montigny's opinion, Alonié de Lestres had made him a despicable and short-sighted character:

> A novelist cannot take his inspiration unduly from real life and reproduce it in interesting images. He must copy nature with propriety. The prototype from which he has borrowed the physical features of his Lantagnac should impose on Alonié de Lestres and his intransigent irredentism a deep respect, since this real life character is also the real champion of the mother tongue that is the guardian of the Catholic faith. Far from playing a stupid and colourless role, as imposed on him in *L'Appel de la race*, his true action, discreet and steadfast, consists in convincing the Anglo-Ontarian elite that solving our school problems is first of all in the interest of national unity. And all the French schools of the province recognize that this strategy is the surest route to winning what the call to the prejudices of the race will never succeed in obtaining.[107]

Groulx always remained categorical on this point. If there was any parallel to be made between the respective trajectories of Belcourt and Lantagnac, he maintained all his life that it was a pure and simple coincidence. As early as September, even before the article by René du Roure appeared, Groulx had told Rodrigue Villeneuve of his apprehension concerning any possible reaction to this matter by Senator Belcourt (and also Father Charlebois). The feeling of anxiety he experienced was all the stronger since *Le Droit* seemed to be taking its time to comment on *L'Appel de la race* in its pages. Was this an indication that the Ottawa nationalists wanted to take their distance from the novel? The silence from the Franco-Ontarian daily, he wrote to Villeneuve, seemed to serve as an endorsement to the detractors of Alonié de Lestres:

> I don't know what has reached the ears of Father Charlebois. They tell me he is quite worried; I have heard that he is even afraid that the novel could offend Monsieur Belcourt.
>
> You know, *mon cher Père*, how much I would dread it if a volume written to serve the Ontario cause ended up doing it a disservice instead. So, let me know if the danger is great. As for *Monsieur* Belcourt, might there be some way to convey to him that Lantagnac's case is quite far from being his and that, in any case, poor Alonié de Lestres was totally unaware, when he wrote it, of the Senator's story?[108]

107. Louvigny de Montigny, "Un mauvais livre," *La Revue moderne*, January 1923, p. 9.
108. Letter from Lionel Groulx to Rodrigue Villeneuve, BAnQ, FLG, P1/A,3696, September 11, 1922.

Villeneuve, in typical fashion, offered Groulx his reassurance and told him he was jumping to conclusions. He reported to him that Charlebois had lent no credence to these unfortunate stories. If *Le Droit* was delaying its promotion of the novel, it was that the only copy available at the newspaper offices was in the hands of Charlebois, who was in Hearst, in Northern Ontario. His subordinates, who were holding the fort in his absence, had only just received a copy of it.[109] The article in *Le Droit* appeared just a few days after these exchanges between Groulx and Villeneuve, that is, on October 14, 1922. As we mentioned above, Charles Gautier, who penned it, would give the novel high praise.

Groulx's worries concerning Senator Belcourt subsided after a few months. But then, when the articles by René du Roure and Louvigny de Montigny appeared in *La Revue moderne*, he turned to Villeneuve again in the hope of obtaining some kind of reassurance: "Is it true that *Monsieur le sénateur* shed tears of sorrow and anger upon reading *L'Appel de la Race* and that he wrote a warm letter of congratulations to du Roure? Father Charlebois, I think, could inform you as to the veracity of this." Villeneuve immediately denied these rumours and indicated to his friend that according to the secretary of ACFEO, Edmond Cloutier, Belcourt had remained "quite indifferent" to this affair and had no hard feelings whatsoever against Alonié de Lestres. The only aspect of the novel with which the Senator was said to be dissatisfied, he added, was the role of "spiritual director" assigned to Father Fabien. That looked like evidence, Belcourt had reportedly said, of the religious obscurantism with which the Orange Lodges liked to label French Canadians. "Well then, his French conversion, if he is Lantagnac, is not complete, as we can see!" was the Oblate's ironic comment. Around the same time, de Montigny gave a speech at the French Canadian Institute in Ottawa in which he reiterated the substance of the article he had published in *La Revue moderne*. Villeneuve informed Groulx, shortly afterwards, that the polemicist's remarks had been greeted by "a deadly silence" and had elicited neither applause nor questions: "Nothing, it seems, could punish this Louvigny more—'damn fool,' they are saying—, which greatly embarrasses *Monsieur Belcourt* and which need not be a source of worry." In his *Mémoires*, Groulx came back on this matter, pointing out that he had continued to be on good terms with Belcourt right up until the Senator's death in 1932. As evidence, he offered the fact that he had been able to deliver his speech without any awkwardness when the *Grand Prix d'Action française* was presented to Belcourt in 1924.[110]

Groulx "resolved to stay outside the quarrel as much as possible" regarding *L'Appel de la race*, as he was "too personally involved."[111] One cannot help but note,

109. Letter from Rodrigue Villeneuve to Lionel Groulx, BAnQ, FLG, P1/A,3696, October 8, 1922.
110. Letters from Lionel Groulx to Rodrigue Villeneuve, BAnQ, FLG, P1/A,3696, January 10, 1923; from Rodrigue Villeneuve to Lionel Groulx, BAnQ, FLG, P1/A,3696, September 15, 1922, January 13, 1923 and January 20, 1923; Lionel Groulx, *Mes Mémoires, Tome II*, p. 90.
111. Lionel Groulx to Rodrigue Villeneuve, BAnQ, FLG, P1/A,3696, January 18, 1923.

however, that his alter ego, Jacques Brassier, was not dogged by the same scruples and did not refrain from coming to the defence of Alonié de Lestres in the pages of *L'Action française*. Groulx also had the satisfaction of seeing several of his friends file past and man the barricades for him.[112] But it was on February 15, 1923 that an event took place in Montréal that put an end to the controversy "in dramatic fashion": Olivar Asselin, the highly respected journalist, took the floor in front of an audience of a thousand persons gathered to hear him give his assessment of "L'Œuvre de l'abbé Groulx." The lecture gave much attention to the dispute over *L'Appel de la race*. Without lapsing into undue praise, Asselin nevertheless stressed the gratuitous nature of the attacks made on Groulx by Louvigny de Montigny, René du Roure and even Camille Roy. "Such was his authority," Groulx wrote several years later, "and such was the fear he inspired in his adversaries, that one hardly dared cross swords with him. Almost everyone laid down their arms."[113]

⋆ ⋆ ⋆

Despite the debates *L'Appel de la race* provoked, or perhaps because of them, the novel helped ensure that the Regulation 17 crisis would remain a primary issue for the French-Canadian intellectual world and, especially, for the nationalist movement. Groulx saw it as an example of the kind of national solidarity that all of French Canada should be demonstrating toward Franco-Ontarians. Throughout the schools conflict, Groulx gave his constant and faithful support to the Franco-Ontarian resistance. He saw the language crisis as a catalyzing event, which, despite its injustice, gave French Canada a perfect opportunity to gather its national energies and awaken from its intellectual torpor. At the same time, it thrust the priest-historian into the foreground of the nationalist movement, making him its principal intellectual leader from the early 1920s. Groulx's influence among Franco-Ontarian militants had become considerable. Even after the schools crisis, they would continue to seek his participation in various activities, such as the annual ACFEO conferences. In September of 1940, at the Côte-des-Neiges cemetery in Montréal, he also said a few words at the tomb of Jeanne Lajoie, the "Maid of Pembroke," on the tenth anniversary of her death. Besides reading some of the pages dedicated to her in his *Enseignement français au Canada*, Groulx sprinkled her coffin with a mixture of soils taken from Pembroke and from the Plains of Abraham. As so many had done before him, he drew a parallel between the deeds of Lajoie and those of Jeanne d'Arc, holding her up as an example for the

112. See, among others, Antonio Perrault, "*L'appel de la race*," *Le Devoir*, September 23, 1922, p. 1–2; Léo-Paul Desrosiers, "Sur un article de M. du Roure," *Le Devoir*, December 21, 1922, p. 1–2; Antonio Perrault, "*L'appel de la race* et ses détracteurs," *Le Devoir*, January 27, 1923, p. 1–2; letter from Damien Saint-Pierre to Lionel Groulx, BAnQ, FLG, P1/A,3346, January 21, 1923.

113. See Olivar Asselin, *L'Œuvre de l'abbé Groulx* (Montréal: Bibliothèque de l'Action française, 1923), 96 p.; Lionel Groulx, *Mes Mémoires*, Tome II, p. 112.

younger generation, who sometimes had difficulty finding heroes or heroines to look to:

> What is it that actually draws us to this figure, to this young woman? It is her heroism. She could easily have given up, like so many others did when they became worn out and had lost their taste for the fight. But she chose to risk everything. If moral flowers grew like other flowers, there would be lilies of heroism blossoming forth from this girl's grave.[114]

In 1928, Napoléon Belcourt, the then president of ACFEO, wrote Groulx personally to inform him of the victory that the Franco-Ontarians had just won from the provincial government. At the same time, the Senator expressed the appreciation that he felt all of French Ontario had for *L'Action française* and, especially, for its director:

> It is a great honour for me to express to you our feelings of gratitude, heartfelt and most sincere, for the immense services that *L'Action française* and you yourself in particular, for fifteen years, have so generously given to the Ontario minority in the struggle to claim French cultural and language rights in this province. We, all of us, recognize that you have been our most powerful, most steadfast and most reliable ally; that without you we would never have won our cause.
>
> On behalf of the Association, myself and the Ontario minority, I come to offer you today this expression of our gratitude for the magnificent and unforgettable succour you brought us.[115]

Shortly afterwards, some of the key leaders of the Franco-Ontarian revolt suffered a treatment that saddened Groulx deeply. In 1934, the general directorate of the Oblates, with the endorsement of the rector of the University of Ottawa, Gilles Marchand, relieved Father Charles Charlebois of his duties at *Le Droit* and sent him to serve as the Superior of the scholasticate in Sainte-Agathe-des-Monts in the Laurentians. He died in Montréal in 1945. Earlier, in January of 1931, Samuel Genest had been removed from the presidency of the Ottawa Catholic School Board, a post he had held since 1913. Historian Robert Choquette attributes the dismissal of these two great Franco-Ontarian leaders to the reversal in the political climate in the federal capital at the start of the 1930s. With the end of the schools conflict and the outbreak of the Great Depression of 1929, "a good number of French Canadians considered that the time had come for cooperation and

114. Consult the report on the ceremony published in *Le Devoir* ("L'hommage à Jeanne Lajoie, la 'Pucelle de Pembroke,'" *Le Devoir*, September 30, 1940). The handwritten outline of Groulx's speech has also been preserved. ("Est-il vrai que nous allons apprendre à nous souvenir ?" BAnQ, P1/MA-266).

115. Letter from Napoléon Belcourt to Lionel Groulx, BAnQ, FLG, P1/A,283, January 17, 1928.

bonne entente with the anglophones."[116] The strategy of confrontation, embodied by Genest and Charlebois, seemed more and more unwise in the mind of certain Franco-Ontarians who preferred to see negotiation and diplomacy.

Groulx witnessed these events as a powerless bystander. In his opinion, the way these two great heroes of the schools crisis were treated was as reprehensible as it was ungrateful and was evidence of the resurgence of the "partisan mentality" that had taken hold again in French-Canadian political and intellectual circles. In his *Mémoires*, Groulx came back on this question time and time again. He wrote that the promoters of *bonne entente* who had orchestrated the marginalization of Charlebois and Genest had been fervent Conservative partisans who were unhappy with the tacit agreement they believed had been made during the schools crisis between the Franco-Ontarian resistance and part of the French-Canadian wing of the Liberal Party. (Let us stress that the Conservatives were far from being completely excluded from the resistance to Regulation 17, as shown by Conservative senator Phlippe Landry's tenure as president of ACFEO.) With the Conservatives' return to power in Ottawa in 1930, certain "old school Tories" wished, Groulx maintained, to deal a major blow to their political adversaries. His opinion of them, in his *Mémoires*, was unequivocal:

> Politics has always, unfortunately, divided French Canadians. The partisan mentality has won out in the judgments and conduct of very good people, over the most serious, and even religious, interests. . . . I note the terrible battle that is consequently being waged. A painful, deplorable battle, if ever there was one. A merciless war, conducted through insinuating shots and perfidious accusations, as in any fratricidal war. A war that pits former comrades-in-arms against one another. . . . The battle will end with the expulsion from *Le Droit* of an eminent cleric, who had directed the newspaper during its most critical hours. It will also end up driving out from the school board the courageous man who, at one point, in order to save the day, had risked prison: Samuel Genest. A team of *politiciens* is ousting a team of fighters.[117]

Among these *politiciens* (a very pejorative term in Groulx's vocabulary), Groulx included Father Georges Simard who, nevertheless, had been one of his most faithful collaborators at *L'Action française*, writing the column on the Franco-Ontarian struggle under the pseudonym Aurèle Gauthier. It is interesting to note that some of the new leaders of the *bonne entente* felt the need to approach Groulx either to try and convince him to rally to their cause or to try to get back into his good graces. The historian had obviously become a public figure whom it was wiser not to alienate unduly. Joseph Charbonneau, for example, future archbishop

116. Robert Choquette, *La Foi gardienne*, p. 197.
117. Lionel Groulx, *Mes Mémoires, Tome I*, p. 360, 361–362.

of Montréal and director of the seminary in Ottawa at the time, paid Groulx a visit to ask him to persuade Charlebois and his chorus to tone down their revolutionary rhetoric. Groulx, needless to say, refused, claiming he was "reluctant to interfere in matters that belong under the jurisdiction of our friends in Ottawa."[118] Later, it would be Father Gilles Marchand's turn to approach Groulx. In a long letter he sent him in January 1934, shortly after the dismissal of Charles Charlebois, in which he had been involved, the rector of the University of Ottawa sought to defend himself against the accusations of betrayal that certain groups were making against him. His only fault, he protested, was "seeking areas where Catholics could agree rather than disagree" and judging "that division and conflict among Catholics should not be seen as the norm."[119]

Groulx sent Marchand no reply of which there is any record. But in his *Mémoires*, he indicated that his personal contact with the leaders of the Franco-Ontarian resistance and his refusal to rally to the cause of the *bonne ententistes* resulted, in 1934, in his losing his post as professor of history at the University of Ottawa, which he had only occupied since the preceding year.[120] Immediately after the schools crisis, in an article which at times sounds like a diatribe, Groulx attributed victory to the true heroes of the Franco-Ontarian crisis, that is to say, to the original militants. Instead of obeying more moderate voices, they had opted to demand, loudly and clearly, that justice be given to Franco-Ontarians:

> Would the government in Toronto do today what it is preparing to do, if the Franco-Ontarians had listened only to those preaching tolerance among them, if they had not, for seventeen years, passionately claimed French school rights, had not debated the issue and even made the question of their schools a question of general politics involving general peace in the country and the fate of the Conservative party? Our good pacifists will not fail to write that peaceful negotiation will accomplish more in a few short months of talks than the militant muddles of so many years of futile battles. That will be false and self-indulgent, just like everything else written by these holy apostles. It is as clear as day, for any sensible person, that the negotiators of these recent times, whose merit must not be denied, have only harvested the fruit of the fight and that these very negotiations would never have taken place if the government of Mr. Ferguson [premier of Ontario] had not been driven to it by demands that could not be resisted.[121]

Groulx, who wrote these lines in 1927, went even further and praised the courage and vigour of *Le Droit* and of ACFEO, to whom, in his eyes, the victory really

118. Lionel Groulx, *Mes Mémoires, Tome I*, p. 361. See also Lionel Groulx, *Mes Mémoires, Tome III*, p. 262–266; Lionel Groulx, *Mes Mémoires, Tome IV*, p. 252–260.
119. Letter from Gilles Marchand to Lionel Groulx, BAnQ, FLG, P1/A,2459, January 8, 1934.
120. Lionel Groulx, *Mes Mémoires, Tome III*, p. 263, 266.
121. Jacques Brassier [pseudonym of L. Groulx], "Les écoles ontariennes," AF, September 1927, p. 178–179.

belonged. The following spring, when the Association held its conference, he was delighted to see that they still seemed to maintain their combative spirit. Victory achieved, ACFEO could have rested on its laurels. Fortunately, Groulx noted, that was far from being the case:

> The Ottawa conference quickly dispelled any such fears. From the beginning it was clear this was a gathering of men who were less keen on celebrating their victory than they were on taking advantage of it. The path before them now cleared, they realized their task as builders was not finished, but had only been made easier.[122]

The "fearful" and the "fainthearted who [we]re bothered by the least bit of resistance," he added, had not been able to gain the advantage. If in writing these lines, Groulx seemed to take the perspective of a privileged witness to the Franco-Ontarian crisis, he never limited his role to being a mere observer. Matching deed to word, he became a full-fledged member of the resistance to Regulation 17, persuaded that this struggle was that of the entire French-Canadian nation. Just as a person could not amputate one of his limbs without becoming disabled, it was unacceptable, in his view, for Québec to turn its back on its "brothers" in the neighbouring province and shirk its duty of national solidarity. When all is said and done, in cultivating his Franco-Ontarian relationships, Lionel Groulx greatly furthered the cause of dialogue and cooperation between nationalist groups in Québec and Ontario at a decisive moment in history.

122. Jacques Brassier [pseudonym of L. Groulx], "Le congrès d'Ottawa," ACF, April 1928, p. 241–242.

Chapter Five

The French Minorities and the "French State": *The* Indépendantiste *Theory During the Interwar Period*

TO WHAT EXTENT did Abbé Groulx contribute to pushing the French-Canadian nationalist movement toward *indépendantisme* or, at least, a more territorial version of nationalism that limited itself to Québec and excluded the French minorities in the other provinces? The minorities, as we have demonstrated, occupied an important place in his historical and polemical work. Groulx was in frequent communication with several of their leading thinkers and had adopted their cause, which was, in his view, that of all French Canadians. This did not, however, prevent certain of his contemporaries from watching him closely and accusing him of "provincialism" and even of "separatism." Could such accusations be justified? Historians have echoed Groulx's critics by sometimes presenting him as the spiritual father of postwar "neo-nationalism" in Québec. Beyond a doubt, Groulx's nationalism was more *canadien-français* than simply *canadien*. Consequently, when historians ignore the French minorities issue in their analyses of his thought, through a highly reductionist approach, they often establish a relationship of equivalence between French-Canadian nationalism and Québec nationalism. This explains in part the confusion surrounding Abbé Groulx's alleged "separatism," at least among historians.

We saw in the third chapter that Groulx attributed to Québec the role of "ancestral home of the nation" in the *survivance* of French Catholic civilization in America. However, this dimension of his thought did not translate into forgetting about the French minorities or leaving them to their own fate. On the contrary, his point was merely to acknowledge the institutional power to which French Canadians in Québec had access and to remind them, as he did repeatedly, that this power should be used to serve the minorities, who did not have the same access and were struggling against far more intractable adversaries. It was his belief that strengthening the "fatherland," sometimes best done by fighting for provincial autonomy, would benefit the entire French-Canadian nation. According to Groulx, Québec was the nourishing breast which, despite the "political sclerosis" it had succumbed to, offered the "sons of the diaspora" the tonic they needed for their survival and development.

In spite of all this, while Abbé Groulx never clearly declared himself a separatist, he did flirt with the idea of independence, especially during the 1920s. At *L'Action française*, assisted by a dozen or so collaborators recruited from among the key figures of the nationalist movement, he undertook a vast study on the political future of French Canada. The review envisaged the possibility of independence in the aftermath of the collapse of Confederation. It believed this to be imminent by virtue, in particular, of the discontent of the Western provinces in the face of Central Canada's mercantilist policies. During the interwar period, the famous "French state" debate earned Groulx accusations of separatism, especially by the French minorities. The minorities, or at least some of their leaders, feared they would be left behind should an independent "French state" be created and a new balance of political power come into being as a result. They jumped to the conclusion that Groulx and his movement had abandoned the "pan-Canadian" concept of the French-Canadian nation and that the nationalist movement was withdrawing to inside the borders of Québec. The "French state" dispute continued until the end of the 1930s. Throughout this period, Groulx had great difficulty shaking off the "separatist" label which certain circles persisted in applying to him.

L'Action française and "Our Political Future": The 1922 Study

One of the best known controversies, and certainly one of the deepest, that Lionel Groulx was ever involved in was undoubtedly the "French state" debate. What set it off, in 1922, was the vast study on the political future of French Canada, organized by *L'Action française*. It did not take long for accusations of "separatism" to be fired at the review from every quarter, at its collaborators and, especially, at its director. Moreover, it has generally been this issue—of the "separatism" of the interwar period nationalists—that has, to date, retained the attention of those historians who have analyzed the place of the French minorities in the ideology of Groulx and *L'Action française*. Of course, Abbé Groulx's interest in the minorities was not limited to exploring what impact the creation of an independent "French state," if that should occur, would have on them. However, this debate does allow us to better grasp Goulx's vision of the French-Canadian nation and the bonds between Québec and the French minorities.

As we noted in the first chapter, several historians, starting with Mason Wade and Michael Oliver, took over, almost word for word, the logic of the anti-separatists who criticized Groulx and the movement he led. Others, such as Susan Mann Trofimenkoff and Jean-Claude Dupuis, provided an in-depth analysis of the "French state" debate and the conflict between Abbé Groulx and Henri Bourassa that it generated. Bourassa indeed had difficulty accepting that his former disciple could be preaching a doctrine he deemed too "seditious." Trofimenkoff states that the divergence of opinion between the two men stemmed from the fact that Groulx's ideology, in contrast to Bourassa's, gave priority to nationalism rather than Catholicism. However, Dupuis seeks, and rightly so, to minimize the extent of the conflict and shows, rather, that their thinking contained far more similarities than differences. As a result, according to Dupuis, the historians exaggerated—as did Groulx and Bourassa themselves—the width of the chasm that separated the two nationalist leaders. The "separatism" of *L'Action française* was quite "timid" and, in the final analysis, its ideology had more in common with that of Bourassa, who favoured a bi-national Canadian state. Theoretically, the review may have fleetingly considered the possibility of an independent "French state," but in analyzing the problems of French Canada more concretely, it hardly strayed from the precepts of *le vieux chef*.[1]

Dupuis is, however, of the opinion that the nationalism of *L'Action française* constituted a turning point, a kind of pivot between the ideology of Bourassa and the idea of a Québec nation-state, an idea that perhaps merits some nuance. The "French state" that *L'Action française* envisaged, although it asked the independence question, would nevertheless remain faithful in all respects to the traditionalist definition of the nation that the review had always professed. Let us recall that according to Groulxist ideology, the nation is a "natural" and "organic" entity, having primacy over any political structures and generated by a supernatural and providential power. According to this reasoning, it was impossible that the creation of a "French state" should on its own generate a new national entity. The essential characteristics of the French-Canadian nation (a common language, culture, history and faith) would have remained unchanged and the French minorities, for their part, would in no way have been excluded from the fold of the nation. It is difficult, then, to ascertain a shift toward the principle of a nation-state when the concepts of state and nation retain full autonomy in relation to each other.

The *L'Action française* study included some dozen articles published between January and December 1922 by several of the great leading figures in the French-Canadian nationalist movement: Louis Durand, Philippe Perrier, Anatole Vanier, Georges Pelletier, Rodrigue Villeneuve and Antonio Perrault, to name just a few.[2] Groulx, for his part, besides taking charge of designing and organizing the study, wrote the conclusion and, it would appear, the overview article as well.[3] Well before the study was published, the director of *L'Action française* anticipated the consternation he would inevitably cause in French Canada's small intellectual world by evoking the possibility, even a hypothetical one, of a rupture with Confederation. He risked sinking into a quagmire that was too dangerous for him not to take certain precautions straightaway. From the time he became director of the review, Groulx wanted his nationalist doctrine to receive the endorsement

1. Susan Mann Trofimenkoff, *Action Française: French Canadian Nationalism in the Twenties* (Toronto: University of Toronto Press, 1975), 157 p.; Jean-Claude Dupuis, *Nationalisme et catholicisme: L'Action française de Montréal* (1917–1928), master's thesis (history), Université de Montréal, 1992, 329 p.
2. The articles included in the study were published the following year as Lionel Groulx, ed., *Notre avenir politique* (Montréal: Bibliothèque de l'Action française, 1923), 269 p.
3. Lionel Groulx, "Notre avenir politique: Conclusion," *AF*, December 1922, p. 333–348; La direction de l'Action française, "Notre avenir politique," *AF*, January 1922, p. 4–25.

of Msgr. Louis-Adolphe Pâquet, the eminent theologian of the Séminaire de Québec. In September of 1920, he asked him for an honest answer to the following question:

> Do you believe I can write, while adhering to sound doctrine, that we in Québec must be more concerned about our French *survivance* than about Canadian unity? Not that I am by any means becoming indifferent to harmony between the races and the coordination of efforts to make this great country more prosperous and successful. But it seems to me that for some time now, a category of French Canadians is, under the pretext of *bonne entente*, in the process of sabotaging the most sacred of our rights and our guarantees . . . Could we therefore maintain that the primary goal of any federation is to obtain the *survivance* of the federated states by means of the union, and that everything else is but a secondary goal? The Canadian provinces, it seems to me, did not abdicate their distinctiveness in 1867. It was through our efforts that the principle of provincialism prevailed over legislative union. It was because we cared enough to defend our national character above all else, and because we did not see fit to sacrifice it on the altar of the great whole.

Pâquet provided Groulx with a reply that must certainly have alleviated some of his anxieties. The *survivance* of the French Canadians, he told him, was in no way incompatible with Canadian unity, the latter needing necessarily to involve respect for the prerogatives of the entities making up the federation. The provinces, in fact, were not subservient to the federal state: it was the federal state, rather, that was subordinate to them. The theologian even added that the *survivance* of the language and culture of the French Canadians was intimately linked to the preservation of their Catholicism: "You are convinced, as am I, and you understand as well as I do, that this fully authorizes us, to be much more concerned for French-Canadian interests than Canadian interests as such."[4]

Why did Groulx think he needed the sanction of a theologian before proceeding with the study of the political future of French Canada? Jean-Claude Dupuis explains that such prudence on Groulx's part stemmed from the intellectual conservatism of the French-Canadian clergy, which came out of the counter-revolutionary thinking of the nineteenth century. The danger was great, in other words, that the study would be viewed as a form of adhesion to the principle of popular sovereignty and a rejection of the idea of the providential order of things. Complementing the analyses of Susan Mann Trofimenkoff and Jean-Pierre Gaboury,[5] Dupuis adds that it is this conservatism that explains the

4. Letters from Lionel Groulx to Louis-Adolphe Pâquet, BAnQ, FLG, P1/A,2857, [September 28, 1920]; from Louis-Adolphe Pâquet to Lionel Groulx, BAnQ, FLG, P1/A,2857, September 29, 1920.
5. Jean-Pierre Gaboury, *Le Nationalisme de Lionel Groulx: Aspects idéologiques* (Ottawa: Presses de l'Université d'Ottawa, 1970), 226 p.

"passive" nature or the "restraint" of the "separatism" espoused by Groulx and *L'Action française*. Thus, it was necessary, in order to dissipate Groulx's theological scruples, that the question of the political independence of French Canada be debated within the limits prescribed by respect for the established order. Authority, regardless of what the democrats or the revolutionaries thought about it, always originated with Providence, according to Groulx and his colleagues: the "people," as such, were not "sovereign." Abbé Groulx wanted to avoid starting down a slippery slope, by ensuring that his brand of nationalism and his review's debate on Canadian Confederation were theologically orthodox. He was preparing to weather the impending storm.

It seemed a foregone conclusion that the *L'Action française* study would spark controversy, so much so that it made certain individuals back out, even some who normally did not run from a challenge. Olivar Asselin, it appears, was one of them. At least that is what we are given to understand from Antonio Perrault's remarks to Groulx stating that the formidable journalist, after some prevarication, had finally declined to provide the article requested of him on the economic obstacles to "the independence of French Canada": "The only reason he gave me for his tardy refusal," Perrault wrote to Groulx, "was that 'he too was becoming prudent.'" In the end, it was Georges Pelletier, a writer with *Le Devoir* at the time, who wrote the article in question.[6]

What did this polemic on the "French state" actually consist in? Without enumerating each of the studies that were part of the 1922 project, suffice it to say that Groulx and his collaborators envisaged that the federal bond would be broken in the more or less immediate future and that French Canada—and this must be emphasized—would not in any way have a hand in this breakup. The review believed, rather, that Confederation was doomed to collapse, what with the discontent of the Western provinces, who were worried about the marginalization of agricultural industry. Farming had long been the basis of the Canadian economy, benefitting the industrial sector that had developed in Ontario and Québec during and after the First World War. But the 1921 census indicated that the majority of Canadians were residing in urban areas. The industrialization process, whose acceleration was enabled by the war, continued well into the 1920s, with the mad rush to exploit the country's natural resources, particularly in forestry, mining and hydroelectricity. The economic growth that followed was, in large measure, the result of the massive intervention of American capital. The United States had become Canada's principal foreign investor, thus outranking Great Britain. In this context, the defenders of agriculture touched off what could cautiously be termed an "agrarian revolt," expressed on the federal political scene by the founding of the Progressive Party in 1920. The Progressives, consisting

6. Letter from Antonio Perrault to Lionel Groulx, BAnQ, FLG, P1/A,2960, January 18, 1922. See Georges Pelletier, "Les obstacles économiques à l'indépendance du Canada français," AF, August 1922, p. 66–82.

of farmers from the Prairies and Ontario as well as dissident Liberals, obtained sixty-five seats in the 1921 elections, which was sufficient to raise them to the rank of Official Opposition.

The popularity of the Progressives faded in the elections of 1925 and 1926, due especially to Prime Minister Mackenzie King's efforts to re-establish the traditional balance between Liberals and Conservatives. But at the start of the decade, this balance seemed very much threatened indeed, if not altogether destroyed. The rise of militant regionalism in the West had been accompanied by a spectacular demographic increase—owing mainly to the upswing in immigration toward the end of the nineteenth century—which allowed the Prairies to have greater influence in the House of Commons. It was no doubt not entirely far-fetched, at the time, to envisage the possible dismantling of the Canadian federation, or to believe it risked collapsing under the weight of diverging economic interests and the radicalization of the political conflict between the Western provinces and Central Canada. This was, in 1922, the premise on which the *L'Action française* study on the political future of French Canada was based. According to the review, French Canadians had the right to prepare for the inevitable backlash that would occur if the bond with Confederation were broken. The review considered itself authorized to envisage, in the event of such a scenario, the creation of an independent state. They were entitled to "prepare for the future" without fear of violating the Catholic principle of respect for the established order: parties other than the French Canadians would have had to bear responsibility for the dismantling of the country. Of all those who worked on the study, it was Abbé Arthur Robert, a theologian at Université Laval, who, in an article analyzing the "philosophical foundations" of the "aspirations" of French Canada, developed this argument most clearly.[7]

What would become of the French minorities in the other provinces in the wake of the dismantling of Confederation? In an overview article in the study, the leadership of the review anticipated the apprehensions of the minorities and wanted to offer them reassurance. It was not Québec that would provoke the fragmentation of the country, but others. What was more, the French-Canadian nation was not a political or state entity in the strict sense. As a community of faith, history, language, culture and tradition, it transcended territorial boundaries:

> Our attitude in no way implies abandonment. We have clearly affirmed this from the start: we are not rushing to bring about any kind of separation; we will accept only the separations imposed on us by necessity or by the twists and turns of history, against which, consequently, neither party can do anything. . . . Our compatriots know as well that our loyal friendship toward them and our ardent desire to cooperate for their wellbeing are in no way conditioned by the current political

7. Arthur Robert, "Aspirations du Canada français: Fondement philosophique," AF, February 1922, p. 66–81.

> ties. These sentiments emanate from a more spontaneous solidarity, from a deeper fraternity.[8]

In the third article of the study, lawyer Louis-D. Durand held that the new state could be made up of Québec, the three Maritime provinces and part of Ontario, no doubt the border regions where there were large groups of French Canadians.[9] Groulx could not logically ignore the question of the French minorities and what relationship they would have with the new state. During the study's planning stages, he told his colleagues of his intention to make this question the subject of an in-depth study.[10] It was to his great collaborator in Ottawa, Oblate Rodrigue Villeneuve, that Groulx entrusted the task of drafting the article on the consequences of a possible dismantling of Canada for "our brothers of the diaspora." Groulx advised him to develop the idea that the creation of a "French state," should that occur, did not in any way signify Québec's abandonment of the minorities. On the contrary, he explained, the greatest service Québec could render to the French Canadians in the other provinces was to demonstrate cultural vitality and political vigour. This responsibility, once again, fell to Québec as "ancestral home" of the French-Canadian nation:

> It seems to me that what a people requires before all else is a life vision, not a general one, not just any vision, but one that is clear, specific and concrete. That is what has been missing in Québec; that is what we need to give it. It does not mean forgetting about our dispersed brothers; on the contrary, it means guaranteeing that the instrument through which we can help them does not fall into disrepair; it means strengthening the heart of the race, so that a richer, warmer blood can pulse through the large arteries and out to the extremities.[11]

Villeneuve, who agreed to draft the article, insisted however that Groulx revise it several times. The Oblate feared it would be considered "a little too revolutionary and anti-British," especially by the Church hierarchy in Ottawa. Groulx intervened to "delete what he could from the compromising passages" by Villeneuve, although we do not know which passages these were. The Oblate continued, nevertheless, to worry about the reactions his article would surely generate and even advised his friend, in a final moment of anxiety, to refuse to publish it. "You did well to make the decision for me, he wrote the day after the piece appeared. "If I am condemned to hang, I will go courageously."[12]

8. Editorial board of *L'Action française*, "Notre avenir politique," *AF*, January 1922, p. 22.
9. Louis-D. Durand, "La croisée des chemins," *AF*, March 1922, p. 148.
10. Letters from Lionel Groulx to Georges Courchesne, BAnQ, FLG, P1/A,889, June 13, 1921; to Omer Héroux, BAnQ, FLG, P1/A,1758, June 13, 1921.
11. Letter from Lionel Groulx to Rodrigue Villeneuve, BAnQ, FLG, P1/A,3696, [1922].
12. Exchange of correspondence between Lionel Groulx and Rodrigue Villeneuve, BAnQ, FLG, P1/A,3696, August 14, 1922.

Villeneuve's article, which he entitled "What of our dispersed brothers?" highlighted many of the arguments mentioned above. The fragmentation of the Canadian federation would result not from any schemes coming out of Québec, but from the dissatisfaction of the Western provinces with Central Canada; the importance of agriculture in the Prairies led these provinces to more readily accept free trade with the United States and, by that very fact, greater Americanization of their way of life. In any event, maintaining the federal bond had not prevented the provincial governments from systematically violating the educational and religious rights of the French minorities. Québec, for its part, had only been able to stand helplessly by as its "dispersed brothers" were being persecuted. Finally, Villeneuve used a philosophical argument to allay the fears of the minorities: if the territory and the form of government of a "nationality" constituted its "body," he explained, its origins and language represented its "soul." The existence of a nation did not depend in any way whatsoever on the political structures to which it was subject.

> Now, if there is such a thing as a duty to individual charity, there is also such a thing as a duty to *national charity*; and if the degree of charity is measured by the degree of union of hearts, not to mention the degree of need, it goes without saying that, even if political unity ceases and territory is divided, *national duty* is in no way extinguished. The better part is left intact: the formal ties, the soul bonds, the connections that make our basic moral temperament the same, that make our community ideals endure, by which hearts and minds are shaped in the same manner under the influence of familiar words and expressions, carrying on their wings the same higher thoughts and sovereign goals. Which shows us that separation by legal borders would not in the least sever the blood ties between us, but would continue to impose on us the obligations of a true fraternity.[13]

The French minorities, whatever the constitutional future of Canada might have been, would always have remained the "co-nationals" of the French Canadians of the new state, Villeneuve concluded. This excerpt reveals clearly, once again, what *L'Action française* considered as the essential foundations of the French-Canadian nation. Villeneuve, like Durand before him, did not dismiss the possibility that the new state could comprise Québec and "member regions." "In our humble opinion," he wrote in conclusion, "our faraway brothers have reason to be somewhat concerned about the political regime currently binding them to us, as heaven does not seem to be affording it much protection."

13. Rodrigue Villeneuve, "Et nos frères de la dispersion ?" AF, July 1922, p. 17. Italics are ours.

Reactions to the 1922 Study

In the conclusion to the study, Abbé Groulx gave a summary of all these arguments. While acknowledging the "legitimate alarm felt by the brothers of our race," he maintained the hope that the study by Villeneuve would put their minds at rest. "Could our brothers of the diaspora really," he asked, "hanker after the influence of a government that was never, in fact, of any support to them?"[14] These remarks were not sufficient to reassure the French minorities, who were visibly shaken by the ramifications of the possible creation of a "French state." And its detractors did not waste any time in making their voices heard either.

The first to man the barricades was Henri Bourassa. Groulx's "separatism," he insisted, condemned the minorities to certain death, and he wanted to defend them. We shall not revisit in detail the conflict between the directors of *L'Action française* and *Le Devoir*, a conflict that aggravated the famous Sentinelle crisis toward the end of the 1920s.[15] But let us recall that Bourassa's sorties against *L'Action française* managed to fuel the anger and resentment felt by its director. In a letter to Rodrigue Villeneuve, Groulx labelled Bourassa's admonishments as "exaggerated" and "crude," and his "polemical methods" as "absolutely deplorable": "Can such a serious person really venture to reproach a colonized people like ours for an excess of nationalism and try to warn of the dangers of intellectualism for our young clergy! This is the height of exaggeration and really goes too far."[16] In November of 1923, Bourassa gave a vitriolic speech that finally caused Groulx to lose his sangfroid. The following month, the editorial board of *L'Action française* prepared for its prestigious detractor a counter-attack in due form. The accusations of "separatism" that Bourassa had fired at them were, in their opinion, unjustified: "Our attitude is determined solely by the probability of a dismantling of the Canadian state." Bourassa was wrong, they went on, to attribute to *L'Action française* the desire to see Québec withdraw into itself. Although Québec would have been its principal nucleus, the "French state" would in all likelihood have encompassed the border regions of the neighbouring provinces: "We refrained from fixing the borders of the future state and our discretion is explained by a motivation that is easily discernible. Nevertheless, we have made it amply clear that these borders could not be those of Québec as it is today." In the final analysis, the strengthening of the ancestral home of the nation, notwithstanding the political regime in place, could only have benefitted "our brothers in the West."[17]

---

14. Lionel Groulx, "Notre avenir politique: Conclusion," AF, December 1922, p. 339.
15. It will be sufficient to consult Jean-Claude Dupuis, *Nationalisme et catholicisme*, p. 198–205, 282–287; Susan Mann Trofimenkoff, *Action Française*, p. 97, 103–107; Damien-Claude Bélanger, *Lionel Groulx et la Franco-Américanie*, master's thesis (history), Université de Montréal, 2000, p. 133–161.
16. Letter from Lionel Groulx to Rodrigue Villeneuve, BAnQ, FLG, P1/A,3696, April 23, 1923.
17. The directors of Ligue d'Action française, "Notre avenir politique: Mise au point," AF, December 1923, p. 351–353.

The French minorities, on the other hand, did not rely on Bourassa alone to express their concerns. Some of their own leaders, deeply worried, approached Abbé Groulx directly to advise him of their fears. Was *L'Action française* really separatist? they asked him. Had the Québec nationalist movement really abandoned all confidence in the *survivance* of the French minorities? The Archbishop of Saint-Boniface, Arthur Béliveau, was among those from the West who reproached Groulx. Commenting on the article by Rodrigue Villeneuve, the prelate indicated to the director of *L'Action française* that "the impression it left one with was: 'You'll have to manage on your own, there is nothing else we can do for you.' . . . We are perhaps being over-sensitive but, when you are suffering and you feel threatened, that happens even to those of us who don't want to be sensitive." Béliveau explained, to Groulx's credit, that he had grasped the subtleties of the study and that, in essence, he did not think that *L'Action française* was really separatist. However, he said he feared that other minds, less able to make fine distinctions and less informed than his, might characterize the 1922 study in such a way as to harm the efforts of those dedicating themselves to the *survivance* and, especially, to the expansion of the French Canadians in Manitoba and the other Western provinces:

> Should we not fear that certain disciples have gone farther than the master, by resolutely taking a stand, already at this time, against all new action in Manitoba and the Canadian West? . . . Our colonizing missionaries tell us that this latest manner of understanding the theory of *L'Action française* invalidates, to a large extent, the work they are doing there.[18]

Groulx sent Béliveau no reply that we know of. However, in a letter he sent to Rodrigue Villeneuve two days later, he expressed sadness that the Franco-Manitoban prelate and Msgr. Joseph-Henri Prud'homme, of Prince-Albert and Saskatoon, had "echoed Mr. Bourassa's attacks" and lamented the fact that some were behaving "as if they had understood nothing of what they had read.[19] A few weeks earlier, in effect, *Le Devoir* had reported that Béliveau, during an evening organized by the ACJC in Montréal, had announced his opposition to the separatist "theory" of *L'Action française*. The Archbishop's position, *Le Devoir* added, was far from ambivalent:

> His Grace differs in opinion here with those who advocate a closed doors government in Québec and who seek one day to be *maîtres chez soi*. "The argument is sound," he said; "those who maintain it are too assiduous in their work for our *survivance* for me to want to cause them any chagrin. However, is it right that we

18. Letter from Arthur Béliveau to Lionel Groulx, BAnQ, FLG, P1/A,286, May 29, 1923.
19. Letter from Lionel Groulx to Rodrigue Villeneuve, BAnQ, FLG, P1/A,3696, May 31, 1923.

> should limit our only efforts as a nation to the Northeastern part of America? A closed doors government does us a grave wrong in the West and I believe it is no longer possible in the face of the immigration of our people from Québec to the United States."[20]

Groulx wrote to Béliveau, through the intermediary of Abbé Sabourin of Saint-Boniface, to clearly explain the position of *L'Action française* on the question of the "French state" and the minorities. He repeated the arguments developed time and again since the beginning of the debate the preceding year to reassure French Canadians in the West: the rupture of the federal bond seemed inevitable to him, sooner or later; the creation of a "French state" did not signify abandonment of the minorities by Quebec; the constitutional status quo had never allowed the old province to protect the educational and religious rights of its "friends" in the West; the ties binding Québec to the minorities were not based on the political structures in place, but on a deeper, "national," solidarity; and finally, the *survivance* of the minorities depended directly on the relative strength of Québec in America.[21]

The "French state" debate was also raised by certain militant nationalists in Ontario, including the president of ACFEO, Senator Napoléon Belcourt. In May of 1924, as we have seen, *L'Action française* awarded Belcourt its *Grand Prix* to honour his contribution to the Franco-Ontarian resistance to Regulation 17. After reading over a copy of the speech that Belcourt was to deliver during the ceremony, Groulx asked the secretary of ACFEO, Edmond Cloutier, if the Senator would agree to modify an excerpt that he deemed too harsh toward the review. Groulx indicated that the passage in question could have been interpreted as an unshakeable profession of faith in the future of Confederation and—especially—as a thumbing of the nose at *L'Action française*, as well as a condemnation, albeit an implicit one, of its political reflections. He concluded by stating once again that he believed "the more or less imminent fall of Confederation to be inevitable" and that it was necessary, as of now, to anticipate this possibility: "This future, we must prepare for it, not only within the borders of Québec, but in Eastern Canada, taking it upon ourselves to stay connected, beyond these borders, with our distant groups, as we are currently trying to do."[22] Belcourt's reply reached Groulx through the publisher of *Le Droit*, Father Charles Charlebois, who conveyed to him that, rather than contradict *L'Action française*, the Senator had decided to delete the compromising passage from his speech. Charlebois, seeking no doubt to respect his friend's sensibilities, added that he believed Belcourt "fundamentally" agreed

20. Charles-Édouard Parrot, "La soirée d'hier au Collège Sainte-Marie," *Le Devoir*, May 8, 1923, p. 4.
21. Letter from Lionel Groulx to Abbé Sabourin [May 1923?], cited in Susan Mann Trofimenkoff, *Abbé Groulx: Variations on a Nationalist Theme* (Toronto: Copp Clark Publishing, 1973), p. 186–188.
22. Letter from Lionel Groulx to Edmond Cloutier, BAnQ, FLG, P1/A,818, May 19, 1924.

with Groulx on the question of the future of Confederaton, but that in the opinion of the president of ACFEO, the review had perhaps been wrong to show its hand so soon: "If, however, there is a divergence of opinion," the Oblate pointed out,

> it is that [Belcourt] is not convinced the time has come to show your attitude *publicly* and it is for that very reason that he expressed in the [deleted] paragraph his conviction that for the time being, it is the federal pact that offers French culture and civilization the only means of survival and expansion and the only way to prepare for the possible future you have foreseen.[23]

If Belcourt showed himself to be conciliatory, it may have been because, as a gentleman, he was reluctant to unnecessarily upset the very people who were about to pay him tribute. Clearly, he did not think the matter settled. A few days after he had received the award, Belcourt returned to the "French state" debate, sending a request to Groulx, again through the intervention of Charlebois, for a meeting with the editorial board of *L'Action française* to discuss it at greater length. Charlebois continued to play a mediating role, advising Groulx that, in his view, there was still no "basic divergence between *L'Action française* and *Monsieur* Belcourt" at all. It seems, however, that the tête-à-tête that the president of ACFEO had asked for did not take place. Groulx answered Charlebois that the crowded schedule of the review's directors made it impossible for them to agree on a date that would suit everyone. He also took the opportunity to ask him, somewhat frostily, to pass on to Belcourt a copy of the 1922 study. As the Senator had not yet read the results of the study in their entirety, the exchanges, according to Groulx, would in any event have been unproductive. Groulx repeated his conviction that "Confederation [was] being swept toward its ruin by powerful forces far superior to human will": "But it was never our intent," he added, "to campaign openly for the immediate founding of a French state." By the following year, it seemed Abbé Groulx had adopted a more moderate theory of the inevitability of the dismantling of Confederation. In February 1925, he had already ceased to speak of a breakup in the strict sense and implied to Charlebois that it was possible to envisage the creation of a "French state" within the federal structures: "If we do not manage to maintain a French state in Québec, no French minority in Canada will be able to survive."[24]

The cruellest rebuff Lionel Groulx and *L'Action française* received was no doubt the one that came from Abbé Denys Lamy of Saint-Boniface. During a talk he gave in Manchester in the fall of 1923, Lamy administered a severe rebuke to *L'Action française*, denouncing its separatist tendencies in no uncertain terms. Lamy,

23. Letter from Charles Charlebois to Lionel Groulx, BAnQ, FLG, P1/A,746, May 20, 1924.
24. Exchange of correspondence between Lionel Groulx and Charles Charlebois, BAnQ, FLG, P1/A,746, June 4, 1924 to February 11, 1925.

whose reputation preceded him, was not unknown to Groulx and must certainly have made him somewhat wary. In 1909, Émile Chartier, one of Groulx's main collaborators in founding the Association catholique de la jeunesse canadienne some twenty years earlier, had already described him as "a nuisance" and "a hothead" when he worked in the Franco-American circles of the ACJC.[25] It may have been Adolphe Robert, of the Association canado-américaine of Manchester, who was the first to report to Groulx on Lamy's schemes. Lamy had accused *L'Action française* of wanting to stop the flow of French-Canadian missionaries, and especially the teaching communities, arriving in New England every year. Robert assured Groulx that he lent no credence to Abbé Lamy's statements, but he advised Groulx nevertheless to print a clarification in the pages of *L'Action française*.[26]

This clarification was indeed published, in the form of a letter from Abbé Groulx to Adolphe Robert, in which he explained that the review had never intended to deprive the minorities of the crucial protection that the religious teaching communities represented for them. At all times, he pointed out, he had recognized their importance and encouraged their efforts. He also formally refuted the fabrications invented by Lamy, who claimed he had the blessing of Msgr. Béliveau in his crusade against *L'Action française*. Groulx countered that he had personally discussed the matter at length with the prelate, the only person entitled to "speak with authority for our brothers in the Canadian West," and that the two men had subsequently found themselves in perfect agreement with each other. In conclusion, he stated that, contrary to what Abbé Lamy had implied, he had never sought to stem the expansion of French Canadians toward the West, even though he might have preferred to see them choose first to populate Québec's virgin territories:

> And, for example, like everyone here, we believe we need to direct French Canadians toward the country rather than toward the cities and that, therefore, a French-Canadian farmer in the West is better than a French Canadian in Montréal. Only, we think that before letting him leave for the West, the US or Montréal, every effort must be made to keep him on Québec soil, the greatest strength of the entire French race in America.[27]

Determined not to be outdone, Lamy continued to look for a fight. Following the publication of that issue of *L'Action française*, he insisted on his right to a riposte and used it to scold both the review and its director: "Let me tell you," he wrote Groulx, "that no one takes seriously your dream of a French state. The sooner you

25. Letter from Émile Chartier to Lionel Groulx, BAnQ, FLG, P1/A,764, March 11, 1909.
26. Letter from Adolphe Robert to Lionel Groulx, BAnQ, FLG, P1/A,3201, September 12, 1923.
27. Lionel Groulx, "Partie documentaire [Letter from Lionel Groulx to Adolphe Robert, September 14, 1923]," AF, September 1923, p. 190–192.

declare your abandonment of it, the better it will be for *L'Action française*." We don't know whether Abbé Groulx replied to Lamy. The review, although it must have wanted to be done with such an agitator, refused to grant his request or welcome him on its pages. Lamy was infuriated and was not going to let himself be treated this way. He returned to the attack, accusing Groulx of having "muzzled" him and begged him to drop his "calamitous project," "this crazy dream of a French state," for fear he might "be ridiculed." He even suggested that a good part of the French-Canadian hierarchy, including Msgrs. Béliveau, Prud'homme and Pâquet, had turned their back on Groulx and his colleagues. The polemicist launched another diatribe shortly afterwards against the director of *L'Action française*, accusing him this time of having destroyed his reputation in the ecclesiastical world and having spread the false impression that he was "at odds" with his archbishop, Arthur Béliveau.[28]

What did Groulx think of this controversy and in particular of the rage that accompanied Abbé Lamy's attacks? Unfortunately, we do not have any of the correspondence that he sent to his detractor. In a letter to Rodrigue Villeneuve, however, he called him a "poor maniac" and did not take great offence at his carrying on. Villeneuve, on the other hand, seemed more sceptical: "this fool is all the same an embarrassment by virtue of his stupidity," he wrote, before confiding that the Archbishop of Saint-Boniface also felt "very much embarrassed" by him. Béliveau had even confided to Villeneuve "that he had no alternative but to consider the priest ill."[29] The Franco-Manitoban prelate was not the only one who thought this. Eugène Jalbert, a lawyer in Woonsocket who was very much involved in the Franco-American nationalist movement, felt the same way, as he told Groulx in October 1923. Shortly before, Lamy had publicly counted Jalbert among his allies in his campaign to denigrate *L'Action française*. Jalbert, feeling that he had been the victim of an injustice, wanted to deny this statement and set the record straight. He wrote Groulx:

> M. l'*abbé* Lamy was certainly wrong to lead you to believe that I was associated with him in the controversy that he seems to want to pursue with you regarding the relationship between our groups. He is wrong, I repeat, but I have nothing to do with this. I know that, ill as he is, he is capable of every aberration, even of misunderstanding those with whom he converses.[30]

Notwithstanding the state of Lamy's mental health, it remains true nevertheless that at *L'Action française*, they were aware that the 1922 study threatened

28. Letters from Denys Lamy to Lionel Groulx, BAnQ, FLG, P1/A,2055, October 5, 1923, October 16, 1923 and November 22, 1923.
29. Letters from Lionel Groulx to Rodrigue Villeneuve, BAnQ, FLG, P1/A,3696, September 21, 1923; from Rodrigue Villeneuve to Lionel Groulx, BAnQ, FLG, P1/A,3696, October 4, 1923.
30. Letter from Eugène Jalbert to Lionel Groulx, BAnQ, FLG, P1/A,1812, October 10, 1923.

to tarnish the image of the review, especially among the French minorities. This no doubt explains why, shortly after the "French state" debate, the review often prominently featured testimonies of confidence and solidarity it received from the French communities in the other provinces. We mentioned earlier that Msgr. Prud'homme visited Montréal in March of 1924 and that Antonio Perrault gave a speech during the luncheon held in honour of the Bishop of Prince-Albert and Saskatoon. It was an unexpected opportunity for *L'Action française* to polish its image. By reiterating its faith in the *survivance* of the minorities before one of their most eminent representatives, it had found the perfect stage from which to announce yet again, to whoever wanted to hear, that its political reflections had in no way diminished its devoted friendship toward them. Groulx, in quoting Perrault's speech, did not fail to highlight this point and, while he was at it, to take a swipe at those who slandered the movement he led:

> *L'Action française*, like any person of stature . . . , has its enemies, and sometimes they try to mar its image. They depict its directors as narrow-minded provincialists who want to erect around our province a wall as thick and as high as the Great Wall of China. We are too familiar with your clear-sightedness, Your Grace, not to assume that you have seen through this imaginary wall or, rather, through these accusations.[31]

The same scenario occurred two years later when a group of French Canadians from the West travelled to Montréal, sponsored by the Société Saint-Jean-Baptiste. The director of *L'Action française* gave the official welcome at a formal ceremony at the Monument-National. He reiterated his faith in their *survivance* and in the apostolic mission of French Canada, to which, in his view, the history of the West testified eloquently. But he also wanted to reassure them regarding the intentions of his review: "On behalf of Québec, it is our duty to . . . help you in your struggle for *survivance*. Let us dispel here any ambiguity that may have persisted too long! No, we do not wish to confine ourselves to the Québec *reserve*." Groulx compared the emigration of French Canadians to a "haemorrhage." But he saw the move to the West as infinitely preferable to the exodus to the big cities of the United States, or even of Québec: ". . . the sons that Québec cannot keep on its soil, take them away: we do not deny you this. Rather than see them throw themselves into the abyss of our big cities or into the maw of the American Moloch, we would rather see them in our fresh country air, growing wheat and raising children."[32]

31. Excerpt from a speech given by Antonio Perrault on March 10, 1924 to the Cercle universitaire de Montréal, cited in Jacques Brassier [pseudonym of L. Groulx], "La vie de l'Action française," AF, March 1924, p. 183. See also Lionel Groulx, *Mes Mémoires, Tome II: 1920–1928* (Montréal: Éditions Fides, 1971), p. 70–71, 318.
32. Lionel Groulx, "Compatriotes de l'Ouest, c'est donc votre droit de vous entêter à survivre," *Le Devoir*, December 21, 1926, p. 4.

At times, the references to the "French state," were more veiled, but no less real. We saw that in 1924 Groulx went on a speaking tour in the counties of Kent and Essex in Southern Ontario. In his account of the trip, published shortly afterwards in *L'Action française*, he reported the friendly welcome and the affectionate words the Franco-Ontarians had had for him. It was proof, if needed, that the libellous accusations of the smear campaign by the review's enemies had not managed to fool anyone:

> These shows of confidence require, like a ransom paid, the acceptance of greater responsibility on our part. But at least these compatriots in Ontario realize that we are far from wanting to keep our efforts contained within the borders of the province of Québec; that we mean for our French action to spread throughout all the regions where groups of our people live. And to receive from them this measure of justice, that does us a world of good.[33]

In 1925, when another group of French Canadians, this time from Saskatchewan, was visiting Montréal, the review had similar comments to make:

> At *L'Action française*, we have never said: Politics first! We are not at all indifferent to the geographic or material frameworks of our existence, but we believe nonetheless that the destiny of an apostolic race must take precedence over all political remedies and interests and that we cannot, as willing believers, be excused from devoting our best efforts to that task.[34]

During the "French state" controversy, and despite the worries of certain Franco-Ontarians, it was mainly the French Canadians situated not west of the Ottawa River, but west of Lake Superior to whom *L'Action française* wanted to offer comfort and reassurance. In February 1927, a few months before the review folded, the directorship issued one last appeal for national solidarity, in the hopes of putting an end to the debate:

> May our compatriots in the West cease to reproach us for leaving them to their own fate. Whatever happens, the French-Canadian nationality will always mean for us all of the groups bound by the same blood and the same history, who, by virtue of that, owe mutual assistance to one another. We are not abandoning anything or anyone.[35]

33. Nicolas Tillemont [pseudonym of L. Groulx], "La vie de l'Action française," AF, May 1924, p. 315–316.
34. L'Action française, "Bienvenue," AF, December 1925, p. 338. See also "Le voyage de la survivance française," AF, October 1926, p. 209.
35. L'Action française, "Le problème national," AF, February 1927, p. 79.

Lionel Groulx, the French Minorities and the Idea of Independence During the 1930s

Abbé Groulx stepped down as director of *L'Action française* at the beginning of 1928 in order, he said, to dedicate himself entirely to his historical works. A few weeks prior, the review had been renamed *L'Action canadienne-française*. The directors wanted, in this way, to avoid being associated in any way with the *L'Action française* of Charles Maurras, in Paris, which had just suffered the disgrace of a papal condemnation. Despite the new identity the Montréal review wanted to create for itself, its days were numbered. *L'Action canadienne-française* managed to survive the departure of its director for only a few months. In December 1928, it published its very last issue. Groulx's departure was not the only reason behind the decline of the review, which also experienced numerous administrative problems.[36] The review was soon to be reborn in another form with the founding in 1933 of *L'Action nationale*. Abbé Groulx, for his part, contributed regularly to it, but, although he was considered, in certain respects, as its éminence grise, he did not play the leading role there that he had had at *L'Action française*.

The context, furthermore, had also changed. Toward the end of the 1920s, nationalism had become highly suspect in the upper echelons of the Catholic hierarchy, as evidenced by the fate reserved by the Holy See for Maurras's newspaper. Closer to home, in New England, the Franco-Americans involved in the "Sentinellist" movement had been given a sentence of excommunication for their boldness in hauling the Bishop of Providence, Rhode Island, William Hickey, before the civil courts. They were contesting the right that Hickey had arrogated to himself to build an English-language diocesan college using the financial reserves of his Franco-American parishes.[37] The "French state" controversy had already brought accusations of radicalism against *L'Action canadienne-française*. And the militant nationalist review, which was, moreover, Catholic and ultramontane, had every reason to show prudence in the intellectual context of the late twenties. Abbé Groulx, for his part, was fully aware of the extent to which nationalism had fallen into disfavour. He felt this was a time for staying level-headed:

> We must ask God to keep our hand steady and our vision clear, he wrote to René Chaloult in 1927. Nationalism is viewed with disdain in Rome, due to the extremes committed in its name in certain countries. We must hope that the crisis will serve to clarify ideas rather than obscure them. And let us be restrained and honest, so that we may be able to face those who have ill intentions and are just waiting for a pretext to denounce us.[38]

36. See Lionel Groulx, *Mes Mémoires, Tome II*, p. 269–383.
37. Consult Yves Roby, *Les Franco-Américains de la Nouvelle-Angleterre, 1776–1930* (Sillery: Septentrion, 1990), 434 p.; Damien-Claude Bélanger, *Lionel Groulx et la Franco-Américanie*, p. 133–161; Jean-Claude Dupuis, *Nationalisme et catholicisme*, p. 282–287; Susan Mann Trofimenkoff, *Action française*, p. 103–107.
38. Letter from Lionel Groulx to René Chaloult, BAnQ, FLG, P1/A,704, February 25, 1927.

The demise of *L'Action canadienne-française* did not, however, bring the "French state" debate to a definitive close. On the contrary, it continued from the twenties right through to the end of the thirties and would haunt Abbé Groulx during that entire period. But he had already started looking at the issue differently in the thirties. In general, his discourse gave less attention to the idea of a more or less imminent breakup of Confedération. Not that he had thrown out the concept of the "French state." This idea continued, just as it did during the twenties, to sustain a good deal of his polemical work. Nevertheless, Abbé Groulx no longer presented it necessarily as a consequence of the dismantling of Canada. He explained, rather, that the "French state" was a project that was realizable by French Canadians right within the federal system. The attitude of mistrust that had made nationalism suspect in certain circles at the start of the 1930s may have played a part in prompting Groulx to watch his ideas and his words. Furthermore, if it is true that the 1922 study on the political future of French Canada was triggered by the more or less real threat posed by the discontent of the West over maintaining Confederation, it is possible that the relative diminishment of regionalist sentiment in the Prairies toward the end of the decade deprived Groulx's "separatism" of some of its conceptual justification. In fact, the popularity of the Progressives declined in the elections of 1925 and 1926, as Prime Minister Mackenzie King succeeded in bringing several of them back into the fold of the Liberal Party. Among those who chose to resist the Prime Minister's efforts, some rallied in 1932 to the newly founded Cooperative Commonwealth Federation. Others joined the ranks of the Conservatives in 1942 to form the Progressive Conservative Party.[39]

In any case, this idea of the "French state" as an "ideal," rather than as a concrete political project to be realized, had already been proposed by Groulx at the start of the twenties during his famous speech on French friendship in America: "If . . . we have kindled like a flame the hope of a French state in North America, it was not that we thought it would be realized immediately or that we were impatient to hasten its reality by even a day."[40] But rather, he went on, the project embodied "a lofty thought, intended to inspire order and action," and was meant to be transformed into an "organizer of French solidarity" for all French groups in America. Groulx did not rule out the possibility that the federal government would fall. But at the same time, he imbued the "French state" with a character that was more "mystical," as it were, than "political," strictly speaking: "It is a word I do not like to steal from its religious usage, but which I will use for lack of a better one and because it is in vogue: what we need is a mystique. There is not a French state, there is not a French people, unless there is a French mystique."[41]

39. See John Herd Thompson and Allen Seager, *Canada 1922–1939: Decades of Discord* (Toronto: McClelland and Stewart, 1985), xiv–438 p.
40. Lionel Groulx, "L'Amitié française d'Amérique," *Dix ans d'Action française*, p. 184–185.
41. Lionel Groulx, "Nos positions," *Orientations*, p. 266.

That was the understanding of the "French state" which, during the 1930s, most often dominated in his discourse. The ambiguity that may have characterized him during the previous decade, although we should not exaggerate the extent of it, was not nearly as present later. Take, for example, this excerpt from a speech Groulx gave in 1936 in Montréal at a Jeunesses patriotes conference:

> When we do speak of a French state, we are not thereby demanding any constitutional disruption whatsoever. In order to create this state, there is no need to change one iota of the constitutions governing us. We ask with one voice today for the realization of that which, through cowardice or lack of intelligence, our political leaders were unable to achieve in 1867. What we ask for is a state which, instead of acting, in so many areas, as if it were a neutral or cosmopolitan state, remembers also, with respect for the rights of all, to govern for the nationals of this province, for the majority of its population which is French-Canadian.[42]

According to Abbé Groulx, it was not Confederation *per se* that was at the root of the ills afflicting French Canada. The real culprits were, on the one hand, the provincial authorities of English Canada, who were quite happy to trample on the religious and educational rights of the French minorities and, on the other, the diffident sense of nation among Québec's political leaders, who were all too ready to collude with the most radical elements of the Anglo-Protestant majority and betray both the letter and the spirit of the pact of 1867. He saw the British North America (BNA) Act as the culmination of a battle waged, since the English Conquest, for the full and complete liberation of the French-Canadian people. From 1760 to 1867, from the Québec Act of 1774 to the beginning of the Parliamentary Era in 1791 to the achievement of responsible government in 1848, the history of French Canada had followed an "upward trend." This was an argument he developed explicitly in his studies on the English Regime.[43] Groulx did not subscribe to the idea that independence was predetermined by History. In his view, the pact of 1867 contained everything necessary to allow French Canadians, wherever they resided in the country, to live normal lives, that is to say, in keeping with their "national genius." All that would have had to happen was for the various political actors, in English as well as French Canada, to bring honesty and loyalty to their interpretation of the BNA Act. According to Groulx, it was not so much the Constitution in itself that posed the problem, as it was the cowardliness of the French and English political elites whose partisan mindset was dividing the life force of the nation. This is what needs to be kept in mind when interpreting

42. Lionel Groulx, "Labeurs de demain," *Directives*, p. 118.
43. Lionel Groulx, *Lendemains de Conquête* (Montréal: Bibliothèque de l'Action française, 1920), 235 p.; *Vers l'émancipation* (Montréal: Bibliothèque de l'Action française, 1921), 308 p.; *Nos luttes constitutionnelles* (Montréal: Le Devoir, published as 5 brochures, 1915–1916); *La Confédération canadienne: Ses origines* (Montréal: Le Devoir, 1918), 265 p.

the often virulent criticism Abbé Groulx directed at the federal system: "I concede therefore without difficulty that with our current race of French Canadians, a race morally weakened by more than half a century of disregard and false orientation, I admit, I say, that Confederation can only be fatal to our nationality."[44]

The "French state" was therefore not in the least incompatible with Confederation. Its "advent," on the contrary, would fit perfectly into the logic of 1867. Speaking to a group of students in 1941, Groulx readily acknowledged that "the highest sentiment of love" on the part of French Canadians should be directed toward Québec, "the old French land, born of New France, land which, more than any other part of Canada, has been for us the source of life, fruitful and abundant." At the same time, however, he added that "within Confederation, provincialism is not insurrection against the central State": he classified as "juvenile" the "equivocation" on this, expressed by circles that were hostile to French-Canadian nationalism.[45] If it were possible to create a "French state" within the federation, that would not entail abandoning the French minorities either. On this point, in any case, Groulx's reasoning remained identical to what it had been during the 1920s. The autonomy and strengthening of the "ancestral home" of the nation, he always repeated, could only improve the chances of *survivance* for the minorities.

> [By French state, I] mean . . . a State which, as Mercier le Grand would have wished, could look beyond its borders and recall that this province is the cradle of a race sorrowfully scattered and that, if mutual aid between brothers of the same origin is not always a political duty, it is a duty of national charity.[46]

In this excerpt, Groulx completely dissociates the "political" and the "national." This shows us once again that he did not consider the existence of the French-Canadian nation to have arisen from any political structures to which it was subject, whatever those might have been. It was therefore not Confederation as such that drew Abbé Groulx's ire, but rather the idea of the "Canadian nation," which he presented as a political abstraction devoid of meaning or organic life. Dominated by English Canadians, the idea of a "Canadian nation" could only, in his view, foster the cultural and linguistic homogenization of the country.

As rightly pointed out by Jean-Claude Dupuis, Groulx's separatism, during the 1920s was very "hesitant." It was even more so during the 1930s. Despite the many explanations he felt obliged to give during this period in order to clarify the true essence of his thought, Groulx was often considered a "separatist" by

44. Lionel Groulx, "Labeurs de demain," *Directives*, p. 130.
45. Lionel Groulx, "Vers l'avenir," *Paroles à des étudiants* (Montréal: Éditions de l'Action nationale, 1941), p. 52–54.
46. Lionel Groulx, "L'éducation nationale," *Directives*, p. 183. See also Lionel Groulx, "Langue et survivance," *AN*, September 1934, p. 60.

both the detractors of the *indépendantisme* theory and those who subscribed it. The fate that would have befallen the French minorities if Confederation had broken up represented a powerful argument to the former group. Running out of patience, Groulx offered the following reply to those who repeatedly "invoked the poignant cohort of the French minorities" in order to "dismiss the spectre of separatism":

> To abandon these brothers, they cry out, would be a crime. Of course, let us not approach such a sensitive question lightly. Let us nevertheless remind our brothers of the diaspora that everything has conspired for seventy years to lead them to complain, and they are infinitely justified in doing so, about the powerlessness of the federal institutions to protect their rights. No one in Canada has gauged more lucidly, and at the same time, more distressingly, than they, the terrible moral decline of their Québec compatriots under the federal regime. To be honest, we have given them ample opportunity to deplore our cowardice in the face of the violations of the rights of the minorities and our supreme indifference toward any form of national solidarity. And so, honestly, do our brothers of the minorities, believe that an independent French state, a true heartland of culture, of a robust and bright life, could serve them any less? For the rest, let us not forget that separatism would not be abandonment and is not intended to be portrayed as such. It is meant, at worst, as reconciliation to the inevitable. When you cannot save everything, you save what you can. And nothing would be gained by all perishing together under the pretext of mutual assistance.[47]

This last remark no doubt represents the harshest comment Abbé Groulx ever made about the French minorities. But for the rest, his reasoning involves nothing original and employs arguments that are by now familiar to us: Confederation has not prevented the English authorities from violating the rights of the minorities; the political elites of Québec have repeatedly shown cowardliness with respect to support for their "dispersed brethren"; a "French state," if it were independent, would not abandon them and would only contribute to French civilization everywhere in America.

Groulx declared these words in 1936. But there would be more harassment to come that he would have to counter. In June of the following year, the "French state" controversy made headlines again, this time during the Deuxième Congrès de la langue française de Québec. Abbé Groulx gave a speech entitled "L'histoire, gardienne des traditions vivantes," which, once again, sowed discord in the French-Canadian intellectual world. "Confederation," he cried, "we support it, but provided that it remains a confederation." He went on to state

47. Lionel Groulx, "Labeurs de demain," *Directives*, p. 126–127. See also Lionel Groulx, "Labeurs de demain," *Directives*, p. 121–126, 131; "L'éducation nationale," *Directives*, p. 177–178.

that the intransigence label, often applied to French-Canadian nationalism, was unfounded and sometimes bordered on hypocrisy, especially when it came from English-Canadian groups who were all too ready to strip the minorities of their educational and religious rights in order to assimilate them. He concluded his presentation with this declaration, which was, to say the least, a provocation: "Whether they wish it or not, our French state, we shall have it; we shall have a young, strong, bright and beautiful spiritual heartland, a dynamic centre for all of French America."[48]

The inevitable reactions were not long in coming. One of the first was from Msgr. Émile Yelle, Auxiliary Archbishop of Saint-Boniface, who was in Québec City at the time of the Congrès. In his *Mémoires*, Groulx recounts that Yelle, "a bishop who is nevertheless intelligent," had added his voice to the chorus of the anti-separatists, thus lapsing into "non-sense."[49] Some newspapers reported with much fanfare that Yelle had condemned Groulx's "separatism." *Le Canada*, for example, in an article with the provocative title, "Separatist doctrine denounced," attributed the following remarks to the Franco-Manitoban prelate: "To talk separatism is not to offer words of encouragement but of resignation. I ask my brothers of Québec to take note of this scandal."[50] Hardly trying to be objective, the newspaper went on to state that "the work of Abbé Groulx offer[ed] more satisfaction to the individual vanity of the Québécois," while that of "Msgr. Yelle involve[ed] more generosity of spirit and humble dedication": "This is why French Canadians who are truly imbued with the civilizing spirit of France cannot help but think that the ideal proposed by the Auxiliary Archbishop of Saint-Boniface is the ideal that is the most French and the most worthy of their efforts."[51] In his *Mémoires*, Groulx indicated, in Yelle's defence, that even before the end of the meeting, the prelate had retracted his words. After verifying with Groulx just exactly what he meant by a "French state," Yelle was able to leave perfectly reassured. *L'Action catholique*, to defend Groulx's reputation, reported the meeting between the two clerics in the following terms:

> One of the wisest and most devoted leaders of the French-Canadian defence in the West, who had not grasped, any better than we had, the meaning of the separatist note in *Monsieur* Groulx's speech, but wanted to have absolute certainty . . . , easily obtained from *Monsieur* Groulx himself a totally reassuring interpretation.[52]

The author of these lines, Eugène L'Heureux, added that Yelle, unlike others, had not misjudged Groulx's real intentions. Groulx had sought only to awaken

48. Lionel Groulx, "L'histoire, gardienne des traditions vivantes," *Directives*, p. 232, 242.
49. Lionel Groulx, *Mes Mémoires, Tome III* , p. 342–343.
50. "Dénonciation de la doctrine séparatiste," *Le Canada*, July 1 1937, p. 1.
51. "L'idéalisme de M. Groulx et celui de Mgr Yelle," *Le Canada*, July 1, 1937, p. 2.
52. Eugène L'Heureux, "Et le juste milieu?" *L'Action catholique*, July 2, 1937, p. 4.

the national sense in Québec so that it could suitably fulfill its role toward the minorities:

> No one among [the minorities] believes Canada's present constitutional formula to be carved in stone until the end of time. [They] entrust to Providence the final fate of Confederation; but [they] count on us to educate Canadians who are truly French and to organize a province of Québec that is truly, for the Race, a heartland radiant with French Catholic culture.
>
> Let us not forget that those who say these things are brothers and friends.

Several newspapers, in Québec and elsewhere in French Canada, even in the United States, dedicated long articles to this affair. Even the Premier of Québec, Maurice Duplessis, got involved in the conflict.[53] Among his apologists, Groulx could rely on Charles Gautier, editor-in-chief of *Le Droit*, who declared that "while *Monsieur* Groulx has not concealed his great desire to see a French Catholic state rise up in the province of Québec that would be 'as independent as possible,' he has not rejected Confederation. He has not burned the bridges between it and his province."[54]

Yelle may have left the 1937 conference fully satisfied with the explanations provided to him by Groulx, but others did not let him off the hook so easily. Another Franco-Manitoban, Donatien Frémont, editor-in-chief of *La Liberté* in Winnipeg, was one of them. Also in attendance at the conference, he published a piece in his paper that described the "malaise" provoked by Groulx's speech, adding that he had even been seen "rubbing shoulders with several separatist leaders." Not long afterwards, Groulx wrote him to reproach him for this "offensive allusion" which, he felt, had distorted his thought. Frémont replied that it had not been his intention to include him among the separatists, but rather to report "as a conscientious journalist" the turmoil his speech had generated. Frémont pointed out that he himself had "applauded" Groulx during his "admirable speech" and that there was in fact no substantial divergence of opinion between them: "The French state (within Confederation), we all support it, here as in Québec. It is from it that we expect fraternal and decisive help to overcome so many obstacles to our *survivance*." However, at the same time, Frémont believed Groulx was committing a monumental error by persisting in mingling with real separatists, "young misguided ones," who claimed, unjustifiably, to have been inspired by his work. He chided him that this behaviour might explain why the unfortunate accusation of "separatism," continually brought against him, persisted:

> I fail to understand why you give the ill-informed and ill-intentioned every pretext to attach your name to this movement. You are not a separatist, that is clear,

53. Lionel Groulx, *Mes Mémoires, Tome III*, p. 342–344.
54. Charles Gautier "Le Congrès de Québec et le séparatisme," *Le Droit*, July 3, 1937, p. 3.

> and everyone who reads you knows this. But there is the blatant fact which speaks louder than your writings: the separatists acknowledge no other leader but you, they proclaim it at every opportunity and no public statement of denial has ever been made that would contradict them in the least.[55]

Frémont implored Groulx to dispel this ambiguity and prevent the real separatists from interpreting his thought in every which way. Who was he talking about? It must have been a reference to the columnists writing for Québec's *La Nation*, a daily which, from 1936 to 1938, was the self-proclaimed "voice of French-Canadian separatism."[56] It is true that these writers fostered unlimited admiration if not worship for Abbé Groulx, and saw in his work the historical and conceptual justification for the separatist theory they held. Neither did they hesitate to repeat this to anyone willing to listen. Paul Bouchard, one of the newspaper's founders expressed in these crudest of terms his complete adherence to Groulx's thought or, rather, the adherence of his intellectual guide to separatist thought:

> I say categorically to all the morons and all the interested parties who impatiently cry that Abbé Groulx is not a separatist: read his works carefully and you will see that separation is the logical conclusion, that Groulx does an admirable job of demolishing the sentimental argument of the scattered French minorities throughout the Dominion, that Groulx tears down all the tall tales used to craft the federal ideal.[57]

Bouchard, like his colleagues Marcel Hamel and Pierre Chaloult, wrote regularly and faithfully to Groulx, at the end of the 1930s, to keep him informed of developments in their movement.[58] Donatien Frémont was correct in saying that Groulx had never publicly repudiated the columnists of *La Nation*. Surely this was because he hesitated to quash the enthusiasm of his young disciples. Their nationalism, although more radical than his, could not be entirely condemned, in his view: at least it had the merit of rising up against the complacency which he felt had taken over the official political world. In his personal correspondence, however, Abbé Groulx felt free to advise the writers of *La Nation* to show greater prudence, to abandon radical separatism and to put "increasing emphasis on [provincial] autonomy." Therefore, when Marcel Hamel asked him to collaborate on a special issue of *La Nation* that was to pay tribute to his work, Groulx refused to lend his support. He answered, although somewhat ironically, that if he accepted,

55. Letter from Donatien Frémont to Lionel Groulx, BAnQ, FLG, P1/A,1426, August 5, 1937.
56. See Robert Comeau, "Lionel Groulx, les indépendantistes de *La Nation* et le séparatisme (1936–1938)," *RHAF*, Vol. 26, No. 1 (June 1972), p. 83–102.
57. Paul Bouchard, "L'abbé Groulx et le séparatisme," cited in *ibid.*, p. 90.
58. Correspondence exchanged between Lionel Groulx and Paul Bouchard (BAnQ, FLG, P1/A,459), Marcel Hamel (BAnQ, FLG, P1/A,1713) and Pierre Chaloult (BAnQ, FLG, P1/A,703).

"I would immediately be mercilessly classified with those who are labelled conceited and smug. And that would spell the end of the little credibility I can bring to serving the ideas we have in common."[59]

In 1935, before *La Nation* was even founded, Groulx had had an honest and serious exchange with Pierre Chaloult on the separatism question. The latter had asked him whether people were right to consider him a real separatist. In a lengthy reply, Groulx tried to enlighten his young disciple: "Have you interpreted my ideas accurately? I think, in short, I can answer that you have. That our future has always appeared to me in the guise of an independent French Canada, it would be very difficult for me to deny."[60] In the next breath, however, Groulx made some subtle distinctions about this statement, which were so significant that they altered its meaning. As he had been doing since 1922, he repeated that for him there had never been any question of "provoking" the fall of Confederation; that circumstances would take care of it without his intervention. Furthermore, he went on, if French Canada found it difficult to flourish within Confederation, "I attribute the blame not so much to institutions as to men. And when I speak of 'men,' I am speaking of us." In the final analysis, Groulx explained that he did not share Chaloult's sense of urgency. In his view, once French Canadians occupied their rightful place in Québec and Ottawa, "Confederation will have become an acceptable framework for us; and we will have burst open this framework through the sheer vitality of our aspirations."

Groulx was clearly trying to be conciliatory in explaining himself to the *La Nation* columnists. Although unable to subscribe fully to their vision, he nevertheless recognized in them a dedication to the nationalist cause which, while more radical than his, did not displease him entirely. Groulx, as we have already noted, advised his young disciples to show moderation and to seek provincial autonomy rather than outright independence. According to historian Robert Comeau, *La Nation* did indeed temper the zealousness of its demands around 1938 and made provincial autonomy its single rallying cry. Groulx, instead of denouncing the separatists, as he had been advised to do by Donatien Frémont, chose to exercise a more discreet influence on them. This strategy, evidently, bore fruit. Comeau stated, quite rightly, that it would be inaccurate to consider the Groulx of the 1930s a separatist in the fullest sense of the term. Independence, in his mind, represented in essence a hypothetical abstraction. The "French state" was rather to be built within the federal structures. Indeed, Comeau explains, his "French state" was the symbol of an ideal to reach for, or, as he points out, of a "national mystique":

> by dissociating his national mystique from political action *per se*, Abbé Groulx maintained the political debate at such an elevated level that everyone, whether

59. Letter from Lionel Groulx to Marcel Hamel, BAnQ, FLG, P1/A,1713, August 15, 1937.
60. Letter from Lionel Groulx to Pierre Chaloult, BAnQ, FLG, P1/A,703, November 8, 1935.

> *autonomiste*, federalist or separatist, could find in it the justification they needed and guiding words for their agenda.[61]

One thing is certain; the young writers for *La Nation* had no difficulty seeing in Abbé Groulx the source of inspiration for their doctrine. They were among the first to applaud him during his speech at the Congrès de la langue française in 1937, a speech which, they believed, had brought significant moral support to the separatist argument. A few days later, Paul Bouchard offered Groulx effusive congratulations: "Your speech of Tuesday evening was an unprecedented success. In Quebec, it is all people are talking about. You have set off a veritable wave of national awakening. As for the official world, it has been quite taken aback."[62] Bouchard even wanted his leader's permission to publish the speech and distribute thousands of copies of it. Evidently, Abbé Groulx refused, because the speech was to appear a few months later in a collection of articles he called *Directives*. It is not difficult to understand why, despite his sympathy for his young followers, he hesitated to let them to use his speech in 1937 to justify *La Nation*'s political vision. In the introductory article to *Directives*, he refers to the "huge stir" his speech had created at the Québec conference. Introduced by the intriguing heading, "Only for those who know how to read," the article was meant to dispel the lingering ambiguity about his political orientation and refute categorically the false idea that he adhered to separatist beliefs:

> My speech at the recent Congrès de la langue française apparently caused a huge stir. But this was not warranted. People believed I was exalting the separatist argument. A reading of *Directives*, chapter by chapter, will show that such an exegesis is arbitrary fantasy. Am I actually going to worry about such a strange misunderstanding? There is not a hint of separatism in that speech; and I defy anyone to find one in it.[63]

Abbé Groulx, however, wished to rehabilitate those who were openly promoting separatism, but would do so within certain limits. Without going so far as to suggest the legitimacy of their option, he stated that the "claim" that was their premise, that is, "the inalienable right of the human personality to national and cultural development" was "legitimate." To his friend, Anatole Vanier, Groulx made similar comments: "Nothing in my speech points to separatism; all my argumentation is intended to show that Québec must be governed with a view to its national and cultural interests and those of its native peoples."[64] But the only

61. Robert Comeau, "Lionel Groulx, les indépendantistes de *La Nation* et le séparatisme (1936–1938)," p. 101–102.
62. Letter from Paul Bouchard to Lionel Groulx, BAnQ, FLG, P1/A,459, July 2, 1937.
63. Lionel Groulx, "Pour ceux-là seulement qui savent lire," *Directives*, p. 12.
64. Letter from Lionel Groulx to Anatole Vanier, BAnQ, FLG, P1/A,3647, July 13, 1937. See also Lionel Groulx, *Mes Mémoires, Tome II*, p. 137–138.

way for separatist ideas never to have come into existence, he insisted, would have been to prevent "the economy from turning against us" in the aftermath of 1867.[65]

* * *

A few years later, Groulx was again reproached, although more discreetly, for the "separatism" in his 1937 speech. The accusing party, this time, was Brother Antoine Bernard, c.s.v., a professor of Acadian history and a member of the Comité permanent de la survivance française.[66] But we have already noted that, despite a certain amount of ambiguity in his speech on this question, to speak of the "separatism" of Abbé Groulx during the interwar period is to make a mountain out of a molehill. The "French state" controversy, sparked in 1922 by the *L'Action française* study on the political future of French Canada, no doubt took on exaggerated proportions and earned Groulx undeserved condemnation, condemnation which was sometimes echoed by historians, as we observed in the first chapter.

In any event, in his mind, the question of independence was relatively secondary. For Groulx, allegiance to nationalism took precedence over allegiance to *indépendantisme*. To understand his work properly, it is his definition of the French-Canadian nation that must be grasped before all else. Whether Groulx was separatist or not does not change one iota of his position on the relations he wanted to see developed between Québec and the French minorities. Even in his most hypothetical reflections about accession to independence, he did not see it as having any sort of impact on the deeper nature of the French-Canadian nation. The creation of a new state, in Groulx's traditionalist perspective, could not have brought about a new "national" entity: that prerogative belonged not to men but to Providence alone. Independence would therefore have been powerless to sever a member of the French-Canadian organism from the whole. The minorities would have, as always, continued to be part of the nation's fold. The theory of the "politicization" of Groulx's nationalism during the 1930s, and even during the 1920s, when the "French state" controversy was at its height, is hard to prove. Groulx's political reflections on independence or on provincial autonomy for Québec did not in any way stem from a wish on his part to reject the foundations of the French-Canadian nation as he had always defined them, that is, language, culture, the Catholic faith and tradition. On this question, Groulx's thinking displayed an impressive continuity, eschewing any radical departure from his earlier ideas. As we shall see in the next chapter, even the ideas of the new generation of nationalists who, after the war, would propose a more "territorial" and "Québécois" definition of the French-Canadian nation, would not manage to shake his faith in the importance of tradition.

65. Lionel Groulx, "Nos positions," *Orientations*, p. 271.
66. Letter from Antoine Bernard to Lionel Groulx, BAnQ, FLG, P1/A,326, December 15, 1941.

In reality, Lionel Groulx's concept of a "French state" was merely the extension of his reflections on the relative places of Québec and of the minorities within the French-Canadian nation. As the national "ancestral home," Québec inherited the duty to come to the aid of its "oppressed brothers" who, in other parts of the country, were waging the same battle to maintain French Catholic civilization in America. It was the responsibility of the French Canadians of Québec to set the example, to become *maîtres chez eux* so they could provide fresh supplies to the "vanguard" fighting in the trenches. In Abbé Groulx's mind, this truth remained deep and immutable, since the political regime in power, whether independent or federal, would be unable to alter it. Groulx did not perceive the decentralization of power and the provincial autonomy of Québec as obstacles to the *survivance* of the minorities. Since 1867, he felt, Ottawa had done little to protect their religious and educational rights. Indeed, we must, when studying this question, avoid the pitfall of anachronism. It was not until the late 1960s, through its language policies and socio-cultural facilitation programs, that the federal government came to be seen as the "great protector"[67] of minority communities. During the Groulx era, on the other hand, there was no such thing: interventions by Ottawa in the affairs of the French Catholic minorities remained very tentative indeed, and centralization, according to Groulx, served only to weaken the ancestral home of the nation, to the detriment of all French Canadians inside as well as outside Québec.

67. Robert Choquette, *L'Ontario français, historique* (Saint-Laurent: Éditions Études Vivantes, 1980), p. 210.

Chapter Six

From the Second World War to the Quiet Revolution: Lionel Groulx, the French Minorities and Québécois Neo-Nationalism (1945–1967)

HISTORIANS OF FRENCH CANADA generally consider the postwar years as a period of extraordinary transformation. Impelled by the young intellectuals of the 1940s and 1950s, the nationalist movement sought to "modernize" the French-Canadian nation. It wanted to see the nation reconciled with the new industrial and urban realities, with the consumer society that, after the war, had begun to expand considerably. At the same time, nationalist discourse centred on Québec, to the great displeasure of the French minorities, who saw themselves being excluded from this rebuilding of the national identity. On a great many questions, breaks with Lionel Groulx's thought were apparent. A significant portion of his intellectual heritage was rejected: Providence, as the directing and regulating force of history and of the existence of peoples, was discarded, as was the theory of the apostolic mission of the French-Canadian nation. The historians of the École de Montréal (Maurice Séguin, Guy Frégault and Michel Brunet), who were nonetheless disciples of Groulx in several respects, and the new enthusiasts of the social sciences sought to retain only factors of a material and structural nature in their interpretations of the historical evolution of French Canada. Groulx had for a long time presented his *petit peuple* as one of the great spiritual entities of North America. After the war, however, the old messianic ideal was marginalized and, in certain circles, roundly ridiculed. Among the young postwar intellectuals, notwithstanding their position on the nationalist question, the watchword was "demystification." This paradigm shift contributed to the nationalist movement abandoning the idea, long cultivated by Groulx, that Québec had responsibilities toward the French minorities of the other provinces.

In the following pages, we shall try to better understand Groulx's position on the metamorphosis the nationalist movement underwent after the war and during the Quiet Revolution of the 1960s. The marginalization of the French minorities, as well as the secularization—or, more aptly, "desacralization"—of French-Canadian society that was at the root of it, provoked in him a profound malaise. From the 1940s to the 1960s, Groulx continued to increase his contact with the French minorities, despite all the opposition prophesying their extinction. Although he sometimes worried about the assimilation problems they faced, he resisted any temptation to dissociate himself from them or abandon them to their own fate, as some of his own disciples were advocating. Just as he had done before the war, in both his polemical work and his historical work, Groulx allotted a large place to the French minorities, displaying in this way an ideological continuity that was quite remarkable.

Anticlericalism, Laicization and Materialism: Challenges to Groulx's Intellectual Legacy

The Intellectual Context of the Postwar Period

World War II (1939–1945) represents a major turning point in the history of Western societies. The upheavals were numerous, politically, economically and culturally. The conflict, in fact, provided a stimulus to the North American economy, which had been devastated by a decade of economic crisis. After 1945, increasing government interventionism, justified by invoking the economic theories of British economist John Maynard Keynes, contributed to several decades during which economic growth was maintained at an unprecedented level. This was owing to several key developments: accelerated industrialization and urbanization, diminished relative importance of agriculture for the gross national product, a spectacular—although temporary—soaring of the birthrate (the baby boom), a significant upswing in immigration and so forth. All this was accompanied by the arrival and ever-increasing presence of technological innovations. The television was certainly not the least impressive of these, profoundly changing the daily lives of the middle class, which was itself expanding. The "democratization" of the automobile, furthermore, brought disruption to the urban landscape of Western societies and led to the rapid development of the suburb, whose existence was directly related to that of another phenomenon that would profoundly transform the consumer habits of North Americans: the shopping centre.[1]

This growth was partly the result of the massive intervention of American capital in all sectors—primary, secondary and tertiary—of the Canadian economy. If, during the 1920s, the United States replaced Great Britain as Canada's principal trading partner, the Second World War enabled the two countries to move toward an unprecedented economic integration that would only increase during the postwar period. During 1950s, the construction of the St. Lawrence Seaway came to symbolize the close relationship and permanence of the ties henceforth binding the economies of Canada and the United States. Similarly, the NORAD air defence treaty sealed their political and military rapprochement. For its part, the Canadian government paid little attention to the consequences of this integration, to which it even gave its blessing. It was not until the pipeline scandal at the end of the 1950s that the simmering discontent in certain English-Canadian circles, hostile to the Americanization of the country, was taken seriously. In 1955,

1. See René Durocher et al., *Histoire du Québec contemporain, Tome II: Le Québec depuis 1930* (Montréal: Boréal, 1989), 834 p.

Parliament created the Gordon Commission on Canada's economic future and it concluded, two years later, that the country's economy had to be "Canadianized," even if only partially. The government of Louis St. Laurent (1948–1957) rejected the Commission's recommendations; but the debate that had just been cut short would resurface a short time later at the instigation of John Diefenbaker's Conservatives (1957–1963) and Pierre Elliott Trudeau's Liberals (1968–1979, 1980–1984).

During the war and the postwar period, then, the Canadian economy experienced structural transformations as drastic as they were numerous, which did not fail to leave a deep imprint on French-Canadian society. The acceleration of the urbanization process and the soaring birth rate, which rose faster than any increase in the number of clergy, led to a certain loosening up of religious and parish structures. Institutions where the clergy had held a primary place, such as the schools and hospitals, had to rely increasingly on the laity to ensure their operation. At the same time, protest movements emerged that criticized what they considered the stagnant and even archaic character of traditional French-Canadian "clerico-nationalism." How could French Canada be reconciled with the industrial and urban realities, with, in a word, modernity? That was the question on the lips of the young reformist intellectuals. They often presented the emerging debate on the destiny of the French-Canadian people in terms of a dichotomy. On the one side, the new generation of intellectuals had identified the forces of progress, resolutely trained on the future, and, of course, this is where they situated themselves. On the other side were the targets of their reform, the traditionalists. They accused them of rejecting modernity, condemning French Canadians to a mediocre existence based on "consoling myths" and keeping them at the fringes of the socioeconomic development seen in other Western societies. The discourse of the traditionalists, turned toward the past and entirely dedicated to an ideology of preservation, had become obsolete in the postwar context. At least, that is what these young reformers seemed to proclaim.

Now, if the new intellectuals were almost all in agreement in their criticism of the "traditionalism" of their elders, there were other issues on which they clashed. They contested the traditional nationalist ideology of the provincial government of Maurice Duplessis and its policies, which they considered retrograde, and this gave birth to two movements, the "neo-liberal" and the "neo-nationalist," as historians have come to refer to them.[2] While both of them acknowledged the need to have French Canada accept modernity and to curb the simplistic liberalism of Duplessis's Unionists, each camp identified different obstacles to the realization of this objective.

2. See Jean Lamarre, *Le Devenir de la nation québécoise selon Maurice Séguin, Guy Frégault et Michel Brunet (1944–1969)* (Sillery: Septentrion, 1993), 561 p.; Michael D. Behiels, *Prelude to Quebec's Quiet Revolution: Liberalism Versus Neo-Nationalism, 1945–1960* (Montréal and Kingston: McGill-Queen's University Press, 1985), 366 p.

For the neo-liberals, the challenge consisted of eliminating the excessive influence of the French-Canadian clergy, as well as the pernicious effects of the nationalist doctrine which, in their view, had kept French Canadians outside the great North American capitalist economy. For the neo-nationalists, the problem was, rather, a structural one: the English Conquest of 1760 had prematurely severed the ties between France and Canada, leaving the Canadian bourgeoisie essentially leaderless. Ever since then, French Canadians been unable to occupy their rightful place among the economic elite of the country. Nationalism was, then, to be preserved, in their view, but on one condition—that it be adapted to the North American economic context. Both movements, the one as well as the other, supported Keynesianism and the principle of government interventionism, although they did not espouse the same vision of a state. For the neo-liberals, the autonomy discourse of the Unionist government contributed to maintaining French Canadians in a state of inferiority by depriving them of the resources of the federal government. The neo-nationalists, for their part, distrusted, as did Duplessis, the centralizing policies of the federal government. In contrast to the Premier, however, they held the firm belief that the Québec state, the only one French Canadians could hope to control, needed to play a more active role in the socioeconomic sphere.

Both movements developed institutions and mechanisms to help disseminate their ideas. The keystone of the neo-liberal movement was the journal *Cité libre*, founded in 1950 by Pierre Elliott Trudeau and Gérard Pelletier. The École des sciences sociales of Université Laval, established in 1938 by Father Georges-Henri Lévesque, also played a major role in its development. The neo-nationalists, for their part, could make use of publications like the daily *Le Devoir* and the monthly review *L'Action nationale*, which had long been associated with traditional nationalism, but wanted to modernize their discourse after the war. The history department at Université de Montréal also represented an important gathering place for the neo-nationalists. The École de Montréal, as it came to be called, headed by Maurice Séguin, Guy Frégault and Michel Brunet, sought a renewal of historical knowledge in French Canada. They wanted to replace the old pillars of traditional historiography with new, more "scientific" foundations. This meant, among other things, that the historians of the École de Montréal would relinquish several of the paradigms found at the heart of Lionel Groulx's work, including the notion of the intervention of Providence in the destiny of nations and minorities. The French-Canadian past would henceforth be explained in terms of men, structures and institutions: the supernatural and, therefore, the idea of the providential mission of the French Canadians, would be eliminated from their conceptual world.

It was undoubtedly historian Maurice Séguin who presented the clearest development of the neo-nationalist position on the "catastrophic" consequences of the Conquest. He maintained that in 1760, Canada (that is to say, what would become French Canada) lost a good part of what any nation needed in order to survive: the ability to determine its own future without being subject to the authority of a colonial power. The political and economic structures imposed by the British authorities in the wake of the Conquest had excluded the French Canadians and had thereby reduced them to colonized minorities in their own country. Seen from this angle, the "national" question was no longer simply linguistic or cultural, but also—and especially—economic and "structural." To recover what Séguin termed the *agir par soi collectif* (the ability to act as an independent collective entity), which had been taken away from them in 1760, the French Canadians of Québec needed, in his opinion, to recover their political and economic independence. In the meantime it was important that they obtain the greatest autonomy possible within the federal system and shed what he considered the "consoling myths" of the traditional nationalists, including the idea of the spiritual reconquest of America. The French-Canadian nationalists of the Groulx school, according to Séguin, had always been content to chase after symbolic trivialities, such as bilingual cheques, rather than attack the real "structural" problems that constituted the obstacle to the development of the French-Canadian nation.

This analysis, which Groulx considered pessimistic and reductionist in the extreme, nevertheless gave the French Canadians of Québec a reason to hope. In spite of everything, they had access to an instrument of development that was not insignificant: the Québec state. But for this state to exercise its powers fully, it needed to escape the sway of the federal government, which French Canadians were powerless to prevent from turning against them, as it had done time and time again. As for the French minorities in the other provinces, the École de Montréal believed them to be almost entirely stripped of political and economic autonomy. They were therefore doomed to assimilation, as the structural obstacles to their development seemed too numerous to overcome.[3] This is what a "scientific" and "objective" analysis of the history of French Canada had apparently made it possible to establish.

The secularization and "desacralization" of Western societies had resolutely conquered French-Canadian intellectual and academic milieus after the war. The historians of Université de Montréal and social scientists of Université Laval would follow this trend, and the fact that both the neo-nationalists and the liberals relied on it to question the traditionalism of their predecessors and bring French Canada into modernity was eloquent testimony to this.[4] Moving forward, the aim would be

3. Consult the following studies on these issues: Jean Lamarre, *Le Devenir de la nation québécoise*; Jean-Pierre Wallot, "L'histoire et le néonationalisme des années 1947–1970," in G. Rocher *et al.*, *Continuité et rupture: Les Sciences sociales au Québec* (Montréal: Presses de l'Université de Montréal, 1984), p. 111–116; Jean-Pierre Wallot, "À la recherche de la nation: Maurice Séguin (1918–1984)," RHAF, Vol. 38, No. 4 (Spring 1985), p. 569–589.

4. On the debate between the *modernité* and the *Grande Noirceur* of the postwar period in Québec, consult Alain-G. Gagnon and Michel Sarra-Bournet, ed., *Duplessis: Entre la grande noirceur et la société libérale* (Montréal: Éditions Québec Amérique, 1997), 397 p.; Kenneth McRoberts, "La thèse tradition-modernité: l'historique québécois," in Mikhaël Elbaz, Andrée Fortin and Guy Laforest, ed., *Les Frontières de l'identité: Modernité et postmodernisme au*

to try to understand the evolution of human societies from a secular and material point of view, through a distancing from the normative framework of Christian morality and the theory of messianism. This represented the rejection of a major part of the intellectual heritage of Lionel Groulx, a figure who had for so long cast his shadow over the French-Canadian historiographic landscape.[5]

These reassessments contributed in a significant way to reconfiguring relations between the nationalist circles in Québec and the French minorities in the other provinces in a way that would lead to a spectacular break with them during the Quiet Revolution of the 1960s. The neo-nationalist movement had gained momentum and the discourse on the chances of *survivance* for the minorities became depressing, their fate being increasingly seen as one of assimilation. Beginning in 1960, the government of Québec began to intervene in the economic, social and cultural spheres on an unprecedented scale. This contributed to the erosion of not only traditional French-Canadian nationalist discourse but also the network of institutions that kept it alive. These were institutions often dominated by the clergy and included, for example, the classical colleges, the national *sociétés*, the hospitals and the charities. The very notion of *Canadien français* had seemingly been abandoned, if not prohibited, at least in Québec: henceforth, one would speak only of the *nation québécoise*, to the great displeasure of the French minorities who were effectively excluded by this "territorialized" identity. It was during the Estates General of French Canada (1966, 1967 and 1969) that the split between Québec and the minorities burst onto the public stage in a sensational manner.[6] Henceforward, French Canadians would follow divergent, if not irreconcilable, strategies, to ensure their development: Québec would advocate the strengthening of its government apparatus, not ruling out accession to complete political independence, while the minorities would put their trust in a strong central government that claimed it was prepared to see to their welfare everywhere in the country. Furthermore, at the end of the 1960s, financial and institutional support from the federal government, launched as part of the anti-separatist fight, would not be long in coming. When the Official Languages Act came into effect in 1969, it marked the beginning of a period of unprecedented socio-cultural development for the French minorities.

Québec (Québec: Presses de l'Université Laval, 1996), p. 29–45; Fernand Ouellet, "La Révolution tranquille, tournant révolutionnaire?," in Thomas S. Axworthy and Pierre Elliott Trudeau, ed., *Les Années Trudeau: La Recherche d'une société juste* (Montréal: Éditions du Jour, 1990), p. 333–362, 420–422.

5. See Ronald Rudin, *Making History in Twentieth-Century Quebec* (Toronto: University of Toronto Press, 1997), 294 p. Additional note: According to Éric Bédard, even though Michel Brunet had been largely won over to Séguin's arguments, he did not entirely reject Groulx's voluntarism (See Éric Bédard, "Michel Brunet: Dix ans après," AN, Vol. 85, No. 7 (September 1995), p. 38–49).
6. See Gaétan Gervais, *Des gens de résolution: Le Passage du Canada français à l'Ontario français* (Sudbury: Prise de parole, 2003), 230 p.; Marcel Martel, *Le Deuil d'un pays imaginé: Rêves, luttes et déroute du Canada français* (Ottawa: Presses de l'Université d'Ottawa, 1997), 204 p.; Michel Bock, *Comment un peuple oublie son nom: La Crise identitaire franco-ontarienne et la presse française de Sudbury (1960–1975)* (Sudbury: Prise de parole and Institut franco-ontarien, 2001), 120 p.

The Estates General, however, only confirmed the "fragmentation" of the French-Canadian nation that had been brewing since the 1940s. According to Marcel Martel, the neo-nationalist movement had already contributed to this in a powerful way right after the war by adopting a "funereal" tone with respect to the minorities.[7] The École de Montréal had played a major role. Michel Brunet, in particular, frequently denounced what he called the "consoling myths" of traditional French-Canadian nationalism, including the myth of messianism and of the spiritual reconquest of America. Brunet claimed to be using, instead, scientific objectivity and a certain historical determinism as the basis for his conclusion of the nonviability of most of the French minorities outside Québec: their assimilation seemed inevitable and "normal" to him, the result of the interplay of the demographic and economic forces that worked against them and the political structures to which they were subject. History had made this decision and the scientific sources could not be questioned; at least this is what Brunet and his neo-nationalist colleagues believed. The idea that Québec could overcome the structural forces operating against the minorities and come to their rescue, an idea that Lionel Groulx had championed for so long, became completely devoid of meaning in the neo-nationalist logic.

Consequently, the discourse on the scientific method gave the neo-nationalist movement and, especially, the historians of the École de Montréal, the conceptual justification they needed to abandon the French minorities.[8] From being *canadien-français*, the nationalist discourse would soon become *québécois*. Given the considerable success of post-structuralist and deconstructionist theories today, this faith in the need to "act independently as a collective entity" through the intermediary of a state, which was founded on a "scientific" vision of society, no longer receives much support. The context of the 1940s and 1950s, however, lent itself very well to the discourse on scientific objectivity, which had also rallied the liberal intellectuals of *Cité libre* and the academics of the École des sciences sociales at Laval. The neo-nationalist historians believed that the movement they were participating in represented a form of progress when compared to the thought of Lionel Groulx. And despite all that they owed to his thought, they felt it gave too large a role to the supernatural and to an entire host of "myths" in the history of the French-Canadian nation. When the neo-nationalists discarded the providential mission theory and started relying on a more materialist interpretation of history, it meant that one of the most powerful arguments ever evoked by Groulx to make Québec responsible and aware of its duties toward the French minorities would be lost. Obviously, the discourse of the neo-nationalists was not any less normative than that of Groulx and the "traditionalists" had been.

7. See Marcel Martel, "'Hors du Québec, point de salut!' Francophone Minorities and Quebec Nationalism, 1945–1969," in Michael D. Behiels and Marcel Martel, ed., *Nations, Ideas, Identities: Essays in Honour of Ramsay Cook* (Toronto: Oxford University Press, 2000), p. 130–140.

8. In the work by Guy Frégault, *Lionel Groulx tel qu'en lui-même* (Montréal: Leméac, 1978), pages 78–81 provide an excellent example of recourse to scientific objectivity to justify Quebec's desertion of the French minorities.

But the so-called "norm" was no longer quite the same. A direct link can be made, then, between, on the one hand, the marginalization of the minorities by the postwar *Québécois* neo-nationalists and, on the other, the growing discourse in intellectual circles about the nation that claimed to be scientifically objective. In his major study on the École de Montréal, historian Jean Lamarre indicates that Michel Brunet, in particular, considered the assimilation of the minorities a "sociological fact" not grasped by preceding generations, in his view, "for lack of proper teaching of the social sciences."[9]

The neo-nationalists thus used what they viewed as the slow death of the French Canadians outside Québec to better ground their analyses: the minorities represented "death," while Québec, on the contrary, represented "life."[10] Among the three historians of the École de Montréal, it was without a doubt Michel Brunet, ironically, the one who had the closest relationship with Groulx, who developed the clearest explanation of this argument. His remarks about the minorities, who revolted against the marginalization they seemed to suffer at the hands of the neo-nationalists, were not particularly kind. In Brunet's estimation, by complaining in this way, the French Canadians in the other provinces were contributing, more or less knowingly, to nothing short of the loss of Québec:

> These people [the minorities] seem to have the idea that we are a minority in the province of Québec. You would think it pains them to know that we are in the majority in this province, to know that we have a government we can count on to serve us as a collective entity, if only our desire to realize it is strong enough. These poor minorities seem to have just one wish: to reduce us to the level of a minority. I have never believed in these associations which have us, here in Québec, tagging along behind these poor *Canadiens* of the diaspora. Their sad fate touches me deeply, but they will never impose on me their understanding of the French-Canadian problem. They should know once and for all that we are not a minority *chez nous*. And what should we say of the French Canadians in Québec who share the mentality of the French-Canadian minorities! Why would we let ourselves be imposed upon by those most assimilated to the Canadian majority? I believe it is urgent to define the actual position of the French Canadians of Québec in their relationship with the minorities. The minorities must not be for us a dead weight, or evidence that can be used against us by English Canada.[11]

One can glean from this passage by Brunet the looming minority state prospect that hung over the nationalist movement in Québec and never left it. The presence

9. Jean Lamarre, *Le Devenir de la nation québécoise*, p. 416.
10. Marcel Martel, "'Hors du Québec, point de salut!'," p. 130.
11. Letter from Michel Brunet to François-Albert Angers (of *L'Action nationale*), August 15, 1956, cited in Jean Lamarre, *Le Devenir de la nation québécoise*, p. 416.

of French Canadians in the other provinces was a vestige of the traditional nationalism that, according to Brunet, excluded all possibility of development for their Québec compatriots, unless it were as a minority group on a pan-Canadian scale. Furthermore, the sentimental attachment of the traditional nationalists to the French minorities continually posed, in his view, the risk of a backlash against Québec: in order to suppress the desire for national affirmation on the part of the French Canadians of Québec, the English-Canadian majority could always blackmail them by holding the minorities hostage. It would be wiser, Brunet felt, to concentrate on Québec, the only state controlled by a French-Canadian majority, even if it meant turning their back on the minorities once and for all.

Groulx, the Neo-Nationalists and the Murial of the French Minorities

Where did Groulx situate himself in relation to the postwar re-evaluations and the Quiet Revolution? Historians have pored over this question. The best study is the master's thesis of Stéphane Pigeon on the thought of Lionel Groulx from 1956 to 1967.[12] The author shows that the way the Canon welcomed the great turmoil of the Quiet Revolution defies easy or reductionist interpretations. To the same extent that Groulx approved of its political and economic aspects, he disapproved of its social and cultural aspect, which he attributed to irreligion and a slackening in morals. Groulx, in fact, was far from considering himself a friend of the Duplessis regime of the 1940s and 1950s. Indeed, his criticism of the Maurice Duplessis government contrasted with the pro-Unionist position of other traditionalist thinkers of his era, including Robert Rumilly, and revealed the diversity of opinions among the intellectuals associated with the nationalist right. Here is what historian Pierre Trépanier has to say about this issue:

> In the aftermath of the Second World War, the shattering of the world of ideas had repercussions on Québec society and even on Groulx's intellectual path. Anticlericalism, the dissociation of the national from the religious, a boldness that bordered on irreligion, and the slackening of morals elicited from him reactions of rejection and dismissal. At the same time, however, he made an effort to recognize signs of hope, even in the new ideas, although most of the time, these bore little relationship to his intellectual tradition.[13]

If Groulx saw in the ideological transformations of the postwar period and the Quiet Revolution an endeavour of national affirmation, he feared that this was being done at the expense of a large part of his own intellectual legacy. The

12. Stéphane Pigeon, *Lionel Groulx, critique de la Révolution tranquille* (1956–1967), master's thesis (history), Université de Montréal, 1999, 117 p. See also Sylvie Beaudreau, "Déconstruire le rêve de nation: Lionel Groulx et la Révolution tranquille," RHAF, Vol. 56, No. 1 (Summer 2002), p. 29–61.
13. Pierre Trépanier, "Le maurrassisme au Canada français," *Les Cahiers des Dix*, No. 53 (1999), p. 203.

materialist trend of the "new history," like the increasingly pronounced materialist trend of the consumer society in which French Canadians were resolutely participating, caused him deep concern. The secularization and laicization project espoused by the new generation of intellectuals proved to him their anticlericalism. He experienced severe anxiety over the split between the national and the religious: one of the principal foundations of the French-Canadian nation, as he had always understood it, had been shoved aside by people who claimed to be nationalists, his own disciples often among them. The fate French Canada was imposing on the French minorities was one of many indications that, as the old leader feared, it was succumbing to materialism.

From the 1940s to the 1960s, Groulx shared his worries with his close friends and with his colleagues in the nationalist movement. The Canon had clearly identified his whipping boys and saved his harshest criticism for the *Cité libre* collaborators who spared no effort in their anti-nationalist and anti-traditionalist crusade. The journal's founder, Pierre Elliott Trudeau, took the hardest beating: Groulx called him a *cerveau indigeste* who had in his youth been too influenced by François Hertel, himself a *brilliant déséquilibré*.[14] But this did not keep him from reprimanding the youth of the neo-nationalist movement, sometimes just as severely. He accused *Le Devoir*, for example, of being "two-faced": it claimed to be nationalist, he said, but time and again, it supported Trudeau's liberalism (a reference to Trudeau's ideas on secularization). In 1963, Groulx wrote personally to the publisher of *Le Devoir*, Gérard Filion, to reproach the daily for its unenthusiastic sense of nation, for its sometimes anticlerical leanings and for seeming to let the French minorities sink into oblivion: "It would not be an exaggeration to say that, in the last three or four years, *Le Devoir* has done more promotion of Frère Un Tel,[15] and the M[ouvement] L[aïque de langue] F[rançaise], than of our national issues and our minorities." When Claude Ryan took it over shortly afterwards, Groulx broke off relations with *Le Devoir* altogether, judging its religious convictions to be too weak.[16]

Le Devoir was not the only publication to draw the Canon's ire. *L'Action nationale* also received its fair share of remonstrations. In 1952, Groulx told the director of the Ligue d'Action nationale, François-Albert Angers, that the imminent

14. Letter from Lionel Groulx to Richard Arès, BAnQ, FLG, P1/A,84, June 5, 1960. Groulx's anxiety about the consequences of Trudeau's thought and that of the other *Cité libristes* frequently surfaces in his correspondence during the 1950s and 1960s (letters from Lionel Groulx to Richard Arès, BAnQ, FLG, P1/A,84, May 8, 1959 and January 8, 1960; to Jean Éthier-Blais, BANQ, FLG, P1/A,1299, January 12, 1965).
15. Frère Un Tel was a pseudonym for Jean-Paul Desbiens, author of a series of letters, initially published in *Le Devoir* and later as a book (translated as *The Impertinences of Brother Anonymous*), which attacked the educational system of the Catholic *collèges*, run by the religious orders, for falling short in preparing students for the real world. Being a member of a religious congregation himself, Desbiens allowed publication of his letters on condition of anonymity.
16. Letters from Lionel Groulx to François-Albert Angers, BAnQ, FLG, P1/A,58, January 8, 1960; to Richard Arès, BAnQ, FLG, P1/A,84, May 8, 1959; to Gérard Filion, BAnQ, FLG, P1/A,1348, March 26, 1963; Stéphane Pigeon, *Lionel Groulx*, p. 20–22.

departure of André Laurendeau as the review's director threatened to open the floodgates. He confided to him at the same time that he did not feel he was any longer on the same wavelength as the younger generation whose only passion seemed to be priest-bashing:

> I will not try to hide from you that along with several other people of my generation, I am very worried about our *Action Nationale*. André definitely wants to leave the REVIEW as director. Who will succeed him? On the team of young people, I see no one with enough authority and judgment to assume the role. The mentality in that camp hardly strikes me as reassuring. It is not with anticlericalism that one can ensure the future of a review more than half of whose subscribers are members of the Church. Nor do I think that the time has come when a nationalist movement has a chance of succeeding in French Canada by displaying loosely camouflaged anticlerical sentiments. Besides, when that day comes, I hardly need to tell you, I will no longer be in the nationalist camp.[17]

Groulx's worries about the fate of *L'Action nationale* came to a head in 1958, when he walked out on the Ligue. The only reason he gave was that he felt there was no longer a place for him among people who were proud of criticizing his understanding of history and portrayed him as one of the principal diffusers of those "baleful myths responsible for landing our people on a false path."[18] If Groulx shared with the Séguins, the Frégaults and the Brunets of the École de Montréal their ideas about the disastrous consequences of the British Conquest of 1760, he did not, however, share their pessimism. He did not hesitate to see, in the next chapter of the history of French Canada, elements of greatness capable of boosting the national pride of his people. Groulx had always defended, when it came down to it, the argument of the "upward trend" mentioned earlier: the French Canadians had been able to improve their fate despite the devastating effects of the Conquest and the obstacles it had placed in their path. For the neo-nationalist historians, however, 1760 had marked the start of an inevitable decline that would remain insurmountable as long as the current political and economic structures remained unchanged. Without minimizing the importance of the structures, Groulx nevertheless maintained his faith in the providential mission of the French Canadians, the pledge that a Catholic people would always be allowed to have hope in the future. He openly deplored that the new generation of historians only saw in this another one of those "consoling" and "baleful myths" that had so urgently to be dispelled.

17. Letter from Lionel Groulx to François-Albert Angers, BAnQ, FLG, P1/A,58, October 20, 1952. The capital letters are Groulx's.
18. Letter from Lionel Groulx to François-Albert Angers, BAnQ, FLG, P1/A,58, December 8, 1958. See also Groulx's review of works by Guy Frégault, *La Guerre de la Conquête* (RHAF, March 1956, p. 579–588) and by Michel Brunet, *Canadians et Canadiens* (RHAF, June 1955, p. 120–129).

Groulx rejoined the Ligue shortly afterward, once François-Albert Angers had steered it into a more orthodox direction.[19] But this episode gives a clear indication of the ideological, and even epistemological, conflict that separated Groulx and his peers at the new nationalist school. At the root of this conflict lay, among other things, the secularization and desacralization of the social sciences. Groulx never gave up his faith in the providential mission of the French Canadians, a key tenet in his analysis of the relationship between Québec and the French minorities in the other provinces. The young nationalists who approached this question so casually were on the wrong track, he felt: in a letter to Angers, in 1958, he made the point again:

> I accuse myself . . . , without any remorse, of having reminded this same [French-Canadian] people of its mission as a Catholic people, and I remain convinced that, in Canada, it is the only people that would have the power, if they take the trouble, to build a civilization in accordance with the most orthodox norms, a modest civilization, if you will, but one that could be a compelling witness to Catholicism and to the Church. Whatever they think, in any case, I refuse to subscribe to this heresy that sees a Catholic and, even more importantly, a Catholic people, as not needing to take any responsibility for the destiny of the Redemption in the world. If that is considered laughable messianism, too bad for messianism.[20]

According to Groulx, by postulating that the inferiority of French Canadians was an inevitable consequence of the Conquest, the new history was posing a grave ethical risk: if all motives for national pride were removed from French-Canadian history, who would prevent his *petit peuple* from jumping headlong into the Anglo-Saxon melting pot? While he conceded that neo-nationalist historians were acting in "absolute good faith," he admonished them for poorly gauging what the "ultimate consequences of [their] philosophy of history" would be. If, in the eyes of the new generation of historians, the *survivance* of the French Canadians depended on the economic and political forces exerted on them, Canon Groulx, without playing down the importance of the structures, ascribed it, in the final analysis, to human will and faith in Providence. He frequently came back on this idea during the postwar years. A talk he gave in Montréal in 1953, entitled "Où allons-nous ?" reveals the anxiety he felt in the face of a French Canada that appeared to him to have lost its moral compass. He had particularly harsh words for the "defeatists." They claimed to be scientifically objective, but were relentless in their humiliation of the French minorities:

> When they scan the horizon, it seems the defeatists have no difficulty observing the losses and defeats of French life in America, its constant setbacks at almost

19. See Stéphane Pigeon, *Lionel Groulx*, p. 19–20.
20. Letter from Lionel Groulx to François-Albert Angers, BAnQ, FLG, P1/A,58, December 8, 1958.

> every turn. If they concede there were victorious advances in New Brunswick, they evoke in contrast the loss of over a million Franco-Americans, some three quarters of them assimilated; the collapse set off in Ontario by the devastating defection of a university institution [the University of Ottawa]; the Essex peninsula more than half lost; the areas of Midland and Penetanguishene, almost entirely lost; those of Pembroke, North Bay and Sault Ste. Marie subjected to systematic erosion; finally, in all of the French West, the absence of any real rallying centres, the gradual disaffection with the too distant old province; and moreover, within all the minorities, slowly undermined by the mandatory practice of full bilingualism and the cruel educational laws, the inexorable weakening of the French spirit and of French life. In short, in Québec: withdrawal and caving in. Outside Québec: a world steadily, implacably, shrinking away.[21]

Noting the adversity did not mean, for Groulx, resigning himself to it or seeing it as inevitable. That was the difference between his analysis and that of the neonationalists. In his view, they yielded too easily to economic determinism and had removed from their conceptual world the principle of the supernatural, of transcendence: Providence would always offer a reason to hope, as long as one was willing to be guided by it.

Groulx took the time to discuss these questions at length with Michel Brunet. In 1957, Groulx advised his former disciple to be less pessimistic and more moderate in his opinions on the viability of the French minorities in the other provinces. Québec should not make its claims on the backs of the minorities, he insisted:

> I asked myself . . . if it might not be a good idea, in order to prevent people from picking a quarrel with you over nothing, to bring some clarification to your argument of the *madness* of a *bi-ethnic* and *bicultural* country of Canada. Understand me well: I don't believe in a bi-ethnic *nation* and a double culture, any more than in the ultra-mad theory of a Canadian people whose masses speak both languages. But does that mean we have to give up on official bilingualism in Ottawa and the rights or privileges of our minorities to learn their language at school? There is some ambiguity here which, no doubt, does not exist in your mind. Why risk having such words put in your mouth?

However, there was very little ambiguity in Brunet's mind. He did not hesitate to see the minorities as "dead weight." Somewhat piqued, he objected to the reprimands of his former mentor. The *survivance* of French Canadians was still possible, he conceded, as long as the necessary measures were taken: "The entire

21. Lionel Groulx, "Où allons-nous ?," *Pour bâtir* (Montréal: Ligue d'Action nationale, 1953), p. 83–84.

problem comes down to a matter of science and will, a complete and dynamic science, capable of offsetting the large numbers and the economic strength." The role of "science" in Brunet's thought appeared, however, to be greater than that of "will." The letter was written in May of 1955, when Groulx was about to take a trip to the Sudbury region where he would give a talk in Verner on the "resistance." "You see that I still have faith," Groulx admonished him rather paternally. That word summarized well the essence of his thought on the *survivance* of the minorities, which in his eyes was first and foremost a matter of "faith" and will: science alone was powerless to ensure it. Brunet nevertheless was courteous enough to wish him *bon voyage*: "I will not be one to rebuke you for going to deliver a message of hope to our brothers in Sudbury."[22]

But Groulx had not had his last say and frequently returned to his attacks against Brunet's pessimism. In 1957, it alarmed him that Brunet "and even to some extent our friend Frégault" had let themselves be too influenced by Maurice Séguin, "poor inhibited fellow who will never be able to exude anything but deep and total pessimism." He then reiterated his faith in Providence, human will and the apostolic mission of his people. He insisted on repeating that the young people in the neo-nationalist movement were wrong to automatically dismiss such key notions: it was these ideas that would save the French-Canadian nation from a downward spiral and, if its desire were strong enough, would allow it to overcome the economic and political obstacles in its path, both outside and inside Québec. Brunet, for his part, stubbornly held his ground by refusing to relinquish his faith in scientific objectivity. He even went so far as to reproach his former teacher for not recognizing the progress that had been made by the science of history: "In order to reach this objective knowledge [of the current situation of French Canadians], we must free ourselves of all romanticism and all messianism."[23] Brunet, moreover, had just published a virulent criticism of traditionalist French-Canadian thought entitled "Trois dominantes de la pensée canadienne-française: l'agriculturisme, l'anti-étatisme et le messianisme."[24] This article must certainly have brought enormous displeasure to his *cher maître*, who did not allow himself to be impressed in this way. The following year, he took an even sterner tone. Brunet's interpretation of the history of French Canada seemed to him to be "too founded on economic determinism. You will agree with me that, under the pretext of destroying myths, it is not recommended, all the same, to invent new ones." The École de Montréal's abandonment of traditionalist philosophy and its blind faith in the structural analysis of history were inducing it to

22. Exchange of correspondence between Lionel Groulx and Michel Brunet, BAnQ, FLG, P1/A,596, August 21, 1954 to May 18, 1955.

23. Letters from Lionel Groulx to Michel Brunet, BAnQ, FLG, P1/A,596, August 2, 1957; from Michel Brunet to Lionel Groulx, BAnQ, FLG, P1/A,596, August 3, 1957.

24. The article, which was originally published in *Écrits du Canada français*, appeared, the following year, in *La Présence anglaise et les Canadiens* (Montréal: Éditions Beauchemin, 1958), p. 112–166).

make rash judgments about the *survivance* of the French Canadians, especially the French minorities. In 1961, Groulx indicated to Brunet that Guy Frégault—who had just been promoted to the level of Deputy Minister of Cultural Affairs—was, in turn, guilty of this great mistake:

> People will forgive you all kinds of opinions, but they have trouble forgiving you certain words that are too bold, too extreme. You are stuck with them until the end of your life. Ask politicians who have made imprudent remarks. You will soon be asking our friend Frégault, whom they are already reminding in whispered voices, while they prepare to remind him out loud—I have experience of this— . . . of his defeatist opinions on the fate of the French minorities across Canada, his premature burial of the Acadians, his lack of faith in any future for his Québec compatriots or for their culture and their civilization.[25]

Michel Brunet and Guy Frégault were not the only ones to question whether it was wise and important for Québec to intervene among the French minorities. There were other actors in the nationalist movement who also seemed to have been converted to the ideas of the younger generation, Rodolphe Laplante, for example. A former journalist with *Le Droit* in Ottawa and with *La Survivance* in Edmonton, Laplante worked, during the 1950s, at the Office de l'électrification rurale du Québec. In 1953, in a letter to Groulx, he upbraided the Conseil de la vie française for devoting itself almost entirely to the *survivance* of the minorities while ignoring Québec, and in his view, pulling the rug out from under its own feet in the process. The interests of the one and of the other were too dissimilar, he felt, for the Conseil to have any chances of success with its endeavours taken as a whole. Laplante stopped short of wanting to leave the minorities to their own devices. However, his pessimism and his funereal vocabulary clearly foreshadowed that he was not far from heading down that path: "In any event, the Conseil de [la] vie française should not be just walking around in a cemetery, running after failing minorities who have given up, regardless of Québec's moral responsibility for the cure of souls."[26]

And sometimes, Groulx's colleagues in the minority milieus let him know of their discontent at how they were being treated at the hands of the neo-nationalists. Right in the midst of the Quiet Revolution, Séraphin Marion, historian and professor at the University of Ottawa, expressed to Groulx his disagreement with some of the ideas of the historians of the École de Montréal:

> As a Franco-Ontarian, I view our problems through a lens of my own which often differs just a tiny bit from the Québécois lens. It is my strict right to act in this way

25. Letters from Lionel Groulx to Michel Brunet, BAnQ, FLG, P1/A,596, December 23, 1958 and April 24, 1961.
26. Letter from Rodolphe Laplante to Lionel Groulx, BAnQ, FLG, P1/A,2096, October 29, 1953.

> and I do not need the permission of anyone whomsoever on that score. This is a point not always understood by the young historians, who certainly do not suffer from a lack of self-assurance or an inferiority complex.[27]

We do not know how, or even whether, Groulx responded to Marion. We do know, however, that he did not hesitate to assure his friends in the minority milieus that they would always have access to his indefatigable support. In 1959, he wanted to show Abbé Adrien Verrette of New Hampshire his solidarity with the minorities there, regardless of all the opposition that, in Quebec, cast doubt on their chances of *survivance*:

> I ask you to believe, in any case, that in the old Québec, often considered forgetful, I remain among those who follow, often passionately, the life and history of all the French groups in America, yours in particular. And among the great memories of my life, there is the modest help which, at certain times, I was able to offer you. May God always be your help! And remember that all peoples live who have chosen to live.[28]

Groulx and the Minorities: Ongoing Relations

Groulx and the Conseil de la vie française en Amérique

It could easily seem that, after the war, Canon Groulx had to some extent retreated from the educational and other minority struggles. It could seem that he was thereby somehow behaving, if not thinking, like the neo-nationalists. Such an analysis would, however, be short-sighted. In studying the relations that Groulx maintained with the minorities from the 1940s to the 1960s, several factors must be taken into account. First, there was no new schools crisis, such as Regulation 17, being reported in the media during the 1910s and 1920s. The only new development in education, notably in Ontario, dealt with the secondary schools and only came at the end of the 1960s, after the Canon had died. Besides, Groulx's advancing years no doubt contributed to slowing his pace: he celebrated his seventy-fifth birthday in 1953 and would not depart this life until 1967 at eighty-nine years of age. Although he remained militant and very active through to the end of his days, the spontaneous zeal of his youth increasingly failed him. Indeed, he continued to speak in public, but it was henceforth in the manner of a leader aware that others had succeeded him in the activist sphere. Finally, the postwar period represented for Groulx a decisive return to his vocation as a historian. It was during that time that he launched some of his biggest projects, including the Institut d'histoire de l'Amérique française, which he directed until his death in 1967, as

27. Letter from Séraphin Marion to Lionel Groulx, BAnQ, FLG, P1/A,2602, January 7, 1966.
28. Letter from Lionel Groulx to Adrien Verrette, BAnQ, FLG, P1/A,3667, November 4, 1959.

we shall see a little further on. It is not surprising, then, that he had less time to devote to direct activism.

Despite all these obstacles, in the last twenty-five years of his life, Canon Groulx found the time to develop numerous contacts with the French minorities. We have already pointed out the influence he exercised among the French minority communities and, in particular, among their intellectual leaders during the interwar period. He had come to be considered as the uncontested *maître* of the French-Canadian nationalist movement, thanks to his historical work, his numerous speeches and, especially, his time at the helm of *L'Action française*. After the war, there continued to be a demand for his endorsement of numerous projects, as people wanted to benefit from his prestige and influence. The Comité permanent de la survivance française, which had in 1952 become the Conseil de la vie française en Amérique, often solicited his services during its campaigns for French minorities community development. It was Groulx whom the Conseil mandated, in 1948, to draft an article in its name to promote the creation of a French radio station in the West. It appeared a month later in *Les Cloches de Saint-Boniface*, a review for which he had written many pieces since the 1920s.[29] During the 1950s and 1960s, Groulx participated in almost every campaign the Conseil launched to support the minorities, including the 1961 campaign, which thumbed its nose at those who wanted to see Québec abandon the minorities once and for all. In an article published in *Le Bulletin de la Société Saint-Jean-Baptiste de Montréal*, the president of the campaign, J.-Émile Boucher, held the neo-nationalist arguments up to ridicule and denounced the "spinelessness" that characterized their adherents.[30] The Fraternité française d'Amérique, which the Conseil had established in 1957 with the Fédération des Sociétés Saint-Jean-Baptiste du Québec to organize fundraising campaigns, sought his services again in 1962 and even asked Groulx to be honorary president of the 1963 campaign which was dedicated to gathering support for French radio in Saint-Boniface and Gravelbourg and to which the Canon contributed out of his own pocket. That same year, Groulx joined a special committee that needed to raise $150,000 for the *Évangéline* of Moncton.[31]

As far as we know, Groulx turned down only one invitation to participate in the activities of the Conseil de la vie française en Amérique, and that was in 1955. The

29. Letter from Gérard Filion to Lionel Groulx, BAnQ, FLG, P1/A,1348, February 16, 1948; Lionel Groulx, "Ceci se passera au Canada . . . à propos de Radio-Ouest," *Les Cloches de Saint-Boniface* [hereinafter CSB], Vol. 47, No. 3 (March 1948), p. 62–63. See also Lionel Groulx, "Lettre du Manitoba," CSB, Vol. 27, No. 9 (September 1928) and Vol. 27 No. 10 (October 1928); Lionel Groulx, "D'Iberville à la Baie d'Hudson," CSB, Vol. 41, No. 6 (June 1942); Lionel Groulx, "Notre peuple canadien," CSB, Vol. 42, No. 9 (September 1943).

30. Letter from J.-Émile Boucher to Lionel Groulx, BAnQ, FLG, P1/A,464, April 10, 1961. See J.-Émile Boucher, "Au diable la fraternité !," *Le Bulletin*, Vol. 10, No. 1 (April 1961), p. 1.

31. Letters from Gérard Pelletier to Lionel Groulx, BAnQ, FLG, P1/A,2941, April 13, 1962; from Armand Godin to Lionel Groulx, BAnQ, FLG, P1/A,1593, November 5, 1962, from Albert Ricard to Lionel Groulx, BAnQ, FLG, P1/A,3157, April 10, 1963, May 14, 1963 and June 28, 1963; from Lionel Groulx to Raymond Dupuis, BAnQ, FLG, P1/A,1241, December 17, 1962.

circumstances surrounding the refusal are not clear, but it seems that Groulx had a disagreement of an ideological nature with some of the members of the Conseil. As usual, J.-Émile Boucher asked him to sponsor the annual campaign, the proceeds of which were to be allocated, this time, to the schools, the newspapers, the radio stations and the educational associations of the minorities. The Conseil had even decided that the Comité de Montréal would bear the name "Comité Lionel-Groulx en faveur des minorités françaises." Groulx, despite this honour, refused to lend his support to the 1955 campaign. Had the Conseil gone too far in yielding to the "defeatist" ideas of the young nationalists to be deserving of his support? Were they neglecting the minorities? Unlikely as that hypothesis may seem, it is what Groulx implied in his reply to Boucher:

> Given the defeatist mindset currently prevailing in many parts of the province and even among our minorities, I cannot associate myself openly with an event that, despite its good intentions, does not fail to be suspected of the same attitude. I have good reason to know that the recent decision, by the bishops of the West, to organize their own fundraiser, is not unrelated to the recent action taken by the Conseil de la vie française.

We do not know what "action" was being referred to, but it seems that it created a chill between the Conseil and the minorities, if one can judge by the French-Canadian episcopate's decision to organize their own campaign, directing the funds to the expansion of the grand séminaire in Saint-Boniface. Groulx had a similar message for Georges Dumont, president of the Conseil:

> I remain convinced, along with many others, that in this matter of the national fundraiser, a wrong move was attempted. And I cannot associate myself with it. We are losing the right, it seems, to keep our work alive through small events. Do not fear, however, that my attitude reflects a break with the "united front."

To both Dumont and Boucher, Groulx added that he did not intend to make a big fuss about it or to bring this mysterious affair to the knowledge of the public. Nor would he be opposed to the Comité bearing his name.[32]

Except for this hazy incident, Groulx participated regularly in the activities of the Conseil de la vie française en Amérique. During its large 1952 conference, he gave a speech about looking ahead to succession, entitled "Pour une relève." While this speech may have provoked less of an uproar than the one he gave at the 1937 conference—no one accused him of separatism—one could be

32. Letters from J.-Émile Boucher to Lionel Groulx, BAnQ, FLG, P1/A,464, April 11, 1955; from Lionel Groulx to J.-Émile Boucher, BAnQ, FLG, P1/A,464, May 16, 1955; from Lionel Groulx to Georges Dumont, BAnQ, FLG, P1/A,1216, May 10, 1955. See also Marcel Martel, *Le Deuil*, p. 90.

sorely tempted to see in it evidence of the calling into question that typified the nationalist movement after the war. Indeed, the speaker presented an alarming portrait of the French minorities in the other provinces and at the same time criticized initiatives by the federal government to centralize the powers which, under the constitution, fell to the provinces. It is also true that he condemned the "scandal" of all the "sons" who had been allowed by Québec to leave, and he stressed the need to work to strengthen the old province. However, this was a speech that Groulx could just as easily have given in 1922 as in 1952. It would be difficult to ascribe his provincial *autonomisme* to the ideological turmoil of the postwar period. Actually, his position on Québec's place within the French-Canadian nation and in Canada had evolved little since the time he headed *L'Action française*. Québec had been and would always remain, in his mind, the source and the heart of French civilization in America: its weakening could only thwart the *survivance* efforts of the French minorities. These were the arguments he advanced to reassure the representatives of the minorities attending the 1952 conference:

> French-Canadian compatriots from all over Canada, there you have the affirmation of our close solidarity. It is a solidarity which we could afford to remember more often in this province, remember at moments other than during conferences on *survivance*. But if we understand that, considering how you have been treated in each of your provinces, it is the same to you whether you deal with an Anglo-Protestant majority in your province or with the Anglo-Protestant majority in Ottawa, you will also understand, we hope, that, being free, we, in our provincial State, masters who govern ourselves as we see fit, we are somewhat reluctant to entrust our fate to the same kind of people who, with no regard for the most formal constitutional documents, have robbed you of your most sacred rights and have never restored them to you. On a point as serious as this, let us take care not to misunderstand one another. Shall I remind you? Rarely does one fortify one's positions by sacrificing the citadel.

At *L'Action française*, some thirty years earlier, Groulx and Rodrigue Villeneuve had said nothing that would contradict this during the study on the political future of French Canada. The orator peppered his speech with frequent references to the courage of the minorities, pointing out that they led "the battle for French *survivance*, often better than we of the old homestead," and calling to mind for his listeners the memory of some of their greatest heroes, among them Msgr. Langevin, Charles Charlebois and Philippe Landry. He concluded his talk by holding forth at length about the apostolic vocation of the French-Canadian nation, which by itself justified its existence. Groulx gave a second talk during the 1952 conference, when he was made a member of the Ordre de la fidélité française, an honour he received at the same time as Joseph-Papin Archambault, Jean-Baptiste Prince and Victor Barrette. It was he who, on behalf of the four laureates, gave the official thank you, revisiting several of the major themes of his first speech. Quite obviously, he had hardly strayed from the orthodoxy of his own brand of nationalism.[33]

Contact Maintained through Lectures, Articles and Travel

Groulx did not rely just on the Conseil de la vie française en Amérique in order to cultivate his relations with the minorities. As he had done countless times before the war, and despite his advancing years, he often found time during the forties and fifties to visit the minorities and contribute to their projects. ACFEO, for example, regularly asked Groulx for copies of his works so they could be given as prizes to the winners of their annual provincial French language competitions.[34] In November 1944, at the invitation of Abbé Antoine d'Eschambault, Groulx went to Saint-Boniface to give a series of five history lectures. According to his *Mémoires*, these courses, which analyzed the "constitutional evolution of Canada up to the present day," drew an audience that averaged about 200 people each evening. D'Eschambault had also wanted his visit to Saint-Boniface to coincide with the festivities set for November 11 to commemorate the birth of Louis Riel. The highlight of the evening was Groulx's talk on "Louis Riel et les événements de la Rivière-Rouge en 1869–1870" (which he gave again the following month at the Monument-National de Montréal). D'Eschambault wanted this celebration to serve as an opportunity to foster closer relations between Franco-Manitobans and the Métis community, which he felt had for too long remained isolated:

> This event will have repercussions among the Métis themselves who feel they are looked upon with condescension by our people and who need a little pride and it would be good to say what service they too have rendered. The Métis youth are inclined toward anglicization because we are too condescending toward them.

A few days later, d'Eschambault confided to Groulx that he had succeeded in "winning the hearts of our good Métis people," and praised their "edifying fidelity." As during his trip there in 1928, this stay among the Franco-Manitobans made Groulx even more aware of the crucial role Québec must play with regard to the minorities, a role it had thus far fulfilled only imperfectly. At least that is what he implied in his *Mémoires* a few years later:

> The priest who is the Rector of the *Collège* [in Saint-Boniface] also recruited me to give a talk to the students there. When I asked him, What shall I talk to them about?

33. Lionel Groulx, "Pour une relève," *Pour bâtir*, p. 49–64; Lionel Groulx, "Crise de fidélité française," *Pour bâtir*, p. 65–77.

34. Exchange of correspondence between Lionel Groulx and Gustave Sauvé, BAnQ, FLG, P1/A,3399, March 1946 to March 1949; exchange of correspondence between Lionel Groulx and Roger Charbonneau, BAnQ, FLG, P1/A,733, March 1948 to January 1963.

he answered, pausing between his words, "Talk to them about Québec, about the old province, which they hardly know." Once again, before these young people, who listen to me eagerly, I observe how little influence the "old province" has outside its borders, how it hardly seeks to make itself known, even among its exiled sons. Here in this Manitoba of 1944, I still find a will to survive. Hope has not been extinguished.[35]

On his way back to Montréal, Groulx stopped in to see the Jesuits of Sudbury. They kept track of his whereabouts, and Father Lorenzo Cadieux, professor at the Collège du Sacré-Cœur and president of the Société historique du Nouvel-Ontario (SHNO), had begged him to take time out to address a few words to his pupils, pointing out how isolated the Franco-Ontarians of the North were and what great good he would accomplish there: "A great many ardent French-Canadian youth wish, at all costs, to see our national historian. And—allow me to share all of my thought and . . . theirs with you—Nouvel-Ontario has been rather left behind, treated like the poor relative who struggles with all her might." Unable to refuse such an invitation, Groulx gave a speech entitled "Confiance et espoir" before a "large audience" of pupils and teachers and for which he received a stipend of one hundred dollars. In his *Mémoires*, he would recall the "atmosphere of warm sympathy" and the "stirring vitality" that had welcomed him. In his talk, he revisited ideas that by now are very familiar to us: after establishing the origins of the educational struggles of the minorities and recalling the importance of history, tradition and Catholicism in the life of the French-Canadian people, he lamented the inadequate sense of nationhood of Québec's political class, who did not live up to their responsibilities toward the minorities as they should. Fortunately, he continued, the new generation offered signs of hope and promised to rectify some of the errors of the past:

> Once awakened to the sentiment of our French solidarity, the old province, I am firmly convinced, will in the end discover its care of souls—for all and for the too oft forgotten brothers of the diaspora. As it becomes aware of its deep originality, of the exceptional values of civilization that it embodies and, then, of the difficult position it will always have in our America and in Canada, Québec will feel more strongly the need to gather up all its strength, all the strength that you are, even if only to bring its minorities into its defence system.

A few days later, Cadieux told Groulx how delighted he was with the turn of events and, especially, with the reaction his visit to Sudbury had elicited: "*Monsieur le*

35. Lionel Groulx, *Mes Mémoires, Tome IV*, p. 139; Lionel Groulx, *Louis Riel et les événements de la Rivière-Rouge en 1869–1870* (Montréal: Éditions de l'Action nationale, 1944), 23 p.; letters from Antoine d'Eschambault to Lionel Groulx, BAnQ, FLG, P1/A,1297, September 19, 1944 and November 15, 1944.

chanoine, I wish you to be persuaded of this: the good that you have done is incalculable. . . . Therefore, you should come back. A great many youth, who struggle, who are on the brink, await words of guidance from you." Later, Cadieux asked to meet with him during a possible trip to Montréal in order to have some advice from him about the teaching of history at the *collège* in Sudbury. Groulx consented to his Franco-Ontarian colleague's request and provided him, a short time later, with the outline of one of his courses. As we will see shortly, the relationship between the two priests grew stronger when Groulx founded his Institut d'histoire in 1946.[36]

The next two trips Groulx made to visit the minorities took place a few years later. In September and November of 1953 he went first to New Brunswick and then to New England. Already during the previous year, Jesuit Father Joseph-Papin Archambault had invited him to give an address in Edmundston during their *Semaine Sociale*, a kind of popular travelling university, founded some thirty years earlier. Archambault told him that it was the Bishop of Edmundston himself, Msgr. Roméo Gagnon, who had expressly asked that Groulx's name appear on the program. The course Groulx offered was called "La paroisse, foyer de vie nationale." This theme had made him hesitate at first, as he indicated to Archambault:

> It is not an easy subject to deal with. I know the parish, centre of religious life. As for whether it is the centre of the life of the nation, I wonder whether that has always been the case and whether it even still is today. How many parishes are there not, in our province, where all they read is *la PRESSE* and where minds are totally indifferent to the deeper life of nationality.

To reassure his friend, Archambault suggested he reread an article on the theme of the parish, published by *L'Action française* in 1918, and some passages in *Études et appréciations* by Msgr. Louis-Adolphe Pâquet. This did not alleviate Groulx's worries. About a month before he left for Edmundston, he confided to Guy Frégault that he did not like the topic he would have to deal with "at all." He added, in the same breath, that he was not any happier about the stop he would be making in Boston a few weeks later. Invited by his friend, Adrien Verrette, he had made a commitment to give a talk entitled "Y a-t-il un avenir ?" at the Société historique franco-américaine. But there would be nothing historical about his lecture: rather, it would have to do with "providing these poor people with a few reasons for French *survivance*." A few days before his departure for Massachusetts, Groulx received a note from Verrette stressing the great good that his trip to Boston would do the Franco-Americans who were going through a difficult time: "I am certain

36. Exchange of correspondence between Lionel Groulx and Lorenzo Cadieux, BAnQ, FLG, P1/A,617, October 30, 1944 to February 28, 1947; Lionel Groulx, *Confiance et espoir* (Sudbury: Société historique du Nouvel-Ontario, 1944), 22 p.; Lionel Groulx, *Mes Mémoires, Tome IV*, p. 140.

that your message will be very beneficial during this distressing time we are going through. For there is no point in hiding it, the slippery slope here is frightening, and we need some powerful vitamins."[37]

Groulx's lecture reviewed several of the great themes he had developed in "Confiance et espoir" but the tone of his remarks betrayed a feeling of urgency that he had not displayed, in 1944, to his Sudbury audience. Clearly he believed the survival of Franco-Americans to be differently threatened, immersed as they were, in the civilization of the United States, made up entirely, in his view, of materialism, pragmatism and hedonism. Not surprisingly then, he appealed once more to the providential mission of the French people of America to justify the fight against acculturation and apostasy. Confronted by the "sudden *compénétration* of the continents" and "universal endosmosis," developments that had been accelerating since World War II, the Franco-Americans of New England, Groulx explained, were caught up in the "whirlwind of assimilation," a plague that did not spare the French minorities of Canada either. He was not lacking in optimism, however, and pointed out that French Catholic civilization, throughout its history, had managed to overcome equally formidable obstacles in the past. The survival of the French-Canadian nation, he concluded, was in the hands of Providence, pending one's willingness to accept its guidance:

> Providence is at the heart of all history. Is it forbidden to us to search its ways? Why this *survivance*? Are we the elect who have been given a mission? Are we the bearers of a message? . . . Sons of the Church: if we understand clearly the grandeur of that title, and if we acknowledge that Providence is involving us in the greatest enterprise of human history, the redemption of the world, no one has the right to extinguish this most humble torch lighted by Christ, and especially not those who carry this torch. The entire message we bring as Christians is at stake. It is the whole reason why we are a Catholic people.

The French Canadians and the Franco-Americans, Groulx continued, embodied the "saving ideal" of Catholicism, their role being to "save the civilizations of the two great countries we cherish." It was sufficient just to place one's trust in Providence and not to be seduced by the "ideal of mere progress or material comfort," which he cited as the cause of the "social levelling that would always entice the *classes populaires*."[38]

37. Exchange of correspondence between Joseph-Papin Archambault and Lionel Groulx, BANQ, P1/A,77, December 9, 1952 to August 2, 1953. Letters from Lionel Groulx to Guy Frégault, BAnQ, FLG, P1/A,1425, August 22, 1953; from Lionel Groulx to François-Albert Angers, BAnQ, FLG, P1/A,58, September 22, 1953; from Adrien Verrette to Lionel Groulx, November 4, 1953, cited in Damien-Claude Bélanger, *Lionel Groulx et la Franco-Américanie*, p. 126. The speech he delivered in Edmundston was published shortly afterwards: Lionel Groulx, "La paroisse, foyer de vie nationale," in *Semaines sociales du Canada (section française): XXXe Session – Edmundston, 1953: La Paroisse, cellule sociale: Compte rendu des cours et conférences* (Montréal: Institut social populaire, 1953), p. 165–178.
38. Lionel Groulx, "Y a-t-il un avenir ?," *Pour bâtir*, p. 162–175.

Groulx, by all accounts, became increasingly disappointed in the materialist dimension of the social transformations that the war had provoked. He believed that these transformations, by contributing to the removal of the principle of Providence, its authority and its intervention in the life of peoples, were chipping away at the foundation of what he saw as the raison d'être of the French-Canadian nation. Groulx brought his crusade against postwar materialism to Northern Ontario once again in May 1955 when he took part in festivities marking the fifty years of priesthood of Oscar Racette, pastor of Verner, near Sudbury. He took the opportunity to deliver a talk entitled "La Résistance." Despite the prosaic title, the theme was far from dull. Why should a people resist? he asked. Because it was a "right" and a "duty" to do so, because the good of humanity was not brought about by the exclusion of the least powerful peoples: "It is not true that the beauty of the world is constituted by uniformity. The homogenization I see in these large contemporary populations, with their frightful intermixture of nationalities, has not, I find, improved the human type." Groulx took leave of his Franco-Ontarian hosts, pleased to have had another stay among them. A few months later, he told Racette that Verner embodied the purest virtues of the French-Canadian traditional parish and that its pastor seemed to him the typical example of the spiritual and national leader: "I deserve no great credit for coming to your town for your celebrations. I was so happy to find there, so far away from Québec, a type of parish that hardly exists here, and to find there also a pastor who is largely responsible for the wonder of Verner."[39]

The Franco-Ontarians continued to seek Groulx's involvement in their activities. In the fall of 1958, *Le Droit* of Ottawa was preparing a special issue to commemorate the one hundredth anniversary of the French-language press in Ontario. The news editor, Charles Bruyère, asked him to provide an article on the importance of the Franco-Ontarian press "because of the sympathetic interest he had tirelessly shown in *Le Droit* and in the cause of the Franco-Ontarian minority." Groulx replied that the need for the French-language press was "obvious" and that, consequently, drafting this article would be "the most difficult thing in the world." He nevertheless accepted willingly, specifying that he would try not to spout too many "platitudes." *Le Droit* published the article in the issue of November 8, 1958. In it, Groulx explained that the role of the French press in Ontario was one of "public salvation." In many respects, he went on, Franco-Ontarians were, of all the minority groups, the best organized, "the best equipped for the resistance" and certainly the most numerous. However, they had to deal with a huge handicap: the terrible distances over which they were spread throughout their province. The independent press, of which *Le Droit* was

39. The handwritten outline of this talk has been preserved: Lionel Groulx, "La résistance: Notes pour une conférence à Verner, Ont., May 1955," BAnQ, P1/MA-393; Letter from Lionel Groulx to Oscar Racette, BAnQ, FLG, P1/A,3117, August 12, 1955.

an excellent example, offered a way to compensate for this dispersal, by bringing together the vital forces of the Franco-Ontarians and setting down a clear direction for them. Nor did Groulx miss this opportunity to upbraid the journalists and intellectuals who insisted on relegating the cultural and spiritual heritage of French-Canadian society to oblivion—something they had been doing for years, alleging all the while that they wanted to democratize it:

> If we really have an attachment to our culture, to our faith, to these sacred assets that an ordinary French-Canadian places above all else, we will support our newspapers and, especially, we will read them. We will not require that they always think as we do, we who so often misinterpret things and think so differently from one another. Have you ever reflected on the kaleidoscopic multiplicity of opinions that a French-Canadian newspaper would have to express each day if it tried to think like each of its readers? Perhaps it could be enough for us that our newspapers be free, that they operate in good faith and that they approach our basic problems intelligently and from a French-Canadian and Catholic perspective.[40]

The Minorities in Groulx's Historical Work

The Minorities and the Theory of Messianism in the Later Works of the Old maître

We have already pointed out that, following World War II, Groulx, progressively withdrew from active militancy and dedicated himself, undoubtedly as never before, to developing his historical work. It was indeed during the fifteen years immediately after the war that the old *maître* produced his major works of historical synthesis. Was it the feeling of having, for such a long time, attended to a myriad of disparate works that led him, in the last twenty years of his life, to dedicate himself to his primary vocation of historian? Certainly, at least, in part. For the rest, how could we not see, in this direction Groulx took after the war, a desire to revalidate his own practice of history? Did not the "new" history of the Brunets, Frégaults and Séguins demand this of him? The historians of the École de Montréal were seeking, as he understood it, to "desacralize" the history of the French-Canadian people: they felt it was time to purge it of the "consoling myths" they believed traditional historians had been relying on for too long. The era of national hero worship seemed to be drawing to a close, at the same time as the idea of the apostolic and providential vocation of the French-Canadian nation was being shelved. This was too much for Groulx. How could he keep silent as he watched the casual dismantling of a large part of the conceptual edifice he had spent many decades constructing? In his opinion, the new generation of

40. Letters from Charles Bruyère to Lionel Groulx, BAnQ, FLG, P1/A,598, September 15, 1958 and October 14, 1958. See Lionel Groulx, "La presse française en terre ontarienne: Son rôle," *Le Droit*, November 8, 1958, p. 34.

historians may not have realized it but they were attacking the spiritual foundations of the French-Canadian nation and threatening its *survivance* as a distinct people. All in the name of a science that seemed to him extremely suspect, as it was too inclined to rely solely on material factors in its analyses. Groulx therefore took advantage of every platform available to him to reiterate his faith in the providential mission of French Canadians. He did not think it necessary to search beyond that truth—profound and immutable, in his mind—to justify the presence of his *petit peuple* in the four corners of America. That is what he explained in 1949 to the graduating class of the *collège* run by the *Sœurs de l'Assomption de Nicolet*:

> What is . . . French Canada? A few men from France who, with the courage and the vision to defy the distances, will carve out for themselves in the vastness of America, on a scale as grand as their era, a country larger than Europe; insatiable adventurers with the ambition to bring half the continent under their dominion; who finally build a kind of empire where the *fleurdelisé* will fly, for a time, from the shores of the Atlantic to beyond the Great Lakes, and from Hudson Bay to the mouth of the Mississippi. . . . Again, what is French Canada? The heroic legion of young *canadienne* missionary sisters, seeking the greatest adventure the world can offer, which is to be found on all roads taken by Canadian missionaries. An adventure that reveals the tremendous energy and drive that remained in the soul of a young nationality nourished for a hundred years by a dream of empire. A spiritual adventure this time, in which the star of the Redeemer still searches out souls to win. And here, among these young people, I see our humble French Canada, swept up by some mystical breeze, associated with the universal missionary movement.[41]

The profession of faith expressed in this speech was something to which Lionel Groulx remained ever faithful, despite the efforts of those who ridiculed him. After the war, the idea of apostolic vocation, at the heart of his analyses of the place of the minorities in the French-Canadian nation, figured more and more frequently among his concerns as a historian. At the end of the 1940s, the Société Saint-Jean-Baptiste suggested he should record a series of French-Canadian history courses for the Montréal radio station CKAC. The scope of the project, however, became much larger: within a short period, Groulx's courses were broadcast throughout all of Québec, but also in Ontario, New Brunswick, Manitoba and Alberta.[42] At the beginning of the fifties, *L'Action nationale* published these courses in four volumes, which then became Groulx's vast synthesis, *L'Histoire du Canada français depuis la découverte*.[43] In this work, the historian traces the trajectory of the

41. Lionel Groulx, "Qu'attend de vous le Canada français ?," *Pour bâtir*, p. 185, 190.
42. Lionel Groulx, *Mes Mémoires*, Tome IV, p. 181–182.
43. Lionel Groulx, *Histoire du Canada français depuis la découverte*, Tome I (Montréal: Éditions de l'Action nationale, 1950), 221 p.; Tome II (Montréal: Éditions de l'Action nationale, 1951), 302 p.; Tome III (Montréal: Éditions de l'Action nationale, 1952), 326 p.; Tome IV (Montréal: Éditions de l'Action nationale, 1952), 273 p. Subsequent

French-Canadian nation from the founding of New France. He emphasizes the apparent conflict between the two imperatives that accounted for its development. There was the call to "explore" and the call to "put down roots." Even when settlement took priority, he explained, the French and, after them, the French Canadians, unstintingly pursued their apostolic vocation throughout the North American continent.

> It is quite significant that in New France, evangelization preceded colonization. Only the mentality of the pioneer leaders can explain this somewhat extraordinary fact. Most of the founders were Catholics of the counter-reformation; some even belonged to the mystical school of France. In the missionary ideal, they saw, as did many of their contemporaries, the vindication promised to the faithful against the ravages of Protestantism.[44]

The ideal behind the foundation of New France, in Groulx's thought, remained first and foremost spiritual. According to this logic, establishing the colony was more than an economic enterprise. Determined to resist the materialist paradigm of the new school of historians, Groulx always observed Providence at work in French Canada's past. We must not conclude from this that he did not appreciate the material dimension of the history of New France. On the contrary, he recognized at the outset that this pressing on into the depths of America had been prompted at the same time by less lofty ambitions, namely, commercial ones, and that this had posed enormous risks to the material survival of the colony. He readily admitted that the colony had been dangerously weakened by being so spread out. Nevertheless, the great men of New France had apparently been powerless to resist the missionary ideal, which, more than anything else, justified the French presence in America. The historian highlighted with obvious pride the work of the numerous missionaries and evangelizers who had crossed the continent bringing the Catholic faith to the indigenous populations and marking these vast territories with the stamp of French civilization.

In his *Histoire du Canada français*—and in particular in the chapters dealing with the period following Confederation in 1867—Groulx frequently returned to the French minorities, their establishment outside Québec and their educational and religious struggles. Although he did not dedicate any one chapter specifically to them, the minorities surface time and again in his account, notably in the general conclusion to the work, containing an absolute refutation of the trend toward the *québécisation* that characterized the neo-nationalist discourse. Groulx repeated that the French-Canadian people existed outside of any territorial or state framework,

references to this work will be taken from the 1960 edition: *Histoire du Canada français depuis la découverte, Tome I: Le Régime français, Tome II: Le Régime britannique au Canada* (Montréal: Fides, 1960), 394 p. and 445 p.

44. Lionel Groulx, *Histoire du Canada français, Tome I*, p. 51.

even though Québec constituted its "ancestral home." His reasoning on these questions remained constant:

> French Canada, we have repeated often enough on these pages, is no longer in any way a geographical entity. A cultural entity is the only way to define it. Either by reconstituting former groups, as is the case in Acadia in the East, or by continuous migrations toward the West, French Canada, along with Québec as principal home and centre of gravity, has branched out and extends today from one ocean to the other, from St. John's, Newfoundland to Vancouver. In 1951, out of a total population of 14,009,429 for all of Canada, the French population accounted for 4,319,167, of which 999,039, almost a million, lived outside Québec.

Although in the lines that followed, Groulx qualified this "dispersal" as "excessive," he did not yield to any pessimism, preferring instead to highlight the numerous battles the minorities had fought successfully over the decades in order to have their linguistic, educational and religious rights recognized:

> A unique and common note is found among all of these migrants of the French race who spread from one province to the other, whether they be *Acadiens* or *Canadiens*. They do not in any way resemble the immigrants who come from outside Canada. They have not left their old provinces, resolved to make a clean break with their past and their traditions, the way one hastily discards one's old clothes. No, along with their material baggage, they have brought other, heavier baggage, their cultural heritage: faith, language, a whole moral and psychological world, a spark of the sacred fire, a relic of the first native land. Everywhere, they become a leaven of liberty.

This "historical continuity," in his view, presupposed "the more or less clear awareness, in the heart of a believing people, of a unique message to be delivered to the world" and it implicated French Canada "in the supreme project, willed and undertaken by Christ twenty centuries ago for the redemption of the world and a new understanding of human history." Groulx ended his defence by enjoining his people not to deny their "missionary past" and to remain faithful to the "path traced by the ancestors."[45]

Groulx rolled up his sleeves again a few years later to undertake another work, *Notre grande aventure*, a historical synthesis, dedicated this time to the French regime.[46] The historian wanted to show that the grandeur of the French Empire was far from illusory, despite having been called "fragile" and "skeleton-like." But if New France had been able to exist, despite the formidable obstacles it faced, it

45. Lionel Groulx, *Histoire du Canada français . . . Tome II*, p. 405–407.
46. Lionel Groulx, *Notre grande aventure: L'Empire français en Amérique du Nord, 1535–1760* (Montréal and Paris: Fides, 1958), 299 p.

was due, he insisted, to the work of the founders, explorers and missionaries, who had devoted themselves to their task with truly heroic faith and zeal. In the St. Lawrence Valley, but also in Acadia, in the Northwest and in the area around the Mississippi, everywhere they went, these pioneers had left the imprint of French Catholic civilization. As Groulx told Gérard Filion of *Le Devoir*, this book was to provide French Canadians with a reason to be proud. That was especially important, he felt, as the new "minimizing" school of history seemed bent on "shrinking our history," stripping it of all its nobility, seeing in it only a series of setbacks and humiliations. He also expressed his disappointment that the press, including *Le Devoir*, had not commented on his *Notre grande aventure* and his sadness that certain groups no doubt judged it to be "teeming with myths." The old leader was deeply upset by this. He told Filion that a friend, back from the West, had reported to him that "terrible harm was being done there by the way history was taught." *Why go on about the accomplishments of the ancestors if they had done nothing that was of any value?* That it had come to asking themselves such a question betrayed, for Groulx, the seriousness of the malady that had been wearing French Canada down for some time. "We are gravely stricken," he explained to Filion. "They have undermined the foundations that our *survivance* depended on, if it is true that to keep the right to survive, a people must have, at the very least, a minimum of culture and civilization and a past of some greatness." Groulx concluded that it was from this *apatriotisme* that French Canadians needed to cure themselves if they still wanted to survive.[47]

However, Groulx made his most eloquent defence of the argument for the apostolic vocation of French Canada once the Quiet Revolution was well under way. In 1962, he published his ambitious and voluminous *Canada français missionnaire*, the fruit of long reflection, the seed of this work having been planted in his mind back in the 1920s. In 1953, he had asked Cardinal Paul-Émile Léger for a special blessing for this project which he thought would be the crowning achievement of his career as a historian.[48] He traced the path of the French-Canadian missionaries on almost all the continents of the planet, from Central America to the Far East and from Africa to Oceania. However, he devoted the first five chapters to the missionaries who had worked in Canada, starting with the time of the founding of New France. Although the analysis remained relatively basic, as Groulx no doubt preferred not to duplicate his earlier studies of the French and English regimes, he treated certain topics at length, among them, the "epic" of the Oblates in the Canadian West during the nineteenth century. Groulx made use of this example to deliver yet another rebuff to the new school of history which, in his view, saw only mythology where they should have recognized some of the greatest heroes of the French-Canadian nation:

47. Letter from Lionel Groulx to Gérard Filion, BAnQ, FLG, P1/A,1348, April 22, 1958.
48. Letter from Lionel Groulx to Paul-Émile Léger, BAnQ, FLG, P1/A,2281, July 10, 1953.

> I write "epic" even though it is fashionable today in history to reduce everything. We no longer want to believe, as was already observed by Péguy, in either heroes or saints. I write "epic" for lack of any other words to designate the persevering, total and heroic giving of oneself, the acceptance of superhuman trials for the love of God and for the love of mankind.[49]

Groulx, the Minorities and the Institut d'histoire de l'Amérique française

For the last twenty years of his life, Lionel Groulx could easily have been content to focus on his own historical writing in peace and tranquility, confident of having made a worthy contribution to French-Canadian historiography, and not troubled himself about the future of his profession. However, being the indefatigable worker that he was, he was not satisfied to rest on his laurels and accumulate honours. After the Second World War, in 1947, at a point in his life when others would no doubt have preferred to consider retiring, Groulx, just shy of seventy years of age, proceeded to initiate another project, one of the biggest he had undertaken in his life, namely, the Institut d'histoire de l'Amérique française (IHAF). That same year saw the publication of the *Revue d'histoire de l'Amérique française*, the first academic periodical in French Canada specifically targeting professional historians. Groulx, whose professional choices had always been guided by his priorities of transmitting knowledge and educating the next generation, and especially by the principle of intergenerational continuity, devoted himself wholeheartedly to the project. Groulx's intent, when he founded his Institut, was not just to protect the integrity of his intellectual heritage. Nor was it limited to ensuring that it was his own understanding of history that would prevail over that of the new practitioners of the discipline. On the contrary, certain historians, like Michel Brunet, Guy Frégault and Maurice Séguin, who had already begun to question his historical work, would occupy important roles. The first two also took advantage of the platform that the *Revue* offered them to publish their writings. We should note also that Groulx took his retirement from Université de Montréal around this same time, partly in order to free up a position that was to go to Maurice Séguin. Although Groulx strongly criticized the methods and, particularly, the materialist paradigm, that rallied the new generation of historians, he did not suffer from any parochialism when it came to historiography and never hesitated to debate the great challenges that historians faced.

Groulx wanted this Institut d'histoire de l'Amérique française to be worthy of its name and to bring together the historians of all the French communities in the country, and even of the continent. However, would this organization serve a scientific or a patriotic purpose? Would the two objectives be incompatible? Right from the beginning, Groulx had to tackle this delicate question. In October

49. Lionel Groulx, *Le Canada français missionnaire: Une autre grande aventure* (Montréal and Paris: Fides, 1962), p. 35.

1946, a journalist from *Le Devoir* asked him if, with this institute, he was seeking to strengthen "the French brotherhood in America." Yes and no, was his answer. Historians, in his opinion, should only be interested in history for the love of history and should "proscribe any utilitarian purpose." He would have had a hard time, however, denying that his own historical works had, throughout his career, fed his activist and polemical work. Therefore, he attempted to nuance his reply: "[Historians] cannot prevent, any more than others can, that their actions should follow them, I mean, cannot prevent their works or their writings from extending into time and life. Yes, I think the Institut d'histoire will serve our French community."[50]

Right from the start, then, it was his aim to bring together historians from all across the vast regions of French America outside Québec: Acadia, Ontario, the Canadian West and New England. The letters patent for the Institut stipulated, moreover, that one of the reasons for its existence was to "organize teams of historians from all parts of America."[51] Of all the historians Groulx tried to recruit, Father Lorenzo Cadieux, of the Collège du Sacré-Cœur in Sudbury, was at the top of his list. In October 1946, he sent him the details of his plan for the historical institute and asked him if the Société historique du Nouvel-Ontario, founded by the Jesuits four years earlier, would agree to be affiliated. He stressed that, even though the objectives were primarily scientific, the organization would not be prevented from helping to strengthen ties between the various French groups of the continent: "Without it being an express aim, you can well imagine that I perceive in the institute another way, an active way, of gathering together all the members of our French community." In the West, Groulx recruited his old friend, Abbé Antoine d'Eschambault, of the Société historique de Saint-Boniface, advising him of his intent to offer all the French minorities their rightful place in IHAF and in the *Revue*: "Surely you know how much I would wish that, in practically every issue of the *Revue*, each of the provinces of French America could be featured in a positive light." It was to Brother Antoine Bernard, c.s.v., that Groulx entrusted the task of representing Acadia at the Institut. Bernard agreed, despite what he considered to be his advancing years (though he was only fifty-six years of age in 1945). As far as he was concerned, seeing the IHAF as a patriotic project did not present a problem: "I will support, as much as I can, an intellectual movement that is perhaps more necessary now than at any other time in the history of the French resistance in America." Just as for *L'Action française* some twenty-five years earlier, Groulx experienced great difficulty recruiting Acadian collaborators. In 1951, he was delighted at the efforts to resurrect the Société historique et littéraire acadienne, which, while founded in 1928, had not been very active since. However, this project was not realized. By 1953, two years later, the

50. Groulx reports these exchanges in *Mes Mémoires, Tome IV*, p. 150–151.
51. Lionel Groulx, "Vie de l'Institut," *RHAF*, June 1947, p. 153.

Institut boasted approximately ten regional sections operating in almost all parts of French Canada and New England. Groulx had difficulty concealing the pride that all these memberships produced in him: "Truly, if we want to cover our entire area, we are only missing a historical society of Acadia, of Louisiana and of the Antilles."[52]

The first issue of the *Revue d'histoire de l'Amérique française* appeared in June of 1947. It listed the names of all the member correspondents of the Institut and Groulx was very pleased that "the entire area of French America was covered." Besides the names Cadieux and d'Eschambault, the list included those of Gérard Gauthier of Vancouver and Burton LeDoux, Adrien Verrette, Adolphe Robert and Gabriel Nadeau, all from New England. Although he indicated that the organization had only one affiliated regional section—namely, the Société historique du Nouvel-Ontario of Sudbury, which operated "under the enthusiastic leadership of Father Lorenzo Cadieux, s.j."—he added that it would not be long before other sections became affiliated (the Société historique franco-américaine and the Société historique de Saint-Boniface were, in fact, slated to join soon). Groulx also announced to his readers that he expected to organize a course to be given each year "on one or the other of the 'provinces' of the French fact" and that d'Eschambault had promised to give the 1948 course, which would be on La Vérendrye.[53]

All this information Groulx provided under the heading "Vie de l'Institut" — which, a bit later, he renamed "Chronique de l'Institut." It resembled in every way "La vie de l'Action française," one of his columns in *L'Action française* during the 1920s, mostly signed by Jacques Brassier (one of his pseudonyms). Just as in *L'Action française*, Groulx used this column to inform his readers of the numerous activities organized and publications issued by the historians of the minorities. He also used it to recruit new member correspondents in the various "provinces" of French America. The projects of the Sudbury section were regularly announced, and Groulx had nothing but praise for its president: "under the dynamic direction of Father Lorenzo Cadieux, s.j., [the Société historique du Nouvel-Ontario (SNHO)] certainly ranks among our most active regional historical societies. And we can expect more good news from this enthusiastic corner of the country."[54] Groulx frequently solicited the SHNO's cooperation for the *Revue*.

52. Letters from Lionel Groulx to Lorenzo Cadieux, BAnQ, FLG, P1/A,617, October 24, 1946; from Lionel Groulx to Antoine d'Eschambault, BAnQ, FLG, P1/A,1297, December 23, 1950; from Lionel Groulx to Antoine Bernard, BAnQ, FLG, P1/A,326, November 8, 1946; from Antoine Bernard to Lionel Groulx, BAnQ, FLG, P1/A,326, November 13, 1946; Lionel Groulx, "Chronique des sections de l'Institut," *RHAF*, March 1951, p. 604; Lionel Groulx, "Vue rétrospective," *RHAF*, June 1953, p. 3.

53. Lionel Groulx, "Vie de l'Institut," *RHAF*, June 1947, p. 155–156; December 1947, p. 474; June 1948, p. 153; June 1947, p. 157.

54. Lionel Groulx, "Vie de l'Institut," *RHAF*, December 1947, p. 474. See also Lionel Groulx, "Vie de l'Institut," *RHAF*, June 1953, p. 148; "Chronique de l'Institut," *RHAF*, March 1958, p. 615–616; December 1958, p. 455; March 1959, p. 605; June 1960, p. 152; June 1961, p. 158.

As early as September 1947, he invited Father Adrien Pouliot, who had just been transferred to Sudbury, to prepare a report on the activities of the SHNO for the *Revue*.[55] Pouliot accepted and provided Groulx with a piece that he co-signed with Lorenzo Cadieux. In addition to rendering an account of the many activities organized by the Sudbury section, the authors alluded, as Groulx himself had often done, to Ontario's ancestral ties to New France. It was the one argument which, of all of them, apparently justified the Franco-Ontarian resistance struggle:

> This region—called *le Nouvel-Ontario*—dates back much farther, note well, than the construction of the Canadian Pacific railway (1880) . . . . The French River, which embraces it, and Lake Huron, in which it sees itself reflected, vie with one another to remind us of the uninterrupted current of glorious expeditions. . . . Our Société, whose field of research extends to all the French history of Ontario, hopes, with time, to honour its other heroes. It wishes especially to show Ontarians that the French civilization achieved by their ancestors lives on today. In this way, the Société expects to both stimulate the pride of Franco-Ontarian groups and fulfil its recent mandate with the Institut d'histoire de l'Amérique française.[56]

In 1952, Groulx also highlighted the fiftieth anniversary of the Société historique de Saint-Boniface, which he ranked, along with that of Sudbury, "among the most active sections of the Institut." In the same issue, he expressed his satisfaction with the fact that the Conseil de la vie française en Amérique was a member of the Institut: "To the Conseil also we offer our sincere thanks for this generosity and for this tribute to a work whose major interest for all of French America they clearly recognize." In the same way, the Institut and the *Revue* seemed to help improve the quality of the projects that the local sections undertook in their "various *petits pays*." Or, so it was implied by Groulx, who, furthermore, was not the only one to conclude this. Back in 1948, in a report presented at the first annual meeting of the Institut, Lorenzo Cadieux had also recognized this development. He pointed out that "under a leader whose erudition and merit were irrefutable," namely, Lionel Groulx, the members of the SHNO had received from the Institut not only "guarantees as to the validity of their [historical] method" and "the sense that they were collaborating on a comprehensive project," but also "increased exposure" for their publications. Cadieux had also expressed the desire to work actively, under the sponsorshop of the IHAF, for the federation of all the historical societies on the continent that were *d'inspiration française*. Let us remember that in 1948, the SHNO was the only regional historical society to be affiliated with the IHAF, which still did not have a single member from Québec. Groulx, for

55. Letter from Lionel Groulx to Adrien Pouliot, BAnQ, FLG, P1/A,3068, September 12, 1947.
56. Lorenzo Cadieux and Adrien Pouliot, "Chronique d'une section de l'Institut: La Société historique du Nouvel-Ontario," *RHAF*, December 1947, p. 472.

his part, had considered his Franco-Ontarian colleague's remarks to be very constructive indeed: "It is to some extent the future and the expansion of the Institut that hangs on this project proposed by Father Cadieux."[57]

We have noted that the IHAF reserved an important place for the historians of the French minorities. So did the *Revue*. Groulx published in its pages several studies dealing with the French fact in the various "provinces" of French America, studies written mostly, though not exclusively, by minority historians. By the time of the director's death in 1967, the *Revue* had published almost sixty of these articles dealing with a plethora of themes, from the exploits of the holy Canadian martyrs on Ontario soil to the schools crises in New Brunswick and in the Canadian West, including the Métis Rebellions and the Deportation of the Acadians. The exploration and colonization, by the French pioneers, of the vast lands of America were among the areas of study that several of the *Revue*'s collaborators favoured most. Groulx, not wanting to be left out, pulled his weight here too, although his numerous responsibilities as the *Revue*'s director, not to mention the tasks that fell to him as president of the IHAF, made him, ironically, a rather irregular contributor. His contributions often took the form of archival material presented under the heading "Previously unpublished documents," an arrangement much appreciated by his collaborators. Groulx often prefaced these selections with contextualization, brief or lengthy, as needed. In September 1947, for example, he presented to his readers some excerpts from correspondence exchanged in the late nineteenth century between the Archbishop of Saint-Boniface, Adélard Langevin—who had stood up to the provincial and federal governments during the Manitoban schools crisis—and Colonel Alphonse Audet, Conservative Party organizer and adviser to Chapleau.[58] This exercise inspired Groulx to write a long article the following year, painting a highly laudatory portrait of the Franco-Manitoban prelate and extolling his sense of justice, patriotic spirit and great faith in Providence and in the "sacred mission of the race." In his conclusion he noted that Langevin was a hero whose greatness of soul was not to be measured by the demographics or material wealth of his Franco-Manitoban *petit peuple*:

> Human greatness is something interior and not exterior. And if it is measured precisely according to the non-material dimensions of the soul, it matters little that Archbishop Langevin was only the leader of a *petit peuple* of some 50,000 souls, half lost in the "far west." In this valiant champion of rights—of rights that have the same dignity and importance everywhere—we must see not only one of the noblest

57. Lionel Groulx, "Chronique de l'Institut," *RHAF*, December 1952, p. 466; June 1955, p. 151; Lorenzo Cadieux, "Mémoire en vue d'un meilleur rendement de nos sociétés d'histoire régionale," *RHAF*, June 1948, p. 149–150, 151; Lionel Groulx, "Vie de l'Institut," *RHAF*, June 1948, p. 154.

58. Lionel Groulx, "Documents inédits. Correspondance Langevin-Audet," *RHAF*, September 1947, p. 271–277.

> sons of Canada, but, and I do not hesitate to write it, one of the great human beings of his time.[59]

Shortly afterwards, Groulx unearthed yet another "unpublished document" drawn from Franco-Manitoban history: this time, a report signed by a Manitoban federal member of Parliament on the parliamentary debates surrounding the central government's intervention in the schools crisis. A few years later, it was the schools affair in New Brunswick that Groulx brought to life when he presented the correspondence between two of the protagonists in the crisis, Cléophas Beausoleil, Liberal member and *merciériste* in the Legislature, and Alphonse Desjardins, a minister in the Bowell and Tupper governments.[60]

The "Books and Periodicals" column rapidly became another means for the *Revue* to let its readers know about the history and historians of the French minorities. Two methods of presentation were used: one listed the historical studies according to specific subjects of history touching on the minorities—regardless of author; the other listed the published works according to their author—regardless of the theme dealt with. Several collaborators took part in this exercise, but no one could hold a candle to Lionel Groulx himself, who almost seemed to carry it out single-handedly. From 1947 to 1967, Groulx alone reviewed more than forty books that related in one way or another to the French minorities of Canada and the United States. While he wanted to assess all these works using the strictest criteria of historical science, he could not help but yield at times to the militant nationalist always vigilant in him, who sometimes got the better of the detached academic. Take, for example, this review he gave of a monograph about the Acadian parish of Saint-Louis-de-Kent: "Classic history of a parish founded by the agricultural land seekers, who labour heroically. Colonists with no help from the State, without roads to connect them to the rest of their province, they live for a long time from their family farms, owing all that they have to their own initiative."[61] Or take this commentary, a veritable panegyric, written in 1963 about a work commemorating the fiftieth anniversary of *Le Droit*:

> Born and raised in battle, the most furious battle ever waged in Canada against a French Catholic minority, *Le Droit* not only survived and won the cause of its founders, but it became one of the great dailies of the French-Canadian press. It became the weapon, the shield, the voice of the largest minority in French Canada, I mean the Franco-Ontarian minority, whose numbers exceed half a million. We must pay

59. Lionel Groulx, "Mgr Adélard Langevin d'après une partie de sa correspondance," *RHAF*, March 1948, p. 569–594.
60. "[Événements des 8, 9, 10, 11 juillet 1895: Affaire des écoles du Manitoba]," *RHAF*, September 1948, p. 275–279; Lionel Groulx, "Documents inédits: Correspondance autour de la question scolaire du Nouveau-Brunswick – 1873," *RHAF*, September 1950, p. 268–275; December 1950, p. 427–431; March 1951, p. 568–575.
61. Lionel Groulx, review of *Histoire de Saint-Louis-de-Kent* (L.-Cyriaque Daigle), *RHAF*, September 1949, p. 276.

> tribute to the Franco-Ontarians who, in resistance to Regulation 17, led . . . the fiercest and most determined struggle ever fought in their country by a minority group. . . . A newspaper like *Le Droit* must be read daily to learn how false are the speeches sometimes made about religious and educational harmony in the country of Canada. And one will also note that it was the good fortune of this daily to always have at its helm publishers and editors-in-chief of rare quality.[62]

In another tribute to French Ontario, Groulx hailed the many merits of the work of the Jesuit folklorist Germain Lemieux of Sudbury. During the fifties, Lemieux took on the immense project of collecting and preserving French-Canadian folklore, stories, songs and legends, as they had circulated in Ontario. In 1965, Groulx congratulated him for reinstating folklore, so often treated with disdain, to its rightful place of dignity, and welcomed the release of his *Chanteurs franco-ontariens et leurs chansons* as a salutary event: Franco-Ontarians, he declared, were doing a better job than their confrères in Québec of respecting this heritage: "[In Sudbury] they have preserved the songs, stories, proverbs and sayings of former days much better than in the old province which, under the pretext of 'being with it,' clothes its old French spirit too easily in American cast-offs."[63]

Sometimes, Groulx was given to more serious reflection, such as when he presented his readers with a collection of writings about the epic journey of the French in the Mississippi, a book "that evokes the nostalgia of a lost paradise."[64] This slightly pessimistic note could only be observed in Groulx when he was speaking about the Franco-Americans. And even then, he refused to definitively throw in the towel and abandon all hope in their *survivance*. Commenting in 1967 on the most recent issue of the *Bulletin de la Société historique franco-américaine*, he admonished the "alarmists" who took a perverse pleasure in prematurely burying compatriots who had not yet given up the ghost:

> Whatever the alarmists may think, this life is not the little still-smouldering ember. Surrounded by men of action . . ., it appears that the ember always remains lit, like those inviolable sacred fires guarded by the ancients. What the future will be no one knows. But there are still men who do not in the least despair over it.[65]

In 1966, a few short months before his death, Groulx launched a final major project at the *Revue*, a vast study that would take stock of French-Canadian history since Confederation, which was about to celebrate its centennial. Like the

62. Lionel Groulx, review of *Entre deux livraisons, 1913–1963* (Laurent Tremblay), RHAF, December 1963, p. 450–451.
63. Lionel Groulx, review of *Chanteurs franco-ontariens et leurs chansons* (Germain Lemieux), RHAF, September 1965, p. 319. See also Lionel Groulx, review of *Contes populaires franco-ontariens* (Germain Lemieux), RHAF, December 1958, p. 434–435.
64. Lionel Groulx, review of *The French in the Mississippi* (John Francis, dir.), RHAF, September 1965, p. 315.
65. Lionel Groulx, review of *Bulletin de la Société historique franco-américaine* [no year], RHAF, March 1967, p. 664–665.

study on the political future of French Canada organized by *L'Action française* some forty-five years earlier, the project brought together some of the big names in the nationalist movement of the time. Also as in 1922, Groulx insisted on dedicating one of the studies to the French minorities in Canada, a study he entrusted this time to Jesuit Father Richard Arès. The director of the *Revue* did not live long enough to see the final version of the study but that did not prevent the editorial committee from going ahead with the publication of it, albeit belatedly. The article by Arès, which he called "A century of French life outside Québec," drew up a discouraging assessment of the historical experience of the minorities since 1867.[66] In short, the author came to the following conclusions: the founding-peoples argument, which the French Canadians had always upheld, had never been respected by their English-language compatriots, who chose instead to see in Canada an essentially English country that included a French enclave—a "reserve"—limited to Québec; the constitutional guarantees the minorities were to have enjoyed had been systematically ignored or interpreted in a minimalist fashion by the courts; finally, the French Canadians in most provinces where they were a minority—with the exception of Ontario and New Brunswick, where the situation was more encouraging—were being assimilated at an alarming rate. All the same, Arès drew attention to signs which he believed still gave reason to hope. Never in a hundred years had Canada appeared more sympathetic toward the French minorities, their network of institutions having expanded considerably since the start of the sixties, owing in particular to the work of the Royal Commission of Inquiry on bilingualism and biculturalism:

> The first century of federal government, which has just ended, has been, for this French life outside Québec, a long hard winter; recent signs have allowed us to glimpse a softening in the climate, a change in temperature and the possible arrival of spring. If this forecast is realized, the stubborn perseverance of the minorities to survive will not have been in vain and perhaps then it will be permitted to them to live a second century of life in the federation under the three-fold sign of peace, justice and fraternity.[67]

Had Arès been won over by the bleak neo-nationalist discourse on the French minorities' chances of survival? According to Marcel Martel, he had been their "accidental embalmer," for he had unwittingly provided the neo-nationalists

66. Letter from Richard Arès to Lionel Groulx, BAnQ, FLG, P1/A,84, April 3, 1966; Richard Arès, "Un siècle de vie française en dehors du Québec," *Cent ans d'histoire, 1867–1967*, special issue of RHAF, [1967], p. 531–571. The study also included contributions by Jean-Charles Bonenfant ("Le Canada et les hommes politiques de 1867"), Robert Boily ("Les hommes politiques du Québec, 1867–1967"), François-Albert Angers ("L'évolution économique du Canada et du Québec depuis la Confédération"), Léon Pouliot ("Un siècle d'expansion religieuse"), as well as pieces by Groulx that had previously been published in 1917 and 1927 in *L'Action française* ("Ce cinquantenaire" and "Les Canadiens français et l'établissement de la Confédération").

67. Richard Arès, "Un siècle de vie française en dehors du Québec," RHAF, p. 569–570.

with the demographic and statistical arguments they had lacked to be able to definitively and "scientifically" seal their coffin.[68] It should be noted, though, that the ideas of the Jesuit intellectual, at least as gleaned from this article in the *Revue d'histoire de l'Amérique française*, were not inspired by the same structural determinism being promoted for several years already by Michel Brunet, for example. Arès certainly refrained from advocating that Québec should abandon the minorities like a "dead weight." Groulx, if he had lived, might have advised him to temper the pessimism in his tone, but, as far as the essential ideas of the study were concerned, he would undoubtedly have found nothing of substance to change.

* * *

It would appear that Lionel Groulx, despite the social, economic and intellectual transformations brought on by the postwar period, maintained the same ideas he had always held regarding the place of the French minorities within the French-Canadian people and the responsibilities that Québec, as the "ancestral home" of the nation, had toward them. The territorialization of neo-nationalist discourse did not influence him, and it is incorrect to see him as supportive of the argument to abandon the French minorities. The voluntarism of the *vieux maître nationaliste* was hard to reconcile with the demographic, economic and structural determinism that the young generation of nationalist intellectuals subscribed to. By expunging from their conceptual world the principles of will, heroism and the role of Providence in the history and existence of the French-Canadian nation, they had undermined the foundation of one of the most powerful arguments ever evoked by Groulx to make Québec aware of its duty toward its "dispersed brethren." The providential mission of the French Canadians always remained, in his mind, the factor that, above all else, explained their spreading throughout the country and the continent (which did not prevent him, let us repeat, from acknowledging that this expansionism was materially motivated as well). By reducing the theory of messianism to a simple "consoling myth," in the interest of a historical approach they deemed more "scientific" and "objective," the neo-nationalist intellectuals had given themselves the conceptual justification they needed to destroy the bonds between Québec and the French minorities, which Groulx had sought, throughout his career, to strengthen. Groulx's admonishment of the "defeatists," some of whom were his own disciples and yet were determined to "shrink" the history of his people, betrayed the profound malaise he felt in the face of a materialism and structural determinism that seemed to condemn French Canada to Americanization in the not too distant future.

68. Marcel Martel, "'*Hors du Québec, point de salut!*'," p. 136–137.

It is true that, after the war, Groulx opted to vigorously defend the autonomy of Québec, given the central government's encroachment on areas of provincial jurisdiction. However, this *autonomisme* was nothing new in his thinking. His position on the problem of relations between Québec and the federal government showed exceptional continuity. His discourse at *L'Action française*, several decades earlier had been the same. In his thought, the autonomy of Québec should not come about, any more than in the 1920s, at the cost of abandoning the French minorities of the other provinces. Similarly, the sympathy he felt for the independence movements of the sixties, at least for those inspired by traditionalist currents of thought, did not induce him to desert the minorities either.[69] If Groulx criticized the neo-nationalists who were willing to subject the minorities to humiliation, he was also severe with the French Canadians of the other provinces whom he reproached for sometimes getting caught up in the illusion of the Canadian nation as such. In 1953, in a lecture delivered in Montréal, he tendered the following remarks:

> As for those of our compatriots of French origin who are easily hypnotized by the mirage of national unity "coast to coast" and who, in this debate, find us deplorably French-Canadian and not Canadian "at large" enough, I will not undertake to demonstrate to them, one more time, that we owe at least our primary emotional allegiance to the historical entity from which we have received these sacred assets of religious faith and cultural inheritance.[70]

Whether Groulx really was separatist or not was irrelevant to some of the leaders of the *indépendantiste* movement who claimed his thought for their own ends. This was the case, in particular, for the organizers of the Estates General of French Canada who conferred on him the title of Honorary President of the assembly. It was indeed during the Estates General that the great French-Canadian "schism" was confirmed. A good portion of the delegates of the French minorities chose to boycott the 1969 assembly in the face of the *indépendantiste* wave that seemed to wash over their Québec colleagues. Groulx, who died in May 1967, did not witness the spectacle of this sensational split. In his message to the 1966 assembly, he had kept his remarks relatively vague and non-committal on the question of independence. He had mentioned, among other things, the need to put an end to the partisan battles and the urgency of gathering together the scattered strength of the nation. He had also enjoined the minorities to show Québec their solidarity by suggesting that the destiny of the old province was not separate from theirs:

69. For an analysis of Groulx's position in relation to the *indépendantiste* movements of the right during the 1950s and 1960s, see Stéphane Pigeon, *Lionel Groulx*, p. 48–53; Lionel Groulx, "Où allons-nous?," *Pour bâtir*, p. 87; Lionel Groulx, *Mes Mémoires, Tome II*, p. 307.
70. Lionel Groulx, "Où allons-nous?," *Pour bâtir*, p. 92.

"[The idea of fraternity and solidarity] will tell us all, even our faraway brothers, that we are the sons of the same past, of the same traditions, of a same country: the State of Québec." In his posthumous message to the 1967 assembly, Groulx appeared sympathetic to the *indépendantiste* option, although his remarks, once again, did not commit him to anything very precise: "The time has . . . passed when this choice could be indicated to us by a political authority other than that of Québec, regardless of how inclusive a certain form of federalism could be."[71]

Despite these rather nebulous comments, Groulx's thought never consisted, even after World War II, of establishing a relationship of equivalence between the French-Canadian nation and the Québec state. The Estates General, set up initially to debate the future of the *French-Canadian* nation, would not take long, however, to be converted to the idea of the *Québécois* nation. Lionel Groulx was present at the start of the assemblies. Present too, at least officially, was the principle of solidarity among French Canadians, wherever in America they might be. But before deliberations ended, the man and the idea had breathed their last breath.

71. [Lionel Groulx], "Message du chanoine Lionel Groulx, président d'honneur des États généraux," *Les États généraux du Canada français: Assises préliminaires tenues à l'Université de Montréal du 25 au 27 novembre 1966* ([no place name given]: [n.p.], [1967]), p. 10; [Lionel Groulx], "Message posthume de M. le chanoine Lionel Groulx," *Les États généraux du Canada français: Assises nationales tenues à la Place des Arts du 23 au 26 novembre 1967*, special issue of *L'Action nationale*, Vol. 57, No. 6 (February 1968), p. 11.

Conclusion

THE POLITICAL AND IDEOLOGICAL UPHEAVALS of the postwar period and the Quiet Revolution in Quebec, provoked a mixed reaction from Lionel Groulx. On the one hand, he applauded the ever-increasing numbers in the French-Canadian political class supporting nationalism (especially with regard to the economy). On the other hand, he watched as a helpless bystander while part of the nationalist doctrine he himself had helped formulate over many decades faded away. The postwar neo-nationalist movement was losing its way, as far as he was concerned, by affirming Québec at the expense of part of its cultural and religious heritage and by reducing the history of the French-Canadian nation to a combination of structural factors. To avoid any misunderstanding, it should be mentioned that the neo-nationalist intellectuals of the 1940s and 1950s were not "materialists" in the strict sense of the term. They did not necessarily deny the existence of spiritual realities in their understanding of the world and humanity. The deeper logic of their thought, however, excluded the action of "Providence" or of any supernatural power from the field of scientific analysis. It was their opinion, therefore, that if historians or other practitioners of the social sciences took such spiritual realities into account, they did so at the risk of lapsing into some form of myth-making.

For Groulx, this distinction made by the young intellectuals between the domains of science and faith entailed grave ethical consequences. By retaining only factors of a structural nature in their historical analyses and by discarding the principle of Providence as the organizing and directing force in human societies, he believed the new historians were depriving the *petits peuples* of the necessary means to overcome the often numerous obstacles to their *survivance* and their development. Groulx therefore reproached the neo-nationalists for seeing French Canada only as prey at the mercy of the goodwill of the wealthier and more numerous Anglo-Saxon powers and depriving their compatriots of any reason to have hope in a better future.

If Groulx and the École de Montréal agreed on the disastrous consequences of the British Conquest of 1760, they differed greatly in their analysis of what followed in the history of the French-Canadian nation. In the Quebec Act (1774), in the establishment of parliamentary government (1791), in the achievement of responsible government (1848) and in Confederation (1867), Groulx saw evidence that the situation of the French Canadians had never ceased to improve and that the political and spiritual leaders of the nation had never abandoned their faith in the beneficent action of Providence. The stance taken by the École de Montréal, however, argued that the Conquest had signalled the start of a long political and economic decline and that the "national victories" that Groulx had found heartening did not add up to much. The old leader denounced this interpretation, repeatedly calling it reductionist. He was therefore not surprised that his young disciples, blind to the role of Providence in the historical experience of nations, seemed to descend into a deep pessimism regarding the future of the French-Canadian people. Against their structural determinism, Groulx set his faith in Providence and human will, which would always make it possible, in his view, to survive all difficulties, insurmountable as they might seem.

It is, in part, this structural determinism that led the neo-nationalist movement to conclude that the assimilation of the French minorities in the other provinces was inevitable. Canon Groulx, for his part, could not tow this line. He was firmly convinced that as long as the French minorities, like the rest of the French-Canadian nation, desired their own *survivance* and maintained their faith in Providence, Providence would not let them down. It was this voluntarism and this validation of spiritual realities that distinguished him from the neo-nationalists. Groulx constructed the national identity in terms of history and tradition. We should not for a moment think that he was unaware of the importance of territorial and geographical realities in the history of French Canada. Indeed, he considered territory as a place that could be marked by the "genius" of the nation. But at no time did he make of it a criterion of national inclusion or exclusion. Groulx believed firmly in the theory of the providential creation of nations. Consequently, it was impossible, in his opinion, that the human person should be able to "choose" his national identity and flout the national context into which he had been born. He saw identity, rather, as something transmitted by heredity (understood here in the genealogical and not the biological sense), which explains the importance of tradition in his thinking, for tradition was the true foundation of identity. "A people does not choose its roots any more than does a tree,"[1] he had stated in 1922 before a group of Franco-Americans who had come to hear him.

Undeniably, there was thus a certain form of determinism in his thought: Providence, which had created them, demanded that nations remain faithful to its designs and to the mission it had entrusted them. According to Groulx, the mission the French-Canadian nation had been entrusted with was to introduce European civilization and the Catholic faith to America. His historical studies, furthermore, seemed to confirm to him that this mission had been constantly

1. Lionel Groulx, "L'Amitié française d'Amérique," *Dix ans d'Action française* (Montréal: Bibliothèque de l'Action française, 1926), p. 181.

and faithfully carried out for over three centuries. In fact, in his historical work, the founding of the immense French colonial empire appears first and foremost as a great mystical epic, even as he acknowledged the political and commercial dimension of it. The evangelizing missionary was, thus, to him, the figure that epitomized New France. Groulx followed the missionary trajectories throughout America over the centuries and felt confident in saying that the French and the French Canadians had been the most faithful apostles of Christianity in the New World. He was glad that even the Conquest of 1760 had been powerless to temper the missionary zeal of his people, as attested, in the nineteenth century, by the French-Canadian clergy taking possession of the immense plains of the West. Therefore, since New France had left the imprint of its civilization on almost the entire continent, the French minorities, in Groulx's opinion, constituted its remnant, its heirs and its still living witnesses. This analysis no doubt revealed the nostalgia that he felt for the former grandeur of the French Empire. But it was also transformed, in his hands, into a powerful instrument in the struggle to defend the right of the French minorities to *survivance*.

He maintained it was the providential and apostolic mission of the French Canadians, and not the 1867 Constitution, that made them a "founding" people. He believed that since this founding work had been initiated during the era of New France, Confederation could only represent its constitutional and political confirmation. Rather than ascribe the religious, linguistic and educational rights of the French minorities to the British North America Act, Groulx saw them as emerging from natural law: Providence had willed and made the diversity of nations and did not accept that the most powerful should be able to absorb the weakest or the smallest. The human person was endowed therefore with the right to develop in accordance with his own "national genius." To seek to place the French Catholic minorities in a situation that would separate them from the national and cultural context into which they had been born would be tantamount, he argued, to a betrayal of natural law. According to Lionel Groulx, if the anti-French and anti-Catholic measures adopted by several provinces with an Anglo-Protestant majority violated Canadian constitutional law, they represented at the same time an affront to the authority of Providence, which he considered infinitely superior to human authority.

This organic construction of the French-Canadian national identity dictated to Québec a duty of national solidarity toward its "dispersed brothers." After the Second World War, the neo-nationalist movement accorded a growing importance to territory and to political structures in the definition of national identity and tended, by that very fact, to exclude the French minorities. It would not be long before the nationalist discourse, which had been "French-Canadian," would become "Québécois." Groulx, for his part, could not find a way to adhere to this change in discourse and semantics. The nation as he understood it was like an "organism." The French Canadians had brought French Canada with them to all the regions where they had spread. A historic, cultural and even spiritual entity, the Groulxist nation could not have one of its members severed without gangrene spreading throughout the entire organism. The notions of responsibility, dedication, solidarity and courage were central to Groulx's thought: Québec needed to adopt them, he believed, even at the price of the greatest sacrifices. The term *survivance*, often associated today with a backward-looking, lacklustre ideology, had a completely different meaning when used by Groulx. For him it was synonymous with a typically romantic nobility and heroism. In the fight to maintain French Catholic civilization in America, the nation could not afford to lose even the smallest of its groups and, even less, to lose any of its entire communities, no matter how small a minority they might be.

Individually, Groulx considered all French Canadians equal. However, he assigned them different roles depending on whether they were in Québec or among the French minorities. Québec was the metropolis or, as Groulx called it, the "ancestral home" and the "citadel" of the French-Canadian nation. The minorities, for their part, represented the vanguard, the reconnaissance troops who gauged the intensity of the threat that hung over their existence. Unlike the postwar neo-nationalists, Groulx saw no incompatibility between invoking the founding peoples principle to protect the rights of the French minorities and defending provincial autonomy for Québec. The interests of the French-Canadian nation were always the same, wherever it was based. In his thinking, provincial autonomy was not a goal in itself: it was useful only to the extent that it facilitated the protection of the rights of the French Canadians inside Québec. It was not acceptable to Groulx that the other provinces should be entitled to deprive the French minorities of their rights. There was no doubt in his mind that the Compact theory should always take precedence over the strategy of provincial autonomy, should there be a conflict between the two.

However, Groulx frequently found cause for deep distress in the attitude of Québec toward its "dispersed brothers," in particular in the attitude of its political class. He believed it was shirking its duty of national solidarity by, time and again, abandoning the minorities to their own fate. This analysis of Groulx's was incorporated into his more general critique of the official world of politics, which he accused of widening the partisan divide, of sacrificing the higher interests of French Canada and of consequently compromising the integrity of the national "organism." The historian considered that this partisan "spinelessness" had begun to appear among politicians immediately after Confederation. He was disappointed, moreover, that it had continued ever since, and gone from bad to worse. When the George-Étienne Cartiers and the Wilfrid Lauriers of this world chose to back away from their national duties, it was the French minorities, he felt, who paid the price. However, there were other segments of French-Canadian society who, in his view, accepted their responsibilities toward the French minorities fully. And Groulx singled out particularly the French-Canadian clergy. Historically, any priests, brothers and nuns that could be spared had always been sent among the minorities to meet their sometimes desperate need for parishes, schools and socio-cultural institutions. Groulx was also delighted at the initiatives of the French-Canadian nationalist movement, whose "awakening," at the start of the century, he attributed to the linguistic and religious crises the minorities had been facing since 1867.

We have been able to observe that Lionel Groulx himself contributed to shaking up Québec opinion toward the sometimes difficult situation of the French minorities. As early as 1912, he threw himself whole-heartedly into the Regulation 17 crisis, going so far as to become an active member of the Franco-Ontarian resistance. By writing countless articles of support, giving numerous speeches and even writing a novel around the theme of the schools crisis, Groulx managed to keep this conflict firmly among the most important intellectual concerns of the French-Canadian nationalist movement. The educational struggle also featured among the principal issues followed by *L'Action française* during the time he was its director, from 1920 to 1928. In effect, the review led the fiercest of battles against the prevailing authorities, who sought to suppress the rights of the French minorities. In doing so, it provided an eloquent example of the kind of national solidarity its director wanted to see established, in a lasting way, between Québec and the other parts of French Canada. The measures proposed by *L'Action française* to achieve the realization of this great project of national rapprochement were many. Groulx fought in particular for the creation of an umbrella organization to encompass all the *sociétés nationales* in Canada and the United States, an organization which came into existence in 1937, during the Deuxième Congrès de la langue française de Québec.

The nation, as Lionel Groulx understood it, depended on neither territory nor any government or state structure. It even transcended boundaries between sovereign states. as shown by the priest-historian's attitude to the Franco-Americans of New England. The survival or the collapse of government structures, according to this reasoning, would in no way have changed the parameters of the French-Canadian nation. The "French state" controversy of the 1920s and 1930s allowed us, once again, to better understand the nature of the bonds which, in Groulx's nationalism, ensured the unity of the French-Canadian people. Panic-stricken, in 1922, by the controversy surrounding the study organized by *L'Action française* on the political future of French Canada, some of the French minorities jumped to the conclusion that the French-Canadian nationalist movement was withdrawing to within the borders of Québec. Groulx and his colleagues strove to reassure the minorities and availed themselves of every platform possible to reiterate the deep sentiment of national solidarity they continued to have for them. Nevertheless, they did not deny that a strong Québec would, at the same time, mean stronger French minorities: reinforcing the powers of the mother province, whatever the political regime in place, could only benefit all members of the nation. Could a weakened Québec live up to its responsibilities toward the minorities? Groulx's reply to this question was a resounding and unequivocal no.

The important thing to remember is that the desire to see Québec obtain the broadest autonomy possible—inside or outside the federation—did not translate, in Groulx's nationalism, into a desire to abandon the French minorities in the other provinces to their own fate, contrary to what the young nationalist intellectuals were advocating after World War II. On this question, the divergence between Groulx's thought and that of the new school was profound. The neo-nationalist historians, by rallying to the theory of structural determinism, believed they had found the scientific justification necessary to abandon the minorities. This fatalism was dictated to them by the material and political conditions in which the minorities were evolving, and which they believed condemned them to being assimilated sooner rather than later: the minorities would never be more for Québec than, to cite Michel Brunet, a burden and a "dead weight."

Groulx, for his part, could not bring himself to share this fatalism. Certainly, he had always been worried for the minorities. He had always been deeply troubled and moved by how hard it was for them to resist acculturation. But the voluntarism element of his nationalism, as well as his unshakeable faith in the beneficent action of Providence, prevented him from giving up and conceding the defeat of the minorities. The opposition between the Groulxist and neo-nationalist schools pointed to a more serious clash, which stemmed partially from the place given to moral and spiritual matters in the field of scientific analysis. For Groulx, these fundamental questions ought not to be left out of the historian's considerations. For the postwar intellectuals, they were too intangible to be included in their analyses without creating myths that would obscure scientific truth as they understood it. The old *maître* saw clearly, however, that by making such a sharp distinction between the domains of science and morality, it would not be long before the neo-nationalist movement lost its sense of responsibility toward its "brothers of the diaspora." Thus, the marginalization of the French minorities became symptomatic, in his opinion, of the deep malady that afflicted a society when it chose to break with its own historical and cultural tradition.

* * *

We have attempted to demonstrate that the profound sentiment of national solidarity that Lionel Groulx and, consequently, a good part of the nationalist movement, had toward the minorities was attributable to an organic understanding of the French-Canadian nation, which accorded greater importance to the notion of tradition than to territory or political structures. Groulx's positions on the duties and responsibilities of Québec toward the French minorities—which displayed a most remarkable continuity from the beginning to the end of his career—have been almost entirely removed from the contemporary nationalist discourse. It was in the wake of the Second World War that this development began to pick up momentum and during the Quiet Revolution of the 1960s that it spread. During this twenty-five-year period, the theme of the "modernization" of Québec and social and economic "catch-up" came to dominate French-Canadian discursive space. In this new intellectual context, the so-called "traditional" nationalists sometimes had a hard time of it. Not that they ignored issues of an economic nature. Abbé Groulx, among others, had for a long time been claiming a greater place for French Canadians in the Québec and Canadian economy. Therefore, he approved unreservedly of the economic nationalism of the Quiet Revolution.[2] (Furthermore, at *L'Action française*, Groulx had been the first to devise the slogan *Maîtres chez nous*, popularized by Jean Lesage, forty years later, during the Québec electoral campaign of 1962.) But Groulx's nationalism did not include the desire to make a clean sweep of the past and abandon the cultural and religious heritage of French Canada.

Seeing this attitude espoused by the postwar generation caused him much anguish. His strongest criticism was directed against the liberal thinkers who rallied around the *Cité libre* journal, but he also lashed out at the neo-nationalist movement with some of his harshest words. To do away with questions of a moral nature, to adopt the theory of structural determinism, to seek to show that the history of French Canada had been one of decline and that French-Canadian tradition had obstructed the path of "progress" and modernity, none of that, in his view, could be called nationalism. On the contrary, Groulx believed that such a project would inevitably lead to contempt for what he considered the foundation of the French-Canadian nation, that is, tradition or, to put it differently, collective memory, and could only signal its demise. In the eyes of this traditionalist historian, presenting the past as something from which one had to be emancipated entailed grave risks. To reject *traditionalism* out of fascination with modernity was for him the equivalent of rejecting the French-Canadian national *tradition*. He wondered whether, by dint of wanting so much to resemble the "other," there was not a great danger that the nation might lose its "soul," its soul being that which made it something unique in the world. He felt it was cultural diversity, as willed by Providence, that was at stake here.

The anti-globalization movements making themselves heard in our day increasingly list among their claims the right of peoples to cultural development.

2. See Jean-Claude Dupuis, *Nationalisme et Catholicism: L'Action française de Montréal (1917–1928)*, master's thesis (history), Université de Montréal, 1992, 329 p.; Stéphane Pigeon, *Lionel Groulx, critique de la Révolution tranquille (1956–1967)*, master's thesis (history), Université de Montréal, 1999, 117 p.

Lionel Groulx, of course, was not a left-wing activist. However, is there not a surprising parallel to be currently made between a part of the left, which no longer sees itself in solely socioeconomic terms, and certain aspects of Groulx's nationalism, an ideology that was nevertheless traditionalist and therefore considered to be on the right? In both cases, the discourse on cultural diversity intervenes to apply the brakes to the cultural hegemony of the great political and commercial empires, a hegemony seen to be fundamentally pernicious. Whether one invokes the designs of "Providence" or the higher interests of "Humanity," to defend the right of *petits peuples* or small nations to exist, only represents perhaps, in some respects, a relatively superficial distinction.

The fear of tradition that has prevailed in nationalist circles in Québec for more than half a century now, has caused solidarity with the minorities to be associated with an ideology that is, at best, backward-looking and, at worst, reactionary. For example, the reintroduction of the concept of tradition into the debate on national identity has Gérard Bouchard quite worried. He wonders, "by what logic could we avoid a return to the former model of a pan-Canadian action program aimed at protecting the French-Canadian nation from coast to coast?"[3] The question pushes the reader to conclude, like Bouchard, that this is an untenable hypothesis. The passage reveals clearly a certain lack of concern for the minorities and the issue they represent. Are Lawrence Olivier and Guy Bédard not correct when they say that the French minorities reflect back to Quebec an image of itself that it would rather forget?[4]

The spirit of solidarity that informed Lionel Groulx's ideology stemmed from a deep sense of responsibility, which was itself grounded in the Catholic intellectual context in which he had been formed. The problems the minorities were sometimes up against as they tried to be the torchbearers of civilization that the old nationalist leader wanted them to be did not constitute for him a reason to conclude that their assimilation was inevitable or that they should be abandoned to their own fate. The more insurmountable the obstacle, he believed, the nobler the cause and the more worthy of one's devotion. In the same way, Goulx's nation was the fruit of a long evolution and it would not easily suffer being restricted to a limited territory or being stripped of its organic nature, of its culture and its history. All those who had received the French-Canadian tradition as their heritage were part of it, wherever they might be and regardless of the obstacles they might encounter along the way.

3. Gérard Bouchard, *La Nation québécoise au futur et au passé* (Montréal: VLB Éditeur, 1999), p. 60–61.
4. Lawrence Olivier and Guy Bédard, "Le nationalisme québécois, les Acadiens et les francophones du Canada," *Égalité: Revue acadienne d'analyse politique*, No. 33 (Spring 1993), p. 81–100.

Selected Bibliography[1]

Works by Groulx

Une Croisade d'adolescents. Québec: L'Action Sociale Limitée, 1912, 264 p.

Nos luttes constitutionnelles I: La Constitution de l'Angleterre: Le Canada politique en 1791. Montréal: Le Devoir, 1915, 18 p.

Nos luttes constitutionnelles II: La Question des subsides. Montréal: Le Devoir, 1915, 17 p.

Nos luttes constitutionnelles III: La Responsabilité ministérielle. Montréal: Le Devoir, 1916, 23 p.

Nos luttes constitutionnelles IV: La Liberté scolaire. Montréal: Le Devoir, 1916, 23 p.

Nos luttes constitutionnelles V: Les Droits du français. Montréal: Le Devoir, 1916, 21 p.

La Confédération canadienne, ses origines. Montréal: Le Devoir, 1918, 265 p.

La Naissance d'une race. Montréal: Bibliothèque de l'Action française, 1919, 294 p.

Chez nos ancêtres. Montréal: Bibliothèque de l'Action française, 1920, 102 p.

Lendemains de conquête. Montréal: Bibliothèque de l'Action française, 1920, 235 p.

Vers l'Émancipation. Montréal: Bibliothèque de l'Action française, 1921, 308 p.

Notre Maître, le passé. Première Série. Montréal: Bibliothèque de l'Action française, 1924, 269 p.

L'Enseignement français au Canada: Tome I: Dans le Québec. Montréal: Éditions Albert Lévesque, 1931, 323 p.

Le Français au Canada. Paris: Librairie Delagrave, 1932, 234 p.

L'Enseignement français au Canada: Tome II: Les Écoles des minorités. Montréal: Librairie Granger Frères, 1933, 271 p.

La Découverte du Canada: Jacques Cartier. Montréal: Librairie Granger Frères, 1934, 290 p.

Notre Maître, le passé. Deuxième Série. Montréal: Librairie Granger Frères, 1936, 305 p.

Notre Maître, le passé. Troisième Série. Montréal: Librairie Granger Frères, 1944, 318 p.

Histoire du Canada français depuis la découverte: Tome I. Montréal: Éditions de l'Action nationale, 1950, 221 p.

Histoire du Canada français depuis la découverte: Tome II. Montréal: Éditions de l'Action nationale, 1951, 302 p.

Histoire du Canada français depuis la découverte: Tome III. Montréal: Éditions de l'Action nationale, 1952, 326 p.

Histoire du Canada français depuis la découverte: Tome IV. Montréal: Éditions de l'Action nationale, 1952, 273 p.

1. For a more detailed bibliography, see Michel Bock, *Lionel Groulx, les minorités françaises et la construction de l'identité canadienne-française: Étude d'histoire intellectuelle*, doctoral thesis (history), Université d'Ottawa, 2002, viii–401 p.

Notre grande aventure. L'Empire français en Amérique du Nord, 1535–1760. Montréal and Paris: Fides, 1958, 299 p.
Dollard est-il un mythe? Montréal and Paris: Fides, 1960, 57 p.
Le Canada français missionnaire: Une autre grande aventure. Montréal and Paris: Fides, 1962, 532 p.
La Grande Dame de notre histoire. Montréal: Fides, 1966, 61 p.
Chemins de l'avenir. Montréal: Fides, 1967, 161 p.
Constantes de vie. Montréal: Fides, 1967, 174 p.
Mes Mémoires, Tome I: 1878–1920, Montréal: Fides, 1970, 438 p.
Mes Mémoires, Tome II: 1920–1928. Montréal: Fides, 1971, 418 p.
Mes Mémoires, Tome III: 1926–1939. Montréal: Fides, 1972, 412 p.
Mes Mémoires, Tome IV: 1940–1967. Montréal: Fides, 1974, 464 p.
Journal, 1895–1911, 2 volumes. Montréal: Presses de l'Université de Montréal, 1984, 1108 p.
Correspondance, 1894–1967. I: 1894–1906. Le Prêtre-Éducateur. Montréal: Fides, 1989, 858 p. (ed. Pierre Trépanier *et al.*)
Correspondance, 1894–1967. II: 1906–1909. Un Étudiant à l'école de l'Europe. Montréal: Fides, 1993, 841 p. (ed. Pierre Trépanier *et al.*)
Correspondance, 1894–1967. III: 1909–1915. L'Intellectuel et l'historien novices. Montréal: Fides, 2003, 1045 p. (ed. Pierre Trépanier *et al.*)

Brochures by Groulx

L'Histoire acadienne. Montréal: Éditions de la Société Saint-Jean-Baptiste de Montréal, 1917, 32 p.
Louis Riel et les événements de la Rivière-Rouge en 1869–1870. Montréal: Éditions de l'Action Nationale, 1944, 30 p.
Jeanne Mance. [no place name], Comité des Fondateurs, 1954, 30 p.
Mère d'Youville, une femme de génie au Canada. [no place name], Comité des Fondateurs, 1957, 30 p.

Collections by Groulx

Dix ans d'Action française. Montréal: Bibliothèque de l'Action française, 1926, 273 p.
Orientations. Montréal: Éditions du Zodiaque, 1935, 310 p.
Directives. Montréal: Éditions du Zodiaque, 1937, 270 p.
L'Indépendance du Canada. Montréal: Éditions de l'Action nationale, 1949, 175 p.
Pour bâtir. Montréal: Éditions de l'Action nationale, 1953, 216 p.
Constantes de vie. Montréal: Fides, 1989, 857 p.

Speeches /Lectures by Groulx

Paroles à des étudiants. Montréal: Éditions de L'Action nationale, 1941, 80 p.
Pourquoi nous sommes divisés. Montréal: Éditions de l'Action nationale, 1943, 30 p.
Confiance et espoir. Sudbury: Société historique du Nouvel-Ontario, 1945, 22 p.
Le Nationalisme canadien-français, sa notion, ses origines, les droits qu'il confère, les devoirs qu'il impose. Ottawa, [n.p.], 1949, 23 p.

Short Stories and Novels by Groulx

Les Rapaillages. Vieilles choses, vieilles gens. Montréal: Le Devoir, 1916, 159 p.

De Lestres, Alonié [pseudonym of L. Groulx]. *L'Appel de la race* [Call of the race]. Montréal: Bibliothèque de l'Action française, 1922, 278 p.

_____. *Au Cap Blomidon*. Montréal: Le Devoir, 1932, 239 p.

Articles by Groulx

"Le Congrès de [la] langue française et le sou des tout petits." *Le Devoir*, March 2, 1912, p. 1.

"Pour la neuvième croisade." *Le Devoir*, May 12, 1914, p. 1.

"La neuvième croisade." *Le Droit*, May 2, 1914, p. 2.

"Aux Acadiens: Discours prononcé à Moncton, le dimanche 15 August, par M. l'abbé L.-A. Groulx." *Le Devoir*, September 11, 1915, p. 9.

"Compatriotes de l'Ouest, c'est donc votre droit de vous entêter à survivre." *Le Devoir*, December 21, 1926, p. 4, 10.

"En revenant de Chicago." *Almanach de la langue française*, 1927, p. 74–76.

"Quelques impressions de voyage [en Louisiane]." In *En Louisiane*, Montréal: [n.p.], 1931, p. 21-27.

"Iberville à la Baie d'Hudson." *Les Cloches de Saint-Boniface*, June 1942, p. 132–137.

"Ceci se passera au Canada . . . à propos de Radio-Ouest." *Les Cloches de Saint-Boniface*, March 1948, p. 62-63.

"La paroisse, foyer de vie nationale." In *Semaines sociales du Canada (section française). XXXe Session – Edmundston, 1953. La Paroisse, cellule sociale. Compte rendu des cours et conférences*, Montréal: Institut social populaire, 1953, p. 165–178.

"La presse française en terre ontarienne: Son role." *Le Droit*, November 8, 1958, p. 34.

"Message du chanoine Lionel Groulx, président d'honneur des États généraux." *Les États généraux du Canada français. Assises préliminaires tenues à l'Université de Montréal du 25 au 27 novembre 1966*, [no place of publication], [n.p.], [1967], p. 9–12.

"Message posthume de M. le chanoine Lionel Groulx." *Les États généraux du Canada français. Assises nationales tenues à la Place des Arts du 23 au 26 novembre 1967*, numéro spécial de *L'Action nationale*, Vol. 57, No. 6 (February 1968), p. 11.

Reviews Consulted

L'Action française (1917–1928).

L'Action nationale (1933–1967).

Revue d'histoire de l'Amérique française (1947–1967).

Handwritten and Unpublished Documents[2]

Correspondance of Lionel Groulx (Fonds Lionel-Groulx, série P1/A)

"Pourquoi nous en sommes fiers." Lecture about the Acadians, [in Acadia, 1915?], BAnQ, FLG, P1/01,03, 2 f.

"Visions acadiennes." Journal kept during a trip to Acadia, August 1915, BAnQ, FLG P1/12,12, 80 f.

2. The handwritten and unpublished documents listed in this section are archived with the Bibliothèque et Archives nationales du Québec in Montreal.

"Conférence de l'automne de 1916 pour le charbon des écoles d'Ottawa." Ottawa, October 15, 1916, BAnQ, FLG, P1/13,06, 44 f.

"Causerie sur la question ontarienne." Vaudreuil, May 19, 1917, BAnQ, FLG, P1/13,17, 14 f.

"Toast au clergé canadien." Delivered at the international Eucharistic Congress in Chicago, June 1926, BAnQ, FLG, P1/17,17, 49 p.

Text of official thank you speech given upon receiving an honorary doctorate in law at Université d'Ottawa, June 17, 1934. BAnQ, FLG, P1/23,06, 7 f.

"Est-il vrai que nous allons apprendre à nous souvenir [Is it true that we shall learn to remember]?" Outline for a speech given in Montréal on September 29, 1940, at the grave site of Jeanne Lajoie. BAnQ, P1/MA-266, 2 f.

"La résistance: Notes pour une conférence à Verner, Ont., May 1954." BAnQ, P1/MA-393, 10 f.

Writings by Authors Other than Groulx[3]

Bourassa, Henri. *Religion, langue, nationalité: Discours prononcé à la séance de clôture du XXIe Congrès eucharistique à Montréal, le 10 septembre 1910*. Montréal: Le Devoir, 1910, 30 p.

Villeneuve, Rodrigue. "Croisade eucharistique." *Le Droit*, May 28, 1914, p. 1–2.

_____. "Pour la neuvième croisade. L'article de M. l'abbé Groulx commenté à Ottawa – Une proposition du R.P. Villeneuve." *Le Devoir*, May 30, 1914, p. 11.

Grenon, Alex. "La Croisade Eucharistique." *Le Droit*, June 2, 1914, p. 2.

Villeneuve, Rodrigue. "La croisade eucharistique." *Le Droit*, June 18, 1914, p. 1.

Perrault, Antonio. "*L'Appel de la race*." *Le Devoir*, September 23, 1922, p. 1–2.

Gautier, Charles. "*L'Appel de la race*." *Le Droit*, October 14, 1922, p. 3.

Boutet, Edgar and Louis-Joseph de la Durantaye. "*L'Appel de la race*." *Les Annales. Lettres, histoire, sciences, arts*, November 1922, p. 1.

Desrosiers, Léo-Paul. "Sur un article de M. du Roure." *Le Devoir*, December 21, 1922, p. 1–2.

Roy, Camille. "*L'Appel de la race*. Un roman canadien." *Le Canada français*, December 1922, p. 308–309.

Du Roure, René. "*L'Appel de la Race*: Critique littéraire." *La Revue moderne*, December 1922, p. 9.

De Montigny, Louvigny. "Un Mauvais Livre." *La Revue moderne*, January 1923, p. 9.

Perrault, Antonio. "*L'Appel de la race* et ses détracteurs." *Le Devoir*, January 27, 1923, p. 1–2.

Gautier, Charles. "L'œuvre de l'Action française." *Le Droit*, February 23, 1923.

Parrot, Charles-Édouard. "La soirée d'hier au Collège Sainte-Marie." *Le Devoir*, May 8, 1923, p. 4.

"Le pèlerinage de l''Action française'." *Le Devoir*, May 25, 1923, p. 4.

Laval, "Chronique de l'Université." *Le Canada français*, February 1924, p. 467.

Dugré, Alexandre. *Notre Survivance française*. Montréal: Imprimerie du Messager, 1937, 15 p.

"Dénonciation de la doctrine séparatiste." *Le Canada*, July 1, 1937, p. 1, 3.

"L'idéalisme de M. Groulx et celui de Mgr Yelle." *Le Canada*, July 1, 1937, p. 2.

L'Heureux, Eugène. "Et le juste milieu?" *L'Action catholique*, July 2, 1937, p. 4.

Gautier, Charles. "Le Congrès de Québec et le séparatisme." *Le Droit*, July 3, 1937, p. 3.

"L'hommage à Jeanne Lajoie, la 'Pucelle de Pembroke'." *Le Devoir*, September 30, 1940.

Boucher, J.-Émile. "Au diable la fraternité!" *Le Bulletin*, April 1961, p. 1.

3. In chronological order of publication.

Secondary Sources

(including monographs, collections and theses)

Asselin, Olivar. *L'Œuvre de l'abbé Groulx*. Montréal: Bibliothèque de l'Action française, 1923. 96 p.

Badour, Mireille. *Le Nationalisme de* L'Action nationale. Master's thesis (economics and political science), McGill University, 1967, 152 p.

Balthazar, Louis. *Bilan du nationalisme au Québec*. Montréal: l'Hexagone, 1986, 217 p.

Behiels, Michael D. *Prelude to Quebec's Quiet Revolution: Liberalism Versus Neo-Nationalism, 1945–1960*. Kingston and Montréal: McGill-Queen's University Press, 1985, 366 p.

Bélanger, A. *L'Apolitisme des idéologies québécoises: Le grand tournant de 1934–36*. Québec: Presses de l'Université Laval, 1974, 392 p.

Bélanger, Damien-Claude. *Lionel Groulx et la Franco-Américanie*. Master's thesis (history), Université de Montréal, 2000, 184 p.

Boily, Frédéric. *La Pensée nationaliste de Lionel Groulx*. Sillery: Septentrion, 2003, 232 p.

Bouchard, Gérard. *Les Deux chanoines: Contradiction et ambivalence dans la pensée de Lionel Groulx*. Montréal: Boréal, 2003, 313 p.

_____. *Entre l'Ancien et le Nouveau Monde: Le Québec comme population et culture fondatrice*. Ottawa: Presses de l'Université d'Ottawa, 1996, 56 p.

_____. *Genèse des nations et cultures du Nouveau Monde: Essai d'histoire comparée*. Montréal: Boréal, 2001, 504 p.

_____. *La Nation québécoise au futur et au passé*. Montréal: VLB Éditeur, 1999, 159 p.

Brunet, Michel. *Québec – Canada anglais: deux itinéraires, un affrontement*. Montréal: Hurtubise HMH, 1968, 309 p.

Choquette, Robert. *L'Église catholique dans l'Ontario français du dix-neuvième siècle*. Ottawa: Presses de l'Université d'Ottawa, 1984, 365 p.

_____. *La Foi gardienne de la langue en Ontario, 1900–1950* [Faith, guardian of the language in Ontario, 1900–1950]. Montréal: Bellarmin, 1987, 282 p.

_____. *Langue et religion: Histoire des conflits anglo-français en Ontario*. Ottawa: Presses de l'Université d'Ottawa, 1977, 268 p.

_____. *L'Autonomie provinciale, les droits des minorités et la théorie du pacte, 1867–1921*. Ottawa: Information Canada, 1969, 82 p.

Cook, Ramsay. *Canada, Quebec and the Uses of Nationalism*. Toronto: McClelland and Stewart, 1986, 224 p.

Coulombe, Danielle. *Coloniser et enseigner. Le rôle du clergé et la contribution des Sœurs de Notre-Dame du Perpétuel Secours à Hearst, 1917–1942*. Ottawa: Éditions du Nordir, 1998, 253 p.

Couture, Yves. *La Terre promise: L'Absolu politique dans le nationalisme québécois*. Montréal: Éditions Liber, 1994, 221 p.

Delisle, Esther. *Le Traître et le juif: Lionel Groulx, Le Devoir et le délire du nationalisme d'extrême droite dans la province de Québec, 1929–1939*. Outremont: L'Étincelle, 1992, 284 p. [The translation, *The Traitor and the Jew: Anti-Semitism and the Delirium of Extremist Right-Wing Nationalism in French Canada from 1929–1939*. Montreal: Robert Davies, 1993 was not used.]

Dion, Léon. *Nationalismes et politique au Québec*. Montréal: Hurtubise HMH, 1975, 177 p.

Dumont, Fernand. *Genèse de la société québécoise*. Montréal: Boréal, 1993, 393 p.

Dumont, Fernand, et al. ed. *Idéologies au Canada français*, 4 volumes, 6 tomes. Québec: Presses de l'Université Laval, 1971–1981.

Dupuis, Jean-Claude. *Nationalisme et catholicisme: L'Action française de Montréal (1917–1928)*. Master's thesis (history), Université de Montréal, 1992, 329 p.

Durocher, René, *et al.* *Histoire du Québec contemporain: Tome I: De la Confédération à la Crise (1867–1929)*. Montréal: Boréal, 1989, 758 p.

_____. *Histoire du Québec contemporain. Tome II: Le Québec depuis 1930*. Montréal: Boréal, 1989, 834 p.

Éthier-Blais, Jean. *Signets IV: Le Siècle de l'abbé Groulx*. Montréal: Leméac, 1993.

Fortin, Gérald. *An Analysis of the Ideology of a French Canadian Magazine: 1917–1954. A Contribution of the Sociology of Knowledge*. Doctoral thesis (sociology), Cornell University, 1956, 251 p.

Frégault, Guy. *Lionel Groulx tel qu'en lui-même*. Montréal: Leméac, 1978, 237 p.

Frenette, Yves. *Brève Histoire des Canadiens français*. Montréal: Boréal, 1998, 211 p.

Gaboury, Jean-Pierre. *Le Nationalisme de Lionel Groulx: Aspects idéologiques*. Ottawa: Éditions de l'Université d'Ottawa, 1970, 226 p.

Gaffield, Chad. *Aux origines de l'identité franco-ontarienne: Éducation, culture, économie*. Ottawa: Presses de l'Université d'Ottawa, 1993, 284 p.

Gaudreau, Guy, ed. *Bâtir sur le roc: De l'ACFÉO à l'ACFO du Grand Sudbury, 1910–1987*. Sudbury: Société historique du Nouvel-Ontario and Prise de parole, 1994, 223 p.

Gervais, Gaétan. *Des gens de resolution: Le Passage du Canada français à l'Ontario français*. Sudbury: Prise de parole, 2003, 230 p.

Giguère, Georges-Émile. *Lionel Groulx: Biographie: "Notre État français, nous l'aurons!"* Montréal: Bellarmin, 1978, 159 p.

Goyette, Julien, ed. *Lionel Groulx: Une Anthologie*. Montréal: Bibliothèque québécoise, 1998, 312 p.

Harvey, Fernand and Gérard Beaulieu, ed. *Les Relations entre le Québec et l'Acadie de la tradition à la modernité*. N.p.: IQRC and Éditions de l'Acadie, 2000, 297 p.

Hébert, Pierre. With the collaboration of Marie-Pier Luneau. *Lionel Groulx et* L'Appel de la race. Montréal: Fides, 1996, 204 p.

Hobsbawm, Eric. *Nations et nationalisme depuis 1780: Programme, mythe, réalité*. Paris: Gallimard, 1992, 371 p.

Jaenen, Cornelius J., ed. *Les Franco-Ontariens*. Ottawa: Presses de l'Université d'Ottawa, 1993, 443 p.

Jones, Richard. *L'Idéologie de* L'Action catholique *(1917–1939)*. Québec: Presses de l'Université Laval, 1975, 359 p.

Lamarre, Jean. *Le Devenir de la nation québécoise selon Maurice Séguin, Guy Frégault et Michel Brunet, 1944-1969*. Sillery: Septentrion, 1993, 561 p.

Lamonde, Yvan. *Histoire sociale des idées au Québec, Volume 1: 1760–1896*. Montréal: Fides, 2000, 574 p.

_____. *Histoire sociale des idées au Québec, Volume II: 1896–1929*. Montréal: Fides, 2004, 330 p.

Levitt, Joseph. *Henri Bourassa and the Golden Calf: The Social Program of the Nationalists of Quebec (1900–1914)*. Ottawa: Éditions de l'Université d'Ottawa, 1969, 178 p.

Luneau, Marie-Pier. *Lionel Groulx: Le mythe du berger*. Montréal: Leméac, 2003, 226 p.

Marcil, Jeffrey. *Franco-Américains, Canadiens français hors Québec et Acadiens dans la grande presse montréalaise de langue française, 1905–1906*. Master's thesis (history), Université d'Ottawa, 1998, 158 p.

Martel, Marcel. *Le Deuil d'un pays imagine: Rêve, luttes et déroutes du Canada français* [Elegy for an imagined country: French Canada's dream, struggles and losses]. Ottawa: Presses de l'Université d'Ottawa, 1997, 203 p.

McRoberts, Kenneth and Dale Posgate. *Développement et modernisation du Québec*. Montréal: Boréal Express, 1983, 350 p.

Monière, Denis. *Le Développement des idéologies au Québec des origines à nos jours*. Montréal: Éditions Québec Amérique, 1977, 381 p.

Oliver, Michael. *The Passionate Debate. The Social and Political Ideas of Quebec Nationalism, 1920–1945*. Montréal: Véhicule Press, 1991, 284 p.

_____. *The Social and Political Ideas of French Canadian Nationalists*. Doctoral thesis (history), McGill University, 1956.

Painchaud, Robert. *Un rêve français dans le peuplement de la Prairie*. Saint-Boniface: Éditions des Plaines, 1986, 303 p.

Paquin, Stéphane. *L'Invention d'un mythe: Le Pacte entre deux peuples fondateurs*. Montréal: VLB Éditeur, 1999, 176 p.

Pelletier-Baillargeon, Hélène. *Olivar Asselin et son temp: Le Militant*. Montréal: Fides, 1996, 780 p.

Pigeon, Stéphane. *Lionel Groulx, critique de la Révolution tranquille (1956–1967)*. Master's thesis (history), Université de Montréal, 1999, 119 p.

Rémillard, Juliette Lalonde. *Lionel Groulx: L'homme que j'ai connu*. Montréal: Fides, 2000, 59 p.

[Rémillard, Juliette and Madeleine Dionne]. *L'œuvre du chanoine Lionel Groulx: Témoignages. Bio-bibliographie*. Montréal: Publications de l'Académie canadienne-française, 1964, 197 p.

Renaud, Laurier. *La Fondation de l'A.C.J.C: L'Histoire d'une jeunesse nationaliste*. Jonquière: Presses collégiales de Jonquière, 1972, 154 p.

Renaut, Alain, ed. *Lumières et romantisme*. Paris: Calmann-Lévy, 1999, 414 p.

Roby, Yves. *Les Franco-Américains de la Nouvelle-Angleterre, 1776–1930*. Sillery: Septentrion, 1990, 434 p.

Roy, Fernande. *Histoire des idéologies au Québec aux XIXe et XXe siècles*. Montréal: Boréal, 1993, 127 p.

Roy, Jean-Louis. *Maîtres chez nous. (Dix années d'Action française) (1917–1927)*. Montréal: Leméac, 1968, 75 p.

Rudin, Ronald. *Making History in Twentieth-Century Quebec*. Toronto: University of Toronto Press, 1997, 294 p.

Saint-Denis, Yves. *Une édition critique de* L'Appel de la race *de Lionel Groulx*. Doctoral thesis (French literature), Université d'Ottawa, 1991, 1422 p.

Savard, Pierre. *Jules-Paul Tardivel, la France et les États-Unis, 1851–1905*. Québec: Presses de l'Université Laval, 1967, 499 p.

Silver, Arthur I. *The French-Canadian Idea of Confederation, 1864–1900*. Toronto: University of Toronto Press, 1982, 297 p.

Simon, Victor. *Le Règlement XVII: Sa mise en vigueur à travers l'Ontario, 1912–1927*. Sudbury: Société historique du Nouvel-Ontario, historical documents No. 78, 1983, 56 p.

Stagni, Pellegrino. *The View from Rome: Archbishop Stagni's 1915 Reports on the Ontario Bilingual Schools Question*. Translated from the Italian and introduction by John Zucchi. Montréal and Kingston: McGill-Queen's University Press, 2002, xlix–131 p.

Stanghieri, Pina. *The Image of the Chef in the Nationalism of Lionel Groulx*. Master's thesis, Université Laval, 1988, 155 p.

Thiboutot, Akim-Isabelle. *La Politisation de l'idée de nation chez Lionel Groulx*. Master's thesis (political science), Université Laval, 1996, 80 p.

Thomson, Dale C. *Jean Lesage et la Révolution tranquille*. Montréal: Éditions du Trécarré, 1984, 615 p.

Trépanier, Pierre. *Qu'est-ce que le traditionalisme? Causerie-débat tenue à Montréal, le samedi 8 June 2002*. N.p.: Club du 3 juillet, [2002], 53 p.

_____. *Une histoire libérale des idées au Québec: Analyse critique. Causerie-débat tenue à Montréal, le samedi 23 February 2002*. [no place of publication], Club du 3 juillet, [2002], 44 p.

Trofimenkoff, Susan Mann. *Abbé Groulx: Variations on a Nationalist Theme*. Toronto: Copp Clark Publishing, 1973, 256 p.

Trofimenkoff, Susan Mann. *Action française: French Canadian Nationalism in the Twenties*. Toronto: University of Toronto Press, 1975, 157 p.

Wade, Mason. *The French Canadians 1760–1945*. Toronto: Macmillan, 1955, 1136 p.

Articles and Chapters

Angers, François-Albert. "Mesure de l'influence du chanoine Lionel Groulx sur son milieu." *Revue d'histoire de l'Amérique française*, Vol. 32, No. 3 (December 1978), p. 357–384.

Balthazar, Louis. "Identity and Nationalism in Québec." In James Littleton, ed., *Clash of Identities: Media, Manipulation, and Politics of the Self*. N.p.: Canadian Broadcasting Corporation, 1996, p. 101–112.

Balthazar, Louis. "Le nationalisme civique d'André Laurendeau." *Les Cahiers d'histoire du Québec au XXe siècle*, No. 10 (Winter 2000), p. 63–70.

Bédard, Éric. "Michel Brunet: dix ans après . . . [Michel Brunet: ten years on]." *L'Action nationale*, Vol. 85, No. 7 (September 1995), p. 38–49.

Bédard, Guy and Lawrence Olivier. "Le nationalisme québecois: Les Acadiens et les francophones du Canada." *Égalité: Revue acadienne d'analyse politique*, No. 33 (1993), p. 81–100.

Beaudreau, Sylvie. "Déconstruire le rêve de nation. Lionel Groulx et la Révolution tranquille." *Revue d'histoire de l'Amérique française*, Vol. 56, No. 1 (Summer 2002), p. 29–61.

Bélanger, Damien-Claude. "Lionel Groulx et la crise sentinelliste." *Mens. Revue d'histoire intellectuelle de l'Amérique française*, Vol. 1, No. 1 (Fall 2000), p. 7–36.

Bellavance, Marcel. "La rébellion de 1837 et les modèles théoriques de l'émergence de la nation et du nationalisme." *Revue d'histoire de l'Amérique française*, Vol. 53, No. 3 (Winter 2000), p. 367–400.

Bergeron, Réjean and Yves Drolet. "Les questions internationales dans les premiers inédits de Lionel Groulx (1895–1909)." *Revue d'histoire de l'Amérique française*, Vol. 34, No. 2 (September 1980), p. 245–255.

Bock, Michel. "Les Franco-Ontariens et le "réveil" de la nation: la crise du Règlement XVII dans le parcours intellectuel de Lionel Groulx." *Francophonies d'Amérique*, No. 13 (Summer 2002), p. 157–177.

_____. "'Le Québec a charge d'âmes': L'Action française de Montréal et les minorités françaises (1917–1928) ["'Quebec has the cure of souls': . . .]." *Revue d'histoire de l'Amérique française*, Vol. 54, No. 3 (Winter 2001), p. 345–384.

_____. "Sociabilité et solidarité: la crise du Règlement XVII et l'insertion de Lionel Groulx dans les milieux nationalistes de l'Ontario français." *Revue du Nouvel-Ontario*, No. 28 (2003), p. 5–49.

_____. "'Suicide de race' ou 'vocation apostolique'? La représentation des Franco-Américains dans *L'Action française de Montréal* (1917–1928)." In Jean-Pierre Wallot, ed., with the collaboration of Pierre Lanthier and Hubert Watelet. *Constructions identitaires et pratiques sociales*. Ottawa: Presses de l'Université d'Ottawa and Centre de recherche en civilisation canadienne-française, 2002, p. 175–200.

Bouchard, Gérard. "Ouvrir le cercle de la nation: Activer la cohésion sociale: Réflexion sur le Québec et la diversité." *L'Action nationale*, Vol. 87, No. 4 (April 1997), p. 107–137.

Bourassa, Joanne. "Le rôle de Lionel Groulx comme éveilleur de conscience nationale de ses compatriots." *Revue d'histoire de l'Amérique française*, Vol. 32, No. 3 (December 1978), p. 449–454.

Brunet, Michel. "Lionel Groulx et l'histoire de notre désassimilation." *L'Action nationale*, Vol. 74, No. 9, May 1985, p. 871–876.

_____. "Trois dominantes de la pensée canadienne-française: l'agriculturisme, l'anti-étatisme et le messianisme." In *La Présence anglaise et les Canadiens*. Montréal: Beauchemin, 1958, p. 112–166.

Caldwell, Gary. "La controverse Delisle-Richler." *L'Agora*, June 1994, p. 17–26.

Cantin, Serge. "Nation et mémoire chez Fernand Dumont: Pour répondre à Gérard Bouchard." *Bulletin d'histoire politique*, Vol. 9, No. 1 (Fall 2000), p. 40–59.

Cecillion, Jack. "Turbulent Times in the Diocese of London: Bishop Fallon and the French-Language Controversy, 1910–1918." *Ontario History*, Vol. 87, No. 4 (December 1995), p. 369–395.

Chouinard, Denis. "Des contestataires pragmatiques: Les Jeune-Canada, 1932–1938." *Revue d'histoire de l'Amérique française*, Vol. 40, No. 1 (Summer 1986), p. 5–28.

Comeau, Robert. "Lionel Groulx, les indépendantistes de *La Nation* et le séparatisme (1936–1938)." *Revue d'histoire de l'Amérique française*, Vol. 26, No.1 (June 1972), p. 83–102.

Dionne, René. "1910: Une première prise de parole collective en Ontario français [Assuming our collective voice for the first time in French Ontario]." In *Cahiers Charlevoix 1: Études franco-ontariennes*. Sudbury: Société Charlevoix and Prise de parole, 1995, p. 15–124.

_____. "*L'appel de la race* est-il un roman raciste [Is *L'appel de la race* a racist novel]?" *Relations*, Vol. 38, No. 441 (November 1978), p. 317–318.

Dupuis, Jean-Claude. "La pensée économique de *L'Action française* (1917–1928)." *Revue d'histoire de l'Amérique française*, Vol. 47, No. 2 (Fall 1993), p. 193–219.

_____. "La pensée politique de *L'Action française* de Montréal (1917–1928)." *Les Cahiers d'histoire du Québec au XXe siècle*, No. 2 (Summer 1994), p. 27–43.

_____. "La pensée religieuse de *L'Action française* (1917–1928)." *Études d'histoire religieuse*, 1993, p. 73–88.

_____. "Pour une éducation nationale: La pensée pédagogique de *L'Action française* (1917–1918)." *Cahiers d'histoire*, Vol. 13 No. 1 (Spring 1993), p. 34–47.

Ferretti, Lucia. "La Révolution tranquille." *L'Action nationale*, Vol. 89, No. 10 (December 1999), p. 59–91.

Frégault, Guy. "Lionel Groulx." *Revue d'histoire de l'Amérique française*, Vol. 22, No.1 (June 1968), p. 3–16.

Gagné, Suzanne. "Lionel Groulx, historien d'hier ou d'aujourd'hui." *Revue d'histoire de l'Amérique française*, Vol. 32, No. 3 (December 1978), p. 455–458.

Gagnon, Alain-G. "La pensée politique d'André Laurendeau: Communauté, égalité et liberté." *Les Cahiers d'histoire du Québec au XXe siècle*, No. 10 (Winter 2000), p. 31–44.

Gélinas, Xavier. "La droite intellectuelle et la Révolution tranquille: Le cas de la revue Tradition et progrès, 1957–1962 ." *Canadian Historical Review*, Vol. 77, No. 3 (September 1996), p. 353–387.

Gervais, Gaétan. "Aux origines de l'identité franco-ontarienne." In *Cahiers Charlevoix 1. Études franco-ontariennes*. Sudbury: Société Charlevoix et Prise de parole, 1995, p. 125–168.

_____. "L'Ontario français et les 'États généraux du Canada français.'" In *Cahiers Charlevoix 3. Études franco-ontariennes*. Sudbury: Société Charlevoix and Prise de parole, 1998, p, 231–364.

_____. "L'Ontario français et les grands congrès patriotiques canadiens-français (1883–1952)." In *Cahiers Charlevoix 2. Études franco-ontariennes*. Sudbury: Société Charlevoix and Prise de parole, 1997, p. 9–155.

_____. "Le Règlement XVII (1912–1927)." *Revue du Nouvel-Ontario*, No. 18 (1996), p. 123–192.

Hamelin, Jean. *Le XXe Siècle: Tome 2: De 1940 à nos jours*, [in Nive Voisine, ed., *Histoire du catholicisme québécois*]. Montréal: Boréal, 1984, 425 p.

Harvey, Fernand. "Le Québec et le Canada français: histoire d'une déchirure." In Simon Langlois, ed., *Identité et cultures nationales: L'Amérique française en mutation*. Québec: Presses de l'Université Laval, 1995, p. 49–64.

_____. "Les relations culturelles Québec – Acadie: Analyse d'une mutation." *Les Cahiers des Dix*, No. 53 (1999), p. 235–250.

_____ and Paul-André Linteau. "Les étranges lunettes de Ronald Rudin." *Revue d'histoire de l'Amérique française*, Vol. 51, No. 3 (Winter 1998), p. 419–424, 429.

Huot, Christiane. "Groulx éveilleur de conscience nationale [Groulx: raising national consciousness]." *Revue d'histoire de l'Amérique française*, Vol. 32, No. 3 (December 1978), p. 435–448.

Huot, Giselle. "De l'esprit, du cœur et des letters: La correspondance Georges-Henri Lévesque – Lionel Groulx (1934–1937)." *Les Cahiers d'histoire du Québec au XX*e *siècle*, No. 2 (Summer 1994), p. 61–83.

Juteau-Lee, Danielle and Jean Lapointe. "The Emergence of Franco-Ontarians: New Identity, New Boundaries." In Jean L. Elliot, ed., *Two Nations, Many Cultures: Ethnic Groups in Canada*. Scarborough: Prentice-Hall, 1979, p. 99–113.

Lacroix, Benoît. "Lionel Groulx, cet inconnu ?" *Revue d'histoire de l'Amérique française*, Vol. 32, No. 3 (December 1978), p. 325–346.

_____. "Lionel Groulx en 1930." *Les Cahiers des Dix*, No. 44 (1989), p. 199–229.

_____. "Lionel Groulx – Georges-Henri Lévesque: Similitudes et affrontements." *Cahiers d'histoire du Québec au XX*e *siècle*, No. 2 (Summer 1994), p. 59–83.

_____. "Pour lire les Mémoires de Lionel Groulx (1878–1967)." *Revue d'histoire de l'Amérique française*, Vol. 24, No. 3 (December 1970), p. 413–419.

Lalonde, A.-N. "L'intelligentsia du Québec et la migration des Canadiens français vers l'Ouest canadien, 1870–1930." *Revue d'histoire de l'Amérique française*, Vol. 33, No. 2 (September 1979), p. 163–185.

Lamonde, Yvan. "Rome et le Vatican: la Vocation catholique de l'Amérique française ou de l'Amérique anglaise?" In Jean-Pierre Wallot, ed., with collaboration by Pierre Lanthier and d'Hubert Watelet, *Constructions identitaires et pratiques sociales*. Ottawa: Presses de l'Université d'Ottawa and Centre de recherche en civilisation canadienne-française, 2002, p. 324–343.

Lavoie, Yolande. "Les mouvements migratoires des Canadiens entre leur pays et les États-Unis au XIXe et au XXe siècles: Étude quantitative." In Hubert Charbonneau, ed., *La Population du Québec: Études rétrospectives*. Montréal: Boréal Express, 1973, p. 73–88.

Létourneau, Jocelyn. "Québec d'après-guerre et mémoire collective de la technocratie." *Cahiers internationaux de sociologie*, No. 90 (January–June 1991), p. 67–87.

Marion, Séraphin. "L'abbé Groulx, raciste?" *Les Cahiers des Dix*, No. 43 (1983), p. 185–205.

Martel, Angéline. "L'étatisation des relations entre le Québec et les communautés acadiennes et francophones: chroniques d'une époque." *Égalité*, No. 33 (Spring 1993), p. 13–79.

Martel, Marcel. "'Hors du Québec, point de salut [Outside Québec, no salvation]!' Francophone Minorities and Quebec Nationalism, 1945–1969." In Michael D. Behiels and Marcel Martel, ed., *Nation, Ideas, Identities: Essays in Honour of Ramsay Cook*. Toronto: Oxford University Press, 2000, p. 130–140.

McRoberts, Kenneth. "La thèse tradition-modernité: L'historique québecois." In Mikhaël Elbaz, Andrée Fortin et Guy Laforest, ed., *Les Frontières de l'identité: Modernité et post-modernisme au Québec*. Québec: Presses de l'Université Laval, 1996, p. 29–45

Morin, Rosaire. "Les États généraux du Canada français: Vingt-cinq (ans) plus tard." In Robert Comeau *et al.*, *Daniel Johnson: Rêve d'égalité et projet d'indépendance*. Sillery: Presses de l'Université du Québec, 1991, p. 315–328.

Olivier, Peter N. "The Resolution of the Ontario Bilingual School Crisis, 1919–1929." *Revue d'études canadiennes*, Vol. 4, No. 4 (November 1969), p. 26–38.

Ouellet, Fernand. "La Révolution tranquille, tournant révolutionnaire?" In Thomas S. Axworthy and Pierre Elliott Trudeau, ed., *Les Années Trudeau: La Recherche d'une société juste*. Montréal: Éditions du Jour, 1990, p. 333–362, 420–422.

Parent, Sébastien. "Ronald Rudin et l'historiographie dite 'révisionniste': Un bilan." *Bulletin d'histoire politique*, Vol. 9, No. 1 (Fall 2000), p. 169–183.

Rémillard, Juliette. "Lionel Groulx: Bibliographie (1964–1979)." *Revue d'histoire de l'Amérique française*, Vol. 32, No. 3 (December 1978), p. 465–523.

Robert, Lucie. "Camille Roy et Lionel Groulx: la querelle de *L'Appel de la race*." *Revue d'histoire de l'Amérique française*, Vol. 32, No. 3 (December 1978), p. 399–405.

Robertson, Susan Mann. "*L'Action française*: L'appel à la race." *Revue d'histoire de l'Amérique française*, Vol. 25, No. 1 (June 1971), p. 94–96.

Roby, Yves. "Les Canadiens français des États-Unis (1860–1900): Dévoyés ou missionnaires?" *Revue d'histoire de l'Amérique française*, Vol. 41, No. 1 (Summer 1987), p. 3–22.

Rudin, Ronald. "Les lunettes différentes." *Revue d'histoire de l'Amérique française*, Vol. 51, No. 3 (Winter 1998), p. 425–428, 429.

_____. "Regards sur l'IHAF et la RHAF à l'époque de Groulx." *Revue d'histoire de l'Amérique française*, Vol. 51, No. 2 (Fall 1997), p. 201–221.

Sénécal, André. "La thèse messianique et les Franco-Américains." *Revue d'histoire de l'Amérique française*, Vol. 34, No. 4 (March 1981), p. 557–567.

Senese, P. M. "Catholique d'abord!: Catholicism and Nationalism in the Thought of Lionel Groulx." *Canadian Historical Review*, Vol. 60, No. 2 (June 1979), p. 154–177.

Sirois, Jean. "Le Chanoine Groulx, historien d'hier et d'aujourd'hui," *Revue d'histoire de l'Amérique française*, Vol. 32, No. 3 (December 1978), p. 459–464.

Smith, Donald. "*L'Action française*, 1917—1921." In Fernand Dumont *et al.*, *Idéologies au Canada français, 1900–1929*. Québec: Presses de l'Université Laval, 1974, p. 345–367.

Stapinsky, Stéphane (presented by). "L'esprit des années trente: Une correspondance André Laurendeau – Lionel Groulx (1936)." *Les Cahiers d'histoire du Québec au XXe siècle*, No. 3 (Winter 1995), p. 81–101.

_____. "Les intellectuels dans l'histoire récente du Québec." *Les Cahiers d'histoire du Québec au XXe siècle*, No. 2 (Summer 1994), p. 147–153.

_____. "L'intégration d'un document historique à un récit de fiction: L'exemple d'*Au Cap Blomidon* de Lionel Groulx." *Voix et Images*, No. 55 (Fall 1993), p. 54–77.

_____. "Quand un 'historien national' en scrute un autre: Lionel Groulx et François-Xavier Garneau." In Gille Gallichan et Denis Saint-Jacques, ed., *François-Xavier Garneau, une figure nationale*. Québec: Éditions Nota Bene, 1998, p. 347–367.

Tousignant, Pierre. "Groulx et l'histoire: Interrogation sur le passé en vue d'une direction d'avenir." *Revue d'histoire de l'Amérique française*, Vol. 32, No. 3 (December 1978), p. 347–356.

Trépanier, Pierre. "L'étudiant idéal vers 1913." *Les Cahiers des Dix*, No. 55 (2001), p. 117–148.

_____. "Le maurrassisme au Canada français." *Les Cahiers des Dix*, No. 53 (1999), p. 167–233.

_____. "Lionel Groulx, historien." *Les Cahiers des Dix*, No. 47 (1992), p. 247–277.

_____. "Notes pour une histoire des droites intellectuelles canadiennes-françaises à travers leurs principaux représentants." *Les Cahiers des Dix*, No. 48 (1993), p. 119–164.

Trofimenkoff, Susan Mann. "Les femmes dans l'œuvre de Groulx." *Revue d'histoire de l'Amérique française*, Vol. 32, No. 3 (December 1978), p. 385–398.

Vallerand, Charles. "De Groulx à Laurendeau: l'héritage nationaliste." In Robert Comeau and Lucille Beaudry, ed., *André Laurendeau: Un intellectuel d'ici*. Sillery: Presses de l'Université Laval, 1990, p. 163–168.

Wallot, Jean-Pierre. "À la recherche de la nation: Maurice Séguin (1918–1984)." *Revue d'histoire de l'Amérique française*, Vol. 38, No. 4 (Spring 1985), p. 569-589.

_____. "Groulx historiographe." *Revue d'histoire de l'Amérique française*, Vol. 32, No. 3 (December 1978), p. 407–433.

_____. "L'histoire et le néonationalisme des années 1947–1970." In G. Rocher *et al.* *Continuité et rupture: Les Sciences sociales au Québec*. Montréal: Presses de l'Université de Montréal, 1984, p. 111–116.

Welch, David. "Early Franco-Ontarian Schooling as a Reflection and Creator of Community Identity." *Ontario History*, Vol. 85, No. 4 (December 1993), p. 321–347.

Index

C

D

G

H

I

J

K

L

Printed in April 2014
by Gauvin, Gatineau (Quebec), Canada.